PRECEPT
UPON
PRECEPT

PRECEPT UPON PRECEPT

Joseph Smith
and the Restoration of Doctrine

ROBERT L. MILLET

DESERET
BOOK

SALT LAKE CITY, UTAH

Library of Congress Cataloging-in-Publication Data

Names: Millet, Robert L., author.
Title: Precept upon precept : Joseph Smith and the restoration of doctrine / Robert L. Millet.
Description: Salt Lake City, Utah : Deseret Book, [2016] | Includes bibliographical references and index.
Identifiers: LCCN 2016021201 | ISBN 9781629722368 (hardbound : alk. paper)
Subjects: LCSH: Smith, Joseph, Jr., 1805–1844. | Restoration of the gospel (Mormon doctrine) | Mormon Church—History—19th century. | The Church of Jesus Christ of Latter-day Saints—History—19th century. | Mormon Church—Doctrines. | The Church of Jesus Christ of Latter-day Saints—Doctrines.
Classification: LCC BX8635.3 .M5555 2016 | DDC 230/.9332—dc23
LC record available at https://lccn.loc.gov/2016021201

Printed in the United States of America
Lake Book Manufacturing, Inc., Melrose Park, IL

10   9   8   7   6   5   4   3   2   1

To my beloved Shauna—
whose friendship, loyalty, sweet companionship,
and love make eternity seem too brief

It is my meditation all the day, and more than my meat and drink, to know how I shall make the Saints of God comprehend the visions that roll like an overflowing surge before my mind.

—Joseph Smith

There is not so great a man as Joseph standing in this generation. The gentiles look upon him as he is a bed of gold concealed from human view. They know not his principles, his spirit, his wisdom, his virtues, his philanthropy, nor his calling. His mind, like Enoch's, expands as eternity, and only God can comprehend his soul.

—Wilford Woodruff

CONTENTS

PREFACE

Jehovah spoke through Isaiah of how divine truth is conveyed to mortals: "For precept must be upon precept, precept upon precept; line upon line, line upon line; here a little, and there a little" (Isaiah 28:10; compare 2 Nephi 28:30). Almost always a merciful God will make known doctrines and principles gradually. Though you and I may occasionally be impatient with the Lord's system of gospel prerequisites, he established it for a wise purpose. It is a quiet illustration of the tender regard and sweet kindness our Father in Heaven has for his children: he gives to us that which we are prepared to receive. This is, in fact, the manner in which the Almighty has dispensed the truths and authorities of the restored gospel. Fourteen-year-old Joseph Smith certainly did not understand in the spring of 1820 what he understood by the time he went to a martyr's death in 1844. His divine schooling, like that of all Saints, was incremental.

It has been observed that doctrine is "the basic body of Christian teaching or understanding (2 Timothy 3:16). Christian doctrine is composed of teachings which are to be handed on through instruction and proclamation. . . . Religious doctrine deals with the ultimate and most comprehensive questions."[1] The central, saving

---

1. *Holman Bible Dictionary,* 374.

doctrine is that Jesus is the Christ, the Son of God, the Savior and Redeemer of humankind; that he lived, taught, healed, suffered, and died for our sins; and that he rose from the dead the third day with an immortal, resurrected body (1 Corinthians 15:1–3; D&C 76:40–42). This core doctrine sets forth what Joseph Smith called the "fundamental principles of our religion."[2]

There is power in doctrine, power in the word (Alma 31:5), power to heal the wounded soul (Jacob 2:8), power to transform human behavior. I have devoted much of my professional and ecclesiastical life to an intense study of the various doctrines of the Restoration and find myself turning to, savoring, and quoting or paraphrasing frequently from Joseph Smith's sermons or writings. In this book we will tell the story of Joseph Smith but not in a typical biographical fashion. Rather, we will look carefully at some of the most significant doctrinal moments and teachings of Joseph's ministry and pursue our study, for the most part, chronologically. In one sense, this work might be described as a kind of doctrinal biography. In some cases we will see how certain theological matters introduced in the Prophet's early ministry were added upon and clarified later by him or by his apostolic and prophetic successors, precept upon precept.

One challenge with a work of this sort is delimitation: everything simply cannot be covered in one book. Consequently, I have selected what I feel to be doctrinal highlights of the founding Prophet. You will notice, for example, that I have not attended to such matters as how the Book of Mormon was translated, the Word of Wisdom, the origins of the book of Abraham, the apostasy in Kirtland, persecution in Missouri and Illinois, the organization of the Relief Society, and the particulars of the Prophet's martyrdom. Further, although I occasionally turn to doctrinal topics as they are presented in the Book of Mormon, Doctrine and Covenants, and the Pearl of Great Price—all of which came through Joseph

---

2. *Joseph Smith* [manual], 49.

Smith—in a volume of this kind it is impossible to cover every doctrinal matter that arises in the Latter-day Saint scriptural canon or to touch on every significant historical moment.

I love and honor Joseph Smith as the Prophet of the Restoration and the head of the dispensation of the fulness of times. I have no hesitation in writing from the angle of faith and commitment; my personal perspective is strongly influenced by my belief. I am persuaded that Joseph was in many ways a prophet's prophet. When I say that, I have in mind the following remark by Joseph's brother Hyrum: "Joseph has the spirit and power of *all the prophets*."[3]

I have chosen to do something that is generally *not* done in a work of this sort—to interact periodically with you, the reader. That is, I will at times insert an experience or a personal insight into a chapter or speak to you as if we were in a conversation. As a reader myself, I find such excursions tend to add warmth and a personal touch to a book.

We have witnessed in recent years a marvelous work in itself in the production of the Joseph Smith Papers, and the results are continually being made available to Latter-day Saints and other interested parties in published form as well as online. It is a deeply significant work, one that is still underway and will be for a number of years to come. The principal sources for quotations from Joseph Smith in this volume are, first, the official Church manual entitled *Joseph Smith* in the Teachings of Presidents of the Church series, and, second, the Joseph Smith Papers themselves. I have occasionally used other sources of the Prophet's words, including the Church newspaper the *Times and Seasons* and *The Words of Joseph Smith: The Contemporary Accounts of the Nauvoo Discourses of the*

---

3. History, 1838–1856, volume E-1 [1 July 1843–30 April 1844], The Joseph Smith Papers, accessed 15 Mar. 2016, http://josephsmithpapers.org/paperSummary/history-1838 -1856-volume-e-1-1-july-1843-30-april-1844&p=397; emphasis added.

Prophet Joseph. Spelling, punctuation, and grammar in many of these quotations have been modernized for readability.

While a prisoner in Liberty Jail in March of 1839, Joseph the Prophet wrote: "Truth is 'Mormonism.' God is the author of it. He is our shield. It is by Him we received our birth. It was by His voice that we were called to a dispensation of His Gospel in the beginning of the fullness of times. It was by Him we received the Book of Mormon; and it is by Him that we remain unto this day; and by Him we shall remain, if it shall be for our glory; and in His Almighty name we are determined to endure tribulation as good soldiers unto the end."[4] Joseph Smith the Prophet believed, as did his followers, that The Church of Jesus Christ of Latter-day Saints was in very deed restored Christianity, the custodian of the fulness of the gospel of Jesus Christ and the only authority-bearing religious institution on earth. Joseph was persuaded, by personal and immediate encounter with the Divine, that what he taught was true, that what was being returned to earth through his efforts was "the ancient order of things." Those who accepted Joseph's witness of the work did so by the power of that Spirit that has been given by a gracious Lord to lead us into all truth (John 16:13).

Among many things that the Prophet Joseph Smith wrote from Liberty Jail is the following: "Thy mind, O man! if thou wilt lead a soul unto salvation, must stretch as high as the utmost heavens, and search into and contemplate the darkest abyss, and the broad expanse of eternity—thou must commune with God. How much more dignified and noble are the thoughts of God, than the vain imaginations of the human heart!"[5] Brother Joseph believed in the power of the human mind and delighted in rigorous thinking,

---

4. *Joseph Smith* [manual], 364.
5. *Joseph Smith* [manual], 267.

contemplation, and reflection on serious and sacred matters. He was also very much aware of the limitations of human rationality and taught repeatedly, in the words of a prophetic successor, that "this latter-day work is spiritual. It takes spirituality to comprehend it, to love it, and to discern it. Therefore, we should seek the Spirit in all we do."[6] It is my hope that you as a reader will find what follows to be rational and to conclude that it makes good sense, that the beliefs and practices of The Church of Jesus Christ of Latter-day Saints are as stimulating and stretching to the mind as they are settling and soothing to the heart (1 Peter 3:15).

In the preparation of this book I am indebted to many, many persons who have through the decades taught me in formal classroom settings, as well as through informal conversations, public lectures, or published writings, to love, revere, and demonstrate loyalty to the Prophet Joseph Smith. Though hesitant to list specific individuals for fear of neglecting others, I yield to the temptation slightly in order to express profound gratitude to Hyrum L. Andrus, Ivan J. Barrett, Robert J. Matthews, Truman G. Madsen, Richard Lloyd Anderson, Karl Ricks Anderson, Larry E. Porter, Milton V. Backman Jr., Larry E. Dahl, Donald Q. Cannon, and Joseph Fielding McConkie. Further, this book would not have materialized without special assistance from two dear friends at Deseret Book Company. First, Lisa Roper, product director, has encouraged and nurtured the book from concept to published work. Second, the careful editorial eye of Suzanne Brady has, once again, scrutinized and improved the product. I am deeply grateful to both.

In expressing thanks, however, I quickly acknowledge that I alone am responsible for the views expressed in this work and the conclusions drawn. This book is a personal endeavor and not an official publication of either The Church of Jesus Christ of Latter-day Saints or Brigham Young University.

6. Benson, *Come unto Christ*, 23.

A DOCTRINAL CHRONOLOGY

23 December 1805	Birth of Joseph Smith Jr.
Spring 1820	Joseph Smith's First Vision
21–22 September 1823	Coming of Moroni
19 November 1823	Death of Alvin Smith
18 January 1827	Joseph Smith and Emma Hale are married
22 September 1827	Joseph receives the gold plates
15 May 1829	John the Baptist confers the Aaronic Priesthood (D&C 13)
Late May 1829	Peter, James, and John confer the Melchizedek Priesthood (D&C 18, 27)
26 March 1830	Book of Mormon published
6 April 1830	Church of Christ formally organized
June 1830	New translation of the King James Bible (JST) begins
June 1830	Revelation of God's appearance to Moses on an unnamed mountain (Moses 1)

In preparing this doctrinal chronology, I am indebted to the staff of *BYU Studies* who, under the direction of Professor John W. Welch, prepared "Chronology of the Life of Joseph Smith" (46, no. 4 [2007]).

June–October 1830	Insights from JST into the premortal existence, Creation, Fall (Moses 2–5)
1831	Principles concerning eternal and plural marriage begin to be revealed (D&C 132)
November 1830–February 1831	Enoch's life and ministry revealed in JST; the revelation of the gospel to Adam; Noah and the Flood (Moses 6–8)
4 February 1831	Edward Partridge called as first bishop of the Church (D&C 41)
9 February 1831	Law of consecration and stewardship begins to be revealed (D&C 42)
7 June 1831	First high priests called and ordained
20 July 1831	Independence, Missouri, named as the site of the New Jerusalem (D&C 57)
3 August 1831	First temple site dedicated in Independence, Missouri
4 December 1831	Newell K. Whitney called as second bishop (D&C 72)
16 February 1832	Vision of the glories (D&C 76)
March 1832	Formal organization of First Presidency (D&C 81)
Between 20 July 1832 and 27 November 1832	Joseph Smith begins to dictate the earliest history of the Church; first account of the First Vision
22–23 September 1832	Revelation on priesthood (D&C 84)
27–28 December 1832, 3 January 1833	Revelation known as the Olive Leaf (D&C 88)
February 1833	School of the Prophets organized
6 May 1833	Revelation on the eternal existence of man (D&C 93)
2 July 1833	Translation of Bible completed
17 February 1834	First high council organized (D&C 102)

14 February 1835	First Quorum of the Twelve Apostles called
28 February 1835	First quorum of seventy called
Winter 1834–35	Lectures on Faith delivered in School of the Elders
28 March 1835	Revelation on priesthood (D&C 107)
July 1835	Church acquires four mummies and Egyptian papyri; Joseph begins translation
17 August 1835	Doctrine and Covenants approved; document on government and laws in general accepted as part of Doctrine and Covenants (D&C 134)
9–11 November 1835	Joseph relates another account of the First Vision
21 January 1836	Joseph receives a vision of the celestial kingdom, the beginnings of revelation concerning salvation for the dead (D&C 137)
21 January–1 May 1836	A Pentecostal season in which visions, revelations, angelic ministrations, and speaking in tongues were enjoyed
27 March 1836	Dedication of Kirtland Temple (D&C 109)
3 April 1836	The Savior accepts the temple; Moses, Elias, and Elijah restore keys of the priesthood (D&C 110)
23 July 1837	Restored gospel first preached in Great Britain; revelation on priesthood government given to Thomas B. Marsh (D&C 112)
26 April 1838	The Church of Jesus Christ of Latter-day Saints receives its name by revelation (D&C 115)

28 May 1843   Joseph and Emma sealed for eternity in the Red Brick Store in Nauvoo; other couples likewise sealed

12 July 1843   Revelation on eternal and plural marriage dictated by Joseph Smith to William Clayton (D&C 132)

13 August 1843   Joseph preaches at funeral of Elias Higbee on how the faithfulness of parents can, through the gospel covenant, secure their children

27 August 1843   Joseph delivers a sermon on the fulness of the blessings of the priesthood; kings and priests unto God

9 October 1843   The Prophet speaks at funeral of James Adams on death, the postmortal spirit world, and the nature and ministry of spirits and angels

7 April 1844   The Prophet delivers a discourse at the funeral of King Follett

16 June 1844   The Prophet delivers a sermon in the grove on the plurality of Gods

25 June 1844   Joseph and Hyrum Smith taken to jail in Carthage, Illinois

27 June 1844   Joseph and Hyrum Smith murdered; John Taylor seriously wounded in Carthage Jail by an armed mob

29 June 1844   Joseph and Hyrum Smith buried in Nauvoo

8 August 1844   Sidney Rigdon speaks to the assembled Saints; Brigham Young speaks, the prophetic mantle descends upon him, and he is transfigured

WHAT SHALL WE DO
WITH JOSEPH SMITH?

M ore than once, friends of other faiths have said to me, in essence, "I simply don't know what to do with Joseph Smith. I
don't believe he was either a liar or a lunatic. But I am not prepared
to accept the First Vision or the supernatural translation of golden
plates." Biographer Richard L. Bushman stated: "I think anyone
who studies the life of Joseph Smith, whether or not they believe he
was divinely inspired, has to acknowledge him as a bold innovator.
He was a man of immense power in creating new religious ideas
and in attracting people to them. That I think is a simple historical
fact."[1]

"Do I personally believe?" historian Robert Remini asked. "No.
[Joseph] may have believed that he did [see God]. But whether he
saw, I have no evidence for that. And since I'm not a Mormon who
by an act of faith believes it, even though it can't be proved, I have
to then make a judgment on the basis of the evidence. However,
you can say, *look what he did. Is one human being capable of doing
this? Without divine help and intervention?*"[2]

Years ago a group consisting of both Latter-day Saint professors

---

1. In Swinton, *American Prophet*, 128.
2. In Swinton, *American Prophet*, 46; emphasis added.

and academics from other Christian faiths met to discuss the role of Joseph Smith and the validity of his claims. The Latter-day Saints offered their perspectives and their convictions. I listened with interest as one of our friends of another faith said: "I'm prepared to believe he was a prophet with a 'small p,' but not a prophet with a 'large 'P.'" I suppose my friend meant by that comment that Joseph wasn't a devil or an impostor and may even have enjoyed some measure of divine direction in his work of restoration. What was more difficult, however, was to place Joseph Smith on the same level as Abraham, Moses, or Isaiah. Another remarked that it wasn't that he didn't believe that theophanies like what Joseph Smith described as happening in the grove of trees in 1820 were not possible, but he just wasn't convinced that that's what happened to young Joseph.

Toward the end of the meeting, one of our Christian colleagues said to the Latter-day Saints, "You folks need to understand that we take seriously the warning of Jesus to beware of false prophets." I replied, "I think we understand very well your concern. No one wants to be misled or deceived. One day, however, you may want to attend just as carefully to the Savior's teaching only one verse later: 'Ye shall know them by their fruits' (Matthew 7:15–16)." At that point, a prominent historian in the group remarked, "I'm not prepared to accept the accounts of the First Vision or the translation of golden plates, but I am haunted by the Christianity to be found in Mormon culture."

The culture. The way of life. The community. The influence. These are indeed some of the fruits of our faith, sweet fruits of the work Joseph Smith set in motion. Certainly these things should not be taken lightly, for they stand as a powerful evidence of the Restoration's truthfulness. In this volume, I have chosen to address what seems to me to be foundational to the culture, what makes Latter-day Saints behave and act as they do. What we *believe* affects what we *do;* what we *profess* affects what we *become.* Stated simply, the success and surprising influence of the Latter-day Saint community is due principally to our theological foundation, the *doctrines we believe,* doctrines that trace themselves almost exclusively to the translations, revelations, writings, and sermons of Joseph Smith. Today we build on the foundation he laid. In an interview with Mike Wallace on the CBS program *60 Minutes,* President Gordon B. Hinckley was asked how God communicates with him as the prophet and president of the Church. He responded: "Let me say first that there is a tremendous history behind this church, a history of prophecy, a history of revelation, and a backlog of decisions which set the pattern of the Church so that there aren't constant recurring problems that require any special dispensation."[3]

Elder Bruce R. McConkie once spoke of a conversation between one of his apostolic colleagues and a religious leader from another faith. "I am told that a high Catholic prelate said to one who held the holy apostleship: 'There are two things which you Mormons have which we as Catholics would like to adopt.' 'What are they?' he was asked. 'They are tithing and your missionary system,' he replied. 'Well, why don't you adopt them?' came the rejoinder. 'We would except for two reasons: our people won't pay tithing, and our people won't go on missions.'" Elder McConkie then offered this commentary on the conversation: "How often have well-meaning and sincere people in the world attempted to adopt our youth programs, our family home evening program, our missionary system, and so on, and yet have not been able to operate them in their situations!

"Why? Because they do not lay a proper foundation; however inspired the programs may be, they do not stand alone. They must be built on the foundation of faith and doctrine. The foundation upon which we build our whole Church system is one of testimony

---

3. In Dew, *Go Forward with Faith,* 585.

and faith and conversion. It is our theology; it is the doctrine God has given us in this day; it is the restored and revealed principles of eternal truth—these are the things that give us the ability to operate our programs and build houses of salvation."[4]

Clearly some of the strongest evidences of Joseph Smith's prophetic call—proofs, if you will, that he was raised up, divinely directed, and empowered to begin and champion a marvelous work and a wonder—are the doctrines that came to him and through him. Every individual is born with the capacity to know and recognize the truths of salvation. Such truths are not incomprehensible mysteries. They are intended to be known, to be felt, and to be believed by all of God's children. Every revelation, every divine communication, carries within it the evidence of its authenticity, and every daughter and son of God—whether low or high, young or old, ignorant of letters or formally educated—is divinely endowed with the ability to see the light and feel its warmth. As we open the Church's doctrinal treasure chest, it is my earnest hope that the reader will in fact see that light and feel that warmth as we sample some of the sweetest fruits of the restored gospel.

---

4. *Doctrines of the Restoration*, 227.

Chapter 1

PREPARATIONS FOR
THE RESTORATION

Before 1820. In revelation after revelation given through the Prophet Joseph Smith, the Lord Jesus Christ stated that "the field is white already to harvest" (D&C 4:4; 6:3; 11:3; 12:3; 14:3). The God who knows all things, from beginning to end, had been laying a foundation for that revolution we call the Restoration. This "marvelous work and a wonder" was not to take place without immense and intricate preparation on the part of the Almighty (2 Nephi 27:26; see also Isaiah 29:14). People would be in place. Concepts and points of view would be in the air. Hearts would be open to a new revelation in an unprecedented manner. Nothing was left to chance.

Less than fifty years before young Joseph Smith went into the grove to pray, the thirteen North American colonies had rebelled against Great Britain and successfully fought the War for Independence. Breaking off the shackles of kingcraft was, however, only part of a much larger intellectual and social process already underway. Soon after the United States was established as an independent nation, there followed the Industrial Revolution, in which Americans began to establish an independent domestic economy and by which society began to be transformed. The population of the United States doubled during the first quarter of the nineteenth century. Linked to that growth in population and opportunity was a strange conglomeration of thought, a most unusual blend of worldviews. Because some of the tenets and sentiments of the preceding Age of Reason persisted, men and women felt no hesitation in uprooting themselves intellectually, socially, economically, and spiritually. A spirit of individualism and self-determination prompted hundreds of thousands to break with tradition and chart a new course for themselves. At the same time and as a kind of reaction to what many considered to be the cold and calculating perspective of a world governed wholly by reason, the spirit of Romanticism impelled persons to look to their feelings, attend to their innermost desires, trust in the Transcendent.

In writing of the profound effects of Romanticism, historian Robert Remini observed: "What had happened was the arrival of a new romantic age that succeeded the age of reason [the Enlightenment] and emphasized the importance of human emotions and feelings. Such sentiments were no longer suspect or frowned upon as they had been in the past. Now they were believed to aid individuals in their search for truth and wisdom. Intuition also served as a tool in the search. . . .

"As this romantic impulse swept across the United States, it helped shape American attitudes about religion. The old Puritan belief in a stern deity poised to punish sin-prone man slowly yielded to the notion that humans were created in the image of God and therefore possessed the touch of divinity that elevated them above the rest of creation. In religious terms these notions translated into the belief that every person could achieve salvation through his or her own volition by submitting to the Lordship of Christ. All it took to win salvation was an act of the will and the desire to obey the commandments and lead a holy life. The idea of an elect chosen by God [the Calvinistic or Reformed doctrine of predestination] no longer had the same force it enjoyed in the colonial era."[1]

The growth in religious sentiment in this country during this era is evident in the fact that in 1825 the American Tract Society was organized and within one year had distributed 65 million religious tracts. Within six years it had twenty-seven vice presidents and thirty-six directors. The American Missionary Society was organized in 1826, and this society had 113 missionaries in New York alone. Both Baptist and Methodist churches grew in numbers quite dramatically during this time. "By the end of the Civil War," historian Grant Wacker pointed out, "the once-tiny sect of Methodists had swollen into the largest Protestant denomination in the United States, more than one million strong. The Methodists would proudly hold that place until they finally dropped behind the Baptists at the turn of the twentieth century."[2]

It was a time of revolution, what some historians have called the second American Revolution, a season of upheaval, of movement—social, political, economic, religious, and even geographical. It was a movement in values and ideology as well as location. Political philosopher Alexis de Tocqueville characterized the age as follows: "In the United States a man builds a house in which to spend his old age, and he sells it before the roof is on; he plants a garden, and leaves it just as the trees are coming into bearing."[3] Orestes Augustus Brownson, a prominent thinker of the time, explained: "No tolerable observer of the signs of the time can have failed to perceive that we are, in this vicinity at least, in the midst of a very important revolution; a revolution which extends to every department of thought, and threatens to change ultimately the whole moral aspect of society. Everything is loosened from its old

---

1. *Joseph Smith*, 4–5.
2. In Butler et al., *Religion in American Life*, 188.
3. *Democracy in America*, 2:164.

fastenings, and is floating no one can tell whither."[4] Ralph Waldo Emerson described this distinctive period as follows: "No one can converse much with different classes of society in New England, without remarking the progress of a revolution. Those who share in it have no external organization, no badge, no creed, no name. . . . They are united only in a common love of truth and love of its work."[5]

People were in search of new ideas, novel endeavors, unusual enterprises. The spirit of utopianism, a yearning for the establishment of Zion or the ideal society, was in the air. Communitarian groups, such as the United Society of Believers in Christ's Second Appearing (the Shakers) and the Oneida Community led by John Humphrey Noyes, sought to establish the model community based on peculiar notions of human sexuality.[6] "In establishing his Zion," Latter-day Saint historian Richard Bushman wrote, "Joseph joined a large company of utopian community builders. Between 1787 and 1860, 137 communitarian experiments were undertaken in the United States. All sought to improve the world by forming miniature societies on ideal principles."[7]

LONGINGS FOR THE PRIMITIVE CHURCH

This was the age of Restorationism, a time of what historians frequently call Christian Primitivism, a time in America's history when individuals read the Bible, believed its story and message, and sought for a return to what they called the ancient order of things. Many longed for the reestablishment of primitive Christianity; others desired to enjoy the spiritual gifts and outpourings that had once

---

4. *Boston Quarterly Review*, 3:265.

5. "The Editors to the Reader," *Dial* 1, no. 1 (July 1840): 2.

6. See Foster, *Religion and Sexuality*; Stein, *Shaker Experience*; Taysom, *Shakers, Mormonism, and Religious Worlds*.

7. *Rough Stone Rolling*, 165.

graced the ancients. Thomas Jefferson, author of the Declaration of Independence and one of America's Founding Fathers, wrote: "I am looking with anxiety to see the dawn of primitive Christianity here, where, if it once appears, it will soon beam like the rising sun and restore reason to her day! 'Thy kingdom come' is therefore my prayer; and my confidence is that it will come."[8]

A notable feature of the age was a desire on the part of many Americans to jettison the theological formulations, the doctrinal creeds and confessions of Christendom, to focus less on *orthodoxy* (correct theology) and more on *orthopraxy* (the practice of religion in daily life). As early as 1756 John Adams, second president of the United States, wrote: "Where do we find a precept in the Gospel requiring ecclesiastical synods, convocations, councils, decrees, creeds, confessions, oaths, subscriptions, and whole cartloads of other trumpery, that we find religion encumbered with in these days?"[9] His wife, Abigail, wrote in 1818: "When will mankind be convinced that true religion is from the heart, between man and his Creator, and not the imposition of man or creeds or tests?"[10] Thomas Jefferson was even more harsh in his denunciation of creeds. "I have never permitted myself to meditate a specified creed," he stated. "These formulas have been the bane and ruin of the Christian church, its own fatal invention which, through so many ages, made of Christendom a slaughter house, and at this day divides it into castes of indistinguishable hatred to one another."[11]

Another example of a person imbued with Restorationist desires was Alexander Campbell. He and his father, Thomas, came

---

8. Jefferson to Benjamin Waterhouse, 15 Oct. 1822; in Hutson, *Founders on Religion,* 58–59.

9. John Adams, Diary, 18 Feb. 1756, in Hutson, *Founders on Religion,* 79.

10. Abigail Adams to Louisa Catherine Adams, 3 Jan. 1818, in Hutson, *Founders on Religion,* 79.

11. Jefferson to Thomas Whittemore, 5 June 1822, cited in Hutson, *Founders on Religion,* 81.

to America from Ireland. Educated and trained as Presbyterian ministers in Scotland, Thomas and Alexander campaigned against creeds and a strict Calvinism. Thomas arrived in America first and, after obtaining a pastorate in a Presbyterian church in southwestern Pennsylvania, incurred the wrath of the synod for teaching what were perceived as heretical doctrines. Thomas Campbell rejected the notion that the church should hold the Westminster Confession of Faith as a term of communion. He denied that faith came through some mystical-emotional experience and taught that faith resulted rather from "an intelligent response to the mind of evidence."[12] After his dismissal by the Presbyterians, Thomas continued to teach his doctrines to the farmers in western Pennsylvania and organized the "Christian Association of Washington" in 1809. This society emphasized "a pure Gospel ministry, that shall reduce to practice that whole form of doctrine, worship, discipline, and government, expressly revealed and enjoined in the word of God."[13]

Alexander Campbell joined his father in America in 1809, learned of the beliefs and practices of the movement, and assumed leadership of it. He accepted the doctrine of baptism by immersion, was baptized, and in 1811 accepted the pastorate at the Brush Run Baptist church in what is now Bethany, West Virginia. His adherence to Restorationist beliefs proved a serious concern to the Baptists, and he was rejected by many Baptist colleagues in the ministry. In 1823 the younger Campbell began editing a magazine called the *Christian Baptist,* the title of which was eventually changed to the *Millennial Harbinger,* evidencing a belief in the imminence of Christ's second coming. Alexander Campbell's dissatisfaction with nominal Christianity is apparent in his statement from the first volume of the *Christian Baptist:* "We are convinced, fully convinced, that the whole head is sick, and the whole heart faint

---

12. See Garrison and DeGroot, *Disciples of Christ,* 133–39.
13. Garrison and DeGroot, *Disciples of Christ,* 146–48.

of modern fashionable Christianity."[14] In addition, Campbell the iconoclast "condemned all beliefs and practices that could not be validated by apostolic mandates. He proclaimed that missionary societies, tract societies, Bible societies, synods, associations, and theological seminaries were inconsistent with pure religion."[15]

The Campbells' disillusionment with nineteenth-century religion was not an isolated sentiment. As late as 1838 Ralph Waldo Emerson stated in his famous "Divinity School Address" at Harvard that "the need was never greater of new revelation than now." Further, "the Church seems to totter to its fall, almost all life extinct." Continuing, Emerson said, "I look forward for the hour when the supreme Beauty, which ravished the souls of those Eastern men, and chiefly of those Hebrews, and through their lips spoke oracles to all time, shall speak in the west also."[16]

CONCLUSION

In light of the characteristics of the age, it is perfectly understandable why Sidney Rigdon, who became a close associate of Alexander Campbell before discovering Mormonism, would become a servant in the hands of the Lord as a kind of Elias, or forerunner: "Behold thou wast sent forth, even as John [the Baptist], to prepare the way before me, and before Elijah which should come, and thou knewest it not" (D&C 35:4). Sidney received the restored gospel himself and then enthusiastically rushed back to his congregations to deliver the glad tidings. Such individuals as Parley P. Pratt, who had come to know Brother Rigdon quite well before he discovered the gospel fulness, went on to become pillars in the

14. *Christian Baptist,* 1:33.

15. Backman, *American Religions and the Rise of Mormonism,* 241.

16. Cambridge, Massachusetts, 15 July 1838, cited in Ahlstrom, *Theology in America,* 306, 315–16.

temple of God, powerful and influential spokespersons for the new revelation.

Many people were watching and waiting and praying for God to bare his arm and make known the ancient order of things (Isaiah 52:10; 1 Nephi 22:10–11). A number of later Latter-day Saint leaders spoke of their own quest for truth and of the frustrations they felt before their encounter with Joseph Smith. Brigham Young stated: "My mind was opened to conviction, and I knew that the Christian world had not the religion that Jesus and the Apostles taught. I knew that there was not a Bible Christian on earth within my knowledge."[17] Wilford Woodruff, fourth President of the Church, said, "I did not join any church, believing that the Church of Christ in its true organization did not exist upon the earth."[18] The God and Father of us all, a Being of perfect mercy and infinite love, did not allow such righteous yearnings to go unanswered for much longer. The heavens were opened. In 1842 Brother Joseph remarked that *the God of heaven has begun to restore the ancient order of His kingdom* unto His servants and His people—a day in which all things are concurring to bring about the completion of the fullness of the Gospel, *a fullness of the dispensation of dispensations,* even the fullness of times."[19]

---

17. In *Journal of Discourses,* 5:75.

18. In *Journal of Discourses,* 4:99.

19. *Joseph Smith* [manual], 510; emphasis added.

Chapter 2

THE HEAVENS ARE OPENED

Palmyra, Spring 1820. In the months preceding the opening of the heavens in the Sacred Grove, upstate New York was in the midst of widespread foment. Talk of religion and truth and sin and salvation was heard throughout the area, which came to be known as the Burnt-Over District. Circuit riders and pastors of various persuasions were engaged in a sobering competition for souls. Men and women, boys and girls, were being pressed, proselyted, and persuaded by preachers to choose what doctrines they should accept and with which denomination they would affiliate. That is the world in which the family of Joseph Smith Sr. and Lucy Mack Smith found themselves, the world in which the Restoration began.

Members of The Church of Jesus Christ of Latter-day Saints are Christian, and it matters very much to us that others understand that. We believe that the Jesus of history, the Jesus of the New Testament, was in very deed the Christ of faith. This is the Jesus we know and worship, the One of whom we bear fervent testimony as Latter-day Saints. We are, however, Christians with a difference. That is to say, we are not a part of traditional or Trinitarian or Nicene Christianity. That difference begins with events in the spring of 1820.

THE WAR OF WORDS

Joseph Smith recalled the spiritual environment in 1820: "My mind at times was greatly excited, the cry and tumult were so great and incessant. The Presbyterians were most decided against the Baptists and Methodists, and used all the powers of both reason and sophistry to prove their errors, or, at least, to make the people think they were in error. On the other hand, the Baptists and Methodists in their turn were equally zealous in endeavoring to establish their own tenets and disprove all others. In the midst of this war of words and tumult of opinions, I often said to myself: What is to be done? Who of all these parties are right; or, are they all wrong together? If any one of them be right, which is it, and how shall I know it?" (Joseph Smith–History 1:9–10).

My colleague Milton V. Backman Jr. provided a brief listing of various doctrinal beliefs at the time of the First Vision, an overview that will assist us to better appreciate what the Prophet meant when he spoke of the "war of words and tumult of opinions" (Joseph Smith–History 1:10).[1]

Baptism

Presbyterians, Methodists, Congregationalists, and Episcopalians believed that infants were proper subjects of baptism and that sprinkling, pouring, and immersion were proper modes of baptism.

Baptists and Eastern Christians (sometimes called Christian Connection) held that only believers should be baptized and that immersion was the only correct mode of baptism.

The Society of Friends or Quakers rejected all sacraments (ordinances).

---

1. *American Religions and the Rise of Mormonism*, 465–78.

Man's Role in Salvation

Calvinist Baptists (the Baptists of Palmyra and Manchester were Calvinist Baptists), Presbyterians, and Congregationalists believed in the Five Points of Calvinism. The "five points of Calvinism," put forward by the followers of John Calvin (1509–1564), are Total depravity, Unconditional election (predestination), Limited atonement (Christ's suffering is efficacious only for the elect, those chosen for salvation before the world was created), Irresistible grace (God will find and make known those who are elect), and Perseverance of the saints (an elect person cannot fall from grace). The five points are often remembered by the acronym TULIP.

Methodists, Freewill Baptists, Quakers, and Episcopalians aligned themselves with the teachings of Arminianism[2]: human depravity (but not total depravity), God's foreknowledge (but not predestination), limited atonement (all believers who persevere to the end benefit from Christ's Atonement), man can reject the call, and man can fall from grace.

Sources of Religious Truth

Baptists, Presbyterians, Methodists, Congregationalists, Episcopalians, and Eastern Christians held that the Bible was the sole source of truth and standard of faith. Most also held that the Bible was without error or flaw.

Quakers accepted the Bible as the word of God but also believed that a primary source of religious truth was personal divine

2. Responses to John Calvin's teachings in the sixteenth century came most strongly from Jacob Arminius (1559–1609) and his followers, known as the Remonstrants. Arminius was a resident of Holland who had been schooled in the Reformed tradition but began to find fault with its premises and conclusions. "The Remonstrance" was a document prepared after Arminius's death in 1609 to set forth the principal views and concerns of Arminius and his followers. For a list of their tenets, see Olson, *Arminianism*, 32.

guidance, contending that the Bible contained errors of omission, additions, and mistranslations.

Godhead

Baptists, Presbyterians, Congregationalists, Episcopalians, and Quakers believed in the Trinity, the triune God consisting of three persons of one essence or substance.

Eastern Christians, most Unitarians, and Universalists held that the Father and Son were separate and distinct spirits.

Divine Authority

Baptists, Presbyterians, Methodists, Congregationalists, and Eastern Christians accepted the notion of a priesthood of all believers. This is a concept that Martin Luther and the Reformers adopted. It stated simply that an individual derives his or her "priesthood," or authority to act or officiate, from the Savior's great commission to go into all the world and make disciples (Matthew 28:19–20), from the holy scriptures, or from a personal call from God to the ministry. It does not come from a priestly hierarchy.

Catholics, Eastern Orthodox, and Episcopalians believed in apostolic succession.

Quakers held that there was no need for authority (no sacraments or ordinances).

Life after Death

Baptists, Presbyterians, Methodists, Episcopalians, Eastern Christians, and Quakers believed in a heaven and hell.

Universalists and most Unitarians believed in universal salvation, the concept that everyone would eventually be received into heaven.

THE BURNT-OVER DISTRICT

Camp meetings and revivals were held throughout what came to be known as the Burnt-Over District because the fires of evangelistic fervor had scorched the area. It is worth noting that at the time of the First Vision only about 11 percent of the people in the United States and in the immediate vicinity where Joseph Smith lived were members of a Christian organization. People were searching, and pastors and ministers were campaigning for converts. There are more reports of revivals in upstate and western New York in 1819 and 1820 than in any other section of the country. In his 1838 account of the First Vision (the authorized account, in the Pearl of Great Price), the Prophet did not state that great multitudes were joining churches in Palmyra but rather in the whole region or district or country. As we have mentioned, Methodism was the fastest growing religion in America at the time: the Methodists held more camp meetings than any other group.[3]

PRELUDE TO THE FIRST VISION

The Joseph Smith Sr. family was certainly inclined toward spiritual things. William Smith, a younger brother to Joseph Jr., spoke of life in the Smith home: "My father's religious habits were strictly pious and moral. . . . I was called upon to listen to prayers both night and morning. . . . My parents, father and mother, poured out their souls to God, the donor of all blessings, to keep and guard their children, and keep them from sin and from all evil works."[4] Indeed, the family was remarkably open to divine manifestations, particularly inspired dreams.[5]

On the other hand, the family was in many ways divided religiously. Mother Smith, who would have been taught the tenets of Calvinism as a child, was drawn toward Presbyterianism. As we know from Joseph Jr.'s own words, Lucy Mack Smith and three of the children (Hyrum, Samuel Harrison, and Sophronia) joined that

---

3. See Backman, *Joseph Smith's First Vision*, 53–89.
4. "Notes on Chambers' *Life of Joseph Smith*," 37.
5. See *History of Joseph Smith by His Mother*, 43–50.

church (Joseph Smith–History 1:7). Father Smith felt suspicious of most organized religion. He and his father, Asael Smith, "came to believe that God was much more loving than they had been taught in church. They rejected the Calvinist idea of limited atonement. 'Jesus Christ,' Asael told his family, 'can as well save all, as any.' This way of thinking became known as Universalism, and Asael and his son Joseph organized a Universalist society the year after Joseph and Lucy were married."[6]

Young Joseph was attracted to the Methodists, by his own report (Joseph Smith–History 1:8). And Methodists, as we mentioned earlier, were Arminian—they believed fully in the freedom of the will and that all persons had a significant role to play in their own salvation. "His confusion," Richard Bushman wrote, "did not prevent him from trying to find a religious home. Two printer's apprentices at the *Palmyra Register* who knew Joseph Jr. remembered Methodist leanings. One said he caught 'a spark of Methodism in the camp meeting, away down in the woods, on the Vienna road.' The other remembered Joseph joining the probationary class of the Palmyra Methodist Church."[7]

Joseph Jr. attended many camp meetings with his family. According to one account, Joseph's "mother and brother and sister got religion. He wanted to get religion too; he wanted to feel and shout like the rest, but could feel nothing."[8] Oh, that we had more detail on what the Smiths heard and saw and experienced in what must have been colorful and eventful revivals. What we do have from Joseph are two reports, one from the official 1838 account (Joseph Smith–History 1:5–12), and this one from the Wentworth Letter

---

6. Harper, *Joseph Smith's First Vision*, 17.
7. *Rough Stone Rolling*, 37. Bushman is citing Tucker, *Origin, Rise and Progress of Mormonism;* Turner, *History of the Pioneer Settlement of Phelps and Gorham's Purchase.*
8. Alexander Neibaur Account, 1844, in Backman, *Joseph Smith's First Vision*, 177; Dodge and Harper, *Exploring the First Vision*, 29.

(1842): "I found that there was a great clash in religious sentiment; if I went to one society they referred me to one plan, and another to another; each one pointing to his own particular creed as the *summum bonum* of perfection: considering that all could not be right, and that God could not be the author of so much confusion, I determined to investigate the subject more fully, believing that if God had a church it would not be split up into factions, and that if he taught one society to worship one way, and administer in one set of ordinances, he would not teach another principles which were diametrically opposed."[9]

In describing this furor, historian Nathan Hatch explained that the Smith family "looked in vain for solace from the institutional church. The church was not absent from their lives; in fact, it was all too present—but in shrill and competing forms. The experience of this intensely religious family is evidence that the proliferation of religious options in the first two decades of the nineteenth century only compounded the crisis of religious authority already so prevalent in popular culture." Sadly, the Smiths "found their hopes for experiencing the divine confused by a cacophony of voices."[10]

Perhaps it would help us visualize this scene of religious excitement by reading the following account of DeWitt Clinton, governor of New York, who visited the area during these tumultuous times: "We stopped in a road to see the camp meeting of Methodists. . . .

"Here, eating and drinking was going on; there, people were drying themselves by a fire. . . . At length four preachers ascended the pulpit and the orchestra was filled with forty more. The people, about two hundred in number, were called together by a trumpet. . . . A good looking man opened the services with prayer. . . . After prayer he commenced a sermon, the object of which was to prove

---

9. Backman, *Joseph Smith's First Vision,* 168; Dodge and Harper, *Exploring the First Vision,* 19–20; Harper, *Joseph Smith's First Vision,* 53–54.

10. *Democratization of American Christianity,* 113–14.

the utility of preaching up the terrors of hell, as necessary to arrest the attention of the audience to the arguments of the ministers. . . . As far as we could hear, the voice of the preacher, growing louder and louder, reached our ears as we departed, and we met crowds of people going to the sermon. On the margin of the road, we saw persons with cakes, beer, and other refreshments for sale."[11]

For those who love the Bible and treasure its teachings, part of the Prophet's story, as recorded in the official 1838 account, is particularly poignant. He states that after reading James 1:5–6, "I reflected on it again and again, knowing that if any person needed wisdom from God, I did; for how to act I did not know, and unless I could get more wisdom than I then had, I would never know." Then followed these sad words: "For the *teachers of religion of the different sects understood the same passages of scripture so differently as to destroy all confidence in settling the question by an appeal to the Bible*" (Joseph Smith–History 1:12; emphasis added). Joseph and his family lived in an essentially Protestant America, and there was no single voice, no arbiter of scriptural truth, no Protestant version of the pope and bishops, no place to turn for help with the Bible. It was a profoundly confusing scene, no doubt one with which hundreds, if not thousands, of God-fearing people in the nineteenth-century Burnt-Over District identified completely.

Latter-day Saint historian Richard L. Bushman offered this perceptive assessment of the situation Joseph faced and what he did about it: "At some level, Joseph's revelations indicate a loss of trust in the Christian ministry. For all their learning and their eloquence, *the clergy could not be trusted with the Bible. They did not understand what the book meant.* It was a record of revelations, and *the ministry had turned it into a handbook. The Bible had become a text to be*

---

11. William W. Campbell, Private Canal Journal, 1849, 105–7, in Kirkham, *New Witness for Christ in America,* 1:42–43.

interpreted rather than an experience to be lived. In the process, the power of the book was lost."[12]

Four accounts of the First Vision were dictated by the Prophet Joseph Smith, in 1832, 1835, 1838, and 1842.[13] From these accounts we learn a number of doctrinal truths.

DOCTRINAL SIGNIFICANCE OF THE VISION

Before discussing some of the timeless lessons we learn from the First Vision, let us consider how unusually important this specific vision was. Elder Joseph F. Merrill of the Quorum of the Twelve Apostles pointed out: "Joseph Smith, the fourteen-year-old lad, saw the Father and the Son and heard Their voices. So far as the records indicate, this was the most glorious vision ever given to mortal man. Never before had both the Father and Son appeared simultaneously to any mortal man." Elder Merrill spoke of Joseph Smith and the First Vision "because of its extreme importance to our faith."[14]

The Power of Pondering

One tradition holds that young Joseph Smith heard Reverend George Lane encourage seekers to "ask of God" and that James 1:5–6 was a part of some of Lane's sermons. In an interview in 1894, Joseph's only surviving brother, William Smith, recalled that one evening, "Rev. Mr. Lane of the Methodists preached a sermon on 'what church shall I join,' and the burden of his discourses was to ask God, using as a text, 'If any man lack wisdom let him ask of God, who giveth to all men liberally.' And of course when Joseph went home and was looking over the text, he was impressed to do just what the preacher had said, and going out into the woods with

---

12. "Joseph Smith for the Twenty-First Century," 167–68; emphasis added; see also Neilson and Woodworth, *Believing History,* 274.

13. See lds.org/topics, "First Vision Accounts."

14. In Conference Report, Apr. 1947, 132–37; or "Joseph Smith Did See God," *Ensign,* Dec. 2015, 70–71.

childlike, simple trusting faith, believing that God meant just what he said, he kneeled down and prayed; and the time having come for the reorganization of His Church, God was pleased to show him that he should join none of these churches, but if faithful he should be chosen to establish the true Church."[15]

There is no more moving and instructive statement on the power of pondering than that contained in the Prophet's words: "I was one day reading the Epistle of James, first chapter and fifth verse, which reads: *If any of you lack wisdom, let him ask of God, that giveth to all men liberally, and upbraideth not; and it shall be given him.* Never did any passage of scripture come with more power to the heart of man than this did at this time to mine. It seemed to enter with great force into every feeling of my heart. I reflected on it again and again, knowing that if any person needed wisdom from God, I did; for how to act I did not know, and unless I could get more wisdom than I then had, I would never know" (Joseph Smith–History 1:11–12).

Notice that Joseph reflected on the scriptural words again and again; he had confidence in the word of God, and so this was no superficial inquiry. Young Joseph took an idea, a phrase written sometime around A.D. 50, and likened it to himself: He appropriately took James's words from their original New Testament context and made specific reference and application to a farm boy in 1820 in upstate New York.

How to Ask in Faith

"The classic example of asking in faith," Elder David A. Bednar explained, "is Joseph Smith and the First Vision. As young Joseph was seeking to know the truth about religion, he read the following

---

15. Briggs and Peterson, "Another Testimony," *Deseret News,* 20 Jan. 1894, 11. Whether the preacher on that occasion was indeed the Reverend George Lane has been questioned; see Harper, *Joseph Smith's First Vision,* 69–70.

verses in the first chapter of James. . . . Please notice [in James 1:5–6] the requirement to ask in faith, which I understand to mean the necessity to not only express but to do, the dual obligation to both plead and to perform, the requirement to communicate and to act.

"Pondering this biblical text led Joseph to retire to a grove of trees near his home to pray and to seek spiritual knowledge. . . . Joseph's questions focused not just on what he needed to know but also on what was to be *done!* His prayer was not simply, 'Which church is right?' His question was, 'Which church should I join?' Joseph went to the grove to ask in faith, and he was determined to act."[16]

The Reality of Satan

A vital lesson to be learned by Joseph Smith early in his prophetic training was a painful and poignant lesson but one that he needed to understand clearly: the reality of Satan and of his eternal hatred for God and His plan of salvation. It was as though the father of lies sensed that he needed to act quickly to confront Joseph Smith directly to frustrate and even stop the marvelous work and a wonder before it had a chance to get off the ground. Joseph explained that after he had knelt in the grove to offer up the yearnings of his soul, he "was seized upon by some power which entirely overcame me, and had such an astonishing influence over me as to bind my tongue so that I could not speak. Thick darkness gathered around me, and it seemed to me for a time as if I were doomed to sudden destruction" (Joseph Smith–History 1:15).

In his 1835 account of the First Vision, the Prophet related that "information was what I most desired at this time, and . . . I made a fruitless attempt to pray. My tongue seemed to be swollen in my mouth, so that I could not utter. I heard a noise behind me like some one walking towards me. I strove again to pray, but could

---

16. "Ask in Faith," *Ensign*, May 2008, 94–95.

not; the noise of walking seemed to draw nearer. I sprang upon my feet and looked around, but saw no person or thing that was calculated to produce the noise of walking. I kneeled again. My mouth was opened and my tongue loosed; I called on the Lord in mighty prayer. A pillar of fire appeared above my head, which presently rested down upon me, and filled me with unspeakable joy. A personage appeared in the midst of this pillar of flame, which was spread all around and yet nothing consumed. Another personage soon appeared like unto the first. He said unto me, 'Thy sins are forgiven thee.' He testified also unto me that Jesus Christ is the Son of God. I saw many angels in this vision. I was about 14 years old when I received this first communication."[17]

The Greater Power of God

Joseph learned by firsthand experience that the power of God Almighty is greater than Satan's power. In the first published account of the First Vision (1840 in Scotland), Elder Orson Pratt stated that "by the time that [glorious light] reached the tops of the trees, the whole wilderness, for some distance around was illuminated in a most glorious and brilliant manner. He expected to have seen the leaves and boughs of the trees consumed, as soon as the light came in contact with them; but perceiving that it did not produce that effect, he was encouraged with the hope of being able to endure its presence."[18] In his account of the vision published in the Wentworth Letter (1842), Joseph said, "I was enwrapped in a heavenly vision and saw two glorious personages who exactly resembled each other in features and likeness, surrounded with a brilliant light

---

17. In Backman, *Joseph Smith's First Vision*, 158–59; Harper, *Joseph Smith's First Vision*, 43; Dodge and Harper, *Exploring the First Vision*, 11.

18. In Backman, *Joseph Smith's First Vision*, 172; Harper, *Joseph Smith's First Vision*, 58–59; Dodge and Harper, *Exploring the First Vision*, 23–24; emphasis added.

which eclipsed the sun at noon day."[19] The First Vision established indelibly in the mind of young Joseph what he would come to know even more forcefully as the years passed: "God Almighty Himself dwells in eternal fire; flesh and blood cannot go there, for all corruption is devoured by the fire. 'Our God is a consuming fire.'"[20]

Redemption through Jesus Christ

Joseph Smith learned firsthand of life beyond the grave and of the immortality of the soul; he became, very early in his ministry, a witness of the Resurrection, for before him stood the resurrected Lord Jesus, attesting that indeed life did continue after death and that immortal life does come through the inseparable union of body and spirit. In fact, according to the earliest account of the First Vision (1832), the testimony of Jesus and the efficacy of his redeeming labor were among the first things Joseph was taught: "While in the attitude of calling upon the Lord . . . a pillar of light above the brightness of the sun at noon day came down from above and rested upon me, and I was filled with the Spirit of God. And the Lord opened the heavens upon me and I saw the Lord and he spake unto me, saying, 'Joseph, my son, thy sins are forgiven thee; go thy way; walk in my statutes; and keep my commandments. Behold, *I am the Lord of glory. I was crucified for the world, that all those who believe on my name may have eternal life. . . .*' My soul was filled with love, and for many days I could rejoice with great joy and the Lord was with me."[21]

---

19. In Backman, *Joseph Smith's First Vision,* 169; Harper, *Joseph Smith's First Vision,* 54; Dodge and Harper, *Exploring the First Vision,* 20.

20. "History of Joseph Smith," *Millennial Star* 23, no. 31 (Aug. 1861): 487.

21. In Backman, *Joseph Smith's First Vision,* 157; Harper, *Joseph Smith's First Vision,* 41; Dodge and Harper, *Exploring the First Vision,* 7; emphasis added. Regarding Joseph's statement in this account that he saw "the Lord," see the section below called "Why Some Question the First Vision."

The Nature of the Father and the Son

Brother Joseph learned that the Father and the Son are separate and distinct personages, as well as separate Beings. At that time, most Christians subscribed to the doctrine of the Trinity (two persons but one divine Being, one God). Only eleven days before his death, the Prophet declared: "I have always declared God to be a distinct personage, Jesus Christ a separate and distinct personage from God the Father, and that the Holy Ghost was a distinct personage and a spirit: and these three constitute *three distinct personages and three Gods.*"[22]

We are uncertain what the young prophet learned at the time of the First Vision relative to the corporeality or physical body of God the Father. Joseph certainly may have been taught or recognized that God has a physical body, but he did not say so. On the other hand, we learn the following from Joseph Smith's translation of Genesis, now in the sixth chapter of Moses, surprisingly early in his ministry (November–December 1830): "In the day that God created man, in the likeness of God made he him; *in the image of his own body, male and female, created he them,* and blessed them" (Moses 6:8–9; emphasis added). We will speak more of the matter of God's physical body in Chapters 12 and 20.

Order in the Kingdom of God

Joseph Smith stated that when the two glorified Beings appeared, the Father called him "by name and said, pointing to the other—*This is My Beloved Son. Hear Him!*" (Joseph Smith–History 1:16–17). There is order in the kingdom of God. Note that the Father introduces the Son. John 1:18 in the King James Version states: "No man hath seen God at any time: the only begotten Son, which is in the bosom of the Father, he hath declared him." Under

---

22. *Joseph Smith* [manual], 41–42; emphasis added.

inspiration, Joseph the Seer altered that verse as follows: "And no man hath seen God at any time; *except he hath borne record of the Son; for except it is through him no man can be saved*" (Joseph Smith Translation, John 1:19; emphasis added; compare JST, Psalm 14:1; JST, 1 John 4:12).

"We have a wonderful illustration," President Joseph Fielding Smith taught, "of how revelation comes through Christ presented to us in the Vision given to the Prophet Joseph Smith. . . .

"Had Joseph Smith come home from the grove and declared that the Father and the Son appeared to him and that the Father spoke to him and answered his question while the Son stood silently by, then we could have [identified] the story as a fraud. Joseph Smith was too young and inexperienced to know this at the time, but he made no mistake, and his story was in perfect harmony with divine truth, with the divine law that Christ is the Mediator between God and man."[23]

The Fulness of the Gospel Was Not on the Earth

Joseph learned that the Church of Jesus Christ, as established by the Savior and his apostles in the meridian of time, had not continued in its pristine purity through the centuries. He was therefore instructed to join none of the churches. "They told me that all religious denominations were believing in incorrect doctrines, and that none of them was acknowledged of God as his church and kingdom. And I was expressly commanded to 'go not after them,' at the same time receiving a promise that the fulness of the gospel should at some future time be made known unto me."[24]

"I was answered that I must join none [of the churches in the area], for they were all wrong; and the Personage who addressed me

---

23. *Doctrines of Salvation*, 1:28.
24. *Joseph Smith* [manual], 438; Backman, *Joseph Smith's First Vision*, 169; Harper, *Joseph Smith's First Vision*, 54; Dodge and Harper, *Exploring the First Vision*, 21.

said that *all their creeds were an abomination in his sight;* that those professors were all corrupt; that 'they draw near to me with their lips, but their hearts are far from me, they teach for doctrines the commandments of men, having a form of godliness, but they deny the power thereof'" (Joseph Smith–History 1:19; emphasis added).

While surely the Prophet Joseph Smith was concerned about false doctrine found within the creeds of Christendom, and more particularly the misrepresentations of God and the Godhead, he may have been almost as exercised with *creedalism* itself. The Prophet's very soul seemed to recoil at the manner in which creeds tended to separate and segregate, pigeonhole, exclude, marginalize, and create a spirit of division, rancor, and even persecution among professing Christians that was and is inconsistent with the gospel of Jesus Christ (D&C 123:7–8). Surely he felt that creeds were one of the greatest hindrances to the accomplishment of our Lord's intercessory plea, "That they all may be one" (John 17:21).

The English word *creed* comes from the Latin *credo,* which means simply, "I believe." There is nothing at all wrong with committing our beliefs to writing or making them more digestible, comprehensible, or even memorable. There is a sense in which the Articles and Covenants of the Church of Christ, which consisted essentially of section 20 of the Doctrine and Covenants, served for a time as a sort of creedal statement, especially verses 17–36; they served as a guide to some of the doctrinal beliefs and priesthood principles of the early restored Church. As we will see in Chapter 12, Lecture Five of the Lectures on Faith is a kind of creedal statement of the perfections and oneness of the members of the Godhead. And, I would suggest, the Articles of Faith are in fact a creedal statement of basic Latter-day Saint teachings and practices.

Why Some Question the First Vision

Disbelief in the Supernatural

The Prophet mentioned in his 1838 report of the First Vision that after the vision he spoke to a Methodist minister about his vision and was startled by his reaction. The man "treated my communication not only lightly, but with great contempt, saying it was all of the devil, that there were no such things as visions or revelations in these days; that all such things had ceased with the apostles, and that there would never be any more of them" (Joseph Smith–History 1:21).

Sadly, a growing number of otherwise believing persons simply cannot accept that such things still occur. There is, of course, a name for this belief—it is called Cessationism, the belief that all visions and revelations ceased with the close of the New Testament. That was the very reaction the young prophet received. In his earliest account of the First Vision (1832) Joseph Smith explained that after the vision, "my soul was filled with love, and for many days I could rejoice with great joy, and the Lord was with me. *But I could find none that would believe the heavenly vision,* nevertheless I pondered these things in my heart."[25] David Nye Whyte, editor of the *Pittsburgh Weekly Gazette,* interviewed the Prophet in 1843 and recorded that Joseph said: "When I went home and told the people that I had a revelation, and that all the churches were corrupt, they persecuted me, and they have persecuted me ever since. They thought to put me down, but they hav'nt succeeded, and they can't do it."[26] Alexander Neibaur also heard the Prophet relate his experience in the Sacred Grove. In 1844 he recorded that Joseph commented, "Told the Methodist priest [who] said this was not an

---

25. See Backman, *Joseph Smith's First Vision,* 157; Harper, *Joseph Smith's First Vision,* 41; Dodge and Harper, *Exploring the First Vision,* 7; emphasis added.

26. In Harper, *Joseph Smith's First Vision,* 65; Dodge and Harper, *Exploring the First Vision,* 29.

age for God to reveal himself in vision; revelation has ceased with the New Testament."[27] This of course confirms the description of Joseph's conversation with the Methodist minister, as given in the official history, in which the young prophet was told that "it was all of the devil, that there were no such things as visions or revelations in these days; that all such things had ceased with the apostles, and that there would never be any more of them" (Joseph Smith–History 1:21).

No doubt there will always be those who doubt the reality of Joseph Smith's experience in the grove. For some it is an inability to accept a display of the supernatural. Consider the following experience of Cotton Mather, the famous New England preacher and community leader. In 1693 Mather, a thirty-year-old who was seeking earnestly to know God's will for him, took seriously the biblical teaching that God does indeed intervene in human affairs. Mather described a "strange and memorable thing":

"After outpourings of prayer, with the utmost fervor and fasting, there appeared an Angel, whose face shone like the noonday sun. He was completely beardless, but in other respects human, his head encircled by a splendid tiara . . . ; his garments were white and shining; his robe reached to his ankles; and about his loins was a belt not unlike the girdles of the peoples of the East."[28] Would traditional Christians doubt that Mather had or could have had such an experience?

Nephi, son of Lehi, warned of such skepticism in the last days: "They shall contend one with another; and their priests shall contend one with another; and . . . they say unto the people: Hearken unto us, and hear ye our precept; for behold there is no God today,

---

27. In Backman, *Joseph Smith's First Vision*, 177; Harper, *Joseph Smith's First Vision*, 66; Dodge and Harper, *Exploring the First Vision*, 30.
28. In Silverman, *Life and Times of Cotton Mather*, 127–28; or in Mouw, *Talking with Mormons*, 84–85.

for *the Lord and the Redeemer hath done his work,* and he hath given his power unto men; behold, hearken ye unto my precept; *if they shall say there is a miracle wrought by the hand of the Lord, believe it not; for this day he is not a God of miracles; he hath done his work*" (2 Nephi 28:4–6; emphasis added).

In a letter to his uncle Silas Smith in 1833, Joseph wrote: "I have no doubt but that the holy prophets and apostles and saints in ancient days were saved in the Kingdom of God. . . . But *will all this purchase an assurance for me, or waft me to the regions of Eternal day with my garments spotless, pure, and white?* Or, must I not rather obtain for myself, by my own faith and diligence, in keeping the commandments of the Lord, an assurance of salvation for myself? *And have I not an equal privilege with the ancient saints?* And will not the Lord hear my prayers, and listen to my cries as soon as he ever did to theirs, if I come to him in the manner they did? Or is he a respecter of persons?"[29]

Various Accounts of the Vision

Some persons are troubled that there is more than one account of the First Vision with differences in detail among the accounts. We need to appreciate that each of the accounts was written to a different audience for different purposes. Milton Backman wrote: "Some have suggested that if a person does not relate an experience in the same manner each time he discusses the event, then he is not to be considered a reliable witness. In an important way, however,

---

29. *Joseph Smith* [manual], 128–30; emphasis added; see also Jessee, *Personal Writings of Joseph Smith,* 322, 324. In a statement that might surprise Latter-day Saints who have read the account of the vision many times, Richard Bushman wrote: "Newly reborn people customarily talked over their experiences with a clergyman to test the validity of the conversion. Standing on the margin of the evangelical churches, Joseph may not have recognized the ill repute of visionaries. The preacher reacted quickly and negatively, *not because of the strangeness of Joseph's story but because of its familiarity.* Subjects of revivals all too often claim to have seen visions" (*Rough Stone Rolling,* 40–41; emphasis added).

the fact that the four recitals of the First Vision are different helps support the integrity of the Mormon Prophet. The variations indicate that Joseph Smith did not deliberately create a memorized version which he related to everyone. . . . While the wordings in Joseph's account are different, a number of basic truths are disclosed in each of his recitals, clearly indicating a rich harmony in many details."[30]

In addition, we have a very close parallel with the writings of the New Testament. This was certainly the case with the writers of the four canonical Gospels of the New Testament. So it was with the apostle Paul's three accounts of his vision of the risen Lord on the road to Damascus (Acts 9; 21; 26). Are Christians, for example, prepared to discount or reject the divinity of Jesus Christ or to deny his miracles, atoning suffering, or resurrection because of variations and inconsistencies in how the Gospel story is told? Should Christians doubt the reality of Paul's conversion because Acts 9 and Acts 22 differ as to who heard the voice of the Lord and who saw the light? Probably not.[31]

Joseph Saw "the Lord"

Some persons have been troubled that Joseph, in his earliest account of his First Vision (1832), stated, "I was filled with the Spirit of God and the Lord opened the heavens upon me and *I saw the Lord* and he spake unto me." Critics are quick to point out that in the subsequent accounts of the vision, Joseph mentions two members of the Godhead. It is worth noting that in March of 1879 President John Taylor said, "The Lord appeared unto Joseph Smith,

---

30. Backman, *Joseph Smith's First Vision*, 201–2.

31. Professor Richard Lloyd Anderson drew an eloquent parallel between Joseph Smith and the apostle Paul in "Parallel Prophets: Paul and Joseph Smith," 178–79. Matthew Christensen demonstrated in his *The First Vision: A Harmonization of 10 Accounts* how the various accounts of the First Vision may be amalgamated into an insightful and inspirational story.

both the Father and the Son."[32] This would be no different from a Latter-day Saint speaking of the First Vision to a person of another faith and saying, "We believe that the heavens were opened in the spring of 1820 and that God appeared to Joseph Smith—both the Father and the Son." People in that day used the words *Lord* and *God* interchangeably, just as we do today. In that early nineteenth-century day, *Lord* meant simply the Supreme Being.[33]

THE WEDGE IS DRIVEN

It was inevitable that Joseph Smith and his followers would be at odds with their religious neighbors. Indeed, as historian R. Laurence Moore wrote, "If sustained controversy denotes cultural importance, then Mormons were as significant as any other religious group in nineteenth-century America."[34] American religious historian Jan Shipps, who has written much on the restored Church, pointed out that "unlike the restorationist understandings of the Campbellite, Seventh-day Baptist, and other primitivist movements, . . . Mormonism's understanding of itself as *the* (not 'a') restoration proceeded from the assumption that restoration could and would come about when *and only when* direct communication between humanity and divinity was reopened. This is to say that before restoration could occur, one who could speak for God, a prophet, would have to come forth."[35]

As the years passed, Latter-day Saint leaders often spoke about what beliefs distinguished the Church from the rest of the Christian world:

- God had chosen to restore the gift and power of revelation or divine communication, institutional and individual;

---

32. In *Journal of Discourses,* 20:166.
33. See Webster, *American Dictionary of the English Language,* s.v. "Lord."
34. *Religious Outsiders and the Making of Americans,* xiii.
35. "Reality of the Restoration and the Restoration Ideal," 183; emphasis added.

- Spiritual gifts, as practiced in the New Testament Church, were once again on the earth and were blessing humankind;[36]
- New scripture, holy scripture beyond the Bible, had been delivered by angels;
- Divine priesthood authority, apostolic authority, the power Jesus had given anciently to Peter and the apostles, was once more on earth;
- Sacred and saving sacraments or ordinances were again being administered by authorized servants of God;
- The restored Church of Jesus Christ had been organized and empowered, and the same organization that existed in the primitive Church was now in operation;
- God's covenant with ancient Israel was now in process of being reestablished among a modern Israel, and God had, in fulfillment of the prophecy of Isaiah, set his hand again to gather scattered Israel (Isaiah 11:11); and,
- The prophetic word of the apostle Paul that God would, in the "dispensation of the fulness of times," gather all things in one, in Christ (Ephesians 1:10), was beginning to be fulfilled.[37]

Now, to be sure, from the point of view of pastors and priests and religionists in proximity to the Latter-day Saints, such claims were audacious. They were not, however, the strongest claims. Richard Mouw of Fuller Theological Seminary pointed out that a person cannot understand the followers of Joseph Smith and what makes them tick by simply discussing, for example, their new books

---

36. In fact, the charismatic gifts—visions, dreams, healing, discernment, prophecy, and even tongues—were alive and well almost a century before they became fashionable once again with the rise of Pentecostalism in the first decade of the twentieth century at the Azusa Street Revival. Joseph Smith stated as an article of faith: "We believe in the gift of tongues, prophecy, revelation, visions, healings, interpretation of tongues, and so forth" (Articles of Faith 1:7).

37. Perhaps the first significant public treatise within Mormonism that spoke boldly of the restoration of all these things was a book published in 1837 by Parley P. Pratt, one of the first Latter-day Saint apostles, a man who has been called "the Apostle Paul of Mormonism" (Givens and Grow, *Parley P. Pratt*, 5).

of scripture. There is more. "For Mormonism, this reliance on writings—sacred 'pages'—is secondary. What they see as primary is *the office of the prophet*. The most important thing to Mormons about their early history isn't that Joseph Smith dug up the golden plates containing the Book of Mormon in the early decades of the nineteenth century. More importantly, Mormonism teaches that *in the person of Joseph Smith the ancient office of prophet was restored.*"[38]

And so The Church of Jesus Christ of Latter-day Saints very early began to be viewed as distinctive, separate and apart from Presbyterians, Methodists, Baptists, and Roman Catholics in the region. What is quite odd today is that it is extremely difficult to find accusations against the "Mormonites," as they were called occasionally, to the effect that they were *not Christian*. They were different, to be sure. Odd. Certainly peculiar. There seemed, however, to be sufficient understanding on the part of critics that the Saints did in fact believe in the redeeming mission of Jesus Christ; that whether or not one accepted the restored gospel's explanation for the origins of the Book of Mormon, the book was filled with teachings about Christ and drenched in what could be called redemptive theology—the nature of fallen humanity, man's inability to save himself, salvation by grace, and the need to be spiritually reborn. In other words, members of the young Church were viewed by most persons of other faiths as unusual and even suspicious but surely Christian. They might not have been Roman Catholic, Eastern Orthodox, or Protestant, but they did profess a belief in Jesus as the Son of God. Christian, but different.

CONCLUSION

Joseph Smith's First Vision is fundamental. It is foundational to the faith of Latter-day Saints. It represents the beginning of the

---

38. *Talking with Mormons,* 62–64; emphasis added.

re-revelation of God to his children in this final dispensation. The revelations that came through Joseph Smith made the latter-day seer acquainted with the mind and voice and will of the Master. Joseph came to know firsthand how to commune with Jehovah.

On a more personal note, I have always believed there is a God. My earliest memories of childhood contain familiar words spoken beside my bed each night: "Now I lay me down to sleep . . ." It felt right to say my prayers, and I sincerely believed that I was being heard by Someone far wiser, greater, and more powerful and loving than anyone here on earth. Further, having grown up in the Southern States, with most of my friends being Baptists, Methodists, or Roman Catholics, I sang with them "Jesus loves me! This I know, / For the Bible tells me so" and "Jesus wants me for a sunbeam" with gusto and feeling.[39] It seems that I have always believed in the living reality of Jesus Christ as the Savior and Redeemer of humankind.

My grandfather joined The Church of Jesus Christ of Latter-day Saints in the 1930s near New Orleans, Louisiana. He had been brought up as a Roman Catholic, and when he left the faith of his fathers, he was basically asked to leave his parents' home. Later he and my grandmother raised their four sons as Latter-day Saints. By the time I was born, my father and mother were not active church attenders, but in time they felt the need to bring up their children in the Church. I recall being asked to speak in church when I was about nine years old. My father did not feel at that early stage of his spiritual development that he was in a position to help me much with my talk, so my Uncle Joseph essentially wrote the talk for me. I memorized it. It was a very simple recitation of Joseph Smith's First Vision—the story of how young Joseph wrestled in 1820 with the

---

39. Verse 1 of "Jesus Loves Me," by Anna B. Warner, 1860; library.timelesstruths.org /music/Jesus_Loves_Me; "Jesus Wants Me for a Sunbeam," by Nellie Talbot, ca. 1900; library.timelesstruths.org/music/Ill_Be_a_Sunbeam.

question of which church to join, how he encountered varying and conflicting views on religious questions, and how he chose to follow the scriptural admonition to ask God for wisdom (James 1:5).

It has now been some sixty years since I looked out at that rather frightening congregation, delivered those halting words (the talk couldn't have lasted more than four or five minutes), and then sat down with a feeling of overwhelming relief. I also remember something else about that occasion—namely, how I felt at the time I spoke about God the Father and his Son Jesus Christ appearing to a fourteen-year-old boy in upstate New York. Although I was, as one might expect, nervous and fidgety behind the pulpit, I began on that occasion to feel the stirrings of testimony, the beginnings of a spiritual witness that what I was speaking about was true and that it had actually happened. The relief I felt at the completion of my talk was not simply the flood of emotion associated with having completed a daunting task but also the quiet and poignant assurance that I had spoken the truth. I knew something when I sat down that I had not known before I stood up to speak.

I have had many, many confirming witnesses of the truthfulness of Joseph Smith's claim since I stood as a child and addressed those people in the old Hiawatha Street chapel in Baton Rouge, Louisiana. And it has been my distinct honor and privilege to bear testimony of that singular event throughout the United States and in several countries throughout the world. Over the decades, I have made it my business to return as often as possible to Palmyra, New York, to the Sacred Grove. In every case, I have come away with the overwhelming sense of responsibility to bear testimony of fundamental and foundational truths, especially Joseph Smith's First Vision.

I have a witness, a solid and sustaining conviction, that Joseph Smith saw the Father and the Son in the spring of 1820 in the grove. That witness is central to all I believe and feel and do as a Latter-day Saint. Times change, people come and go, and circumstances and challenges change, but for me the First Vision is a constant, a foundation stone, a pillar of my personal religious life. As President Ezra Taft Benson taught, "The first vision of the Prophet Joseph Smith is bedrock theology to the Church."[40]

President Gordon B. Hinckley, one of Joseph Smith's prophetic successors, rejoiced: "To me it is a significant and marvelous thing that in establishing and opening this dispensation our Father did so with a revelation of himself and of his Son Jesus Christ, as if to say to all the world that he was weary of the attempts of men, earnest though these attempts might have been, to define and describe him. . . . The experience of Joseph Smith in a few moments in the grove on a spring day in 1820, brought more light and knowledge and understanding of the personality and reality and substance of God and his Beloved Son than men had arrived at during centuries of speculation."[41]

"When God the Father and his Son Jesus Christ came to earth, as they did in 1820 when they appeared to the young boy prophet, Joseph Smith," President Benson explained, "it is not something that concerns only a handful of people. It is a message and a revelation intended for all of our Father's children living upon the face of the earth. *It was the greatest event that has ever happened in this world since the resurrection of the Master.*"[42] It is the starting point, the foundation on which the Restoration is built.

---

40. *Ezra Taft Benson* [manual], 105.
41. *Teachings of Gordon B. Hinckley*, 236.
42. *Ezra Taft Benson* [manual], 105; emphasis added.

Chapter 3

ANOTHER TESTAMENT

New York and Pennsylvania, September 1823. Young Joseph Smith had been promised by the Lord that the marvelous work and a wonder was at hand and that he would play a significant role in that grand enterprise. Three years had passed, however, with no word from on high. Joseph went before the Lord once again in a spirit of contrition and inquiry. The visitation and revelation that followed would change the world and certainly the small world of the seventeen-year-old seeker.

After the First Vision, nothing was nor ever could be the same again for young Joseph Smith. Joseph knew then that the fulness of the gospel of Jesus Christ was not on the earth, nor was the Lord's true church. He also knew that something magnificent was about to take place and that he would serve a significant role in accomplishing that grand endeavor. I have always been fascinated by the Prophet's words regarding his affiliation with existing religious groups: "He again forbade me to join with any of them; and *many other things did he say unto me, which I cannot write at this time*" (Joseph Smith–History 1:20; emphasis added). We can only wonder at that expression and contemplate soberly on what the first and second members of the Godhead must have shared with this spiritually hungry, impressionable youth. Was he instructed about the revelations he would receive, the visions he would see, the divine personages who would visit him? Was he forewarned of the challenges that he and his followers, the Lord's agents, would face as they sought to carry out the will of their Principal? For now we can only contemplate and speculate. Perhaps one day the contents of that sacred session will be made known.

THE COMING OF MORONI

The three years that passed between the appearance of the Father and the Son in the Sacred Grove and the coming of Moroni must have seemed to the boy prophet like an eternity. When a mortal is allowed to come into the very presence of the Almighty Elohim and the Everlasting Jehovah, something that very few persons have ever experienced, the weeks and months that followed must surely have been filled with long periods of contemplation and extraordinary introspection and soul searching. Being excited about what had happened to him, he would have shared the experience with some of his friends, many of whom would have thought him to be at best possessed of a fertile imagination and at worst delusional, perhaps mentally unstable. There is a loneliness known only to those who have tasted of the powers of heaven that those who have not so tasted cannot comprehend, a loneliness that creates interpersonal distance, that drives one inward. Such would be a natural course of one who was shut up in a plastic bubble and kept from the world and from worldly things. Joseph, however, was not isolated from daily life, nor was he spared the temptations and distractions that come quite naturally to a teenager.

"Having been forbidden to join any of the religious sects of the day, and being of very tender years, and persecuted by those who ought to have been my friends and to have treated me kindly, . . . I was left to all kinds of temptations; and, mingling with all kinds of society, I frequently fell into many foolish errors, and displayed the weakness of youth, and the foibles of human nature." Then being more specific, he added that "I was guilty of levity and sometimes associated with jovial company, etc., not consistent with that character which ought to be maintained by one who was called of God as I had been" (Joseph Smith–History 1:28). Or, as he put it on another occasion, "During this time, as is common to most of all youths, I fell into many vices and follies; but . . . I have not, neither can it be sustained, in truth, been guilty of wrongdoing or injuring any man or society of men." He added that his foibles included "a light and too often vain mind, exhibiting a foolish and trifling conversation."[1] It may be the case that young Joseph was being overly critical of himself, much as persons he encountered in his later ministry would be when they saw him and judged his "native cheery temperament" as incompatible with the lofty office of prophet, seer, and revelator.

It was in a spirit of contemplation that Joseph found himself on the evening of 21 September 1823. Mother Smith wrote: "He retired to his bed in quite a serious and contemplative state of mind. He shortly betook himself to prayer and supplication to Almighty God, for a manifestation of his standing before Him."[2] In his 1835 history, the Prophet described the scene as follows: "When I was about 17 years old, I saw another vision of angels in the night season after I had retired to bed. I had not been asleep, but was meditating upon my past life and experience. I was very conscious that I had not kept the commandments, and I repented heartedly for all my sins and transgression and humbled myself before Him whose eyes are over all things."[3]

---

1. Letter to Oliver Cowdery, 6 Nov. 1834, "Millennium. No. X," *Messenger and Advocate* 1, no. 3 (Dec. 1834): 40.

2. *History of Joseph Smith by His Mother*, 74.

3. Journal account dictated 9 Nov. 1835 to Warren Parrish.

In describing the young prophet, Oliver Cowdery related that "his heart was drawn out in fervent prayer, and his whole soul was lost to everything of a temporal nature, that earth, to him, had lost its charms, and all he desired was to be prepared in heart to commune with some kind of messenger who would communicate to him the desired information of his acceptance with God. . . .

"In this situation hours passed unnumbered . . . but supposes it must have been eleven or twelve, and perhaps later, as the noise and bustle of the family, in retiring, had long since ceased. While continuing in prayer . . . on a sudden a light like that of day, only of a purer and far more glorious appearance and brightness, burst into the room. Indeed, to use his own description, the first sight was as though the house was filled with consuming and unquenchable fire. This sudden appearance of a light so bright, as must naturally be expected, occasioned a shock or sensation, visible to the extremities of the body. It was, however, followed with a calmness and serenity of mind, and an overwhelming rapture of joy that surpassed understanding, and in a moment a personage stood before him."[4]

Latter-day Saints know well the story that follows. Moroni introduced himself as an angel dispatched from the presence of God, "sent to bring the joyful tidings that the covenant which God made with ancient Israel was at hand to be fulfilled, . . . that the time was at hand for the gospel in all its fullness to be preached in power, unto all nations that a people might be prepared for the Millennial reign. I was informed that I was chosen to be an instrument in the hands of God to bring about some of His purposes in this glorious dispensation."[5]

Please note that in this initial moment of introduction nothing is said about the Book of Mormon. As a participant in the Nephite story, as a military and spiritual leader, and as a record

4. "Letter IV," *Messenger and Advocate* 1, no. 5 (Feb. 1835): 78.
5. *Joseph Smith* [manual], 439.

keeper himself, Moroni was of course a specific authority on the matters related to obtaining the golden plates and translating them. But he was also a general authority, an angel sent to accomplish a monumentally important task—to prepare Joseph Smith Jr. for his assignment as prophet, seer, revelator, translator, President of the restored Church of Jesus Christ, modern Abraham, and head of the dispensation of the fulness of times. Obviously Moroni would teach young Joseph all about the Nephite peoples and how to translate a record written in reformed Egyptian. He would, in addition, ready this remarkable young soul to take upon him the responsibility to reestablish the kingdom of God on earth with all of its priesthood powers, keys, covenants, ordinances, offices, quorums, and councils. Such training would take place through frequent visits with Moroni before Joseph could obtain the plates. "I went at the end of each year," Joseph reported, "and at each time I found the same messenger there, and *received instruction and intelligence from him at each of our interviews, respecting what the Lord was going to do, and how and in what manner his kingdom was to be conducted in the last days*" (Joseph Smith–History 1:54; emphasis added).

One other matter. It is important to me as a teacher of the gospel that of all the things Moroni chose to do during his first four visits to the young prophet, he chose to quote scripture passages from the Old and New Testaments. One might wonder why an angel, a messenger sent directly from the presence of God, would need to use other prophets' words. But only a moment's reflection on the matter brings to remembrance that when the risen Lord visited his American Hebrews, he did exactly the same thing: He quoted such prophets as Moses (3 Nephi 20:23, 27), Isaiah (3 Nephi 20:39–45; 3 Nephi 22), Micah (3 Nephi 21:12–18), Habakkuk (3 Nephi 21:8–9), and Malachi (3 Nephi 24–25). What a recommendation, what a model, to those of us called to speak and teach within the Church of Jesus Christ!

We learn from the Prophet's official history that Moroni quoted such prophets as Malachi, Isaiah, and Joel (Joseph Smith–History 1:36–41). In addition, Oliver Cowdery wrote that in his conversations with Joseph Smith about the visits of Moroni, he learned that many other scriptural passages were quoted, including the following:[6]

> Deuteronomy 32:23–24, 43
> Psalms 100:1–2; 107:1–7; 144:11–13
> Isaiah 1:23–26; 2:1–4; 4:5–6; 11:15–16; 29:11–14; 43:6
> Jeremiah 31:1, 6, 8, 27–28, 32–33; 16:16; 31:9; 50:4–5
> 1 Corinthians 1:27–29

One discovers that these scriptural references deal with such topics as the sorrowful condition of scattered Israel; the gathering of the people of Israel out of strange lands; God's new covenant in the latter days; the mountain of the Lord's house being set up in the tops of the mountains; Israel's becoming the Lord's people and his firstborn; the establishment of Zion as a defense; God's vengeance to be answered upon his adversaries; and Jehovah's everlasting reign on earth. In short, Joseph Smith was being tutored by heavenly messengers, was becoming more than a distant acquaintance with holy scripture, and was beginning to see his place in God's prophesied latter-day work.

THE TRANSLATION OF THE PLATES

Much has been spoken and written in recent years about how the Prophet Joseph Smith was able to translate the golden plates. Considering that everyone imaginable from the nineteenth century who might have seen this or heard that was interviewed, historians have sifted and sorted, compared and contrasted, pooled and amalgamated, and come to what for them are final conclusions on the matter, and they all appear to have worked out the details for

---

6. "Letter IV," *Messenger and Advocate* 1, no. 5 (Feb. 1835): 77–80.

themselves. Ironically, the two persons who were most closely and intimately involved in the inspired work of translation—Joseph Smith and Oliver Cowdery—are the ones who spoke the least on how the translation took place.

Joseph Smith said: "I would inform you that I translated, by the gift and power of God, and caused to be written, one hundred and sixteen pages, the which I took from the Book of Lehi, which was an account abridged from the plates of Lehi, by the hand of Mormon" (Preface to the 1830 edition of the Book of Mormon). In explaining how he received and then translated the plates, Joseph later related, "Moroni, the person who deposited the plates . . . in a hill in Manchester, Ontario County New York, being dead, and raised again therefrom, appeared unto me, and told me where they were; and gave me directions how to obtain them. I obtained them, and the Urim and Thummim with them, by the means of which, I translated the plates; and thus came the Book of Mormon."[7] Also: "By the power of God I translated the Book of Mormon from hieroglyphics, the knowledge of which was lost to the world, in which wonderful event I stood alone, an unlearned youth, to combat the worldly wisdom and multiplied ignorance of eighteen centuries, with a new revelation."[8]

Oliver Cowdery recorded the following: "Br. Hyrum Smith said that he thought best that the information of the coming forth of the Book of Mormon be related by Joseph himself to the Elders present that all might know for themselves. Br. Joseph Smith Jr. said that *it was not intended to tell the world all the particulars of the coming forth of the Book of Mormon, & also said that it was not expedient for him to relate these things.*"[9] In the Wentworth Letter (1842) the Prophet explained simply that "with the records was

---

7. *Elders' Journal* 1, no. 3 (July 1838): 42–43.

8. *Joseph Smith* [manual], 60.

9. *Far West Record,* 23; emphasis added.

found a curious instrument which the ancients called 'Urim and Thummim,' which consisted of two transparent stones set in the rim of a bow fastened to a breastplate. Through the medium of the Urim and Thummim I translated the record by the gift and power of God."[10]

Oliver Cowdery wrote to W. W. Phelps: "These were days never to be forgotten—to sit under the sound of a voice dictated by the *inspiration* of heaven, awakened the utmost gratitude of this bosom! Day after day I continued, uninterrupted, to write from his mouth, as he translated, with the *Urim and Thummim,* or, as the Nephites would have said, 'Interpreters,' the history, or record, called 'The Book of Mormon.'"[11] Oliver explained on another occasion that "while [Joseph] looked through the stone spectacles another sat by and wrote what he told them, *and thus the book was all written.*"[12] And what to me is perhaps the most powerful statement by Brother Cowdery after he had determined to return to the Church (1848): "I wrote with my own pen the entire Book of Mormon (save a few pages) as it fell from the lips of the Prophet, *as he translated it by the gift and power of God, by the means of the Urim and Thummim, or, as it is called by that book, holy interpreters.* I beheld with my eyes and handled with my hands the gold plates from which it was translated. I also beheld the interpreters. That book is true. Sidney Rigdon did not write it. Mr. [Solomon] Spaulding did not write it. I wrote it myself as it fell from the lips of the Prophet."[13]

---

10. *Joseph Smith* [manual], 440–41; "Church History," *Times and Seasons* 3, no. 9 (Mar. 1842): 707.

11. "Letter I," *Messenger and Advocate* 1, no. 1 (Oct. 1834): 14; italics in original.

12. Josiah Jones, "History of the Mormonites," *Evangelist* 9 (1 June 1841): 132–34, in Welch and Carlson, *Opening the Heavens,* 142; emphasis added.

13. Reuben Miller Journal, 21 Oct. 1848, in Welch and Carlson, *Opening the Heavens,* 143; emphasis added. For current views on the process of translation, see Turley and Slaughter, *How We Got the Book of Mormon,* 13–25; MacKay and Dirkmaat, *From Darkness unto Light,* 61–139; Turley, Jensen, and Ashurst-McGee, "Joseph the Seer," *Ensign,* Oct. 2015, 49–55.

A Doctrinal Treasure

Sometimes when we have read a book of scripture many times, we lock into the story, or narrative—which is vital, for it contains the context for the inspirational teachings—but never get deep enough into the doctrinal messages, the theological presentations, to enjoy that unusual endowment of the Spirit that comes as we contemplate, reconsider, and reflect seriously on pure doctrine. If, as President Boyd K. Packer taught, "true doctrine, understood, changes attitudes and behavior,"[14] then surely immersing ourselves in the principles and precepts of the Book of Mormon should purify our motives and desires and elevate our perspective. "The richness of the Book of Mormon," Elder Neal A. Maxwell observed, "is basically spiritual, not historical. It is one thing to focus on stage and scenery and quite another to focus on substance."[15]

Not long ago, I sat down and began to browse the Book of Mormon, looking exclusively for great doctrinal truths. Soon I began making notes to myself. Despite my having read the Book of Mormon many, many times and searched and studied and taught its doctrines for over four decades, I was stunned and delightfully surprised by what I found.

Let me reminisce for a moment to make my point. I remember very well the week of February 21–27, 1967. It was the week I spent in what was then called the Mission Home on Main Street in Salt Lake City. Together with about three hundred young men and women, I had come to be taught and prepared in some manner for what we were about to experience over the next eighteen or twenty-four months. When I reflect now on what took place, I am both thrilled and saddened—thrilled by the privilege of sitting at the feet of a surprising number of general authorities (in those days

14. "Little Children," *Ensign*, Nov. 1986, 17.
15. *Plain and Precious Things*, 2.

the Brethren did most of the teaching of the missionaries) and saddened that I probably did not appreciate at that time what a feast was being served up. Instruction was given by members of the First Presidency, the Quorum of the Twelve Apostles, the Assistants to the Twelve, and the members of the First Council of the Seventy.

I remember that we received instruction from Elder Bruce R. McConkie, then one of the seven presidents of the Seventy. I had heard him speak in general conference before 1967 and was somewhat acquainted with his well-known reference work, *Mormon Doctrine.* Elder McConkie spoke on the power of the Book of Mormon. He said, in essence, that if we want to understand the doctrines of the restored gospel of Jesus Christ, we must turn to the Book of Mormon, our most powerful source for doctrine.

I remember thinking to myself, "Wait a minute. Why the Book of Mormon? Why not the Doctrine and Covenants? Isn't that really where most of the doctrine is?"

My unspoken queries reveal just how much I knew about the Book of Mormon at the time. Our family had for a time listened to the Book of Mormon records, and that was a good beginning, but, I am ashamed to admit, until I entered the mission field, I had not read the actual book myself. Oh, if at that impressionable time I could have realized the import of Elder McConkie's words! Well, of course, he was right on target. For a sampling of just some of the doctrines and precepts taught in the Book of Mormon, see Appendix 1 at the end of this book.

We are given little indication in the biblical record that the prophet-writers delivered and preserved their messages for any day other than their own. There is no doubt that Isaiah, Jeremiah, Ezekiel, Daniel, Malachi, Peter, Paul, John, and others spoke of the distant future; by the power of the Spirit, they saw and described the doings of peoples of another time and place. Their words were given to the people of their own time. Their words have found and will yet find application and fulfillment for future times. And yet we never encounter a particular prophet from the stick of Judah addressing himself directly to those who will one day read his pronouncements.

The Book of Mormon is different. It was prepared and preserved by men who saw and knew our day and addressed themselves to specific issues that a people in the last days would confront. The poignant words of Moroni alert us to the contemporary relevance of the Book of Mormon: "Behold, I speak unto you as if ye were present, and yet ye are not. But behold, Jesus Christ hath shown you unto me, and I know your doing" (Mormon 8:35). Later Moroni said: "Behold, I speak unto you as though I spake from the dead; for I know that ye shall have my words" (Mormon 9:30). In the words of President Ezra Taft Benson, the Book of Mormon "was written for our day. *The Nephites never had the book; neither did the Lamanites of ancient times.* It was meant for us. Mormon wrote near the end of the Nephite civilization. Under the inspiration of God, who sees all things from the beginning, he abridged centuries of records, choosing the stories, speeches, and events that would be most helpful to us."[16]

Remembering the significant statement from President Boyd K. Packer that "true doctrine, understood, changes attitudes and behavior,"[17] let us speak of how the Book of Mormon doctrine and its messages may be applied to individual lives. For example, do we desire to know how to handle wayward children; how to deal justly yet mercifully with transgressors; how to bear pure testimony; how to teach and preach in such a manner that people cannot go away unaffected; how to detect the enemies of Christ and how to withstand those who seek to destroy our faith; how to discern and expose secret combinations that seek to destroy the works of the

---

16. *A Witness and a Warning,* 19; emphasis added.
17. "Little Children," *Ensign,* Nov. 1986, 17.

Lamb of God; how to deal properly with persecution and assaults on the faith; and how to establish Zion?

Do we desire to know more about how to avoid pride and the perils of the prosperity cycle; how to avoid priestcraft and acquire and embody charity, the pure love of Christ; how our sins may be remitted and how we can know when they have been forgiven; how to retain a remission of sins from day to day; how to come unto Christ, receive his holy name, partake of his goodness and love, be sanctified by his Spirit, and eventually be sealed to him? Do we desire to know how to prepare for the second coming of the Son of Man? The Book of Mormon is stunningly relevant. This surely is at least partially what Joseph Smith meant when he taught that a person could get nearer to God by abiding by the precepts of the Book of Mormon than by any other book.[18]

But there is more. The Book of Mormon is far more than a theological treatise, more than a collection of great doctrinal sermons. (It would be beyond valuable even if that were all it was.) It is not just a book that helps us feel good; it is a heavenly document that has been given to help us *be* good. It is as if the Nephite prophet-leaders were pleading to us from the dust: "We sought for the Lord. We found him. We applied the gospel of Jesus Christ and have partaken of its sweet fruits. We know the joy of our redemption and have felt to sing the song of redeeming love. And now, O reader, go and do thou likewise!" The Book of Mormon is not only an invitation to come unto Christ but a pattern for the accomplishment of that consummate privilege. That invitation is extended to all of the earth's inhabitants, the rank and file as well as the prophets and apostles.

The Book of Mormon does more than teach with plainness and persuasion the effects of the Fall and the absolute necessity for an

---

18. *Joseph Smith* [manual], 64.

atonement; it cries out to us that unless we acknowledge our fallen state, put off the natural man, apply the atoning blood of Christ, and be born again, we can never—worlds without end—be with or become like our Lord. Nor can we ever hope to establish Zion, a society of the pure in heart. The Book of Mormon is not just a book about religion. *It is religion.* Our challenge, therefore, is not just to read and study the Book of Mormon; we must live it and accept and apply its doctrines and philosophy (D&C 84:57).

FREQUENTLY ASKED QUESTIONS

Scripture beyond the Bible?

One reason some people contend that Latter-day Saints are not Christian is our acceptance of the Book of Mormon, as well as the Doctrine and Covenants and Pearl of Great Price, as holy scripture. That is, we couldn't possibly be Christian because we expand the Christian canon of scripture. For those critics of the Church who state that the Latter-day Saints are not Christian, the words of Stephen Webb, a Roman Catholic scholar, relative to the Book of Mormon, may be of some interest. "Whatever one thinks about Joseph Smith's claims regarding the origins of the Book of Mormon," Webb wrote, "it is impossible to deny that the book is full of a Jesus who is very divine. . . . The Book of Mormon . . . has stories about and sayings by Jesus that do not appear in the New Testament. The really crucial question, then, is the following: Does the Book of Mormon add to the Gospels in a way that is consistent with the New Testament, or does it damage or deface the Gospel portrait?"

Webb suggests an analogy, a scenario that should cause most non-Mormon readers—particularly those who look upon the Book of Mormon with suspicion—to at least be a bit reflective: "Your family gathers at the funeral of your dearly beloved grandfather, a world traveler. Your relatives begin telling the familiar stories about

his legendary adventures. Soon, however, you notice another group
of mourners at the other end of the room. As you eavesdrop on
them, you realize that they are talking about your grandfather as if
they knew him well, yet you have never met these people or heard
some of the stories they are telling. . . .

"There is . . . no need for you to react to this other group's
love for your grandfather as if they are trying to threaten or harm
you. Whether or not you decide to expand your family to include
this group, you can still welcome them for their sincere efforts to
honor and respect your grandfather's memory. And the more you
love your grandfather, the more you will be drawn to discover for
yourself whether these new stories are true.

"Of course, Jesus Christ is not your grandfather, and the stories
Christians tell about him are grounded in scripture, not legends
and lore. Still, the Book of Mormon raises a very awkward question
for Christians: Can you believe too much about Jesus?"[19]

The Fulness of the Gospel?

Now, having established that the Nephite-Jaredite record is
saturated in doctrine, let us address ourselves to a few of the questions raised occasionally both by staunch believers and by skeptical
critics. The first is this: If the Book of Mormon contains the "fulness of the gospel of Jesus Christ" (D&C 20:9; 27:5; 42:12; 135:3),
how is it that there is no mention made within the book of such
singularly Latter-day Saint beliefs as the teaching of the gospel in
the postmortal spirit world; three degrees of glory hereafter; eternal
marriage; the vital place of temples; and deification, or *theosis,* the
notion that mortals may become as God?

We begin our response by observing that the Book of Mormon
is a story, a running narrative, "the saga of a message, a testament."[20]

---

19. *Mormon Christianity,* 114–21.
20. Packer, *Let Not Your Heart Be Troubled,* 282.

The Book of Mormon is not intended to be a kind of systematic theology, any more than are the Old and New Testaments. It contains the fulness of the gospel, though not in the sense that it contains every doctrinal feature of Mormonism—for it is not, strictly speaking, a book about The Church of Jesus Christ of Latter-day Saints. Rather, the prophets in the Book of Mormon teach powerfully and persuasively the good news, or glad tidings, that Jesus Christ came into the world to redeem fallen humanity from the Fall of our first parents and from our own sins on condition of repentance. The prophets bear repeated testimony that the infinite atonement is to be accessed through faith in Christ, repentance from sin, an authorized baptism by immersion, the reception of the Holy Ghost by the laying on of hands, and enduring faithfully to the end. This is the gospel. It is Christ crucified and risen from the dead. It is the first principles and ordinances.

President Ezra Taft Benson explained that to say that the Book of Mormon contains the fulness of the gospel of Jesus Christ "does not mean it contains every teaching, every doctrine ever revealed. Rather, it means that in the Book of Mormon we will find the fulness of those doctrines required for our salvation. And they are taught plainly and simply so that even children can learn the ways of salvation and exaltation. The Book of Mormon offers so much that broadens our understandings of the doctrines of salvation. Without it, much of what is taught in other scriptures would not be nearly so plain and precious."[21]

Joseph Smith's Use of the Book of Mormon?

Another question that arises occasionally is, If the Book of Mormon is so significant, so replete with wisdom and theological truths, why did the Prophet Joseph Smith quote from it so seldom? That is a worthwhile observation and an excellent query. If one were

---

21. *A Witness and a Warning,* 18–19.

to read the many sermons delivered by Brother Joseph, particularly in Nauvoo, it doesn't take long to discover that his remarks are laced with biblical quotations or paraphrases. He clearly relied heavily upon the New Testament, for example, and focused a great deal on the writings of the apostle Paul.[22] Only a moment's reflection is necessary to appreciate that young Joseph was brought up with the Bible. His family studied it, and he heard its passages read and commented on at revivals and camp meetings and church services.

In addition, as we will consider in more detail in Chapter 7, Joseph spent three years, from June 1830 to July 1833, in an intense study of the King James Bible while engaged in his work of preparing an inspired "new translation." The Bible was in his soul, and it would make perfect sense that the Prophet would draw upon biblical phrases and stories and personalities to make many of his points as he taught the gospel to the Saints. Orson Spencer, a Baptist minister who joined the Church, wrote, "I have never known [Joseph] to deny or depreciate a single truth of the Old and New Testaments; but I have always known him to explain and defend them in a masterly manner."[23]

The Church of Jesus Christ of Latter-day Saints is steeped in the Bible and in its teachings. Because we are blessed to have in our possession a marvelous library of latter-day revelation and modern scripture, we, as well as those who are critical of the Church, are sometimes prone to overlook the fact that our faith and way of life are inherently biblical. This truth may be illustrated informally but quickly by analyzing one of our recent general conferences for the number of times the Holy Bible is quoted or paraphrased or referred to. For that matter, notice in any given sacrament meeting sermon how freely we move from Mosiah to Hebrews to 2 Nephi to

---

22. See Jackson, *Joseph Smith's Commentary on the Bible.*
23. Letter to an unknown person, 17 Nov. 1842, in *Joseph Smith* [manual], 500; "Letter of Orson Spencer," *Times and Seasons* 4, no. 4 (2 Jan. 1843): 56–57.

Romans to the Doctrine and Covenants to Genesis. In other words, we frequently and without much forethought tend to follow the risen Lord's pattern for teaching the Nephites—we seek to expound all the scriptures in one (3 Nephi 23:14). And right in the middle of that is the Bible.

Perhaps more important for our present consideration, I suggest that Joseph did not quote very often from the Book of Mormon because it was not something he created, brought forth from his own imagination, or devised as a result of his own genius. "Clearly," Elder Neal A. Maxwell explained, "this book came *through* a 'choice seer'—Joseph Smith—but not *from* that seer. Some, desperate for an alternative explanation, almost seem to suppose Joseph was getting help from some theological mail-order supply house. To the human mind it is amazing that such rich revelations and translations should come through an untrained individual such as Joseph was. The reason, of course, is that though Joseph did not spell perfectly, he came to know the grammar of the gospel, because he was God's apt pupil."[24]

The Book of Mormon Outgrown?

Some persons, both within the faith and outside it, have suggested that though the Book of Mormon served an important role in the early days of the Restoration, by and large the Mormon prophet and his followers outgrew the book as time went by and as deeper and more distinctive doctrines, particularly those in Nauvoo, were made known. Such persons claim that while the Book of Mormon presents a doctrine that is focused on an infinite Deity, fallen humanity, and the need to be saved by the grace of Jesus Christ (all paramount teachings in the Book of Mormon), later Mormonism, especially the Nauvoo developments, moved more toward a belief in

---

24. *But for a Small Moment*, 44.

a finite God, the innate goodness of man, and exaltation and glory through human works.[25]

For me, this is a false dichotomy. The Joseph Smith who repudiated *ex nihilo* creation, who built temples and taught his people to perform baptisms in behalf of those who had not received the gospel in this life, and who taught that mortal beings had the potential to become like God—*that* Joseph Smith was the same man who translated the Book of Mormon, was schooled in its doctrine and precepts, and taught them until his death in 1844. Joseph Smith did not outgrow or transcend the Book of Mormon and its teachings, nor did his people. The Book of Mormon was not superseded by Joseph's progressive or sophisticated ideas. Indeed, he was teaching and bearing testimony of that book to the prison guards the night before his death in the jail in Carthage, Illinois. According to Dan Jones, who was at the jail and heard the Prophet speak, "Joseph bore a powerful testimony to the guards of the divine authenticity of the Book of Mormon, the restoration of the Gospel, the administration of angels, and that the kingdom of God was again established on the earth, for the sake of which he was then incarcerated in that prison, and not because he had violated any law of God or man."[26]

That is to say, a modern Latter-day Saint may comfortably believe in the God described in the Book of Mormon—one who is "infinite and eternal, from everlasting to everlasting the same unchangeable God, the framer of heaven and earth, and all things which are in them" (D&C 20:17)—and at the same time accept the God described in the Prophet's closing and, for some, more controversial sermons. I certainly do, as do millions of other Latter-day Saints throughout the world. A modern Saint may deny the doctrine of original sin and at the same time believe, as taught in the

---

25. See, for example, White, *Mormon Neo-Orthodoxy*.

26. *Joseph Smith* [manual], 336.

Book of Mormon, that "all mankind [are] in a lost and in a fallen state, and ever [will] be save they should rely on this Redeemer" (1 Nephi 10:6) and that "because of the fall our natures have become evil continually" (Ether 3:2). Last but not least, Latter-day Saints in the twenty-first century can believe wholeheartedly that salvation comes "only through the merits, and mercy, and grace of the Holy Messiah" (2 Nephi 2:8) and at the same time believe that true faith is always manifest by faithfulness, that discipleship and obedience to God's commandments are the walk and talk of true Christians (Matthew 7:21; 16:27; Romans 2:6, 13; 2 Corinthians 5:10; Titus 3:8; James 1:22; 2:19–20, 26; Revelation 20:12). These doctrinal matters are not mutually exclusive. That they can and do exist in the mind and theology of Latter-day Saints concurrently is an indication that typical members of the Church can manage comfortably what is in reality a dynamic tension.[27]

Inspired Fiction?

Finally, some have chosen to reject the Book of Mormon as a historical record and to label it as "inspired fiction." Of that group there are those who accept the book as holy scripture but do not believe there was a real Nephi, Abinadi, or Alma. I believe that in regard to faith (and thus faithfulness and adherence to a cause), it matters very much whether there is an actual event, an objective occurrence toward which we look and upon which we build our faith. One cannot exercise saving faith in something untrue (Alma 32:21) or that did not happen, no matter how sweet the story, how sincere the originator or author, or how committed the followers. Though it is true that great literature, whether historically true or untrue, may lift and strengthen in its own way and even contain great moral lessons, such works cannot result in the spiritual transformation of

---

27. For a discussion of this dynamic tension, see Millet and Hopkin, *Mormonism*, 99–110.

the soul that only scripture can achieve. Scripture becomes a divine channel by which personal revelation comes, a significant means by which we may hear the voice of the Lord (D&C 18:34–36; 88:66).

The power of the word, whether spoken or written, is in its source—even God our Father and his Son, Jesus Christ. We are able to exercise faith in a principle or doctrine taught by real people who were moved upon by the power of the Holy Ghost, actual persons in time and space whose interactions with the Lord and his Spirit were genuine and true and whose spiritual growth we may imitate. Huck Finn may have given the world some sage advice, but his words cannot sanctify. Even the sweet testimonies of Demetrius the slave and Marcellus the Roman centurion from Lloyd Douglas's *The Robe* cannot enliven the soul in the same way that the teachings of Alma to Corianton or the letters of Mormon to Moroni do. There is a difference, a big difference. Doctrinal fiction may be entertaining. Its characters may demonstrate wisdom and their lives provide noble examples. But doctrinal fiction cannot engage and enliven the sons and daughters of God as does scripture.

Our faith in Christ is grounded in the work of redemption that was accomplished in a specific garden and on a designated cross during a particular moment in our earth's history. It is not the exact site that matters so much as it is that there was such a site. If Jesus did not in reality suffer and bleed and die and rise from the tomb, then we are spiritually doomed, no matter how committed we may be to the "faith event" celebrated by the first-century Christians. And so it is in regard to the occasion in Palmyra. It matters very much that the Eternal Father and his Only Begotten Son did appear to a young boy in a grove of trees in New York State. Exactly where the Sacred Grove is, as well as what specific trees or ground were hallowed by the theophany, is much less significant. If Joseph Smith did not see in vision the Father and the Son, if the First Vision was only the "sweet dreams" of a naïve boy, then no amount of goodness and civility on the part of the Latter-day Saints will save us.

And so it is in regard to the people and events and teachings of the Book of Mormon. That there was a Nephi and an Alma and a Gidgiddoni is vital to the story and, in my view, to the relevance and truthfulness of the Book of Mormon. That the prophetic oracles from Lehi to Samuel preached and prophesied of Christ and taught and administered his gospel is vital in establishing the concept of dispensations restored through Joseph Smith. These items reveal far more about the way things are and have been among the people of God in all ages than they do about the way things were in the nineteenth century.[28]

There is room in the Church for all types and shapes and sizes of people, and certainly all of us are at differing stages of intellectual development and spiritual maturity. Further, there are many doctrinal issues over which discussion and debate may lead to diverse conclusions, particularly in matters that have not been fully clarified in scripture or by living prophets. At the same time, there are certain well-defined truths—matters pertaining to the divine Sonship of Christ, the reality of the Atonement, the appearance of the Father and the Son in 1820, and the truthfulness of the Book of Mormon—that in the uncompromising language of President J. Reuben Clark Jr. "must stand, unchanged, unmodified, without dilution, excuse, apology, or avoidance; they may not be explained away or submerged. Without these two great beliefs"—the reality of

---

28. Some who have questioned the historicity of the Book of Mormon account have suggested that the book reflects nineteenth-century ideas, doctrines, and cultural challenges. Richard L. Bushman demonstrated, however, that Book of Mormon views on government, war and peace, and deliverance reflect far more of ancient Israelite thinking and culture than a nineteenth-century context (see Reynolds, *Book of Mormon Authorship,* 189–211.

the resurrection and atonement of Jesus Christ and the divine call of Joseph Smith—"the Church would cease to be the Church."[29]

In the end, as we have been counseled repeatedly, the reality of golden plates and Cumorah and angels may be known only by an independent and individual revelation. Such an experience, as well as the reinforcing and renewing ones thereafter, comes to those who demonstrate patience and faith. "The finished mosaic of the history of the Restoration," Elder Neal A. Maxwell taught, "will be larger and more varied as more pieces of tile emerge, adjusting a sequence here or enlarging there a sector of our understanding. . . . There may even be," he added, "a few pieces of the tile which, for the moment, do not seem to fit. We can wait, as we must." One day, he promised, "the final mosaic of the Restoration will be resplendent, reflecting divine design. . . . At the perfect day, we will see that we have been a part of things too wonderful for us. Part of the marvel and the wonder of God's 'marvelous work and a wonder' will be how perfect Divinity mercifully used us—imperfect humanity. Meanwhile, amid the human dissonance, those with ears to hear will follow the beckoning sounds of a certain trumpet."[30]

Any Proofs or Evidences for the Book of Mormon?

The question of proofs or evidences for the Book of Mormon arises quite often, especially on the part of those who are offended by what they perceive to be a kind of arrogant presumption that we as Latter-day Saints are in possession of extrabiblical scripture. Yes, there have been many efforts on the part of believers to discover tangible, physical evidences for the Book of Mormon, meaning specifically evidence for the existence of an ancient Hebrew people in America both before and after the time of Jesus Christ. Some examples include studies of geography and anthropology, suggesting

29. "The Charted Course of the Church in Education," in *J. Reuben Clark*, 245.
30. "Out of Obscurity," *Ensign*, Nov. 1984, 11.

a meso-American context for the Book;[31] Book of Mormon authorship[32]; word print studies to determine authorship[33]; literary studies of the Book[34]; chiasmus in the Book[35]; intertextual studies[36]; ancient Israelite festivals and coronations within the Book[37]; and, simply, the phenomenon of the Book of Mormon.[38]

Evidences do matter, since we are speaking in the Book of Mormon of real people in real time and actual locations and events. As we stated earlier, much of our conviction of the Restoration is grounded in historical events, things that actually took place. But believers do not rest their faith upon what geographers or archaeologists or anthropologists or historians have or have not discovered to date. More and greater proofs will arise, to be sure, but in the meantime the evidence that is of greatest worth is that evidence that comes to the heart, to the soul, by the power of the Holy Ghost— the witness of the Spirit. As the apostle Paul taught so powerfully, the things of God are known only by the power of the Spirit of God (1 Corinthians 2:11–14). Elder Neal A. Maxwell put it this way: "It is the author's opinion that all the scriptures, including the Book of Mormon, will remain in the realm of faith. Science will not be able to prove or disprove holy writ. However, enough plausible evidence

31. See Sorenson, *Ancient American Setting for the Book of Mormon;* Sorenson, *Mormon's Codex;* Meldrum, *Exploring the Book of Mormon in America's Heartland Photobook.*

32. Reynolds, *Book of Mormon Authorship;* Reynolds, *Book of Mormon Authorship Revisited.*

33. Keller, *Book of Mormon Authors.*

34. Hardy, *Book of Mormon;* Hardy, *Understanding the Book of Mormon;* Rust, *Feasting on the Word.*

35. Welch, *Chiasmus in Antiquity.*

36. Hilton, "Jacob's Textual Legacy," 52–65; "Textual Similarities in the Words of Abinadi and Alma's Counsel to Corianton," 39–60; Hilton and Johnson, "Who Uses the Word *Resurrection* in the Book of Mormon and How Is It Used?" 30–39; Hopkin and Hilton, "Samuel's Reliance on Biblical Language," 31–52.

37. Welch and Ricks, *King Benjamin's Speech;* Welch, *Illuminating the Sermon at the Temple and the Sermon on the Mount.*

38. Givens, *By the Hand of Mormon;* Gutjahr, *The Book of Mormon.*

will come forth to prevent scoffers from having a field day, but not enough to remove the requirement of faith. Believers must be patient during such unfolding."[39]

CONCLUSION

How did Joseph Smith learn the gospel? How did he become the mighty prophet that he was, not only a legal administrator charged to be the instrument for restoring priesthood powers and keys to the earth but also the great revealer of truth, the dispenser and clarifier of doctrine? In his early ministry, was it not through his translation of the Book of Mormon?

First of all, as a seer and translator, he learned to operate by and through God's Holy Spirit. He leaned upon a most useful device, the Urim and Thummim, but with patient maturity and by divine tutorials he became, as it were, a living urim and thummim.

Second, consider what it must have been like for him to translate the golden plates and dictate to a scribe, not just a rather fascinating story but also, and perhaps much more important, page after page of profound Christian doctrine, principles, and precepts, all couched within a historical narrative. If only a portion of the doctrinal principles listed in Appendix 1 had lodged within the Prophet's

---

39. *Plain and Precious Things,* 4. President Gordon B. Hinckley put things in perspective when he taught: "I can hold [the Book of Mormon] in my hand. It is real. It has weight and substance that can be physically measured. I can open its pages and read, and it has language both beautiful and uplifting. The ancient record from which it was translated came out of the earth as a voice speaking from the dust. . . . The evidence for its truth, for its validity in a world that is prone to demand evidence, lies not in archaeology or anthropology, though these may be helpful to some. It lies not in word research or historical analysis, though these may be confirmatory. The evidence for its truth and validity lies within the covers of the book itself. The test of its truth lies in reading it. It is a book of God. Reasonable individuals may sincerely question its origin, but those who read it prayerfully may come to know by a power beyond their natural senses that it is true, that it contains the word of God, that it outlines saving truths of the everlasting gospel, that it came forth by the gift and power of God" (*Faith, the Essence of True Religion,* 10–11).

soul, it is no wonder that he was able to walk the streets of Nauvoo, followed closely by anxious secretaries William Clayton or Willard Richards, no longer dictating revelations at a Kirtland-like pace but instead speaking and discoursing left and right on profound eternal truths. Can there be any doubt but that his supernal seasoning with the Book of Mormon was fundamental to the schooling of his soul?

Too much effort has been expended over too many centuries, too much blood has been shed, too many tears have watered too many pillows, too many prayers have ascended, too great a price has been paid for the Book of Mormon record to be discarded or relegated to the category of some beloved but dated theological relic. No less a being than God himself has borne solemn witness of the Book of Mormon. To Oliver Cowdery, who was raised up to serve as the principal scribe in the translation, the Lord affirmed: "I tell thee, that thou mayest know that there is none else save God that knowest thy thoughts and the intents of thy heart. I tell thee these things as a witness unto thee—that *the words or the work which thou hast been writing are true*" (D&C 6:16–17; emphasis added; compare 18:2).

President Boyd K. Packer stated: "We do not have to defend the Prophet Joseph Smith. The Book of Mormon: Another Testament of Jesus Christ will defend him for us. Those who reject Joseph Smith as a prophet and revelator are left to find some other explanation for the Book of Mormon. And for the second powerful defense: the Doctrine and Covenants, and a third: the Pearl of Great Price. Published in combination, these scriptures form an unshakable testament that Jesus is the Christ and a witness that Joseph Smith is a prophet."[40] The Almighty set his own seal of truthfulness upon the Nephite record by a sacred oath when he said: "And he [Joseph Smith] has translated the book, even that part which I have commanded him, and *as your Lord and your God liveth it is true*"

40. "The Book of Mormon: Another Testament of Jesus Christ," *Ensign*, May 2005, 9.

(D&C 17:6; emphasis added). In the words of a modern apostle, Elder Bruce R. McConkie: "This is God's testimony of the Book of Mormon. In it Deity himself has laid his godhood on the line. Either the book is true or God ceases to be God. There neither is nor can be any more formal or powerful language known to men or gods."[41]

President Ezra Taft Benson put things into proper perspective when he stated: "The most singular evidence in support of Joseph Smith's claim to being a spokesman for Almighty God was the publication of a scriptural record, the Book of Mormon."[42]

President Benson also explained that "*if we really do our homework and approach the Book of Mormon doctrinally,* we can expose the errors and find the truths to combat many of the current false theories and philosophies of men." He then drew this significant conclusion: "I have noted within the Church a difference in discernment, insight, conviction, and spirit between those who know and love the Book of Mormon and those who do not. The book is a great sifter."[43]

The fruits of The Church of Jesus Christ of Latter-day Saints cannot be severed from its roots, for our manner of life is forever linked to the historical events and the translations and revelations that came from and through its initial revelator. "Take away the Book of Mormon and the revelations," Joseph declared, "and where is our religion? We have none."[44] Joseph is reported to have said, even more personally, "The Book of Mormon is true, just what it purports to be, and for this testimony I expect to give an account in the day of judgment."[45] And so might we all.

---

41. "The Doctrine of the Priesthood," *Ensign,* May 1982, 33.

42. *Ezra Taft Benson* [manual], 107.

43. *Ezra Taft Benson* [manual], 132; emphasis added.

44. Kirtland High Council Minutes, 21 Apr. 1834, 43–44; Minute Book 1, The Joseph Smith Papers, accessed 15 Mar. 2016, http://josephsmithpapers.org/paperSummary /minute-book-1&p=48.

45. Quoted by David Osborn, in "Recollections of the Prophet Joseph Smith," *Juvenile Instructor* 27, no. 6 (Mar. 1892): 173; *Joseph Smith* [manual], 64.

Chapter 4

DIVINE AUTHORITY RESTORED

Harmony, Pennsylvania, May 1829. Emma Smith accompanied her husband to receive the golden plates from Moroni in September 1827. The translation of the plates proceeded with various persons serving as scribe. Joseph and his principal scribe, Oliver Cowdery, made their way into that segment of the Nephite narrative in which the risen Lord ordained, commissioned, and counseled the Nephites regarding baptism for the remission of sins. Having learned in the translation process that all must be baptized, and now knowing that such a rite must be performed by one having proper authority (3 Nephi 11:18–26), the translators once again sought heavenly guidance.

Joseph Smith was called upon to restore doctrine, to bring back to earth plain and precious truths and many covenants of the Lord that had been excised from the Bible during its centuries-long period of transmission (1 Nephi 13:20–40). Thus he was appointed before the foundations of this earth were laid to be a *revealer of truth*. He was also selected by the God of heaven to be the means of restoring divine priesthood authority, authority that had been lost following the deaths of the ancient apostles and the gradual but very real loss of the keys of the kingdom. Thus he was chosen and selected, like Jeremiah of old (Jeremiah 1:5). Only weeks before his martyr's death, Joseph Smith stated: "Every man who has a calling to minister to the inhabitants of the world was ordained to that very purpose in the Grand Council of heaven before this world was. I suppose I was ordained to this very office in that Grand Council."[1] Thus Joseph was appointed to be a *legal administrator*.

A distinguishing feature of The Church of Jesus Christ of Latter-day Saints is its organization—its priesthood hierarchy from the most recently ordained deacon in Recife, Brazil, to the President of the Church in Salt Lake City; its lay ministry but intricate organizational structure with callings, assignments, and officers; and its powers to communicate, spread the word, and mobilize its resources in a matter of hours in times of natural disaster. Joseph Smith explained his philosophy of leadership simply: "I teach them correct principles, and they govern themselves."[2]

This organization is not accomplished solely because of a kind of spontaneous, service-oriented Latter-day Saint propensity that just takes shape naturally but rather because divine authority has been restored to earth at the hands of heavenly messengers. "Priesthood is the central power in the Church," President Thomas S. Monson explained, "and the authority through which the Church is administered."[3] The priesthood is the power of God, delegated to man on earth, to act in all things pertaining to the salvation of God's children. It is not a person or a group of people, particularly males or male administration;[4] rather, it is the divine authorization and organizing principle that must be in place if the

---

1. *Joseph Smith* [manual], 511.
2. *Joseph Smith* [manual], 284.
3. *Teachings of Thomas S. Monson*, 232.
4. See Faust, "Father, Come Home," *Ensign*, May 1993, 35–37; Oaks, "Priesthood Authority in the Family and the Church," *Ensign*, Nov. 2005, 25–26; "The Keys and Authority of the Priesthood," *Ensign*, May 2014, 49–52.

church and kingdom of God are to move forward on the earth to accomplish its foreordained purposes.

Clearly, today's priesthood organization did not exist in the nineteenth century. How, then, did we get to this point? How did a young Joseph Smith—who would have had much more immediate contact with a world of Protestantism (there is little evidence that Joseph had much contact with Roman Catholics in his area), a society of people whose break with Roman Catholicism had resulted in a "priesthood of all believers"—come to establish a church that was so very different in organization from the Methodists, the Baptists, the Presbyterians?

THE BOOK OF MORMON AND PRIESTHOOD ORGANIZATION

Joseph Smith's encounter with the Book of Mormon had a profound effect upon his theological mindset and, in particular, his ecclesiology (his study of the work and workings of the Church). Consider how, precept upon precept, significant truths were made known in the Book of Mormon narrative concerning how the Lord's Church should be organized to best carry out its mission.

In the first chapter of the Book of Mormon, Lehi receives in a vision his commission to call the people to repentance. He sees the heavenly hosts worshipping Deity, is given a book to read in which he learns of the coming destruction of Jerusalem at the hands of the Babylonians, and learns the prophetic word affirming the coming of the promised Messiah in six centuries. Although there is no mention of Lehi receiving his prophetic mantle by the laying on of hands, his becomes a prophetic role, and, as Joseph Smith explained, "All the prophets [of the Old Testament era] had the Melchizedek Priesthood."[5]

---

5. *Joseph Smith* [manual], 109; compare Ehat and Cook, *Words of Joseph Smith*, 59.

Some forty years later, Nephi observed: "And it came to pass that I, Nephi, did consecrate Jacob and Joseph [his younger brothers], that they should be priests and teachers over the land of my people" (2 Nephi 5:26; compare Jacob 1:17–18). This is not a reference to Nephi's brothers receiving the lesser, or Aaronic, priesthood, for there were no Levites in the Lehite colony. Rather, it refers to their ministerial duties within the higher, or Melchizedek, priesthood.[6] Alma later responded to the prophetic warnings of Abinadi, separated himself from the wayward majority, and established a "church in the wilderness." He taught and baptized more than two hundred people in a relatively hidden part of the wilderness called Mormon.[7]

At the waters of Mormon, his baptismal prayer for the first initiate into the faith began with these words: "Helam, I baptize thee, *having authority from the Almighty God*" (Mosiah 18:13; emphasis added). Later Jesus instructed the one performing the baptism to use the following words, first calling the person by name: "Having authority given me of Jesus Christ, I baptize you in the name of the Father, and of the Son, and of the Holy Ghost. Amen" (3 Nephi 11:24–25).

The narrator of the record, Mormon, having himself been given authority from God (Moroni 8:16), wrote that the people were called a church and denominated themselves as the Church of God or the Church of Christ. He then adds: "Alma, *having authority from God,* ordained priests; even one priest to every fifty of their number." Further, Alma instructed those priests that "they should teach nothing save it were the things which he had taught, and which had been spoken by the mouth of the holy prophets"

---

6. See Smith, *Answers to Gospel Questions,* 3:123–26; McConkie, *Promised Messiah,* 412, 427; *New Witness for the Articles of Faith,* 348.

7. For insight into how Alma may have received the priesthood, see Smith, *Answers to Gospel Questions,* 3:203–4.

(Mosiah 18:17–19; emphasis added). Later in the story, however, another group of people had been taught the gospel and desired to enter the Church through baptism, "but there was none in the land that had authority from God" (Mosiah 21:33).

Eventually Alma and his followers joined with a larger group of believers who were governed by King Mosiah. Mosiah, who served as both king and priest over the people, seemed to be impressed with what Alma had accomplished and asked that Alma implement his ecclesiastical system among all the believers. Mosiah delegated to Alma the office of high priest, or president, of the Church (Mosiah 26:8; Alma 5:3). "And it came to pass that king Mosiah granted unto Alma that he might establish churches throughout all the land . . . ; and *gave him power to ordain priests and teachers over every church.* . . . And thus, notwithstanding there being many churches they were all one church, yea, even the church of God; for there was nothing preached in all the churches except it were repentance and faith in God" (Mosiah 25:19, 22; emphasis added). In fact, "none received authority to preach or to teach except it were by [Alma, the high priest] from God. Therefore he consecrated all their priests and all their teachers; and none were consecrated except they were just men. Therefore they did watch over their people, and did nourish them with things pertaining to righteousness" (Mosiah 23:17–18).

Nephi, son of Lehi, had earlier made it clear that baptism was an essential ordinance, one necessary for entrance into the Church and kingdom of God. In speaking of the baptism of Jesus at the hands of John the Baptist (which he had seen in vision), Nephi wrote: "And now, if the Lamb of God, he being holy, should have need to be baptized by water, to fulfil all righteousness, O then, how much more need have we, being unholy, to be baptized, yea, even by water! . . . Know ye not that he was holy? But notwithstanding he being holy, he showeth unto the children of men that, according to the flesh he humbleth himself before the Father, and witnesseth unto the Father that he would be obedient unto him in keeping his commandments" (2 Nephi 31:5, 7; see also vv. 9–12).

What is clear also in the Nephite-Jaredite record is the necessity of persons being properly ordained (2 Nephi 6:2; Alma 5:44; 6:8; 43:2; Helaman 8:18; Ether 12:10) and that such ordination come through the laying on of hands. Mormon recorded that Alma "ordained priests and elders, *by laying on his hands according to the order of God,* to preside and watch over the church" (Alma 6:1; emphasis added). When the resurrected Lord appeared to the Nephites, "he touched with his hand the [apostles] whom he had chosen, one by one, even until he had touched them all, and spake unto them as he touched them." These later affirmed "that he gave them power to give the Holy Ghost" (3 Nephi 18:36–37). Later in the account, Mormon writes of this occasion: "And [Jesus] called them by name, saying: Ye shall call on the Father in my name, in mighty prayer; and after ye have done this ye shall have power that to him upon whom ye shall lay your hands, ye shall give the Holy Ghost; and in my name shall ye give it, for thus do mine apostles" (Moroni 2:2).[8]

Twenty years before the coming of Jesus to the Old World, Nephi in the New World taught the gospel with great power, warned the people of coming destruction if they did not repent, and even demonstrated signs and wonders among them. Most of his listeners, however, remained unconverted and rebellious. While Nephi was pondering the plight of his world, a voice came to him, saying: "Blessed art thou, Nephi, for those things which thou hast

---

8. One account of a long preaching ministry began as follows: "Now it came to pass that when Alma had said these words [offered a prayer in behalf of those to whom they were called to preach], that *he clapped his hands upon all them who were with him.* And behold, as he clapped his hands upon them, they were filled with the Holy Spirit" (Alma 31:36; emphasis added). Latter-day Saints have generally assumed that the phrase "clapped his hands upon them" means that he laid his hands upon them, set them apart for their assignment, and thereby empowered them for the ministry.

done; for I have beheld how thou hast with unwearyingness declared the word. . . . And now, . . . I will make thee mighty in word and in deed, in faith and in works; yea, even that all things shall be done unto thee according to thy word, for thou shalt not ask that which is contrary to my will. Behold, thou art Nephi, and I am God. Behold, . . . *ye shall have power over this people. . . . I give unto you power, that whatsoever ye shall seal on earth shall be sealed in heaven; and whatsoever ye shall loose on earth shall be loosed in heaven;* and thus shall ye have power among this people" (Helaman 10:4–7; emphasis added).

It appears that Nephi is here granted the same power that Peter and the early apostles received to govern the Church, the sealing power, the power to perform an ordinance on earth that will be recognized and accepted in heaven (Matthew 16:18–19; 18:18). Linked with that idea is that in the Book of Mormon, after the Nephite Twelve had passed away, "other disciples [were] ordained in their stead" (4 Nephi 1:14), thus setting up, at least for a season, apostolic succession in the New World,[9] just as it had operated in the Old World when Matthias was chosen to succeed Judas Iscariot (Acts 1:15–26).

Without question, the most detailed description of priesthood in the Book of Mormon is found in Alma 13, right in the middle of a series of fiery sermons directed to an extremely wicked and rebellious group of people. This chapter speaks at some length of people who bear the priesthood in this life, having been foreordained to it in a premortal existence. The speaker, Alma, referred to the ancients who had been ordained to the "holy order of God," and

---

9. We generally speak of the Twelve who were called in the Book of Mormon as *disciples*. Yet it is clear from Moroni 2:2 that they were *apostles*. In the Wentworth Letter (1842), Joseph explained that the risen Lord "planted the Gospel here in all its fulness, and richness, and power, and blessing; that they had Apostles, Prophets, pastors, Teachers, and Evangelists" (*Joseph Smith* [manual], 441). See also Pratt, *Key to the Science of Theology*, 15, 42, 69.

who, through the purifying work of the Atonement and through the priesthood of God, "were sanctified, and their garments were washed white through the blood of the Lamb. Now they, after being sanctified by the Holy Ghost, having their garments made white, being pure and spotless before God, could not look upon sin save it were with abhorrence; and there were many, exceedingly great many, who were made pure and entered into the rest of the Lord their God" (Alma 13:11–12).

Alma used as a specific example of a person who attained unto this level of holiness the man Melchizedek, the king of Salem and a contemporary of Abraham: "Now this Melchizedek was a king over the land of Salem; and his people had waxed strong in iniquity and abomination. . . . But Melchizedek having exercised mighty faith, and received the office of the high priesthood according to the holy order of God, did preach repentance unto his people. And behold, they did repent; and Melchizedek did establish peace in the land in his days. . . . Now, there were many before him, and also there were many afterwards, but none were greater; therefore, of him they have more particularly made mention" (Alma 13:17–19).

BUILDING ON THE BOOK OF MORMON FOUNDATION

In his 1838 history of the Church, Joseph Smith indicated that on 5 April 1829 he met Oliver Cowdery in Harmony, Pennsylvania. Two days later, Oliver began to serve as scribe in the translation of the Book of Mormon, a work Joseph had begun months earlier. "We still continued the work of translation," Joseph stated, "when, in the ensuing month (May, 1829), we on a certain day went into the woods to pray and inquire of the Lord respecting *baptism for the remission of sins, that we found mentioned in the translation of the plates.* While we were thus employed, praying and calling upon the Lord, a messenger from heaven descended in a cloud of light, and having laid his hands upon us, he ordained us" to the Aaronic, or lesser, Priesthood (Joseph Smith–History 1:68; emphasis added). The messenger identified himself as John the Baptist and explained that he acted under the direction of Peter, James, and John, the ancient apostles, who would come shortly to restore the Melchizedek, or higher, Priesthood, including the holy apostleship, which held the power to confer the gift of the Holy Ghost and perform sacred, saving ordinances. John commanded Joseph and Oliver to baptize and ordain one another (Joseph Smith–History 1:70–71).

In October 1834 Oliver Cowdery described the coming of John the Baptist in much more colorful detail in the Church newspaper in Kirtland, Ohio, the *Messenger and Advocate.* In speaking of the work of translation, Brother Cowdery stated: "These were days never to be forgotten—to sit under the sound of a voice dictated by the inspiration of heaven, awakened the utmost gratitude of this bosom!" Then, he wrote of the specific portion of the Book of Mormon narrative that elicited the greatest curiosity concerning ordinances and the power to perform them: "After writing the account given of the Savior's ministry to the remnant of the seed of Jacob, upon this continent, it was easy to be seen, as the prophet said it would be, that darkness covered the earth and gross darkness the minds of the people. On reflecting further it was as easy to be seen that amid the great strife and noise concerning religion, none had authority from God to administer the ordinances of the Gospel. For the question might be asked, have men authority to administer in the name of Christ, who deny revelations, when His testimony is no less than the spirit of prophecy, and His religion based, built, and sustained by immediate revelations, in all ages of the world when He has had a people on earth?"

Continuing, Oliver described hearing the voice of Jesus Christ and feeling thereafter the hands of an angel, a heavenly messenger, John the Baptist, upon their heads. "The assurance that we were in the presence of an angel, the certainty that we heard the voice of Jesus, and the truth unsullied as it flowed from a pure personage, dictated by the will of God, is to me past description, and I shall ever look upon this expression of the Savior's goodness with wonder and thanksgiving while I am permitted to tarry; and in those mansions where perfection dwells and sin never comes, I hope to adore in that day which shall never cease."[10]

In his 1839 history, the Prophet recorded that "we had for some time made this matter [the promise by John the Baptist that the higher priesthood would be conferred] a subject of humble prayer, and at length we got together in the Chamber of Mr. [Peter] Whitmer's house in order more particularly to seek of the Lord what we now so earnestly desired: and here to our unspeakable satisfaction did we realize the truth of the Saviour's promise; 'Ask, and you shall receive, seek, and you shall find, knock and it shall be opened unto you;' for we had not long been engaged in solemn and fervent prayer, when *the word of the Lord, came unto us in the Chamber, commanding us; that I should ordain Oliver Cowdery to be an Elder in the Church of Jesus Christ, and that he also should ordain me to the same office, and then to ordain others to the same office* as it should be made known unto us, from time to time: we were however commanded *to defer this our ordination until such time as it should be practicable to have our brethren, who had been and who should be baptized, assembled together, when we must have their sanction to our thus proceeding to ordain each other, and have them decide by vote whether they were willing to accept us as spiritual teachers,* or not, when also we were commanded to bless bread and break it with them, and to take wine, bless it, and drink it with them, afterward proceed to ordain each other according to commandment, then call out such men as the Spirit should dictate, and

---

10. *Messenger and Advocate* 1, no. 1 (Oct. 1834): 16.

ordain them, and then attend to the laying on of hands for the gift of the Holy Ghost."[11]

Within weeks following the 15 May 1829 ordination under the hands of John the Baptist, the higher priesthood was indeed conferred upon them (D&C 18:9; 27:12). Elder Erastus Snow of the Quorum of the Twelve declared: "In due course of time, as we read in the history which he [the Prophet Joseph] has left, Peter, James and John appeared to him—it was at a period when they were being pursued by their enemies and they had to travel all night, and in the dawn of the coming day when they were weary and worn who should appear to them but Peter, James and John, for the purpose of conferring upon them the Apostleship, the keys of which they themselves had held while upon the earth, which had been bestowed upon them by the Savior. This priesthood conferred upon them by those three messengers embraces within it all offices of the Priesthood from the highest to the lowest."[12]

"The priesthood is here," Oliver Cowdery testified in 1848. "I was present with Joseph when an holy angel from God came down from heaven and conferred or restored the Aaronic Priesthood, and said at the same time that it should remain upon the earth while the earth stands. *I was also present with Joseph when the Melchizedek Priesthood was conferred by the holy angels of God;* this was the more necessary in order that [we might confirm on each other this power] by the will and commandment of God. This priesthood is also to remain upon the earth until the last remnant of time."[13] Elder Parley P. Pratt thus summarized the process by which mortal

11. History, 1838–1856, volume A-1 [23 December 1805–30 August 1834], The Joseph Smith Papers, accessed 15 Mar. 2016, http://josephsmithpapers.org/paperSummary /history-1838-1856-volume-a-1-23-december-1805-30-august-1834?p=33; emphasis added.

12. In *Journal of Discourses,* 23:183.

13. Reuben Miller, Journal, 21 Oct. 1848, in Welch and Carlson, *Opening the Heavens,* 244; emphasis added.

men were once again divinely authorized by referring to Joseph and Oliver, "who profess to have received their authority and priesthood, or apostleship, by direct revelation from God—by the voice of God—by the ministering of angels—and by the Holy Ghost."[14]

In the years that followed, the Church and its organization came into place "precept upon precept; line upon line; . . . here a little, and there a little" (Isaiah 28:10). At the formal organization of the Church at Fayette, New York, on 6 April 1830, Joseph Smith was named the first elder and Oliver Cowdery the second elder; in March 1832 the First Presidency was organized; in February 1835 the Quorum of the Twelve Apostles and the quorums of the seventy were put in place. In May 1842 Joseph began to deliver to the Church covenants and ordinances associated with the temple, and, in conjunction with the rites of the temple, began in the fall of 1843 to confer upon individuals the fulness of the blessings of the priesthood, the power that makes of men and women kings and queens, priests and priestesses.

With the growing complexity of the Church organization, Joseph the Prophet began to teach principles of priesthood government, tenets that clearly grew out of his work with the Book of Mormon, concepts that addressed the needs of the Church in the nineteenth century and that still form the foundation for the operation of The Church of Jesus Christ of Latter-day Saints today. Some of these include the following:

1. "The Priesthood is an everlasting principle, and existed with God from eternity, and will to eternity, without beginning of days or end of years. The keys [the right of presidency, the directing power] have to be brought from heaven whenever the Gospel is

---

14. *Late Persecution of the Church of Jesus Christ of Latter Day Saints* (New York: J. W. Harrison, 1840), iii, in Welch and Carlson, *Opening the Heavens,* 247.

sent." This priesthood was first given to Adam, and the kingdom of God was set up in that earliest age.[15]

2. "There are two Priesthoods spoken of in the Scriptures, namely, the Melchizedek and the Aaronic or Levitical. Although there are two Priesthoods, yet the Melchizedek Priesthood comprehends the Aaronic or Levitical Priesthood, and is the grand head, and holds the highest authority which pertains to the priesthood, and the keys of the Kingdom of God in all ages of the world to the latest posterity on the earth; and is the channel through which all knowledge, doctrine, the plan of salvation and every important matter is revealed from heaven. Its institution was prior to 'the foundation of this earth.'"[16]

3. John the Baptist held the keys of the Aaronic Priesthood and was what Joseph Smith called a "legal administrator" of the priesthood.[17] John taught the same gospel and performed the same ordinances as those who succeeded him—Christ and the apostles.[18]

4. Jesus Christ held the keys of the Melchizedek Priesthood and was also a legal administrator.[19] He conferred the keys of the kingdom upon Peter, James, and John on the Mount of Transfiguration.[20]

5. Although the Bible is the word of God and may be relied upon as a guide for our lives, "there is no salvation between the two lids of the Bible without a legal administrator."[21] In other words, although the accounts of miracles and signs and wonders and the performance of ordinances in the Old and New Testaments are

---

15. *Joseph Smith* [manual], 104.
16. *Joseph Smith* [manual], 108–9.
17. *Joseph Smith* [manual], 81–82.
18. *Joseph Smith* [manual], 83.
19. *Words of Joseph Smith*, 158.
20. *Joseph Smith* [manual], 105.
21. *Words of Joseph Smith*, 235.

historical and real, they do not convey the necessary authority to us to act in the name of the Almighty.

6. There has been no change in the ordinances (either in the necessity or the mode) since the beginning of time. Adam and Eve were earth's first Christians. By extension, Christian prophets have taught Christian doctrine and administered Christian ordinances since the dawn of time. "Ordinances instituted in the heavens before the foundation of the world, in the priesthood, for the salvation of men, are not to be altered or changed. All must be saved on the same principles."[22] Even as pertaining to the temple, "The order of the house of God has been, and ever will be, the same, even after Christ comes; and after the termination of the thousand years it will be the same; and we shall finally enter into the celestial kingdom of God, and enjoy it forever."[23]

In speaking of Noah, Joseph Smith observed: "Now taking it for granted that the scriptures say what they mean, and mean what they say, we have sufficient grounds to go on and prove from the Bible that the gospel has always been the same; the ordinances to fulfil its requirements, the same; and the officers to officiate, the same; . . . therefore, as Noah was a *preacher* of righteousness he must have been *baptized* and ordained to the priesthood by the laying on of the hands, etc. For no man taketh this honor upon himself except he be called of God as was Aaron [Hebrews 5:4]."[24]

7. Though salvation is in Christ and his is the only name by which eternal life comes to us, the ordinances of the gospel are not optional: they are required. "All men who become heirs of God and joint-heirs with Jesus Christ," Joseph stated, "will have to receive the fulness of the ordinances of his kingdom; and those who will not receive all the ordinances will come short of the fulness of that

22. *Joseph Smith* [manual], 417.
23. *Joseph Smith* [manual], 419.
24. "Baptism," *Times and Seasons* 3, no. 21 (Sept. 1842): 904; emphasis added.

glory."[25] Joseph later declared, "The question is frequently asked, 'Can we not be saved without going through with all those ordinances, etc.?' I would answer, No, not the fullness of salvation."[26]

8. God works through his legal administrators on earth. He will seldom if ever become personally involved in the performance of a priesthood ordinance (sacrament) or send an angel if someone on earth can perform it. "No wonder the angel told good old Cornelius that he must send for Peter to learn how to be saved: Peter could baptise, and angels could not, *so long as there were legal officers in the flesh holding the keys of the kingdom, or the authority of the priesthood.* There is one evidence still further on this point, and that is that Jesus himself when he appeared to Paul on his way to Damascus, did not inform him how he could be saved. He had set in the church first Apostles, and secondarily prophets, for the work of the ministry, . . . so Paul could not learn so much from the Lord relative to his duty in the common salvation of man, as he could from one of Christ's ambassadors called with the same heavenly calling of the Lord, and endowed with the same power from on high."[27]

9. It matters very much that an ordinance be performed and performed properly, but it must be done by one who is duly authorized. Elder Orson Hyde explained that the Saints were "not under the necessity of tracing back the dark and bloody stream of papal superstition to find their authority, neither were they compelled to seek for it among the floating and transient notions of Protestant reformers; but God has sent his holy angel directly from heaven with this seal and authority, and confirmed it upon men with his own hands."[28]

---

25. *Joseph Smith* [manual], 419.

26. *Joseph Smith* [manual], 418.

27. "Baptism," *Times and Seasons* 3, no. 21 (Sept. 1842): 905; emphasis added.

28. "Letter from Elder O. Hyde," *Times and Seasons* 2, no. 23 (Oct. 1841): 551.

Joseph Smith was especially drawn to the story in Acts 19 of the apostle Paul encountering certain disciples at Ephesus who claimed to be Christians but who had not heard anything concerning the bestowal of the Holy Ghost. They indicated that they had been baptized "unto John's baptism. Then said Paul, John verily baptized with the baptism of repentance, saying unto the people, that they should believe on him which should come after him, that is, on Christ Jesus. When they heard this, they were baptized in the name of the Lord Jesus. And when Paul had laid his hands upon them, the Holy Ghost came on them; and they spake with tongues, and prophesied" (Acts 19:2–6).

The Prophet of the Restoration explained concerning these disciples at Ephesus that "some sectarian Jew had been baptising like John, but had forgotten to inform them that there was one to follow by the name of Jesus Christ, to baptise with fire and the Holy Ghost: *which showed these converts that their first baptism was illegal,* and when they heard this they were gladly baptised."[29] From the journal of Wilford Woodruff under the date of 10 March 1844, Joseph took the part of Paul and said: "No, John did not baptize you, for he did his work right. And so Paul went and baptized them, for he knew what the true doctrine was and he knew that John had not baptized them."[30]

My favorite recitation of this story by the Prophet is as follows: "Unto what were you baptized? And they said, Unto John's baptism. Not so, not so my friends; if you had, you would have heard of the Holy Ghost. But you have been duped by some designing knave who has come in the name of John, an imposter. . . . John's baptism stood good, but these had been baptized by some imposter."[31]

10. The powers of the priesthood span the veil of death and

---

29. "Baptism," *Times and Seasons* 3, no. 21 (Sept. 1842): 904; emphasis added.

30. *Words of Joseph Smith,* 328.

31. *Words of Joseph Smith,* 333.

continue into the world to come. Under inspiration, Joseph confronted one of the most vexing issues of Christian history and theology: If indeed the name of Jesus Christ is the only name by which salvation comes (Acts 4:12), then what of the untold billions of souls who come to earth and die without so much as ever hearing of him, much less having the opportunity to receive his message of salvation? We will discuss this matter at length in Chapter 14.

CONCLUSION

There is little reference to priesthood in the Old Testament except for the consecration of the tribe of Levi and the descendants of Aaron, brother of Moses. We know there were prophets and holy men in the Old Testament, that they stood as covenant spokesmen and mouthpieces for Deity to the people, and, presumably, that they were called by God and empowered by him. But as to how and in what manner they were ordained, set apart, or commissioned or how they related to one another—such as in the days of Jeremiah when there were many prophets in the land (1 Nephi 1:4)—the biblical record is silent.

The Book of Mormon, on the other hand, is a record of God's dealings with his children in ancient America, the greater portion of which takes place during a period that roughly parallels the time from Jeremiah to Malachi, as well as the first four centuries of the Christian era. References to priesthood and authority and covenants and ordinances are found throughout the text, and one sees, in fact, a seamless narrative running between it and the New Testament.

The Book of Mormon contains either direct mention of principles associated with divine authority or passing allusions to it throughout the record. It was inevitable that Joseph Smith and the Latter-day Saints should begin to view biblical history and teachings and practices through the lens of the Book of Mormon and that many of these teachings should stand in stark contrast to a nineteenth-century religious world made up largely of a priesthood of all believers. In addition, further revelations through Joseph Smith, as found in the Doctrine and Covenants and in a surprising number of sermons, expanded upon the Book of Mormon foundation of priesthood government. As described by Elder Jeffrey R. Holland, "the priesthood of God, with its keys, its ordinances, its divine origin and ability to bind in heaven what is bound on earth, is as *indispensable* to the true Church of God as it is *unique* to it and that without it there would be no Church of Jesus Christ of Latter-day Saints."[32]

The power that is in our midst in the Church, the authority and power we know as the priesthood, is found nowhere else. Joseph "told an anecdote of [an] Episcopalian priest who said he had the Priesthood of Aaron, but not Melchizedek, and bore this testimony that" he had never "found the man who claimed the Priesthood of Melchizedek."[33] We as Latter-day Saints believe we are living in the dispensation of the fulness of times, a period when the God of heaven is restoring truths from ages past and bringing all things to consummation in Christ (Ephesians 1:10). For the early Saints, all the streams and rivers of the past were now flowing into the ocean of revealed truth and divine power. Joseph was authorized to establish the kingdom of God on earth and to empower its citizens to carry on the work of salvation long after he, the founder, had gone on to his reward.

---

32. "Our Most Distinguishing Feature," *Ensign*, May 2005, 43.
33. *Words of Joseph Smith*, 244.

Chapter 5

THE WORK OF THE HOLY SPIRIT

Harmony, Pennsylvania, April 1829. Even before the formal organization of the restored Church in April 1830, the Lord had given revelations to the Prophet Joseph Smith on such matters as the translation of the Book of Mormon and the "marvelous work" that was about to come forth (D&C 3, 5, 17). Oliver Cowdery had come to Harmony, Pennsylvania, on 5 April 1829 to meet the Prophet, and by 7 April he was engaged as a scribe for Joseph the translator. During April and into October, a number of divine directives were received that pertained to the receipt of revelation itself—how it was to come, through whom revelations for the Church were to come, and how individual revelation was to be obtained and understood (D&C 6; 8–9; 11; 28; 43). In addition, in the months and years that followed, Joseph and the Saints became acquainted with the vital role of the Spirit as the Sanctifier, the agent of the new birth, the means by which sins are remitted and human souls are cleansed and by which the gifts and fruits of the Spirit come.

The apostle Paul taught powerfully that the things of God can be received and valued only through the power of God's Spirit, through what we know as the gift of the Holy Ghost. Truly, the only way to gain what Paul called "the mind of Christ" is through the medium of this Spirit (1 Corinthians 2:11–14, 16). Joseph Smith's translation of the Book of Mormon, coupled with his receipt of many revelations, makes it crystal clear that another work of the Holy Spirit is cleansing and purifying the human soul. Because the Holy Ghost is both a revelator and a sanctifier, we will in this chapter attend to what the Prophet Joseph Smith learned and then conveyed to the Latter-day Saints about both of these vital functions.

THE SPIRIT OF REVELATION

"Salvation cannot come without revelation," Brother Joseph taught. "It is vain for anyone to minister without it."[1] It should thus come as no surprise to Latter-day Saints to learn that when the time had fully arrived for the promised restitution of all things, when the glorious day of restoration had dawned, it was necessary for God to make known through his chosen prophet a myriad of pertinent truths. Not the least of these was the nature and scope of revelation itself—from whence it comes, the manner in which it is to be received, and how it is to be understood. Thus numerous passages in the Doctrine and Covenants describe, some almost as a passing comment, what we must do to qualify for the gifts and guidance of the third member of the Godhead. "It remained for Joseph Smith to announce to a disbelieving world," Joseph Fielding McConkie wrote, "that that same God who spoke so freely in times past not only could speak, but had spoken again, and that the promise of James that any who sought the wisdom of heaven in faith still had claim upon it."[2]

---

1. *Joseph Smith* [manual], 195.
2. "The Principle of Revelation," in Millet and Jackson, *Doctrine and Covenants*, 81.

Revelation for the Church

The restored Church was less than six months old when difficulties about revelation arose. "Brother Hiram Page had in his possession a certain stone," Joseph the Prophet recorded, "by which he had obtained two revelations, concerning the upbuilding of Zion, the order of the Church, etc., all of which were entirely at variance with the order of God's house, as laid down in the New Testament, as well as in our late revelations."[3] In describing this incident, Newel Knight observed that "even Oliver Cowdery and the Whitmer family had given heed to them. . . . Joseph was perplexed and scarcely knew how to meet this new exigency. That night I occupied the same room he did," Brother Knight continued, "and the greater part of the night was spent in prayer and supplication. After much labor with these brethren, they were convinced of their error, and confessed the same, renouncing [Page's] revelations as not being of God."[4] It was because of Hiram Page's claims to revelation for the Church that the Lord spoke through Joseph Smith to Oliver Cowdery, giving what we now know as section 28 of the Doctrine and Covenants:

"Behold, I say unto thee, Oliver, that it shall be given unto thee that thou shalt be heard by the church in all things whatsoever thou shalt teach them by the Comforter, concerning the revelations and commandments which I have given.

"But, behold, verily, verily, I say unto thee, no one shall be appointed to receive commandments and revelations in this church excepting my servant Joseph Smith, Jun., for he receiveth them even as Moses" (D&C 28:1–2).

---

3. History, 1838–1856, volume A-1 [23 December 1805–30 August 1834], The Joseph Smith Papers, accessed 15 Mar. 2016, http://josephsmithpapers.org/paperSummary /history-1838-1856-volume-a-1-23-december-1805-30-august-1834?p=60.

4. From Newel Knight's journal, in Cook, *Revelations of the Prophet Joseph Smith,* 39–40.

Some five months later, another episode provoked a similar directive from the Lord. A Mrs. Hubble, presumably a recent convert to the Church, "professed to be a prophetess of the Lord and professed to have many revelations, and knew the Book of Mormon was true, and that she would become a teacher in the Church of Christ. She appeared to be very sanctimonious and deceived some who were not able to detect her in her hypocrisy: others however had the spirit of discernment, and her follies and abominations were made manifest."[5] Again, in response to this incident the Lord spoke of Joseph Smith as "him whom I have appointed unto you to receive commandments and revelations from my hand. And this ye shall know assuredly—that there is none other appointed unto you to receive commandments and revelations until he be taken, if he abide in me." And then, in summarizing the course the Saints were to follow in that day and forevermore, the Master said: "And this shall be a law unto you, that ye receive not the teachings of any that shall come before you as revelations or commandments; and this I give unto you that you may not be deceived, that you may know they are not of me" (D&C 43:2–3, 5–6).

Joseph taught a vital principle. If it were properly understood, much of the confusion that frequently ensues when some new tenet, interpretation, or supposed revelation comes forth would not exist. "I will inform you that *it is contrary to the economy of God,*" he said, "*for any member of the Church, or any one, to receive instruction for those in authority, higher than themselves.*" He explained that "if any person have a vision or a visitation from a heavenly messenger, *it must be for his own benefit or instruction;* for the fundamental principles, government, and doctrine of the Church are

---

5. John Whitmer, History, 1831–circa 1847, The Joseph Smith Papers, accessed 27 Jul. 2016, http://josephsmithpapers.org/paperSummary/john-whitmer-history-1831-circa-1847?p=22.

vested in the keys of the kingdom."[6] On a later occasion he pointed out that it is the "privilege of any officer in this Church, to obtain revelations, *so far as relates to his particular calling and duty in the Church.*"[7]

The principle is clear and the doctrine certain: only the President of the Church—the prophet, seer, and revelator for the Church—has the right to receive divine direction for the whole Church, for he is the person the Lord will inspire "to move the cause of Zion in mighty power for good" (D&C 21:7). "He alone," President J. Reuben Clark explained, "has the right to receive revelations for the Church, *either new or amendatory, or to give authoritative interpretations of scriptures that shall be binding on the Church, or change in any way the existing doctrines of the Church.* He is God's sole mouthpiece on earth for The Church of Jesus Christ of Latter-day Saints, the only true church. He alone may declare the mind and will of God to His people."[8] This principle and practice ensure orthodoxy, constancy, and consistency in the Church and kingdom of God, an institution guided and led by him whose "house is a house of order" (D&C 132:8).

Revelation for the Individual

"No man can receive the Holy Ghost," Brother Joseph explained, "without receiving revelations," for "the Holy Ghost is a revelator."[9] Building upon the foundation laid by his prophet-uncle, Joseph F. Smith taught that "every individual in the Church has just

6. *Joseph Smith* [manual], 197–98; emphasis added.

7. History, 1838–1856, volume B-1 [1 September 1834–2 November 1838], accessed 15 Mar. 2016, http://josephsmithpapers.org/paperSummary/history-1838-1856-volume-b-1-1-september-1834-2-november-1838?p=210; emphasis added.

8. From "When Are the Writings and Sermons of Church Leaders Entitled to the Claim of Being Scripture?" address delivered to Church Educational System personnel at Brigham Young University, 7 July 1954; in *J. Reuben Clark*, 101; emphasis added.

9. *Joseph Smith* [manual], 132.

as much right to enjoy the spirit of revelation and the understanding from God which that spirit of revelation gives him, for his own good, as the bishop has to enable him to preside over his ward."[10] Consequently we should not be surprised to find a number of early revelations detailing how and in what manner God may choose to speak to his children.

An important insight pertaining to the spirit of revelation came to Oliver Cowdery in April of 1829. He desired to translate and thus do more than act as scribe to the Prophet in their work with the gold plates. He was told: "Oliver Cowdery, verily, verily, I say unto you, that assuredly as the Lord liveth, who is your God and your Redeemer, even so surely shall you receive a knowledge of whatsoever things you shall ask in faith, with an honest heart. . . . Yea, behold, *I will tell you in your mind and in your heart, by the Holy Ghost, which shall come upon you and which shall dwell in your heart. Now, behold, this is the spirit of revelation;* behold, this is the spirit by which Moses brought the children of Israel through the Red Sea on dry ground" (D&C 8:1–3; emphasis added). This is significant information. Moses was the head of a dispensation. Of him the Lord Jehovah said to Aaron and Miriam: "If there be a prophet among you, I the Lord will make myself known unto him in a vision, and will speak unto him in a dream. My servant Moses is not so, who is faithful in all mine house. With him will I speak mouth to mouth" (Numbers 12:6–8; compare Exodus 33:11). Yet the revelation to Oliver Cowdery indicates that Moses—like all prophets, and, for that matter, potentially all men and women—walked with and was led most often and most surely by the kindly light and whisperings of the Holy Spirit. It was by means of those thoughts (in his mind) and feelings (in his heart) that Moses knew to part the Red Sea and enable the children of Israel to cross over on dry ground.

---

10. In Conference Report, Apr. 1912, 9.

In commenting on these verses in the Doctrine and Covenants, Joseph McConkie wrote: "We observe that neither [Oliver] nor Joseph was to experience any suspension of their natural faculties in the process of obtaining revelation. Quite to the contrary, their hearts and minds were to be the very media through which the revelation came. Prophets are not hollow shells through which the voice of the Lord echoes, nor are they mechanical recording devices; prophets are men of passion, feeling, and intellect. One does not suspend agency, mind, or spirit in the service of God. It is . . . with heart, might, mind, and strength that we have been asked to serve, and in nothing is this more apparent than the receiving of revelation. There is no mindless worship or service in the kingdom of heaven."[11]

In a sense, the mind and the heart serve as a kind of check and balance, a system of witnesses, a means whereby one may not be deceived or misled to trust one's eternal salvation solely to either the rational processes or to the feelings and emotions.

As to the workings of the Spirit of God and as to the matter of things coming into the mind, almost always a revelation from God will be rational, will make sense, will be in harmony with the commonly accepted standards and ideals set down by God and prophets and the laws of the land. "In the Church," President Boyd K. Packer pointed out, "we are not exempt from common sense. You can know to begin with that you won't be prompted from any righteous source to steal, to lie, to cheat, to join anyone in any kind of moral transgression."[12] Yes, God did command Abraham to sacrifice Isaac and Nephi to slay Laban, but these were rare exceptions, and both Abraham and Nephi were prophets and seers; they knew the voice of the Lord implicitly and thus could converse with the Spirit, which had come to be a constant companion. We would be well served to abide by the rule and leave the exception to God and

---

11. "The Principle of Revelation," 83.
12. "Prayers and Answers," *Ensign,* Nov. 1979, 21.

his prophets. The Lord will not reveal to an individual member of the Church anything that is out of harmony with law and order and good judgment or in conflict with the order of the Church.[13]

As to how revelation may come through the mind, the Prophet declared: "A person may profit by noticing the first intimation of the spirit of revelation; for instance, when you feel pure intelligence flowing into you, it may give you sudden strokes of ideas, so that by noticing it, you may find it fulfilled the same day or soon; (i.e.) those things that were presented unto your minds by the Spirit of God will come to pass; and thus by learning the Spirit of God and understanding it, you may grow into the principle of revelation, until you become perfect in Christ Jesus."[14]

In regard to the feelings, President Ezra Taft Benson taught: "We hear the words of the Lord most often as a feeling. If we are humble and sensitive, the Lord will prompt us through our feelings. That is why spiritual promptings move us on occasion to great joy, sometimes to tears. . . . The Holy Ghost causes our feelings to be more tender. We feel more charitable and compassionate. We are calmer. We have a greater capacity to love. People want to be around us because our very countenances radiate the influence of the Spirit."[15]

One of the precious but often overlooked aspects of revelation through our feelings is peace. In a sense, to be at peace is to have received a meaningful revelation, to have the inner awareness that God is pleased with one's life and that the course charted by the individual is in harmony with the divine will (D&C 59:23). In another sense, peace is a means by which the Lord responds to petitions and answers prayers. "Blessed art thou," the Savior said to Oliver Cowdery, "for what thou hast done; for thou hast inquired

---

13. Smith, "Try the Spirits," *Times and Seasons* 3, no. 11 (Apr. 1842): 745.

14. *Joseph Smith* [manual], 132.

15. *Come unto Christ*, 20.

of me [concerning the truthfulness of the Restoration], and behold, as often as thou hast inquired thou hast received instruction of my Spirit. . . . Behold, thou knowest that thou hast inquired of me and I did enlighten thy mind; and now I tell thee these things that thou mayest know that thou hast been enlightened by the Spirit of truth."

The Lord continued with his instructions and an invitation: "Verily, verily, I say unto you, if you desire a further witness, cast your mind upon the night that you cried unto me in your heart, that you might know concerning the truth of these things" (D&C 6:14–15, 22). That is a reference to the occasion when, while residing in the Joseph Smith Sr. home, Oliver had inquired of the Lord about the truthfulness of the family's claims concerning Joseph Jr. and the coming forth of the Book of Mormon. This information is found in the earliest (1832) history prepared by the Prophet Joseph. The account speaks of the Prophet receiving once again the plates after being chastened by God for allowing the 116 manuscript pages to be lost. "After much humility and affliction of soul, I obtained them again when *the Lord appeared to a young man by the name of Oliver Cowdery and showed unto him the plates in a vision and also the truth of the work* and what the Lord was about to do through me, his unworthy servant."[16] "Did I not speak peace to your mind concerning the matter?" the Lord asked Oliver. "What greater witness can you have than from God?" (D&C 6:23).

One of the keys to *individual* revelation is *institutional* revelation. That is, holy scripture can become both the *means* by which God speaks to us as well as the *message* to us. Many answers to personal and family challenges are to be found in the inspired principles taught and the poignant stories told within the standard works. In addition, scripture is in a sense a sacrament, a sacred

---

16. Jessee, *Personal Writings of Joseph Smith,* 14; emphasis added.

avenue, a channel by which we are brought closer to God. "When we want to speak to God," Elder Robert D. Hales taught, "we pray. And when we want Him to speak to us, we search the scriptures, for His words are spoken through His prophets."[17]

Joseph Smith learned precept upon precept, and he taught the Saints that divine responses to the prayerful, humble seeker of truth are many and varied, as are the ways in which those answers may be delivered: a personal appearance of the Lord (D&C 110:1–10); personal appearances of other heavenly messengers (D&C 110:11–15; 128:20); a vision (D&C 76; 137; 138); the voice of God (D&C 128:21); the Urim and Thummim (D&C 3; 6; 11; 14); the still, small voice (D&C 85:6); and the Holy Ghost speaking to our minds and hearts (D&C 8:2–3; 9:7–9; 128:1). It would be a mistake for Latter-day Saints to suppose that answers and confirmations come only in one way—as a burning in the bosom, for example. The Lord desires to communicate with his children and will choose the means that will more clearly and persuasively convey his holy words and his perfect will to those who seek him diligently (D&C 1:24; compare 2 Nephi 4:15). "If thou shalt ask," the promise is stated, "thou shalt receive revelation upon revelation, knowledge upon knowledge, that thou mayest know the mysteries and peaceable things—that which bringeth joy, that which bringeth life eternal" (D&C 42:61).

"We believe all that God has revealed, all that He does now reveal, and we believe that He will yet reveal many great and important things pertaining to the Kingdom of God" (Articles of Faith 1:9). This statement of belief is as true of individuals as it is of the institutional Church. Joseph Smith the Prophet parted the veil, turned the key, and opened the door for those who earnestly and sincerely desire to know the mind and will and hear the voice of the

---

17. *Return*, 347.

Lord their God. There are great and important things to be made known to those Latter-day Saints who search, ponder, and pray. The Lord is no respecter of persons (Acts 10:34; Romans 2:11; Colossians 3:25). He does not bless only office holders, nor does he endow with knowledge from on high only those called to direct the destiny of his Church and kingdom. "God hath not revealed anything to Joseph," the Prophet himself observed, "but what he will make known unto the Twelve, and even the least Saint may know all things as fast as he is able to bear them."[18]

Sometime after his death, Joseph Smith appeared to Brigham Young and gave specific and pointed instructions about why the members of the Church must labor to acquire and keep the Spirit of the Lord. "'Tell the people to be humble and faithful and be sure to keep the Spirit of the Lord and it will lead them right. . . . They can tell the Spirit of the Lord from all other spirits; it will whisper peace and joy to their souls; it will take malice, hatred, strife and all evil from their hearts; and their whole desire will be to do good, bring forth righteousness and build up the kingdom of God. . . . Be sure to tell the people to keep the Spirit of the Lord; and if they will, they will find themselves just as they were organized by our Father in heaven before they came into the world.'" Joseph again said: "'Tell the people to be sure to keep the Spirit of the Lord and follow it, and it will lead them just right.'"[19]

God spoke to and through Joseph Smith. One may begin to grasp, to some degree at least, how familiar the Prophet became with the things of God by reflecting seriously on this statement: "It is my meditation all the day, and more than my meat and drink, to know how I shall make the Saints of God comprehend the visions that roll like an overflowing surge before my mind."[20] Through

---

18. *Joseph Smith* [manual], 268.

19. *Joseph Smith* [manual], 98; Journal History, 23 Feb. 1847.

20. *Joseph Smith* [manual], 520.

learning the spirit of revelation, the Saints learned also that those who decry or deny new visions, new revelation, even new scripture, do not really know the God they claimed to worship. Moroni taught: "And again I speak unto you who deny the revelations of God, and say that they are done away, that there are no revelations, nor prophecies, nor gifts; . . . Behold I say unto you, he that denieth these things knoweth not the gospel of Christ; yea, he has not read the scriptures; if so, he does not understand them" (Mormon 9:7–8).

President Henry B. Eyring made this observation: "More than for any other prophet, we have *a clear and lengthy record from Joseph Smith of how we can communicate with God.* Because of Joseph's example and teaching, I can hear what God would have me hear from a living prophet, a bishop of my ward, a home teacher, a child asking a question in my family home evening, or an impression to my heart and mind as I pray.

"Your problem and mine is not to get God to speak to us; few of us have reached the point where he has been compelled to turn away from us. Our problem is to hear. The Prophet Joseph is our master example in that art."[21]

"The plea of many in this day," Joseph Smith said, "is that we have no right to receive revelations; but if we do not get revelations," he affirmed, "we do not have the oracles of God; and if they have not the oracles of God, they are not the people of God."[22] In that sense, to receive revelation is not merely what the Saints of God can do; it is what they *ought to do.* It is our duty and obligation, our spiritual birthright.

SPIRITUAL REBIRTH

There came to Jesus by night a man named Nicodemus, a "ruler of the Jews," presumably a member of the Sanhedrin, a man who

---

21. *To Draw Closer to God,* 29; emphasis added.
22. *Words of Joseph Smith,* 156.

was a "master in Israel," meaning a master teacher or an acknowledged scholar among the Jews. He and others had been impressed with the miracles of Jesus. He said: "Rabbi, we know that thou art a teacher come from God: for no man can do these miracles that thou doest, except God be with him." Jesus then did two things. First, he pointed out to Nicodemus that more was required of him than a verbal recognition of Jesus as a miracle worker. Second, he anticipated the unasked question that must have lurked in the shadows of Nicodemus's mind, namely, "What must I do to inherit eternal life?" Jesus answered: "Except a man be born again, he cannot *see* the kingdom of God" (John 3:1–3; emphasis added).

This was no new idea, no novel concept revealed for the first time, for the doctrine of rebirth was as old as the world. God had taught this truth to Adam and Eve (Moses 6:58–59), as well as to Jeremiah (Jeremiah 31:33) and Ezekiel (Ezekiel 36:25–26), and surely to all of the prophets. Either Nicodemus did not understand what Jesus was teaching or he sought to prolong an otherwise interesting discussion, for he asked: "How can a man be born when he is old? Can he enter the second time into his mother's womb, and be born?" (John 3:4). Jesus responded to Nicodemus's questions: "Except a man be born of water and of the Spirit, he cannot *enter* into the kingdom of God" (John 3:5; emphasis added).

In the early days of the Restoration, the Christian world was largely divided over this matter of the new birth, very similar to how they are divided today. A large segment of Christianity believed then and believes now that being born again consists of having a personal spiritual experience with Jesus, of being converted, of being saved, of accepting him as Lord and Savior. Another even larger segment of Christianity holds that being born again consists of receiving the prescribed sacraments (ordinances) of the church. And what do the Latter-day Saints believe? Is it enough to receive the revelation, the spiritual conviction that God lives, that Jesus is the Christ, and that the gospel of Jesus Christ has been restored to the earth in its fulness through a modern prophet? Or is it sufficient to receive the proper ordinances? The Prophet Joseph Smith stated simply but powerfully that "being born again comes *by the Spirit of God through ordinances.*"[23]

Joseph explained on another occasion that it is one thing to *see* the kingdom of God and another thing to *enter into* that kingdom. A person must have a "change of heart" to *see* the kingdom; that is, he or she must be awakened spiritually to recognize that The Church of Jesus Christ is the custodian of the fulness of the gospel and the requisite priesthood authority to perform the specified ordinances, and he or she must acknowledge that the fulness of salvation is to be had through acceptance of and participation in those principles and ordinances. Further, the Prophet taught, a person must "subscribe the articles of adoption"—the first principles and ordinances of the gospel, the means by which individuals are adopted into the family of the Lord Jesus Christ—to *enter* into the kingdom.[24]

One man heard Joseph Smith discourse on the doctrine of spiritual rebirth as given in the third chapter of John. Joseph pointed out that the birth spoken of in John 3:3 "was not the gift of the Holy Ghost, which was promised after baptism, but was *a portion of the spirit, which attended the preaching of the gospel by the elders of the Church.* The people [investigating the Church] wondered why they had not previously understood the plain declarations of scripture, as explained by the elders, as they had read them hundreds of times. When they read the Bible [now] it was a new book to them. *This was being born again to see the Kingdom of God.* They were not in it, but could see it from the outside, which *they could not do until the Spirit of the Lord took the veil from before their eyes. It was a change of*

---

23. *Joseph Smith* [manual], 95; emphasis added.
24. *Words of Joseph Smith,* 256.

heart but not of state; they were converted, but were yet in their sins. Although Cornelius [in Acts 10] had seen an holy angel, and on the preaching of Peter the Holy Ghost was poured out upon him and his household, they were only born again to see the Kingdom of God. Had they not been baptized afterwards they would not have been saved."[25]

Latter-day Saints, as well as other Christians, speak occasionally of "having our sins washed away" in the waters of baptism. This, however, is a figurative expression to describe the larger and more comprehensive process by which one's sins are remitted by the Savior and the person placed in a proper standing before God (being justified). Nephi, son of Lehi, provided the more accurate perspective. Having foreseen and spoken of the baptism of Jesus at the hands of John the Baptist and having spoken of the narrow way to salvation prescribed by Christ, Nephi counseled his people and us: "Wherefore, do the things which I have told you I have seen that your Lord and your Redeemer should do; for, for this cause have they been shown unto me, that ye might know the gate by which ye should enter. For the gate by which ye should enter is repentance and baptism by water; and *then cometh a remission of your sins by fire and by the Holy Ghost*" (2 Nephi 31:17; emphasis added).[26] In harmony with that counsel and that clarification, the latter-day seer explained: "You might as well baptize a bag of sand as a man, if not done in view of the remission of sins and getting of the Holy Ghost.

---

25. Daniel Tyler, in "Recollections of the Prophet Joseph Smith," *Juvenile Instructor* 27, no. 3 (Feb. 1892): 93–94; emphasis added; in Andrus and Andrus, *They Knew the Prophet,* 50.

26. Elder Bruce R. McConkie wrote: "Sins are remitted not in the waters of baptism, as we say in speaking figuratively, but when we receive the Holy Ghost. It is the Holy Spirit of God that erases carnality and brings us into a state of righteousness. We become clean when we actually receive the fellowship and companionship of the Holy Ghost. It is then that sin and dross and evil are burned out of our souls as though by fire. The baptism of the Holy Ghost is the baptism of fire" (*New Witness for the Articles of Faith,* 290; see also 239).

Baptism by water is but half a baptism, and is good for nothing without the other half—that is, the baptism of the Holy Ghost."[27]

Truly, to choose Christ is to choose to be changed. "Those who have felt the touch of the Master's hand," President Thomas S. Monson explained, "somehow cannot explain the change which comes into their lives. There is a desire to live better, to serve faithfully, to walk humbly, and to live more like the Savior." These have "glimpsed the promises of eternity."[28]

GIFTS OF THE SPIRIT

As we mentioned earlier, Sidney Rigdon and Alexander Campbell finally separated as a result of their doctrinal differences. Sidney felt, for example, that the Lord's Church should live according to the pattern set forth in the book of Acts—the people should have all things in common (see 2:44). The other point of difference was over spiritual gifts: Sidney was emphatic that even Jesus himself had promised that signs should follow those who believed. Campbell, more intent on establishing the rationality of Christian belief, was not prone to press for spiritual gifts. A popular Methodist itinerant preacher named Peter Cartwright spoke of a conversation he had with Joseph Smith in Nauvoo. "He [Joseph] believed that among all the Churches in the world the Methodists was the nearest right. But they had stopped short by not claiming the gift of tongues, of prophecy, and of miracles, and then quoted a batch of Scriptures to prove his position correct. . . . 'Indeed,' said Joe, 'if the Methodists would only advance a step or two further, they would take the world. We Latter-day Saints are Methodists, as far as they have gone, only have advanced further."[29]

When Elder Parley P. Pratt published one of the first extended

---

27. *Words of Joseph Smith,* 230.
28. *Teachings of Thomas S. Monson,* 34.
29. *Autobiography of Peter Cartwright,* 342.

treatises on Mormonism, *A Voice of Warning* (1837), he addressed himself first to the apostasy of the early Christian Church and thus the manner in which God would begin to restore the gospel fulness. He pointed out that the offices of the meridian Church "consisted of apostles, prophets, evangelists, pastors, and teachers, all inspired and set in the Church by the Lord himself for the edifying of the saints, for the work of the ministry, etc. And they were to continue in the Church, wherever it was found, until they all came to the unity of the faith and unto the measure of the stature of a man in Christ [see Ephesians 4:11–14].

"Secondly," Elder Pratt explained, "the gifts of the Spirit, which some call supernatural, were the powers and blessings which pertained to that covenant wherever it existed, among the Jews or the Gentiles, so long as the covenant was of force. . . . And it must be through the breaking of that covenant that they were lost."[30]

In November of 1839, when Joseph Smith and Elias Higbee were asked by President Martin Van Buren how Mormonism differed from other Christian denominations, the Prophet replied that the Saints differed in "mode of baptism, and the gift of the Holy Ghost by the laying on of hands." All other considerations, Joseph declared, are "contained in the gift of the Holy Ghost."[31] In an editorial that appeared in the *Times and Seasons,* Joseph explained why this was the case. "It is not to be wondered at that men should be ignorant, in a great measure, of the principles of salvation, and more especially of the nature, office, power, influence, gifts, and blessings of the gift of the Holy Ghost, when we consider that the human family have been enveloped in gross darkness and ignorance for many centuries past, without revelation, or any just criterion [by which] to arrive at a knowledge of the things of God, which can only be known by the Spirit of God. . . .

---

30. *Voice of Warning,* 28.
31. *Joseph Smith* [manual], 97.

"We believe in the gift of the Holy Ghost being enjoyed now, as much as it was in the apostles' days; we believe that [this gift] is necessary to make and to organize the priesthood; that no man can be called to fill any office in the ministry without it; we also believe in prophecy, in tongues, in visions, and in revelations, in gifts, and in healings; and that these things cannot be enjoyed without the gift of the Holy Ghost; we believe that the holy men of old spake as they were moved by the Holy Ghost, and that holy men in these days speak by the same principle; . . . but *whilst we do this we believe in it rationally, reasonably, consistently, and scripturally,* and not according to the wild vagaries, foolish notions and traditions of men." The Prophet then cautioned that "to say that men always prophesied and spoke in tongues when they had the imposition of hands [for the gift of the Holy Ghost], would be to state that which is untrue, contrary to the practice of the Apostles, and at variance with holy writ."[32]

When the apostle Paul addressed himself to the Corinthians, he pointed out that not all of the gifts of the Spirit are of equal spiritual value, and that some of the gifts, though "less comely" or attractive or enviable, are in fact among the most valuable. He encouraged the meridian Saints, for example, to seek earnestly to obtain the gift of prophecy, meaning the gift to speak the word of God by the gift and power of the Holy Spirit. He also commended those who had enjoyed the gift of tongues but warned them that such a gift had a limited utility and would probably do more to mystify and even repel those not of the faith than entice them (1 Corinthians 14).

Joseph the Prophet took a similar course. He noted that "there are only two gifts that could be made visible—the gift of tongues and the gift of prophecy. These are things that are the most talked about, and yet if a person spoke in an unknown tongue, according to Paul's testimony, he would be a barbarian to those present. They

32. *Joseph Smith* [manual], 118–19; emphasis added; see also "Gift of the Holy Ghost," *Times and Seasons* 3, no. 16 (June 1842): 823.

would say that it was gibberish."[33] He also provided sound and solid counsel to his people relative to the need to avoid the drama and sensationalism that we so often witness in our own Spirit-starved world: "The Lord cannot always be known by the thunder of his voice; by the display of his glory, or by the manifestation of his power; and those that are the most anxious to see these things, are the least prepared to meet [receive] them."[34] As to spiritual gifts in the Church, the Prophet pointed out that "every Latter-day Saint had a gift, and by living a righteous life, and asking for it, the Holy Spirit would reveal it to him or her."[35]

Paul taught powerfully that the "more excellent way" was the gift of charity, what Mormon called the "pure love of Christ" (Moroni 7:47). In his abridgment of the Jaredite record, Moroni offered the magnificent insight, one he shares with Paul, that charity is first and foremost the love that Christ offers to us through his sufferings and death and resurrection. Note his words as he speaks with the Lord: "And again, I remember that thou hast said that thou hast loved the world, even unto the laying down of thy life for the world, that thou mightest take it again to prepare a place for the children of men. And now I know that *this love which thou hast had for the children of men is charity;* wherefore, except men shall have

---

33. *Joseph Smith* [manual], 121. Indeed, the Prophet offered far more caution than recommendation when it came to the gift of tongues: to be careful lest they be deceived (383); that it is not necessary for tongues to be taught to the Church (383); the devil will often take advantage of the innocent and unwary, and so if anything is taught in the Church by the gift of tongues, it is not to be received as doctrine (384); it is the smallest gift of all, but it is the one most sought after ("Gift of the Holy Ghost," *Times and Seasons* 3, no. 16 [June 1842]: 825).

34. "Gift of the Holy Ghost," *Times and Seasons* 3, no. 16 (June 1842): 825.

35. Amasa Potter, "Reminiscence of the Prophet Joseph Smith," *Juvenile Instructor* 29, no. 4 (Feb. 1894): 132; *Joseph Smith* [manual], 117.

charity they cannot inherit that place which thou hast prepared in the mansions of thy Father" (Ether 12:33–34; emphasis added).[36]

This was the kind and quality and depth of love to which Joseph Smith called and summoned the Latter-day Saints. "Love is one of the chief characteristics of Deity," he explained, "and ought to be manifested by those who aspire to be the sons of God. A man filled with the love of God, is not content with blessing his family alone, but ranges through the whole world, anxious to bless the whole human race."[37] He also taught: "It is one evidence that men are unacquainted with the principles of godliness to behold the contraction of affectionate feelings and lack of charity in the world. . . . *God does not look on sin with allowance, but when men have sinned, there must be allowance made for them.*

"All the religious world is boasting of righteousness," Joseph declared; "it is the doctrine of the devil to retard the human mind, and hinder our progress, by filling us with self-righteousness." Now notice this transcendent expression, one beautifully reflective of the soul of the Prophet of the Restoration: "*The nearer we get to our heavenly Father, the more we are disposed to look with compassion on perishing souls;* we feel that we want to take them upon our shoulders, and cast their sins behind our backs. . . . There should be no license for sin, but mercy should go hand in hand with reproof."[38]

Joseph Smith understood quite well, however, that this kind of love must not be confined to the household of faith but was to be the means by which the truthfulness of Latter-day Saint Christianity could be discerned by those of other faiths (John 15:12). "There is a tie [love] from God," he said on one occasion, "that should be exercised towards those of our faith, who walk uprightly, which is

---

36. An excellent treatment of this dimension of charity is Holland, *Christ and the New Covenant*, 336–37. See also Hafen, *The Broken Heart*, 189–99.

37. *Joseph Smith* [manual], 426.

38. *Joseph Smith* [manual], 428–29; emphasis added.

peculiar to itself; but *it is without prejudice; it gives scope to the mind, which enables us to conduct ourselves with greater liberality towards all that are not of our faith, than what they exercise towards one another.* These principles approximate nearer to the mind of God, because [they are] like God, or Godlike."[39]

It is exactly this kind of love that enabled and empowered Brother Joseph to act and feel toward those of other faiths kindness, consideration, and genuine respect. He declared that the reason he was able to gain so many followers was because "I possess the principle of love. All I can offer the world is a good heart and a good hand." He went on to say that he was just as willing to lay down his life in defense of the religious liberties of Presbyterians or Baptists or Roman Catholics as he was to do the same for his own people. He then made a point that would no doubt surprise many—that Latter-day Saints "did not differ so far in our religious views, but that we could all drink into one principle of love." Then comes a statement that might well serve as a guide, if not a constitution, in defining how members of The Church of Jesus Christ of Latter-day Saints ought to relate to persons of other faiths: "If I esteem mankind to be in error, shall I bear them down? No. I will lift them up, and in their own way too, if I cannot persuade them my way is better; and I will not seek to compel any man to believe as I do, only by the force of reasoning, for truth will cut its own way. Do you believe in Jesus Christ and the Gospel of salvation which he revealed? So do I. Christians should cease wrangling and contending with each other, and cultivate the principles of union and friendship in their midst."[40]

One wonders what would happen if twenty-first-century Saints

---

39. History, 1838–1856, volume C-1 [2 November 1838–31 July 1842], The Joseph Smith Papers, accessed 15 Mar. 2016, http://josephsmithpapers.org/paperSummary /history-1838-1856-volume-c-1-2-november-1838-31-july-1842?p=93; emphasis added.

40. *Joseph Smith* [manual], 287, 345; emphasis added.

acquired and incorporated the feelings of the Prophet toward our brothers and sisters of the world: "I have no desire but to do all men good. I feel to pray for all men. We don't ask any people to throw away any good they have got; we only ask them to come and get more."[41]

THE PROMISE OF ETERNAL LIFE

The Lord has declared in our dispensation that "he who doeth the works of righteousness shall receive his reward, even peace in this world, and eternal life in the world to come" (D&C 59:23). Isaiah had written some twenty-six hundred years earlier, "The work of righteousness shall be peace; and the effect of righteousness quietness and assurance for ever" (Isaiah 32:17). Those in this life who conduct themselves with fidelity and devotion to God and his gospel will eventually know that peace "which passeth all understanding" (Philippians 4:7), the calming but powerful assurance that they have successfully met the challenges of mortality.

These are they who have lived by every word of God and are willing to serve the Lord at all hazards. They have, according to Joseph Smith, made their calling and election sure.[42] For them the day of judgment has been advanced, and the blessings associated with the glories of the celestial kingdom are assured. They receive what the prophets have called the "more sure word of prophecy" (2 Peter 1:19). "The more sure word of prophecy," Joseph explained, "means a man's knowing that he is sealed up unto eternal life, by revelation and the spirit of prophecy, through the power of the Holy Priesthood. It is impossible for a man to be saved in ignorance" (D&C 131:5–6). Though it is true, as President Marion G. Romney observed, that "the fulness of eternal life is not attainable in mortality, . . . the peace which is its harbinger and which comes as a result

---

41. *Joseph Smith* [manual], 155.
42. *Words of Joseph Smith*, 5.

of making one's calling and election sure is attainable in this life."[43] The Prophet Joseph extended a challenging invitation to the Saints: "I would exhort you to go on and continue to call upon God, until you make your calling and election sure for yourselves, by obtaining this more sure word of prophecy, and wait patiently for the promise until you obtain it."[44]

Latter-day Saints who have received the ordinances of salvation—including the blessings of the temple endowment and eternal marriage—may thus press forward in the work of the Lord and with quiet dignity and patient maturity seek to be worthy of gaining the certain assurance of salvation before the end of their mortal lives. Should an individual not formally receive the more sure word of prophecy in this life, however, he or she has the scriptural promise that faithfully enduring to the end—keeping the covenants and commandments from baptism to the end of his or her mortal life (Mosiah 18:8–9)—eventuates in the promise of eternal life, whether the fulfillment of that promise be received here or hereafter (D&C 14:7; 53:7; 2 Nephi 31:20; Mosiah 5:15). "But blessed are they who are faithful and endure, whether in life or in death, for they shall inherit eternal life" (D&C 50:5; see also 58:2). Why? Because "if we die in the faith, that is the same thing as saying that our calling and election has been made sure and that we will go on to eternal reward hereafter."[45]

CONCLUSION

For Joseph Smith, spirituality was a state of being, a condition achieved through the merging of the temporal and the spiritual,

---

43. In Conference Report, Oct. 1965, 20.

44. History, 1838–1856, volume D-1 [1 August 1842–1 July 1843], The Joseph Smith Papers, accessed 15 Mar. 2016, http://josephsmithpapers.org/paperSummary/history -1838-1856-volume-d-1-1-august-1842-1-july-1843?p=193.

45. McConkie, Address at the funeral for Elder S. Dilworth Young, 5.

the finite and the infinite. Spirituality was essentially the result of a righteous life coupled with heightened perspective, an increased affinity toward the Holy Spirit, sensitivity to things of God.[46] To possess spirituality was to recognize that in the end all things are spiritual and that God has never given a purely temporal (time-bound or temporary) command or directive (D&C 29:34). Spirituality consisted of tying the heavens to the earth, imbuing man with the powers of God, and thereby elevating society. Such a change in one's nature was to be undertaken in the world, amidst the throes of spiritual opposition: one need not resort to monasticism in order to come out of the world. It was to be accomplished by every individual, not just priests or ministers. It could come to the Saints for one overriding reason: the Melchizedek Priesthood had been restored, and thus the right to confer the gift of the Holy Ghost was available once more among God's children. Truly, as Joseph Smith and Elias Higbee explained to United States president Martin Van Buren, the Mormons differ from other faiths "in mode of baptism, and the gift of the Holy Ghost by the laying on of hands," and any other differences "were contained in the gift of the Holy Ghost."[47]

As the revelations of God began to elevate his perspective on reality, Joseph Smith came to understand the infinite and eternal God, as well as the nature of mortal men and women. The profundity of his thinking was evident early, and by 1834 he could speak of the capacity of human beings to mature in spiritual things: "We consider that God has created man with a mind capable of instruction, and a faculty which may be enlarged in proportion to the heed and diligence given to the light communicated from

---

46. An apostolic successor, Elder Dallin H. Oaks explained: "Spirituality is a lens through which we view life and a gauge by which we evaluate it. . . . To be spiritually minded is to view and evaluate experiences in terms of the large perspective of eternity. How we interpret our experiences is . . . a function of our degree of spirituality" (*Pure in Heart,* 111–13).

47. *Joseph Smith* [manual], 97.

heaven to the intellect; and that *the nearer man approaches perfection, the clearer are his views, and the greater his enjoyments, till he has overcome the evils of his life and lost every desire for sin;* and like the ancients, arrives at that point of faith where he is wrapped in the power and glory of his Maker and is caught up to dwell with Him. But we consider that this is a station to which no man ever arrived in a moment."[48] Like so many of the principles of spiritual progression, that station would be arrived at line upon line, precept upon precept.

Gaining the mind of God and cultivating the sanctifying influence of the Holy Ghost was serious business to Joseph Smith, and it required sober mental and spiritual exertion, as well as personal resolve and discipline. It did not come easy. "The things of God are of deep import," he wrote from Liberty Jail, "and time, and experience, and careful and ponderous and solemn thoughts can only find them out. Thy mind, O man! if thou wilt lead a soul unto salvation, must stretch as high as the utmost heavens, and search into and contemplate the darkest abyss, and the broad expanse of eternity— thou must commune with God."[49]

A modern apostle, Elder Robert D. Hales, offered the following

---

48. *Joseph Smith* [manual], 210–11; emphasis added. Joseph would no doubt have been the first to acknowledge, however, that one who has risen to such spiritual heights will have done so through a great deal of opposition. The night before their first baptism of British converts in Preston, England, Heber C. Kimball and Orson Hyde were attacked by a horde of evil spirits for an extended period of time. Years later Heber discussed this excruciating experience with the Prophet, perhaps troubled that he and his brethren had done something wrong. "No, Brother Heber," Joseph replied, "at that time you were nigh unto the Lord; there was only a veil between you and Him, but you could not see Him. When I heard of it, it gave me great joy, for I then knew that the work of God had taken root in that land. It was this that caused the devil to make a struggle to kill you." The Prophet then explained some of his own battles with evil and remarked: "The nearer a person approaches the Lord, a greater power will be manifested by the adversary to prevent the accomplishment of His purposes" (Whitney, *Life of Heber C. Kimball,* 131–32; see also Kimball, *Heber C. Kimball,* 47–48).

49. *Joseph Smith* [manual], 267.

insight and charge: "Choose to put yourself in a position to have experiences with the Spirit of God through prayer, in scripture study, at Church meetings, in your home, and through wholesome interactions with others. *When you feel the influence of the Spirit, you are beginning to be cleansed and strengthened.* The light is being turned on, and where that light shines, the darkness of evil cannot be."[50]

On 7 April 1844, during a time when, many believe, the Prophet was at his spiritual and intellectual pinnacle, he said: "When you climb up a ladder, you must begin at the bottom, and ascend step by step, until you arrive at the top; and so it is with the principles of the gospel—you must begin with the first, and go on until you learn all the principles of exaltation. But it will be a great while after you have passed through the veil before you will have learned them. It is not all to be comprehended in this world; it will be a great work to learn our salvation and exaltation even beyond the grave."[51] Thus we can perhaps appreciate the simple but deeply profound directive delivered frequently to Latter-day Saints, one that in reality makes all the difference in growing in the grace of God: "Seek the Spirit."

---

50. *Return,* 37–38; emphasis added.
51. *Joseph Smith* [manual], 268.

Chapter 6

JESUS CHRIST AND THE ETERNAL GOSPEL

*Manchester, New York, and Harmony, Pennsylvania, 1829–1830.
Very early in the process of translating the Book of Mormon, Joseph encountered a doctrinal concept that would have been completely foreign to lay persons as well as pastors and theologians—that the gospel of Jesus Christ preceded Jesus Christ, that long before the Son of Man was born in Bethlehem of Judea, God's people understood that redemption would come only in and through the Holy Messiah. Subsequent revelations and translations would confirm and expand upon this doctrine.*

J oseph Smith taught that God our Father has a plan for his children, a program established to maximize our growth and ensure our happiness. And yet that fact alone—that there is some divine plan to life—is not as obvious from the Bible as from latter-day scripture. Knowing what we know, we as Latter-day Saints are able to recognize divine design, but seldom can we turn to a specific Old or New Testament passage that speaks with clarity of a plan. On the other hand, Book of Mormon prophets speak with grateful hearts for the merciful plan of the great Creator (2 Nephi 9:6), the plan of our God (2 Nephi 9:13), the great plan of mercy (Alma 42:15, 31), the plan of redemption (Jacob 6:8; Alma 12:25–26, 30, 32; 17:16; 18:39;

22:13–14; 29:2; 34:31; 39:18; 42:11, 13), the eternal plan of deliverance (2 Nephi 11:5), the plan of salvation (Jarom 1:2; Alma 24:14; 42:5), and the great plan of happiness (Alma 42:8, 16). We know that the plan of salvation is "always and everlastingly the same; that obedience to the same laws always brings the same reward; that the gospel laws have not changed . . . ; and that always and everlastingly all things pertaining to salvation center in Christ."[1]

AN ETERNAL ATONEMENT

Jesus is truly the "Lamb slain from the foundation of the world" (Revelation 13:8; Moses 7:47). That is, the atoning sacrifice is not only timely (for us who need its redeeming and enabling powers) but *timeless*. Though the act of atonement would not take place until Jesus suffered in Gethsemane and on Golgotha in the meridian of time, earth's earliest inhabitants were taught to call upon God in the name of his Beloved Son for deliverance (Moses 5:5–8). Again, this central truth is no longer to be had in traditional Christendom. Indeed, one fascinating attack on the Book of Mormon is that it is too Christ-centered! That is, critics contend, the Book of Mormon has too much Christ within it, long before there was a Christ.

Brother Joseph declared that God has revealed himself, his plan, and the Mediator of his sacred covenant to his children from the beginning. The voice of the Father came to Adam: "If thou wilt turn unto me, and hearken unto my voice, and believe, and repent of all thy transgressions, and be baptized, even in water, in the name of mine Only Begotten Son . . . , which is Jesus Christ, the only name which shall be given under heaven, whereby salvation shall come unto the children of men, ye shall receive the gift of the Holy Ghost" (Moses 6:52). Further, Adam was commanded to teach his children that all mankind, because of the effects of the

---

1. McConkie, *Promised Messiah*, 4–5.

Fall, "must be born again into the kingdom of heaven, of water, and of the Spirit, and be cleansed by blood, even the blood of mine Only Begotten; that ye might be sanctified from all sin, and enjoy the words of eternal life in this world, and eternal life in the world to come, even immortal glory" (Moses 6:59).

The Prophet observed that "we cannot believe that the ancients in all ages were so ignorant of the system of heaven as many suppose, since all that were ever saved, were saved through the power of this great plan of redemption, as much before the coming of Christ as since; if not, God has had different plans in operation (if we may so express it), to bring men back to dwell with Himself; and this we cannot believe, since there has been no change in the constitution of man since he fell."[2] And so it is that we learn through the scriptures of the Restoration that, in addition to Adam, such biblical personalities as Enoch (Moses 7), Noah (Moses 8), Abraham (JST, Genesis 15:9–12), and Moses (Moses 1) had revealed unto them the particulars of the Father's plan and knew and taught of the coming redemption in and through Jesus Christ. Truly, as the apostle Peter proclaimed, "To [Christ] give all the prophets witness" (Acts 10:43).

It was no different in the western hemisphere. Very early in the Book of Mormon account Nephi stated that "six hundred years from the time my father left Jerusalem, a prophet would the Lord God raise up among the Jews—even a Messiah, or, in other words, a Savior of the world" (1 Nephi 10:4). Nephi saw in vision that Jesus would be "lifted up upon the cross and slain for the sins of the world" (1 Nephi 11:33). Almost six hundred years before the birth of Jesus in Bethlehem, Lehi taught his son Jacob that "redemption cometh in and through the Holy Messiah; for he is full of grace and truth." Further, he explained, "there is no flesh that can dwell in the presence of God, save it be through the merits, and mercy, and

2. *Joseph Smith* [manual], 48–49.

grace of the Holy Messiah, who layeth down his life according to the flesh, and taketh it again by the power of the Spirit, that he may bring to pass the resurrection of the dead, being the first that should rise" (2 Nephi 2:6, 8). Alma taught an erring son that because the souls of individuals who lived before the meridian of time are just as precious in the sight of God as those who lived during or after that age, it is necessary that redemption in Christ should be made available to people of all ages (Alma 39:17–19). Indeed, "none of the prophets have written, nor prophesied, save they have spoken concerning this Christ" (Jacob 7:11; compare 4:4; Mosiah 13:33).

ETERNAL COVENANTS AND ORDINANCES

Because we know that the great plan of happiness is eternal and that salvation in any age is accomplished only in and through the mediation of the Redeemer, we also know that the covenants and ordinances are likewise eternal and unchanging. "Now taking it for granted that the scriptures say what they mean and mean what they say," the Prophet Joseph noted, "we have sufficient grounds to go on and prove from the Bible that the gospel has always been the same; the ordinances to fulfill its requirements, the same, and the officers to officiate, the same; and the signs and fruits resulting from the promises, the same." He continued with an illustration of this principle: "Therefore, as Noah was a preacher of righteousness he must have been baptized and ordained to the priesthood by the laying on of the hands."[3] In short, the Lord "set the ordinances to be the same forever and ever."[4] That is, "ordinances, instituted in the heavens before the foundation of the world, in the priesthood, for the salvation of men, are not to be altered or changed. All must be saved on the same principles."[5]

---

3. *Joseph Smith* [manual], 93; "Baptism," *Times and Seasons* 3, no. 21 (Sept. 1842): 904.

4. *Joseph Smith* [manual], 107.

5. *Words of Joseph Smith*, 210.

It is in this light that we speak of the restored gospel as comprising the new and everlasting covenant. Modern revelations affirm: "Wherefore, I say unto you that I have sent unto you mine everlasting covenant, even that which was from the beginning" (D&C 49:9). "Verily I say unto you, blessed are you for receiving mine everlasting covenant, even the fulness of my gospel, sent forth unto the children of men, that they might have life and be made partakers of the glories which are to be revealed in the last days, as it was written by the prophets and apostles in days of old" (D&C 66:2; compare 1:22; 39:11; 45:9; 49:9; 133:57). In the words of President Joseph Fielding Smith, "The new and everlasting covenant is the sum total of all gospel covenants and obligations."[6] The gospel covenant is *new* in a given time, often following a period of apostasy. It is *everlasting* in the sense that it was taught from the beginning.

Understanding what we do about the everlasting nature of the gospel, the Church and kingdom, and the principles and ordinances pertaining thereto, we know that many of the ancients had the gospel. Many of them knew the Lord, taught his doctrine, and officiated as legal administrators in his earthly kingdom. Isaac, Israel, Joseph, and all the patriarchs enjoyed personal revelation and communion with their Maker. We would suppose that Eve and Sarah and Rebekah were baptized, that Jacob received the temple endowment, that Micah and Malachi stood in the prophetic office by divine call and not because they assumed that role on their own. Surely Nephi, son of Lehi, was baptized by water and received the gift of the Holy Ghost, as well as the high priesthood, although an account of the same is not stated directly in the Nephite record. The Saints of God in all ages have been commanded to build temples (D&C 124:37–41), and the keys associated with eternal marriage were held by those charged to lead the ancients (D&C 132:39).

---

6. *Doctrines of Salvation*, 1:156.

That the blessings of the holy temple were available to Former-day Saints is also made clear in the Prophet's translation of the Egyptian papyri. We are told that one particular figure represents "the grand Key-words of the Holy Priesthood, as revealed to Adam, in the Garden of Eden, as also to Seth, Noah, Melchizedek, Abraham, and all to whom the Priesthood was revealed" (Explanation of Figure 3 in Facsimile #2). Because of what has been made known through Joseph Smith—principles of doctrine and priesthood government—we know what it takes to operate the kingdom of God and what things the people of God must do to comply.

"ALL THAT HE SEETH FIT THAT THEY SHOULD HAVE"

One has only to wrestle personally with the challenge of a wandering child or other loved one, or feel the pain of someone who does, to realize that we do not cease to love the straying or the ignorant. And surely he who is the embodiment of love and mercy does not cease to love those of his children who do not enjoy the fulness of gospel blessings in their lives. Our Father in Heaven surely will do all that is appropriate during our mortal probation to inspire, lift, edify, and encourage individuals, families, communities, and whole nations. It was to Nephi that the Lord Jehovah spoke on this matter: "Know ye not that there are more nations than one? Know ye not that I, the Lord your God, have created all men, and that I remember those who are upon the isles of the sea; and that I rule in the heavens above and in the earth beneath; and that *I bring forth my word unto the children of men, yea, even upon all the nations of the earth?* . . . For behold, I shall speak unto the Jews and they shall write it; and I shall also speak unto the Nephites and they shall write it; and I shall also speak unto the other tribes of the house of Israel, which I have led away, and they shall write it; *and I shall also speak unto all nations of the earth and they shall write it*" (2 Nephi 29:7, 12; emphasis added).

Alma explained that "the Lord doth grant unto all nations, of their own nation and tongue, to teach his word, yea, in wisdom, all that he seeth fit that they should have" (Alma 29:8). One body of people may be prepared for the fulness of light and knowledge; another body will be prepared only for a glimmer of that ray of truth. God suits his blessings according to the present readiness of the children of men. Elder B. H. Roberts, a serious student of Joseph Smith, offered the following counsel on this principle: "While the Church of Jesus Christ of Latter-day Saints is established for the instruction of men; and is one of God's instrumentalities for making known the truth, yet he is not limited to that institution for such purposes, neither in time nor place. God raises up wise men . . . of their own tongue and nationality, speaking to them through means that they can comprehend; not always giving a fulness of truth such as may be found in the fulness of the gospel of Jesus Christ; but always giving that measure of truth that the people are prepared to receive. Mormonism holds, then, that all the great teachers are servants of God, among all nations and in all ages. They are inspired men, appointed to instruct God's children according to the conditions in the midst of which he finds them. . . . Wherever God finds a soul sufficiently enlightened and pure, one with whom his Spirit can communicate, lo! he makes of him a teacher of men. . . . While the path of sensuality and darkness may be that which most men tread, a few . . . have been led along the upward path; a few in all countries and generations have been wisdom seekers, or seekers of God. They have been so because the Divine Word of Wisdom has looked upon them, choosing them for the knowledge and service of himself."[7]

President Ezra Taft Benson observed: "God, the Father of us all,

---

7. *Defense of the Faith and the Saints*, 1:512–13.

uses the men of the earth, especially good men, to accomplish his purposes. It has been true in the past, it is true today, it will be true in the future."[8] President Benson then quoted the following from a conference address delivered by Elder Orson F. Whitney in 1928: "Perhaps the Lord needs such men on the outside of his Church, to help it along. They are among its auxiliaries, and can do more good for the cause where the Lord has placed them, than anywhere else. . . . Hence, some are drawn into the fold and receive a testimony of the Truth; while others remain unconverted . . . , the beauties and glories of the [restored] gospel being veiled temporarily from their view, for a wise purpose. The Lord will open their eyes in his own due time." Now note this particularly poignant message: "*God is using more than one people for the accomplishment of his great and marvelous work. The Latter-day Saints cannot do it all.* It is too vast, too arduous for any one people. . . . We have no quarrel with [those of other faiths]. They are our partners in a certain sense."[9]

It is but reasonable, therefore, that elements of truth, pieces of a much larger mosaic, should be found throughout the world in varying cultures and among diverse religious groups. Further, as the world has passed through phases of apostasy and restoration, relics of revealed doctrine remain, albeit in some cases in altered or even convoluted forms. Persons lacking spiritual insight and the faith that derives from a knowledge of Christ's eternal plan of salvation may tend to cast doubt on the true gospel, may point to legends and traditions of creation epics or flood stories that presumably predate the Pentateuch, may eagerly note similarities between ordinances of the temple and practices in pagan cultures, and may thereby suggest that Christianity has but copied from the more ancient sources.

Joseph F. Smith, a nephew of the Prophet, had much to say to those who seek to upstage Christianity. Jesus Christ, he taught,

---

8. "Civic Standards for the Faithful Saints," *Ensign*, July 1972, 59.
9. In Conference Report, Apr. 1928, 59; emphasis added.

"being the fountain of truth, is no imitator. He taught the truth first; it was his before it was given to man." Further, "let it be remembered that Christ was with the Father from the beginning, that the gospel of truth and light existed from the beginning, and is from everlasting to everlasting. The Father, Son, and Holy Ghost, as one God, are the fountain of truth. . . . If we find truth in broken fragments through the ages, it may be set down as an incontrovertible fact that it originated at the fountain, and was given to philosophers, inventors, patriots, reformers, and prophets by the inspiration of God. It came from him through his Son Jesus Christ and the Holy Ghost, in the first place, and from no other source. It is eternal." In summary, President Smith pointed out, "men are mere repeaters of what he has taught them. He has voiced no thought originating with man."[10]

REMNANTS OF THE FAITH

Knowing what we know concerning God our Father—that he is a personal being, that he has a body of flesh and bones as tangible as our own, that he is an exalted and glorified being, and knowing that this knowledge was had by many of the ancients—should we be surprised to find legends and myths concerning gods who have divine power but human attributes and passions? Knowing that Adam and Seth and Enos and Cainan and Mahalaleel and others of the antedeluvians spoke of the coming of the Messiah and that the Messiah would come to earth as a man but possessing the powers of a god, is it not likely that they also knew that he would be born of a virgin? Should we be surprised to find pagan traditions of virgin births and divine humans?

Adam heard the heavenly voice saying, "I am God; I made the world, and *men before they were in the flesh*" (Moses 6:51). That is, men and women in the earliest ages knew of a first estate, a

---

10. *Gospel Doctrine*, 31, 395, 398–400; see also Joseph F. Smith, in *Journal of Discourses*, 15:325.

premortal existence.[11] Therefore, is it any wonder that several religious traditions are wedded to an idea of past lives? Inasmuch as the doctrines of rebirth, regeneration, resurrection, and the immortality of the soul were taught to Adam and his posterity, why should we flinch when we discover the misshapen doctrines of reincarnation, transmigration of souls, and rebirth in such traditions as Hinduism, Jainism, and Sikhism, or when we encounter a people like the ancient Egyptians who were almost obsessed, not with death (as some suppose), but with life after death?

Of particular interest to Latter-day Saints is the resemblance between what goes on in our own temples and things that transpire in sacred structures of other faiths. In many cases those resemblances may originate with earnest truth seekers who act without authority, as did Pharaoh, great-grandson of Noah. "Pharaoh, being a righteous man, established his kingdom and judged his people wisely and justly all his days, seeking earnestly to imitate that order established by the fathers in the first generations, in the days of the first patriarchal reign, even in the reign of Adam, and also of Noah, his father" (Abraham 1:26).

Professor Hugh Nibley spent a lifetime studying such parallels. He wrote: "Latter-day Saints believe that their temple ordinances are as old as the human race and represent a primordial revealed religion that has passed through alternate phases of apostasy and restoration which have left the world littered with the scattered fragments of the original structure, some more and some less recognizable, but all badly damaged and out of proper context." More specifically, Nibley asked, "But what about the Egyptian rites? What are they to us? They are a parody, an imitation, but as such not to be despised. For all the great age and consistency of their rites and

---

11. See Chapter 11.

teachings, which certainly command respect, the Egyptians did not have the real thing, and they knew it. . . .

"The Mormon endowment . . . is frankly a model, a presentation in figurative terms. As such it is flexible and adjustable; for example, it may be presented in more languages than one and in more than one medium of communication. But since it does not attempt to be a picture of reality, but only a model or analog to show how things work, setting forth the pattern of man's life on earth with its fundamental whys and wherefores, it does not need to be changed or adapted greatly through the years; it is a remarkably stable model, which makes its comparison with other forms and traditions, including the more ancient ones, quite valid and instructive."[12]

And what is true of sacred practices and beliefs throughout the ancient non-Christian world is also true in today's modern Christian world. We know that divine priesthood authority was taken away by God and that many plain and precious truths were lost or kept back following the deaths of the meridian apostles. We know that God began the restoration of truths and powers through Joseph Smith and will continue to do so into and through the Millennium. But this does not mean that Protestants or Catholics have no truth or that any scriptural interpretation from them is automatically suspect, incorrect, or corrupt. As noted earlier, elements of enlightenment, remnants of truth, and aspects of the faith of Former-day Saints may be found in modern Christianity. The Lord loves his children, all of them, and he delights to "honor those who serve [him] in righteousness and in truth unto the end" (D&C 76:5). "Have the Presbyterians any truth?" Joseph the Prophet asked in 1843. "Yes. Have the Baptists, Methodists, etc., any truth? Yes. They all have a little truth mixed with error. We should gather all

---

12. *Message of the Joseph Smith Papyri*, xii–xiii. See also Nibley, *Temple and Cosmos;* Nibley and Rhodes, *One Eternal Round.*

the good and true principles in the world and treasure them up, or we shall not come out true 'Mormons.'"[13]

CONCLUSION

There are good people in the world who love God, who are earnestly striving to be true to the standards of decency and integrity they have been taught. Indeed, everyone has access to some measure of light and truth from the Almighty. President Brigham Young thus declared that there has never been "a man or woman upon the face of the earth, from the days of Adam to this day, who has not been enlightened, instructed, and taught by the revelations of Jesus Christ."[14] The prophets teach that if people will be true to the light within them—the Light of Christ—they will be led to the higher light of the Holy Ghost found in the covenant gospel, either in this life or in the life to come. "And the Spirit giveth light to every man that cometh into the world; and the Spirit enlighteneth every man through the world, that hearkeneth to the voice of the Spirit" (D&C 84:46).[15]

Joseph Smith revealed that Christ's gospel is eternal. It was delivered to earth's inhabitants in the beginning. It has been preached through the ages by Christian prophets who knew their Lord and sought to be true to divine covenants and ordinances. In The Church of Jesus Christ of Latter-day Saints we attend to sacred matters, matters that are ancient and eternal, matters that were taught and foreordained from before the foundations of the world, matters that will prepare this earth to abide the coming of the King of kings. What Latter-day Saints believe is what Former-day Saints

---

13. *Words of Joseph Smith*, 234.

14. In *Journal of Discourses*, 2:139.

15. See Smith, *Gospel Doctrine*, 67–68; McConkie, *New Witness for the Articles of Faith*, 260–61.

believed. The covenants we make and the ordinances we perform thereby link us to the past and point us to a glorious future. God loves all his children and is eager to enlighten them in whatever ways he can. We rejoice in our Father and God, and we rejoice in the knowledge that we are all part of his royal family.

Chapter 7

A NEW TRANSLATION
OF THE BIBLE

Harmony, Pennsylvania, June 1830. Sometime in June 1830 the Prophet began work on his new translation of the Bible. Joseph Smith and Oliver Cowdery had learned while translating 1 Nephi that plain and precious truths and covenants of the Lord would be taken from or kept back from the Holy Bible and that because of these actions, many would stumble spiritually. Nephi had also beheld that the Lord, the Author of scripture, would provide a means whereby many of those precious truths would be made known in the latter days. At some point, though the specific date is unknown, the Prophet was "appointed" to undertake a "new translation" of the Bible. In obedience to that directive, Joseph and Oliver purchased a large King James Bible from E. B. Grandin, on 8 October 1829.

Moses the ancient lawgiver was given prophetic direction: "And in a day when the children of men shall esteem my words as naught and take many of them from the book which thou shalt write, behold, I will raise up another like unto thee; and they shall be had again among the children of men—among as many as shall believe" (Moses 1:41). Through the opening of the heavens in modern times, Joseph Smith was called as a prophet, a seer, a revelator, and a modern lawgiver. In addition, he was commissioned as a *translator,* the means whereby the mind and word of God were made known to a generation in the midst of spiritual calamity (D&C 1:17). To the young prophet-leader the Lord disclosed: "This generation shall have my word through you" (D&C 5:10).

PREPARATIONS FOR THE NEW TRANSLATION

A number of events seem to have been critical in the preparation of Joseph Smith for his labor as Bible translator. As early as 1820 young Joseph recognized that confusion and uncertainty were the obvious results of unilluminated minds and undirected study, even when the object of study was the Holy Bible. Seeking for both personal fulfillment and the one system of religious practice that would lead him back to the divine presence, Joseph Smith discovered that not all of the answers were to be found in the Bible alone (Joseph Smith–History 1:11–12).

A further lesson was taught to the seventeen-year-old Prophet by the angel Moroni in the year 1823. Moroni quoted numerous passages of scripture to Joseph, particularly Malachi 4, though "with a little variation from the way it reads in our Bibles" (Joseph Smith–History 1:36). Whether Moroni gave detailed instructions concerning specific passages of scripture or taught Joseph how to interpret biblical verses is unknown. The young prophet did learn, however, that the Authorized Bible of the day (the King James Version) was not the only way scriptural passages could be rendered.

Theological darkness and spiritual stumblings in the Judeo-Christian world were due in large measure to a willful tampering with some of the earliest Bible texts. That was the bad news. Joseph also became aware (through Nephi's prophetic vision) that through the Restoration things would be made known once again to those willing to receive them (1 Nephi 13:20–40). That was the good news. The Prophet was to observe many years later: "I believe the

Bible, as it ought to be, as it came from the pen of the original writers."[1]

As we remember from Chapter 4, on 15 May 1829, Joseph and Oliver Cowdery "went into the woods to pray and inquire of the Lord respecting baptism for the remission of sins," which was mentioned in the Nephite record (Joseph Smith–History 1:68). John the Baptist appeared, delivered the keys and powers associated with the Aaronic Priesthood, and gave instructions concerning the baptism and priesthood ordination of Joseph and Oliver. The Prophet Joseph remarked that immediately upon coming up out of the waters of baptism, both men enjoyed a rich endowment of the Holy Ghost, and each had the spirit of prophecy and revelation. Joseph further explained: "Our minds being now enlightened, *we began to have the scriptures laid open to our understandings, and the true meaning and intention of their more mysterious passages revealed unto us in a manner which we never could attain to previously, nor ever before had thought of*" (Joseph Smith–History 1:74; emphasis added). No doubt such spiritual understanding would have given to the Prophet not only the ability to grasp "true meaning and intention" but also the divine perspective to recognize and correct faulty or incomplete biblical texts.

On 8 October 1829 Joseph and Oliver purchased a large, pulpit-style edition of the King James Bible (containing the Old and New Testaments and Old Testament Apocrypha) from E. B. Grandin in Palmyra, New York, for $3.75. The Bible had been printed in 1828 by the H. and E. Phinney Company at Cooperstown, New York. It was this Bible that was used in the translation.

---

1. *Words of Joseph Smith*, 256.

THE PROCESS OF TRANSLATION

There was nothing particularly unusual about a new translation, or version, of the Bible in the 1830s. Religious revivalism reached a peak in the New York area in the early nineteenth century, and with it came a heightened awareness of the need for the Bible as a divine standard for living. In fact, New England was not the only section of the country that manifested an intense interest at this time in a study and scrutiny of the biblical record. From 1777 to 1833, more than five hundred separate editions of the Bible (or parts thereof) were published in America. Many of these represented new translations or "modern translations," often with an attempt to prepare paraphrased editions or alternate readings based on comparisons with Hebrew and Greek manuscripts.[2]

Joseph Smith's translation of the scriptures was, however, highly unusual. The Prophet had no formal training in ancient languages until some years later, when he studied Hebrew with a number of the leaders of the Church. Nor did he work with manuscripts written in the biblical languages in undertaking his study. What, then, was the nature of this "translation," and how was it effected? Many in our own day, including some Latter-day Saints, are eager to point out that Joseph's work with the Bible was not a translation per se but rather something of a rewording or a biblical targum (paraphrase) or midrash (commentary). We will deal more specifically with the nature of the translation later in this chapter. For the present, however, it is essential that we recognize that Joseph Smith himself called the labor a translation, the members referred to the labor as a translation, and (perhaps most important) the Lord himself made frequent reference to his servant's work as a translation. As indicated earlier, the Prophet was divinely called and appointed as a "seer, a revelator,

---

2. See Hills, *English Bible in America*.

a translator, and a prophet, having all the gifts of God which he bestows upon the head of the church" (D&C 107:92).

Joseph's mission as translator was not terminated when he had finished translating the Book of Mormon. In his serious study of the Bible, he sought to harmonize himself with the Spirit of God (and surely with the minds and intentions of the ancient writers) so as to recognize and correct faulty translations, as well as deficient or ambiguous passages of the Bible that had suffered the long and painful process of transmission of texts. In one sense, Joseph Smith was translating the Bible by attempting to interpret it by revelation, to explain it by the use of clearer terms or a different style of language. In another sense, Joseph was translating the Bible by restoring in the English language ideas and events and sayings that were originally recorded in Hebrew or Greek. The Prophet translated the King James Bible by the same means he translated the Book of Mormon—by revelation. His knowledge of Hebrew or Greek or his acquaintance with ancient documents was no more essential in making the Joseph Smith Translation than a previous knowledge of Reformed Egyptian or an access to more primitive Nephite records was essential to the translation of the Book of Mormon. Not infrequently the Lord chooses and calls the unlearned, the "weak things of the world," to bring about Joseph's purposes (2 Nephi 27:15–20; D&C 1:19, 23; 35:13).

June of 1830 is the earliest date of translation given in any of the Prophet's records. From his own journal history we have the following entry: "I will say . . . that amid all trials and tribulations we had to wade through, the Lord, who well knew our infantile, and delicate situation, vouchsafed for us a supply [of strength], and granted us 'line upon line, here a little and there a little['] [of knowledge]; of which the following was a precious morsel."[3] Joseph then recorded some "selections from the book of Moses" (Moses 1), containing "the words of God, which he spake unto Moses at a time when Moses was caught up into an exceedingly high mountain" (Moses 1:1). Moses 1 is indeed a fascinating chapter. It is an account of an experience that Moses had with the Lord Jehovah that is not recorded in the Bible but seems to have taken place some time between the burning bush experience and Moses's leading of the Israelites out of Egyptian bondage (Moses 1:17, 26). In some ways, it is an appropriate prelude to Joseph's inspired translation of Genesis and even the entire Bible.

The translation of the book of Genesis continued for many months, and significant doctrinal truths were revealed concerning premortal existence, the Creation, the Fall, and the Atonement. In December of 1830 the following was recorded in the Prophet's journal: "It may be well to observe here, that the Lord greatly encouraged, and strengthened the faith of his little flock which had embraced the fulness of the everlasting gospel, as revealed to them in the book of Mormon, by giving some more extended information upon the Scriptures; a tran[s]lation of which had already commenced. Much conjecture and conversation frequently occurred among the saints, concerning the books mentioned and referred to, in various <places> in the old and new testaments, which were now no where to be found. The common remark was, they are "*lost books*"; but it seems the apostolic churches had some of these writings, as Jude mentions or quotes the prophecy of Enoch the seventh from Adam [Jude 1:14–15]. To the joy of the little flock . . . did the Lord reveal the following doings of olden time from the [prophecy]

---

3. History, 1838–1856, volume A-1 [23 December 1805–30 August 1834], The Joseph Smith Papers, accessed 15 Mar. 2016, http://josephsmithpapers.org/paperSummary /history-1838-1856-volume-a-1-23-december-1805-30-august-1834?p=54.

of Enoch."[4] The Prophet then recorded his inspired translation of Genesis 7 (also known to us as Moses 7), containing many of the remarkable details of the ministry and eventual translation of Enoch and his city.

Work on the Old Testament continued until 7 March 1831. On that date, Joseph Smith received the revelation known to us as Doctrine and Covenants 45, in which he was told the following: "And now, behold, I say unto you, it shall not be given unto you to know any further concerning this chapter [the Savior has been speaking at length concerning the signs incident to his second coming], until the New Testament be translated, and in it all these things shall be made known; wherefore I give unto you that ye may now translate it, that ye may be prepared for the things to come. For verily I say unto you, that great things await you" (D&C 45:60–62). The manuscript of the work with the first chapter of Matthew is dated 8 March 1831. By that time, the translation of the Old Testament had progressed through Genesis 19:35.[5]

By early April the Old Testament was put aside temporarily in order that the New Testament might receive full attention. During the months that followed, Joseph the Prophet continued the translation of the New Testament and labored as time would permit. As was so often the case, the problems associated with a growing church, as well as providing the necessities of life for his own family, precluded more frequent work with the Bible. At this point (by 7 April) the translators had progressed through Genesis 24:42a and Matthew 9:2.[6]

---

4. History, 1838–1856, volume A-1 [23 December 1805–30 August 1834], The Joseph Smith Papers, accessed 15 Mar. 2016, http://josephsmithpapers.org/paperSummary/history-1838-1856-volume-a-1-23-december-1805-30-august-1834?p=86; emphasis added.

5. See Matthews, *"Plainer Translation,"* 96. A more recent historical and textual study of the translation is Faulring, Jackson, and Matthews, *Joseph Smith's New Translation of the Bible;* see especially page 64.

6. Matthews, *"Plainer Translation,"* 96.

Worthy of note at this point is that major revelations (now recorded in our Doctrine and Covenants) were being received concurrently with the translation of the Bible; in fact, it is critical to recognize that such sections as 76 (the vision of the glories), 77 (insights into the Revelation of John), 91 (information concerning the Old Testament Apocrypha), and 132 (eternal and plural marriage) were received as a direct outgrowth of the Prophet's work of Bible translation. In addition, matters in the Doctrine and Covenants pertaining to the Creation, the Fall, and the Atonement (e.g., D&C 29) were also being revealed through the inspired translation of Genesis (e.g., Moses 2–6). In other words, what we are witnessing here is a concurrent revelatory process.

In December 1830 the translation of the Bible revealed many great things pertaining to the ancient city of Enoch, a historical moment that became the scriptural prototype for the people of God in all ages. Joseph learned that the Lord "called his people Zion, because they were of one heart and one mind, and dwelt in righteousness; and there was no poor among them" (Moses 7:18). In February of 1831, only two months later, the Lord began to make known through revelation the plan by which his people in the latter days could establish a society of the pure in heart, and could build economic and spiritual equality in a modern Zion society (D&C 42).[7] In summary, Robert J. Matthews explained: "The Prophet's work with the Bible was a primary source for much of the doctrinal content and the instructional information of the D&C. Consequently, one could not adequately understand either the background or the content of those parts of the D&C without an acquaintance with the history and content of the JST. The two volumes, when placed in tandem, enable the student to gain a

---

7. Chapters 8 and 9 will discuss these principles in greater detail.

clearer picture of how the gospel was restored in this dispensation, and gives the reader an insight as to how divine revelation comes."[8]

Early in 1833 the translator wrote: "I completed the translation and reviewing of the New Testament, on the 2[d] of February 1833, and sealed it up."[9] At this point, work with the Old Testament resumed. By 8 March 1833 the translators had moved through the Old Testament as far as the Prophets (D&C 90:13). On the very next day, 9 March, Joseph inquired of God concerning the Old Testament Apocrypha (which is between the Old and the New Testaments in the King James Bible Joseph was using) and received what is now Doctrine and Covenants 91. Joseph's journal entry for 2 July 1833 is as follows: "We are exceedingly fatigued owing to a great press of business. *We this day finished the translating of the scriptures,* for which we returned gratitude to our heavenly Father."[10]

THE SCRIBES

Joseph the Prophet was assisted in his translation of the Bible by a number of persons who served as scribe. His wife, Emma Smith, labored in that capacity for a short time. In a revelation given to Emma in July of 1830 she was instructed: "And thou shalt go with him at the time of his going, *and be unto him for a scribe,* while there is no one to be a scribe for him, that I may send my servant, Oliver Cowdery, whithersoever I will" (D&C 25:6; emphasis added). The Book of Mormon had been published in March of 1830, and so this directive could not have had reference to further

---

8. "The Joseph Smith Translation," 90.

9. History, 1838–1856, volume A-1 [23 December 1805–30 August 1834], The Joseph Smith Papers, accessed 15 Mar. 2016, http://josephsmithpapers.org/paperSummary /history-1838-1856-volume-a-1-23-december-1805-30-august-1834?p=277.

10. History, 1838–1856, volume A-1 [23 December 1805–30 August 1834], The Joseph Smith Papers, accessed 15 Mar. 2016, http://josephsmithpapers.org/paper Summary/history-1838-1856-volume-a-1-23-december-1805-30-august-1834?p=322; emphasis added.

work with the Nephite record. Oliver Cowdery served for a time in the work of translation, but his scribal activities were interrupted by a call to serve a preaching mission to the Lamanites (D&C 28; 32). John Whitmer also worked in the role of scribe for a time. He later was given an assignment to assist the Prophet in transcribing and recopying the Bible translation (D&C 47:1). The bulk of the scribal activity was accomplished by Sidney Rigdon. After being baptized into the Church in Ohio, Sidney joined Joseph Smith and the Saints in New York in December of 1830. He became involved that very month in the work with the Bible and labored consistently until the formal work of translation came to an end in July of 1833.

The work of the scribe seems to have consisted in writing on sheets of paper that which was dictated by Joseph Smith. Joseph would read directly from the Bible and through the spirit of inspiration note the need for a revision of a text. An examination of the manuscripts reveals different approaches or methods to the work of translation. For example, the biblical text is written out in full in longhand on the manuscripts for Genesis 1–24 and Matthew 1–John 5. A shorter method was later employed, in which only the passages to be revised were noted by the scribe on the manuscript pages.

Of equal importance in the process of translation was Joseph's marking of the large Bible. A check or an X or some other symbol was placed before or after many of the passages to be altered. Additional marks in the Bible (dots, slanted lines, circled words, or lined-out words) were discovered to be essential in conjunction with the manuscripts in discerning exactly what Joseph Smith intended with particular passages and exactly where the change was to be made.[11]

---

11. See Matthews, *"Plainer Translation,"* chapters 3 and 4; Faulring, Jackson, and Matthews, *Joseph Smith's New Translation of the Bible,* 7.

THE NEW TRANSLATION, 1830–1844

The Prophet's interest and involvement did not cease when he had made his way through the King James Bible in July of 1833. Joseph spent his remaining years (until the time of his death in 1844) reviewing and revising the manuscripts, seeking to find appropriate words to convey what he had come to know by revelation. Robert Matthews wrote concerning revisions in the original manuscript: "In the face of the evidence it can hardly be maintained that the exact words were given to the Prophet in the process of a revelatory experience. Exact words may have been given to the mind of the Prophet on occasion, but the manuscript evidence suggests that generally he was obliged to formulate the words himself to convey the message he desired. Consequently, he might later have observed that sometimes the words were not entirely satisfactory in the initial writings. They may have conveyed too much or too little. Or they may have been too specific or too vague, or even ambiguous. Or the words may have implied meanings not intended. Thus through (1) an error of recording, (2) an increase of knowledge, or (3) an inadequate selection of words, any passage of the New Translation might be subject to later revision."[12] Some of the revisions were written directly on the original manuscripts; others were written on separate sheets of paper pinned to the original manuscript pages.

Portions of Joseph Smith's translation were published before the martyrdom of the Prophet.[13] The entire translation was not made available until 1867, when the Reorganized Church of Jesus Christ of Latter Day Saints, known today as the Community of Christ, printed the first edition, calling it the Holy Scriptures. Some of Joseph's new translation was available through *The Evening and the Morning Star* in Independence, Missouri (1832–33). In the Lectures

---

12. *"Plainer Translation,"* 86.
13. *"Plainer Translation,"* 52.

on Faith, Joseph quoted a number of scriptural passages according to the new translation. In addition, what is now known as Joseph Smith–Matthew (Joseph Smith's translation of Matthew 24) was published sometime between 1832 and 1837, while the visions of Moses (Moses 1) were published in the *Times and Seasons* in 1843.

One thing is clear regarding the Joseph Smith Translation during Joseph Smith's lifetime: the Prophet had every intention of publishing the entire translation and of making the valuable truths contained therein accessible to the Latter-day Saints. Inasmuch as a person is saved no faster than he gains knowledge,[14] Joseph the Prophet was eager to make known to the people the marvelous insights that had come to him through his work with the Bible. Both the Prophet and the Saints viewed the labor of translation and certainly the product as matters of profound gravity. In a revelation given to Frederick G. Williams in January of 1834 the Lord explained: "Now I say unto you, *my servant Joseph Smith Jr. is called to do a great work and hath need that he may do the work of translation for the salvation of souls.*"[15] Thus on numerous occasions throughout the closing years of Joseph Smith's ministry, the Prophet himself and the Twelve made frequent requests of the Saints for financial assistance, in order that Joseph might "devote himself exclusively to those things which relate to Spiritualities of the church," particularly the New Translation.[16]

In July of 1840 the First Presidency and the Twelve appointed two men to go throughout the Church to seek donations and offerings for the printing of various Church books, including the Joseph Smith Translation. An editorial in the *Times and Seasons* noted:

---

14. *Joseph Smith* [manual], 266.

15. Revelation given to Frederick G. Williams, 5 Jan. 1834, Joseph Smith Collection, Letters 1834, Church History Library, Salt Lake City, Utah; emphasis added.

16. Memorial to High Council, 18 June 1840, The Joseph Smith Papers, accessed 15 Mar. 2016, http://josephsmithpapers.org/paperSummary/memorial-to-high-council -18-june-1840?p=2.

"The authorities of the church here, having taken this subject into consideration, and viewing the importance of Publishing a Hymn Book, and a more extensive quantity of the Books of Mormon, *and also the necessity of Publishing the new translation of the scriptures, which has so long been desired by the Saints;* have appointed and authorized Samuel Bent and Geo. W. Harris, as traveling agents, to make contracts and receive monies &c. for the accomplishment of this glorious work."[17] On 19 January 1841 the Lord gave specific directions and promises to William Law: "If he will do my will let him from henceforth hearken to the counsel of my servant Joseph, and with his interest support the cause of the poor, *and publish the new translation of my holy word unto the inhabitants of the earth.* And if he will do this I will bless him with a multiplicity of blessings, that he shall not be forsaken, nor his seed be found begging bread" (D&C 124:89–90; emphasis added). The pleadings of the leaders of the Church in this regard were not heeded, and the Prophet was murdered before the entire translation was printed in full.

The question of the completeness of the JST is an important one. Did Joseph Smith actually complete his work with the Bible? In one sense the Prophet completed his task in that he moved from Genesis to Revelation—that is, made his way through the King James Version of the Bible. We remember the entry in Joseph's journal for 2 July 1833: *"We this day finished the translating of the scriptures,* for which we returned gratitude to our heavenly Father."[18] If, however, we are asking whether Joseph Smith made every change in the King James Version that could have or should have been made,

---

17. "Books!!!" *Times and Seasons* 1, no. 9 (July 1840): 140; emphasis added.

18. History, 1838–1856, volume A-1 [23 December 1805–30 August 1834], The Joseph Smith Papers, accessed 15 Mar. 2016, http://josephsmithpapers.org/paperSummary /history-1838-1856-volume-a-1-23-december-1805-30-august-1834?p=322; emphasis added.

we are dealing with another matter entirely, so far as completeness is concerned.

One of the strongest evidences of the incomplete status of the translation is to be found in Joseph Smith's sermons from 1833 to 1844. On numerous occasions the Prophet clarified and corrected biblical passages, which alterations were not reflected in his earlier inspired translation. For example, the second verse of the King James Bible describes the state of things in the morning of creation: "And the earth was without form, and void" (Genesis 1:2). In the original manuscript of the Joseph Smith Translation, this verse is exactly the same as it appears in the King James Version. In a sermon delivered on 5 January 1841 in Nauvoo, however, Joseph taught that the phrase "without form and void" should be translated "empty and desolate."[19]

The apostle Paul explained in his first epistle to the Corinthians that "no man can say that Jesus is the Lord, but by the Holy Ghost" (1 Corinthians 12:3). In an address to the Relief Society late in April of 1842, Joseph explained that no man can *know* that Jesus is the Lord but by the Spirit.[20] Just five months before his death, the Prophet clarified another biblical passage that had received no alteration in the original manuscript: "The question is frequently asked, 'Can we not be saved without going through with all those ordinances?' I would answer, No, not the fullness of salvation. Jesus said, There are many mansions in my Father's house, and I will go and prepare a place for you. *House* here named should have been translated kingdom; and any person who is exalted to the highest mansion has to abide a celestial law, and the whole law too."[21] Other examples could be given to further illustrate this point.[22]

19. *Words of Joseph Smith,* 60.
20. *Words of Joseph Smith,* 115.
21. *Words of Joseph Smith,* 319.
22. See Matthews, *"Plainer Translation,"* 210–13.

There is another very significant angle from which to view the matter of how much of the Bible the Lord permitted Joseph Smith to translate—the Saints' and the world's lack of readiness to receive all that might have been given through the Prophet. According to a conversation held in the Salt Lake City School of the Prophets in 1868, "George A. Smith testified that he had heard Joseph say before his death that *the new translation was not complete, that he had not been able to prepare it, and that it was probably providentially so.*"[23] President George Q. Cannon observed: "Joseph did not live to give to the world an authoritative publication of these translations. But the labor was its own reward, bringing in the performance a special blessing of broadened comprehension to the Prophet and a general blessing of enlightenment to the people through his subsequent teachings." President Cannon also noted: "We have heard Brigham Young state that the Prophet before his death had spoken to him about going through the translation of the scriptures again and perfecting it upon points of doctrine *which the Lord had restrained him from giving in plainness and fullness at the time of which we write.*"[24]

President Joseph Fielding Smith wrote in 1914 that the Prophet "revised, as it is, a great deal more than the world can, or will, receive. In the 'translation' of the scriptures, he gave to the world all that the Lord would permit him to give, and as much as many of the members of the Church were able to receive. He therefore finished all that was required at his hands, or, that he was permitted to revise, up to July, 1833, when he discontinued his labors of revision."[25] Elder Bruce R. McConkie also wrote: "In many passages all necessary changes were made; in others he was 'restrained' by the Spirit from giving the full and clear meaning. As with all revealed knowledge,

---

23. Journal History, 20 June 1868; emphasis added.
24. *Life of Joseph Smith the Prophet,* 148 and note; emphasis added.
25. "Joseph Smith's 'Translation' of the Scriptures," *Improvement Era* 17, no. 6 (Apr. 1914): 595.

the Lord was offering new truths to the world, 'line upon line, precept upon precept. . . . ' *Neither the world nor the saints generally were then or are now prepared for the fullness of Biblical knowledge.*"[26]

THE TRANSLATION:
1844 INTO THE TWENTIETH CENTURY

The Bernhisel Manuscript (1845)

After the death of the Prophet, the manuscripts of the New Translation were held by Emma Smith, Joseph's widow, and thus eventually came into the possession of the RLDS Church.[27] Not long after the martyrdom, however, Dr. John M. Bernhisel, a trusted friend of the Prophet and Emma, was given an opportunity to examine the original manuscript. In describing the occasion in the spring of 1845 when Dr. Bernhisel examined the manuscript, L. John Nuttall recorded: "Elder John M. Bernhisel called at the request of Pres. Taylor and explained concerning his manuscript copy of the New Translation of the Bible as taken from the Manuscript of the Prophet Joseph Smith. Bro. Bernhisel stated: 'I had great desires to see the New Translation, but did not like to ask for it; but one evening, being at Bro. Joseph's house about a year after his death, Sister Emma to my surprise asked me if I would not like to see it. I answered, yes. She handed it to me the next day, and I kept it in my custody about three months. She told me it was not prepared for the press, as Joseph had designed to go through it again. I did not copy all that was translated leaving some few additions and changes that were made in some of the books. But so far as I did copy, I did so as correctly as I could do. The markings in my Bible correspond precisely with the markings in the Prophet Joseph's Bible, so that all the books corrected in his Bible so far as I now know are marked

---

26. *Mormon Doctrine*, 384; emphasis added.
27. See Matthews, *"Plainer Translation,"* chapter 4; Faulring, Jackson, and Matthews, *Joseph Smith's New Translation of the Bible,* 29–32.

in my Bible: but as I stated, the additions are not all made in my Manuscript of those books that I did not copy.'"[28]

The limitations of what has come to be known as the Bernhisel Manuscript are clear from John Bernhisel's own words: the copy made by him is incomplete and thus inadequate in representing exactly what the Prophet Joseph Smith and his scribes recorded. The following are some errors that were committed unintentionally by Dr. Bernhisel:[29]

1. Bernhisel did not copy *all* of the corrections noted on the original manuscripts. Joseph altered 3,410 verses; Bernhisel noted only 1,463.

2. Bernhisel's copy is interpretive, in the sense that he seems to be thinking for himself, rather than simply copying from Joseph's manuscript.

3. Sometimes Bernhisel recorded *more* than he should have; that is, he anticipated corrections that were not there.

It is no doubt the case that had Bernhisel known in the spring of 1845 that the original manuscripts would be unavailable to The Church of Jesus Christ of Latter-day Saints for such a long period (about 125 years), he would have taken greater care to record everything that Joseph had recorded. His was intended as a personal copy and was never envisioned by him as becoming an official document. John Bernhisel arrived in the Salt Lake Valley on 24 September 1848, and it is assumed that he brought his manuscript with him. A copy of this manuscript was made by direction of the First Presidency in 1879. The original Bernhisel Manuscript is now available in the Church Historian's Library in Salt Lake City. It is significant as a historical relic, and its early date of 1845 does much toward verifying the present accuracy of the original manuscripts.

---

28. Diary, 20 Sept. 1879, 1:335.
29. See Matthews, *"Plainer Translation,"* chapter 6.

The Pearl of Great Price (1851)

In 1850 Franklin D. Richards of the Council of the Twelve succeeded Orson Pratt as president of the British Mission. One of the first things Richards noticed about the state of things in his mission was the paucity of Church reading material. Few of the Saints even had copies of the standard works. Knowing the necessity of regular reading of good books, particularly the scriptures, President Richards compiled and published a mission tract, a booklet made up of a number of gems of doctrinal and historical worth, many of which were revelations and writings of the Prophet Joseph Smith. This booklet, which came to be known as *The Pearl of Great Price* and which was first printed in 1851, contained such items as Joseph's translations of the Egyptian materials (Abraham's writings and the facsimiles); several revelations from the Doctrine and Covenants (all or part of sections 20; 27; 77; 87; 107); excerpts from Joseph Smith's history of the Restoration (Joseph Smith–History); the Articles of Faith, as given in the Wentworth Letter; and a poem by John Jacques, a British convert, called "Truth" (we know it as "Oh Say, What Is Truth?").[30] *The Pearl of Great Price* also contained the following items from Joseph Smith's translation of the Bible, as given in the table of contents of that first edition:

> Extracts from the Prophecy of Enoch, containing also a Revelation of the Gospel unto our father Adam, after he was driven out from the Garden of Eden. Revealed to Joseph Smith, December, 1830 [Moses 6:43–7:69]
>
> The words of God, which he spake unto Moses at the time when Moses was caught up into an exceeding high mountain, and he saw God face to face, and he talked with him, and the glory of God was upon Moses; therefore Moses could endure his

---

30. *Hymns*, no. 272.

presence. Revealed to Joseph Smith, June, 1830 [Moses 1:1–5:16, part; Moses 5:19–40; Moses 8:13–30] . . .

An Extract from a Translation of the Bible—being the twenty-fourth chapter of Matthew, commencing with the last verse of the twenty-third chapter. By the Prophet, Seer, and Revelator, Joseph Smith [Joseph Smith–Matthew]

As can be seen, not all of the Moses material was contained in the 1851 *Pearl of Great Price*. President Richards seems to have drawn upon Joseph Smith's translation materials from earlier manuscripts (that is, not the final versions prepared by the Prophet Joseph), as were published earlier in *The Evening and the Morning Star* and the *Times and Seasons*.[31]

The First Printing of Joseph Smith's Translation (1867)

At a conference of the RLDS Church held in April 1866, plans were made to publish the Prophet Joseph Smith's translation of the Bible. A committee approached Emma Smith Bidamon on 3 May 1866 regarding the use of the original manuscripts, and Emma delivered the manuscripts to them. She wrote later to her son Joseph Smith III: "Now as it regards the Ms of the New Translation if you wish to keep them you may do so, but if not I would like to have them. I have often thought the reason our house did not burn down when it was so often on fire was because of them, and I still feel there is a sacredness attached to them."[32]

An RLDS publication committee had the manuscript ready for publication by 1 July 1867, and the first shipment of the

---

31. See *The Evening and the Morning Star* 1, no. 3 (Aug. 1832): 17–24 (Moses 7:1–69); no. 10 (Mar. 1833): 73–80 (Moses 6:43–68); no. 11 (Apr. 1833): 81–88 (Moses 5:1–16; 6:52, 58–61; 7:5–11; 8:13–30); *Times and Seasons* 4, no. 5 (Jan. 1843): 65–80 (Moses 1:1–42).

32. Letter from Emma Smith Bidamon to Joseph Smith III, 2 Dec. 1867, original in the possession of the Community of Christ, Independence, Missouri; see also Launius, *Joseph Smith III*, 43.

printed edition (five hundred copies) arrived in Plano, Illinois, on 7 December 1867. The book was called The Holy Scriptures. Subsequent editions followed, including a 1936 teacher's edition, which was the first edition to have the words *Inspired Version* as a part of the title of the book. In 1944 a "New Corrected Edition" was published, in which 352 corrections were made to the original (1867) edition. In that edition, it appears that the publication committee had discovered how to merge the manuscripts with the marked Bible. In 1970 a parallel-column edition was introduced in which the student could compare the King James Version with Joseph Smith's translation at a glance. The 1991 printing of the new corrected edition seems to be the most accurate printing to be released to date.

The 1867 edition is important not only because of its historical value as the apparent realization of the Prophet's desires that the entire new translation be accessible to all Church members but also because it was the source upon which Orson Pratt drew in his production of the second (American) edition of the canonized Pearl of Great Price in 1878.[33] Though it would have been marvelous for the Utah Church to have access to the original manuscripts much sooner in our history, we owe a debt of gratitude to the RLDS Church (Community of Christ) for printing the Prophet Joseph Smith's translation of the Bible and preserving the manuscripts to the degree they were able.

The Work of Robert J. Matthews

Interest in the Joseph Smith Translation, or Inspired Version, of the Bible continued in both the LDS and RLDS churches. Studies in the history of Joseph Smith's translation,[34] comparisons between

---

33. Matthews, *"Plainer Translation,"* 225, 278–79.
34. Examples include Clark, *Story of the Pearl of Great Price;* Durham, "History of Joseph Smith's Revision of the Bible."

it and the King James Version,[35] and major textual analyses[36] were undertaken from 1940 to 1969. The spirit of inquiry and the desire to discover and probe the meaning and significance of Joseph Smith's work with the Bible prompted numerous theses, dissertations, articles, and books for many years.

In the summer of 1944 Robert J. Matthews listened to a radio address over station KSL delivered by President Joseph Fielding Smith.[37] In that sermon President Smith quoted John 1:18, "No man hath seen God at any time," as well as 1 John 4:12, "No man hath seen God at any time, except them who believe." President Smith said: "These two passages under discussion were corrected by the Lord in a revelation to Joseph Smith," and then he read the words of the Prophet's inspired translation: "And no man hath seen God at any time, *except he hath borne record of the Son; for except it is through him no man can be saved*" (JST John 1:19; emphasis added). Robert Matthews was at that time only eighteen years of age and had never before heard of the JST. Suddenly, however, he was struck with a deep sense of significance regarding what President Joseph Fielding Smith had just spoken and at the same time gained a desire to know more about this facet of the Prophet's ministry.

No printed edition of Joseph Smith's translation of the Bible was available in Brother Matthews's hometown of Evanston, Wyoming, nor was there anyone who knew much about the work. Those who did know something were negative towards it, indicating on the one hand that Joseph Smith had never finished the

---

35. Sperry and Van Wagoner, "Inspired Revision of the Bible," *Improvement Era* 43, no. 4 (Apr. 1940): 206–7; Bartholomew, "Comparison of the Authorized Version and the Inspired Revision of Genesis."

36. Harris, "Study of the Changes in the Content of the Book of Moses"; Matthews, "Study of the Doctrinal Significance of Certain Textual Changes"; Matthews, "Study of the Text of the Inspired Revision of the Bible"; Howard, *Restoration Scriptures;* Nyman and Millet, *Joseph Smith Translation;* Millet and Matthews, *Plain and Precious Truths Restored.*

37. The address was delivered on 9 July 1944; see Smith, *Restoration of All Things,* 57.

translation and on the other that the printed edition was unreliable, as it had probably been altered by the RLDS Church. Finally young Brother Matthews was able to obtain a 1947 printing of the Inspired Version from N. B. Lundwall of Salt Lake City, a man who had formerly belonged to the RLDS Church and who was also known for numerous important compilations and publications in the LDS book market. From 1947 to 1950 Brother Matthews compared the King James Version and Joseph Smith's translation. He quoted from it frequently in talks and lessons, but he was often told by people in his ward and at Brigham Young University that the Church did not accept the book and that it was inappropriate for him even to cite it.

The introduction in 1944 of the "new corrected edition" of the Inspired Version had confirmed in the minds of many Latter-day Saints that the RLDS Church had tampered with the original manuscripts of Joseph Smith's translation of the Bible. Such attitudes heightened Robert Matthews's desire to examine the manuscripts himself to check for accuracy of the printed editions. Brother Matthews began to inquire of the leaders of the RLDS Church about the possibility of his examining the original documents. He continued his requests for fifteen years before permission was finally granted in 1968.

Meanwhile, Brother Matthews had learned that a partial copy of the manuscripts—the Bernhisel Manuscript—was held by the Church in Salt Lake City. Largely through the efforts of Reed C. Durham and the graciousness of President Joseph Fielding Smith, the Church historian at the time, the Bernhisel Manuscript became available for research in 1965. In 1960 Robert Matthews had written a master's thesis at Brigham Young University on the four Gospels and Joseph Smith's translation of the Bible, but in that study he did not have access to the original manuscripts. In 1968 he completed a Ph.D. at BYU, his doctoral dissertation examining the printed editions of Joseph Smith's translation and the Bernhisel Manuscript. This study opened the way for the RLDS Church to permit Brother Matthews to have access to the original manuscripts, beginning in 1968. In 1975 he published his book *"A Plainer Translation": Joseph Smith's Translation of the Bible, a History and Commentary,* and therein discussed the historical and doctrinal significance of Joseph Smith's translation, drawing on not only printed sources (the Inspired Version and earlier published editions of Joseph Smith's translation of the Bible) but also the original manuscripts.

Among the many critical contributions of Robert J. Matthews's work with the original documents, the following points were discovered or confirmed:

1. The Prophet's corrections were made not on the pages of the Bible but on sheets of paper.

2. Various scribes worked with the Prophet in recording the corrections.

3. Some passages were corrected more than one time, with additional information being provided each time. This helped to demonstrate how revelation comes.

4. The manuscripts disclosed key dates, which gave a clearer indication of the time when the Prophet was translating certain chapters. Such findings also established the doctrinal relationship of Joseph Smith's translation to the Doctrine and Covenants.

5. Through access to the dates on the manuscripts, it became clear that the work of Bible translation was a principal activity of the Prophet and a significant matter in Latter-day Saint history and in the unfolding of truth in this dispensation.

6. Finally, Brother Matthews's work substantiates and verifies the text of Joseph Smith's translation as it was printed in the Inspired Version, giving evidence that readers may feel comfortable

with what they now find in print. With very few exceptions,[38] the printed text follows the manuscripts in content and meaning.

The Latter-day Saint Edition of the King James Bible (1979)

In 1972 President Harold B. Lee organized a Bible Aids Committee to prepare an edition of the Bible that would provide doctrinal and historical helps for Latter-day Saint students of the scriptures. Among the first matters proposed in the preparation of the LDS edition of the Bible was that significant changes from the Prophet Joseph Smith's translation of the Bible be included. As work went forward on this edition of the King James Bible, it became clear that such a project would lead naturally to a consideration of the status of the triple combination as well. The Bible Aids committee became the Scriptures Publications Committee, consisting finally of Elders Thomas S. Monson, Boyd K. Packer, and Bruce R. McConkie. These three members of the Council of the Twelve Apostles were assisted primarily by three members of the BYU Religious Education faculty: Ellis T. Rasmussen, Robert C. Patch, and Robert J. Matthews. In addition, hundreds of members of the Church Educational System aided in producing the Topical Guide and a complex cross-referencing system among all the books within the standard works.

There is much to recommend the ground-breaking LDS edition of the King James Bible, first published in 1979 and again in 2013 with updated spelling and study aids and a new introduction to the Joseph Smith Translation. One of its profound strengths is the marvelous light shed by the changes made in Joseph Smith's translation, either in the footnotes on each page or in the Appendix at the end of the book. Elder Packer observed in 1982 concerning the new editions of the scriptures: They "will be regarded, in the perspective of history, as the crowning achievement in the administration of

---

38. See Matthews, *"Plainer Translation,"* chapter 7.

President Spencer W. Kimball." Continuing, Elder Packer taught, "With the passing of years, these scriptures will produce successive generations of faithful Christians who know the Lord Jesus Christ and are disposed to obey His will.

"The older generation has been raised without them, but there is another generation growing up. The revelations will be opened to them as to no other in the history of the world. Into their hands now are placed the sticks of Joseph and of Judah. They will develop a gospel scholarship beyond that which their forebears could achieve. They will have the testimony that Jesus is the Christ and be competent to proclaim Him and to defend Him."[39]

WHAT IS THE JOSEPH SMITH TRANSLATION?

Unfortunately, Joseph Smith did not explain the nature of his inspired translation of the King James Bible. Just as we are uncertain as to exactly how he translated the Book of Mormon, so we are not informed by the Prophet himself about what was involved as he studied and pondered upon the biblical text. The following have been suggested[40] as possibilities in explaining what Joseph Smith's translation of the Bible represents:

1. "Inspired prophetic commentary" by the Prophet Joseph Smith, insights he provided to assist a latter-day world to better understand a former-day message. This might be similar to what Nephi referred to as likening the scriptures unto ourselves (1 Nephi 19:23–24; 2 Nephi 11:8). Prophetic documents may be interpreted and explained by prophets, and we owe a deep debt of gratitude to Joseph Smith in this regard.

2. A harmonization of doctrinal concepts that were revealed to Joseph Smith independent of his work with the Bible but which

---

39. "Scriptures," *Ensign*, Nov. 1982, 53.
40. Matthews, *"Plainer Translation,"* 253; Faulring, Jackson, and Matthews, *Joseph Smith's New Translation of the Bible*, 8–11.

proved to be the means whereby he came to recognize a biblical inaccuracy.

3. A restoration of content, ideas, events, and sayings either not recorded by the biblical authors or recorded by them but since omitted from the record. In a very real sense we question the integrity of Joseph Smith unless we seriously consider the proposition that many of the Prophet's changes in his translation of the Bible may well be a restoration of lost content. One response I receive occasionally from those within the LDS faith and others outside it when they learn of the Prophet's Bible translation is this: "But wasn't Joseph Smith simply 'Mormonizing' the Bible?" It doesn't take long, however, to realize that there was very little with which to Mormonize the Bible by 1833. Many Latter-day Saint doctrines that today are typically associated with Mormonism didn't come until later.

In his translation of two of the Gospels, the Prophet changed the titles to read "The Testimony of St. Matthew" and "The Testimony of St. John." Such an alteration is not without significance. I have great difficulty imagining him adding words to the Savior's sermons, creating discussions between Jesus and the Twelve, and producing settings and recreating events of which we have no other record—except as those words and events were once part of the testimonies of the Gospel writers. Would it not suggest dishonesty (or pride or arrogance) to insert or create or conjure up episodes or dialogue that have no basis in historical fact? The words of Joseph Smith himself are poignant in regard to pretending to a divine work: "After [D&C 67] was received, W[illiam] E. McLellin, as the wisest man in his own estimation, having more learning than sense, endeavored to write a commandment like unto one of the least of the Lord's, but failed; *it was an awful responsibility to write in the name of the Lord.* The elders, and all present, that witnessed *this vain attempt of a man to imitate the language of Jesus Christ,* renewed their faith in the fulness of the gospel, and in the truth of the commandments and revelations which the Lord had given to the church through my instrumentality; and the elders signified a willingness to bear testimony of their truth to all the world."[41]

My personal conviction is certain as to the integrity of Joseph Smith. I believe that many of the alterations made in Joseph's translation represent commentary or harmonization. I likewise believe that as a divinely called translator and restorer, Joseph Smith restored that which had once been recorded but later was removed intentionally and also incorporated that which had occurred or was said anciently but was not recorded by the ancient writers. We must always keep in mind that Joseph, the translator of the Book of Mormon and recipient of the revelations in the Doctrine and Covenants, was the same man called and empowered as a translator of the Bible.

Some hesitate to recognize or use the Joseph Smith Translation as a true restoration because the changes often do not reflect the readings or more obvious meanings in some of the oldest extant texts. The Saints, of all people, should use caution in avoiding superficial assumptions regarding the oldest available manuscripts. Textual variants through the centuries are of two kinds—unplanned and planned. Unplanned variants are frequently the unintentional ones, resulting from human error; they are in some ways the simplest to deal with and the ones to which a sincere textual critic might devote a lifetime of study. Planned variants resulted when a scribe consciously decided to add to or omit from the manuscript. In many cases, those might be well-intentioned additions or omissions, but they are nonetheless damaging to the accurate transmission of the earlier manuscript. In other cases the additions or omissions might

---

41. History, 1838–1856, volume A-1 [23 December 1805–30 August 1834], The Joseph Smith Papers, accessed 15 Mar. 2016, http://josephsmithpapers.org/paperSummary /history-1838-1856-volume-a-1-23-december-1805-30-august-1834?p=168; emphasis added.

be less well-intentioned, such as when valuable truths have been altered, taken away, or withheld. Even this latter type of error could be corrected if we had access to original manuscripts or subsequent but unaltered documents from an earlier time. But we don't.

Nephi's prophetic vision deals with intentional, dramatic alterations to the earliest texts. Brother Matthews observed: "As we read the words of the angel [in 1 Nephi 13], we discover that the world has never had a complete Bible, for it was massively, even cataclysmically, corrupted *before* it was distributed."[42] It requires no greater faith to suppose that the Prophet Joseph Smith saw well beyond the texts now available to an earlier or more complete text (or perhaps even to an episode or statement not previously recorded) than it does to accept that he translated golden plates that contained a language known only to the Nephites (Mormon 9:34). In short, "the plain and precious missing parts have not yet been made known through manuscripts and scholars, but are available only through the Book of Mormon, the Joseph Smith Translation, and modern revelation through the instrumentality of a prophet."[43]

CONCLUSION

Few matters in the history of The Church of Jesus Christ of Latter-day Saints demonstrate more dramatically how doctrinal treasures have generally come to us line upon line, precept upon precept, than the process by which the New Translation came from Joseph Smith, through the Reorganized Church, to the Saints in the twentieth century. In looking carefully at the history of the Joseph Smith Translation, we are able to see the hand of the Lord in a significant way: not only did the Lord direct the labors of his noble servant Joseph Smith in the translation itself but he also

---

42. "The Book of Mormon As a Co-Witness with the Bible," 57.
43. Ibid.

opened doors and intervened where necessary in order that a monumental work might be delivered intact to modern Israel.

The attitude with which Joseph Smith approached his assignment of Bible translation is evident in statements by the Prophet himself. For example, in a letter to W. W. Phelps, Joseph wrote: "We have finished the translation of the New Testament. Great and glorious things are revealed, we are making rapid strides in the old book and in the strength of God we can do all things according to his will."[44] That Joseph and his scribe recognized that the work of Bible translation was far more than a mental exercise is apparent in a simple entry at the top of page 1 of the manuscript of Joseph Smith's translation of Matthew: "A Translation of the New Testament Translated by the power of God."[45] In a revelation to Sidney Rigdon, the principal scribe for the translation, Jesus Christ gives to us His own perception of the nature and scope of the Joseph Smith translation: "And a commandment I give unto thee—that thou shalt write for him; and *the scriptures shall be given, even as they are in mine own bosom, to the salvation of mine own elect*" (D&C 35:20; emphasis added).

In 1832 the Lord warned the Saints that unless they took seriously the "new covenant" of the Book of Mormon, the Church would remain under condemnation (D&C 84:54–57). In 1831 Joseph Smith had taught in a similar manner concerning his Bible translation: "God had often sealed up the heavens because of covetousness in the Church. Said that the Lord would cut his work

---

44. Letter to William W. Phelps, 31 July 1832, in Jessee, *Personal Writings of Joseph Smith*, 274.

45. See a copy of this New Testament Manuscript page (8 Mar. 1831) in Matthews, *"Plainer Translation,"* 267; Howard, *Restoration Scriptures*, 171; Faulring, Jackson, and Matthews, *Joseph Smith's New Translation of the Bible*, following p. 406.

short in righteousness and *except the Church receive the fulness of the Scriptures that they would yet fall.*"[46]

There is so much beauty and depth of doctrine and insight to be had within the Joseph Smith Translation of the Bible that it is foolish to study and teach without it; to do so is tantamount to choosing what we will receive from the Lord and what we will not. Such an attitude is certainly foreign to the genuine truth-seeker. Those who love and revere the name and labors of Joseph Smith should be pleased and enthusiastic to receive whatever God has chosen to reveal through his modern seer and lawgiver.

It should be obvious that we live in a day wherein the effects of the removal of precious truths are being felt in the religious world. In fulfillment of the glorious prophecy of Moses, however, God has indeed raised up in our day a modern Moses, one through whose instrumentality the truths of heaven are "had again among the children of men—among as many as shall believe" (Moses 1:41).

---

46. From an entry dated 25 Oct. 1831, in Cannon and Cook, *Far West Record,* 23; emphasis added.

Chapter 8

ZION, THE PURE IN HEART

Fayette, New York, and Kirtland, Ohio, November–December 1830. *The Prophet Joseph and his scribes in the Bible translation had, between June and September 1830, made their way through the very early chapters of Genesis and learned significant details regarding the Lord's work and glory, the Creation and the Fall, and the eternal atonement of Jesus Christ. In November and December 1830 insights that had been lost from the biblical record hundreds of years earlier were made known concerning the life, ministry, and eventual translation of the antediluvian prophet-patriarch Enoch. Enoch's Zion provided a pattern, a model, by which a latter-day Zion could be established.*

While acceptance of Jesus Christ and his message of salvation is an individual undertaking, heaven on earth and heaven hereafter are to be brought to pass through the establishment of unity among people of good will. Though ultimate peace and righteousness on earth cannot come until the King of kings returns in glory and majesty and power, it is incumbent upon the people of God to rid their souls of pride and envy and thereby establish meaningful spiritual union in society. Respected New Testament scholar N. T. Wright wrote: "It seems that we humans were designed to find our purpose and meaning not simply in ourselves and our own inner lives, but in one another and in the shared meanings and purposes of a family, a street, a workplace, a community, a town, a nation."[1]

GROWTH AND COMMUNITY

As I have witnessed the growth of The Church of Jesus Christ of Latter-day Saints since the year of my own birth (1947, when the Church had grown to include its first million members) to the present, I am stunned but inspired by how bold early Latter-day Saint leaders were, how confident they were, how optimistic they were about the future growth of the Lord's kingdom. Try to imagine how a small group of Latter-day Saints must have felt as they gathered together at the home of Peter Whitmer Sr. for the formal organization of the Church on 6 April 1830. Try to imagine what went through the minds of the early missionaries as they were told by revelation that "the voice of the Lord is unto all men, and there is none to escape; and there is no eye that shall not see, neither ear that shall not hear, neither heart that shall not be penetrated. . . . And the voice of warning shall be unto all people, by the mouths of my disciples, whom I have chosen in these last days" (D&C 1:2, 4).

Try to imagine the wonder and amazement that must have overcome the little flock as they were instructed that "the sound must go forth from this place unto all the world, and unto the uttermost parts of the earth—the gospel must be preached unto every creature, with signs following them that believe" (D&C 58:64). Truly, the arm of the Lord would be revealed "in convincing the nations . . . of the gospel of their salvation. For it shall come to pass in that day, that every man shall hear the fulness of the gospel in

---

1. *Simply Christian,* 31.

his own tongue, and in his own language, through those who are ordained unto this power" (D&C 90:10–11).

Wilford Woodruff described an early meeting of the Saints in Kirtland, Ohio: "On Sunday night the Prophet called on all who held the Priesthood to gather into the little log school house they had there. It was a small house, perhaps 14 feet square. But it held the whole of the Priesthood of the Church of Jesus Christ of Latter-day Saints who were then in the town of Kirtland, and who had gathered together to go off in Zion's Camp. . . . When we got together the Prophet called upon the Elders of Israel with him to bear testimony of this work. . . . When they got through the Prophet said, 'Brethren I have been very much edified and instructed in your testimonies here tonight, but I want to say to you before the Lord, that you know no more concerning the destinies of this Church and kingdom than a babe upon its mother's lap. You don't comprehend it.' I was rather surprised. He said 'it is only a little handful of Priesthood you see here tonight, but this Church will fill North and South America—it will fill the world.'"[2]

Joseph Smith stated only weeks before his death: "I calculate to be one of the instruments of setting up the kingdom of [God envisioned by] Daniel by the word of the Lord, and I intend to lay a foundation that will revolutionize the whole world." And how was this to be realized? "It will not be by sword or gun that this kingdom will roll on," the Prophet said. "The power of truth is such that all nations will be under the necessity of obeying the gospel."[3]

Joseph Smith's vision of the kingdom of God was cosmic. It consisted of more than preaching and study and Sabbath services; it entailed the entire renovation of the order of things on earth, the transformation of man, and the elevation of society. And at the heart of that sublime scene was the doctrine of Zion, a doctrine and

2. In Conference Report, Apr. 1898, 57; see also *Discourses of Wilford Woodruff*, 30.
3. *Joseph Smith* [manual], 512.

a worldview that would shape the early Church and point the Saints of the twentieth and twenty-first centuries toward the ideal community. In this chapter, we will consider more broadly the idea and the ideal of Zion as a people or community of believers, Zion as a specific place, and Zion as a state of being, the pure in heart.

ZION DISCOVERED

Joseph Smith seems to have first encountered the concept of Zion (in a sense other than the holy mount or holy city in Jerusalem) in his translation of the Book of Mormon. The Book of Mormon prophets spoke of Zion as a holy commonwealth, a *society* of the Saints, *a way of life* that was to be established or brought forth under God's direction; those who fought against it were to incur God's displeasure. The citizens "labor for the welfare of Zion" rather than for money. In addition, in the words of the resurrected Jesus found in the Book of Mormon, Zion was identified as a specific *place* in the land of America, a land of promise and inheritance for the descendants of Joseph of old (1 Nephi 13:37; 2 Nephi 10:11–13; 26:29–31; 28:20–24; 3 Nephi 16:16–18).

As we have mentioned, a key moment in Latter-day Saint history in regard to the discovery of the concept of Zion came during Joseph Smith's translation of the early chapters of Genesis. By the time Sidney Rigdon joined the Prophet in December 1830 and became the principal scribe in the Bible translation, particulars concerning the patriarch Enoch and his ancient city of Zion were beginning to be made known. A King James text of three verses on Enoch and his people was expanded to more than one hundred verses, setting forth knowledge concerning the manner in which an entire society of persons living before the Flood was spiritually awakened to transcendent righteousness; the means by which this ancient people, formerly bent on selfishness and pride, had their souls changed, saw to the needs of the poor, and became "of one heart and one mind"

(Moses 7:18); and how, through the application of such a divine philosophy, they were translated, taken from the earth into the bosom
of God (Moses 7). Enoch's Zion became the pattern, the scriptural
prototype, for the Latter-day Saints. In the months that followed,
several revelations that we now have in the Doctrine and Covenants
spoke of the ancient Zion of Enoch (D&C 38:4; 45:12–14; 107:49)
and also provided the broad framework for the Latter-day Saints to
begin to build a modern Zion society.

MULTIPLE MEANINGS OF ZION

Among the earliest revelations recorded in the Doctrine and
Covenants was the repeated command, "Now, as you have asked,
behold, I say unto you, keep my commandments, and seek to
bring forth and establish the cause of Zion" (D&C 6:6; see also
11:6; 12:6; 14:6). Zion thus came to be associated with the restored *Church* and the work of the Restoration. The faithful could
take heart in the midst of their troubles, for Zion was the city of
God (D&C 97:19). Indeed, in speaking of the sacred spot where
the people of God congregated, the Lord said, "Behold, the land
of Zion—I, the Lord, hold it in mine own hands" (D&C 63:25).
Surely the King of Zion (Moses 7:53) would deal mercifully with
his subjects.

That there was a specific location for the city of Zion in the
Americas was made known very early. Oliver Cowdery was called
in September 1830 to preach among the Lamanites, the native
Americans. He was instructed that the specific location of the city
of Zion "is not revealed, and no man knoweth where the city Zion
shall be built, but it shall be given hereafter." The Lord then added
that the location "shall be on the borders by the Lamanites" (D&C
28:9). On 20 July 1831, just as the leaders of the Saints had begun to arrive in Missouri, the early members of the Church learned
that the land of Missouri was "the land which I have appointed

and consecrated for the gathering of the saints. Wherefore, this is the land of promise, and the place for the city of Zion. . . . The place which is now called Independence is the center place" (D&C 57:1–3).

Zion is spoken of in scripture as a banner, or *ensign,* around which a weary or beleaguered people can rally. It is also a *standard* against which the substance and quality of all things are to be evaluated. The Saints are expected to judge all things by a set of guidelines from a source beyond that of unenlightened man. Note the language of the revelation: "Behold, I, the Lord, have made my church in these last days like unto a judge sitting on a hill, or in a high place, to judge the nations. For it shall come to pass that the inhabitants of Zion shall judge all things pertaining to Zion" (D&C 64:37–38). As an illustration of this principle, Joseph Young, brother of Brigham Young, explained that Joseph Smith the Prophet "recommended the Saints to cultivate as high a state of perfection in their musical harmonies as the standard of the faith which he had brought was superior to sectarian religion. To obtain this, he gave them to understand that the refinement of singing would depend upon the attainment of the Holy Spirit. . . . When these graces and refinements and all the kindred attractions are obtained that characterized the ancient Zion of Enoch, then the Zion of the last days will become beautiful, she will be hailed by the Saints from the four winds, who will gather to Zion with songs of everlasting joy."[4]

In addition, Zion is the focus, the convergence, and the concentration of all that is good, all that is ennobling, all that is instructive and inspirational. In Zion all things are to be gathered together in one in Christ (Ephesians 1:10). In short, according to Brigham Young, "every accomplishment, every polished grace, every useful

---

4. *History of the Organization of the Seventies,* 14–15.

attainment in mathematics, music, in all science and art belong to the Saints."[5] The Saints "rapidly collect the intelligence that is bestowed upon the nations," President Young said on another occasion, "for all this intelligence belongs to Zion."[6]

Zion is people, the people of God, those people who have come out of the world of Babylon into the marvelous light of Christ. The Lord encouraged his little latter-day flock: "Verily, thus saith the Lord, let Zion rejoice, for this is Zion—THE PURE IN HEART; therefore, let Zion rejoice, while all the wicked shall mourn" (D&C 97:21). Thus Zion is *a state of being,* a state of purity of heart that entitles one to be known as a member of the household of faith. Brigham Young therefore spoke of the Saints having Zion in their hearts: "Unless the people live before the Lord in the obedience of His commandments," he said, "they cannot have Zion within them." Further, "as to the spirit of Zion, it is in the hearts of the Saints, of those who love and serve the Lord with all their might, mind, and strength."[7] On another occasion President Young affirmed: "Zion will be redeemed and built up, and the saints will rejoice. This is the land of Zion; and *who are Zion? The pure in heart are Zion; they have Zion within them.* Purify yourselves, sanctify the Lord God in your hearts, and have the Zion of God within you."[8] Finally, President Young asked: "Where is Zion? *Where the organization of the Church of God is. And may it dwell spiritually in every heart;* and may we so live as to always enjoy the Spirit of Zion."[9]

Isaiah the prophet had spoken some seven hundred years before Christ of the "mountain of the Lord's house" being established in the tops of the mountains (Isaiah 2:2). In July 1840 Joseph Smith

---

5. In *Journal of Discourses,* 10:224.

6. In *Journal of Discourses,* 8:279.

7. In *Journal of Discourses,* 2:253.

8. In *Journal of Discourses,* 8:198.

9. In *Journal of Discourses,* 8:205; emphasis added.

declared (in harmony with the teachings in the Book of Mormon; see 3 Nephi 16:16–18) that "the land of Zion consists of all North and South America, but that *any place where the Saints gather is Zion*."[10] The latter part of this statement—that Zion represented more than a place, a single location, but rather any place of gathering—is significant. It broadens the notion of Zion to include areas around the world where people of the covenant congregate. This larger vision of Zion is reflected in the following scripture: "Zion shall not be moved out of her place, notwithstanding her children are scattered. They that remain, and are pure in heart, shall return, and come to their inheritances, they and their children, with songs of everlasting joy, to build up the waste places of Zion—and all these things that the prophets might be fulfilled. And, behold, there is none other place appointed than that which I have appointed; neither shall there be any other place appointed than that which I have appointed, for the work of the gathering of my saints—until the day cometh when there is found no more room for them; and then I have other places which I will appoint unto them, and *they shall be called stakes, for the curtains or the strength of Zion*" (D&C 101:17–21; emphasis added).

In the prayer dedicating the Kirtland Temple, the Prophet pleaded in behalf of the Saints "that they may come forth to Zion, or *to her stakes, the places of thine appointment,* with songs of everlasting joy" (D&C 109:39; emphasis added). The revelations are clear in their pronouncement that safety and refuge are to be found in the stakes of Zion. "Arise and shine forth," the Lord implored, "that thy light may be a standard for the nations; and that the gathering together upon the land of Zion, *and upon her stakes,* may be for a defense, and for a refuge from the storm, and from wrath

---

10. *Words of Joseph Smith,* 415; emphasis added.

when it shall be poured out without mixture upon the whole earth" (D&C 115:5–6; emphasis added).

As to the future of Zion, Elder Bruce R. McConkie wrote: "The center place! Let Israel gather to the stakes of Zion in all nations. Let every land be a Zion to those appointed to dwell there. . . . But still there is a center place, a place where the chief temple shall stand, a place to which the Lord shall come, a place whence the law shall go forth to govern all the earth in that day when the Second David reigns personally upon the earth. And that center place is what men now call Independence in Jackson County, Missouri, but which in a day to come will be the Zion of our God and the City of Holiness of his people."[11] Although the Church will establish a significant presence in Independence, Missouri, and though Jackson County will become the center place, yet there will always be, as suggested above, a need for the stakes of Zion throughout the earth far and wide, a need for the Saints to gather to their own lands and congregate with their own people.

Like the Church, the concept of Zion has grown and expanded over time. Elder Erastus Snow, a member of the Quorum of the Twelve, pointed out in 1884 that when the early Saints "first heard the fullness of the Gospel preached by the first Elders, and read the revelations given through the Prophet Joseph Smith, our ideas of Zion were very limited. But as our minds began to grow and expand, why we began to look upon Zion as a great people, and the Stakes of Zion as numerous. . . . We ceased to set bounds to Zion and her Stakes."[12] Likewise, Elder Joseph Young explained that many Saints of the nineteenth century misconstrued and miscalculated on a number of matters, including the time when the Saints should return to Missouri and redeem Zion. "The Holy Spirit brought many things close to their minds—they appeared right

---

11. *New Witness for the Articles of Faith*, 595.
12. In *Journal of Discourses*, 25:30–31.

by, and hence many were deceived. . . . I knew that faith and the Holy Ghost brought the designs of Providence close by, and by that means we were enabled to scan them, . . . but we had not knowledge enough to digest and fully comprehend those things."[13]

Zion is the City of God; Babylon is the city of Satan. Both work upon the souls of their citizens. Both seek to build an allegiance and a loyalty among their people. While Zion looks to the Almighty God for strength and direction, Babylon specializes in idolatry: the people of Babylon "seek not the Lord to establish his righteousness, but every man walketh in his own way, and after the image of his own god, whose image is in the likeness of the world, and whose substance is that of an idol, which waxeth old and shall perish in Babylon, even Babylon the great, which shall fall" (D&C 1:16).

While in the end Babylon will produce withered and benighted souls whose chief aim is self-aggrandizement, Zion seeks to reconcile the irreconcilable, to produce both social union and also mature and dynamic individualism. Stephen L Richards, then a counselor in the First Presidency, observed that "there is no fence around Zion or the world, but to one of discernment, they [Zion and Babylon] are separated more completely than if each were surrounded with high unscalable walls. Their underlying concepts, philosophies, and purposes are at complete variance one with the other. The philosophy of the world is self-sufficient, egotistical, materialistic, and skeptical. The philosophy of Zion is humility, not servility, but a willing recognition of the sovereignty of God and dependence on his providence."[14]

CONCLUSION

Although it is true that salvation is an individual matter, some significant facets of the Christian character can be developed only

13. In *Journal of Discourses*, 9:230.
14. In Conference Report, Oct. 1951, 110.

in community. And from the Prophet Joseph's perspective, that community was Zion. Zion is a place. Zion is a people. Zion is a holy state of being. In the words of President Spencer W. Kimball, Zion is the "highest order of priesthood society."[15] It is the heritage of the Saints. "The building up of Zion," Joseph Smith taught, "is a cause that has interested the people of God in every age; it is a theme upon which prophets, priests and kings have dwelt with peculiar delight; they have looked forward with joyful anticipation to the day in which we live; and fired with heavenly and joyful anticipations they have sung and written and prophesied of this our day; but they died without the sight; we are the favored people that God has made choice of to bring about the Latter-day glory."[16] That is the destiny of those who endure faithfully to the end. For that reason, "we ought to have the building up of Zion as our greatest object."[17] Thus the duty and responsibility of the Saints of God is to establish the City of God, the holy commonwealth, the place where the Almighty can come and dwell with his people (Moses 7:69).

---

15. "Welfare Services: The Gospel in Action," *Ensign*, Nov. 1977, 78.
16. *Joseph Smith* [manual], 186.
17. *Joseph Smith* [manual], 186.

Chapter 9

ALL THINGS IN COMMON

Kirtland, Ohio, February 1831. Utopian societies were numerous in early America. A significant part of the quest for the holy community, the city on a hill (Matthew 5:14), was a yearning to return to the ancient order of things, particularly to implement an economic system that would enable Christian seekers to pattern themselves after the followers of Jesus in the first century (Acts 2:44–45; 4:32–37; 5:1–11). The combination of inspired translation from the Bible (Moses 6–7) and revelations to the Prophet Joseph (D&C 42, 51, 83) would provide a solid doctrinal and economic foundation upon which to build the latter-day city of God.

The early nineteenth century is often characterized as a time of significant movement: in geography, in values, in institutions. This movement of body and mind was not purposeless, however; many were shaking themselves loose from their moorings and were busily in search of new ideas, of a better way. Similarly, individuals were traveling from one part of the country to another, seeking to understand every social effort that was being tried. It was a period of utopianism, and men and women everywhere were yearning for the holy community.[1] Historian Carl Russell Fish wrote concerning this era: *"Never before in America were people so much out of their homes and on the move.* Never before were there so many travellers to observe them, with so easy a market for their observations when put into print. Never had the busy reporters of the newspapers been so numerous and so alert to catch the mass or the individual in some unusual pose, some amusing gesture."[2]

THE SETTING

A common idea of the times was that paradise on earth, or Eden, or utopia, was to be had only through changing society; some were committed to the axiom that human behavior is altered only through the manipulation of the human environment. From this posture flowed the idea of a "beloved community," a model city, a pure society. "Confident that men would follow the right if only the right were clearly shown to them, reformers who believed in a total reconstruction of social institutions pinned their faith upon model communities. . . . Once successfully established, a model community would be initiated far and wide until at length—and perhaps at no great length—society would be transformed in its image. . . . Sometimes referred to as 'utopian socialism,' for it undertook to use the model community as a lever for the wholesale reform of society—not merely in the economic sphere, but in education, morals, and social life generally."[3]

At the same time, many reformers still sought to restore the *practices* as well as the beliefs of New Testament Christianity. One set of scriptural passages that held special significance to those seeking change and restoration is found in the early chapters of the Acts of the Apostles. Here is described a group of Christian believers

---

1. See Andrus, "Field Is White," 4.

2. *Rise of the Common Man,* 137; emphasis added.

3. Bestor, "Ferment of Reform," 6.

who were "of one heart and of one soul," who "had all things [in] common," who so structured their social world that there were not "any among them that lacked" (Acts 4:32–34). In the minds of a number of social experimenters, therefore, a perfect spiritual union was to be achieved only through a communal organization.

Latter-day Saint historian Milton Backman characterized the communal societies of the nineteenth century. First, almost all of the groups were led by charismatic leaders who claimed a vision or a revelation from God or at least felt a spirit of destiny and direction in their work. Second, they believed in the importance of gifts of the Spirit. Third, theirs was a millennial consciousness, a belief that the second coming of Christ was imminent. Fourth, they believed in future rewards and punishments. Fifth, they adhered to health codes. Sixth, they practiced communal forms of living. And seventh, they believed in public confession of sins, pacifism, simplicity of living, and frugality.[4]

An interesting prelude to the establishment of an economic system among the Latter-day Saints is the organization of "the family." Sidney Rigdon had broken with Alexander Campbell over certain doctrinal matters—specifically, Rigdon's belief in the importance of gifts of the Spirit and his commitment to the establishment of a Christian society like the one described in Acts. Before joining with the Saints, Rigdon helped to organize a group based upon the pattern found in the New Testament. This group, called "the family," settled on a farm owned by Isaac Morley near Kirtland, Ohio. The situation at the Morley farm in early 1831 was a common stock arrangement, and members of "the family" were expected to love one another, share all things, and thereby become a people "of one heart and one soul." "In this organization," one historian wrote, "they followed the prevailing man-made concept of what it means to have

---

4. *American Religions and the Rise of Mormonism,* 232–37.

all things in common. For example, everyone wore everyone else's shirts, shoes, etc. The first one up in the morning was often the best dressed that day."[5]

Such practices soon led to discord. John Whitmer wrote of the experiment: "The disciples had all things common, and were going to destruction very fast as to temporal things; for they considered from reading the scripture that what belonged to a brother, belonged to any of the brethren. Therefore they would take each other's clothes and other property and use it without leave, which brought on confusion and disappointment, for they did not understand the scripture."[6]

One convert to the Church wrote in his journal of his own encounter with "the family": "Isaac Morley . . . was a cooper by trade and one of the most honest, patient men I ever saw. The company he maintained looked large enough to bring on a famine. I do not know if they lived on him all the time or not. While I was in the room at 'Father Morley's' as we all called him, Heman Bassett came to me and took my watch out of my pocket and walked off as though it was his. I thought he would bring it back soon but was disappointed as he sold it. I asked him what he meant by selling. 'Oh,' said he, 'I thought it was all in the family.' I told him I did not like such family doings and I would not bear it."[7]

"The family" was dissolved as word of the Restoration through Joseph Smith was spread through the area around Kirtland. Joseph the Prophet recorded simply in his journal: "The plan of 'common

5. Andrus, "Field Is White," 7.
6. John Whitmer, History, 1831–circa 1847, The Joseph Smith Papers, accessed 27 Jul. 2016, http://josephsmithpapers.org/paperSummary/john-whitmer-history-1831-circa-1847?p=15.
7. Journal of Levi Hancock, 27.

stock,' which had existed in what was called 'the family' . . . was readily abandoned for the more perfect law of the Lord."[8]

THE LORD SPEAKS

For Joseph Smith and the early Latter-day Saints, Zion represented the fusion of the temporal and the spiritual: seemingly temporal matters had a spiritual basis and were given to achieve divine purposes; spiritual laws were kept and spiritual goals attained through the proper use of temporal resources. A revelation given in 1830 stated that all things were spiritual to the Almighty and that a truly temporal law or commandment had never been given to his earthly servants (D&C 29:34). Brigham Young explained that "the order of Enoch . . . is in reality the order of heaven. It was revealed to Enoch when he built up his city and gathered the people together and sanctified them, so that they became so holy that they could not live among the rest of the people and the Lord took them away."[9] In the Zion of Enoch the people were not only righteous but fair, just, and equitable. That is, the ancient city of Zion—that which became the scriptural prototype for Joseph Smith and the Saints—was translated, not only because they were "of one heart and one mind," or just because they "dwelt in righteousness," but also because "there was no poor among them" (Moses 7:18). The Latter-day Saints soon began to apply the axiomatic expression that "a religion that has not the power to save a man temporally has not the power to save him spiritually,"[10] for "if ye are not equal in earthly things ye cannot be equal in obtaining heavenly things" (D&C 78:6).

On 9 February 1831 Joseph Smith dictated what has come

8. History, 1838–1856, volume A-1 [23 December 1805–30 August 1834], The Joseph Smith Papers, accessed 15 Mar. 2016, http://josephsmithpapers.org/paperSummary /history-1838-1856-volume-a-1-23-december-1805-30-august-1834?p=99.

9. In *Journal of Discourses,* 13:2.

10. Smith, *Gospel Doctrine,* 208.

to be known as a revelation "embracing the law of the church." In Doctrine and Covenants 42 is introduced the law of consecration and stewardship, some of the principles of the economic order the Saints believe were implemented by Enoch and his people. It is a system intended to minimize and eventually to eliminate inequalities and class distinctions. It is dramatically different both from what we experience in present-day society and from what nineteenth-century Saints experienced.

In the words of the Lord to the Latter-day Saints, "It is not given that one man should possess that which is above another, wherefore the world lieth in sin" (D&C 49:20). "It is my purpose," the members of the Church were later instructed, "to provide for my saints, for all things are mine. But it must needs be done in mine own way; and behold this is the way that I, the Lord, have decreed to provide for my saints, that *the poor shall be exalted, in that the rich are made low*" (D&C 104:16; emphasis added). The Saints were to be engaged constantly in "searching after the poor to administer to their wants by humbling the rich and the proud" (D&C 84:112).

The basis of consecration and stewardship was self-denial and brotherly love. As Adam Smith, author of *The Wealth of Nations* (1776), had written, "To feel much for others, and little for ourselves, that to restrain our selfish, and to indulge our benevolent affections, constitutes the perfection of human nature."[11]

CONSECRATION AND EQUALITY

The law of consecration was to be entered into by choice, as a matter of free will. In speaking years later of those who entered into a variation of this system in the Great Basin, President Brigham Young said: "We are trying to unite the people together in the order that the Lord revealed to Enoch, which will be observed and

---

11. *Theory of Moral Sentiments*, 71.

sustained in the latter days in redeeming and building up Zion; . . . but I want to tell you, my brethren and sisters, that . . . the saints are not prepared to see everything at once. They have got to learn little by little, and to receive a little here and a little there."[12]

In Ohio and Missouri, members of the Church entered this system by consecrating, or giving, to the Lord, through the local bishop, all personal property or holdings. "Behold, thou wilt remember the poor, and consecrate of thy properties for their support that which thou hast to impart unto them, with a covenant and a deed which cannot be broken" (D&C 42:30). The consecration was to be a matter of *covenant* between the Church member and God and was to be acknowledged by a *deed* from the bishop of the Church to the member. "Their covenant of consecration made their act officially binding before God and the Church, and the deed bound it legally according to the law of the land. Zion's economic law, therefore, was founded both in the religious powers of faith and conscience and in the legal power of civil law, that by each it might be given sanction and protection."[13]

According to Elder Orson Pratt, consecration was the first step in the achievement of equality. From his perspective, once a man has *given back* to God all possessions (since all belongs to God anyway; Psalm 24:1), then he owns nothing. When all the members in the society of Zion have nothing (that is, when all have consecrated), then all thereafter are equal, owning nothing. Even that which is deeded back as a stewardship is not one's own: it is God's. Therefore, he believed, initial equality is assured through a transition from ownership to consecration.[14]

Latter-day Saints understood that the act of consecration was a restoration of the pattern given in the New Testament in which

---

12. In *Journal of Discourses,* 18:245.
13. Andrus, *Doctrines of the Kingdom,* 229.
14. In *Journal of Discourses,* 2:99.

early Christians, "as many as were possessors of lands or houses sold them, and brought the prices of the things that were sold, and laid them down at the apostles' feet" (Acts 4:34–35). Though a consecration was a free-will offering, yet the members were taught that the full blessings of Zion were available only to those who chose to enter this order. "A man is bound," Joseph said, "by the law of the Church, to consecrate to the Bishop, before he can be considered a legal heir to the kingdom of Zion."[15] Wilford Woodruff recorded in his journal: "Be it known that I, Wilford Woodruff, freely covenant with my God that I freely consecrate and dedicate myself, together with all my properties and effects unto the Lord, for the purpose of assisting in building up his kingdom, even Zion, on the earth, that I may keep his law and lay all things before the bishop of his Church, that I may be a lawful heir in the kingdom of God, even the Celestial Kingdom."[16]

RECEIVING THE STEWARDSHIP

Having consecrated all to Zion, members then counseled with the bishop to determine an appropriate stewardship, or inheritance. The idea of stewardship was prevalent in early American thought and had a great deal to do with the Puritans' attitude toward possessions. "In the Puritan mind the biblical idea of the stewardship was coupled with the idea of the covenant. The doctrine of stewardship held that God had given to his faithful servants a special charge to oversee not just their own material possessions, but the Lord's vineyard (in their case, New England) in its entirety. In other words, the Puritans believed themselves to be responsible for the well-being of the whole commonwealth. It comes as no surprise, then, to learn

---

15. History, 1838–1856, volume A-1 [23 December 1805–30 August 1834], The Joseph Smith Papers, accessed 15 Mar. 2016, http://josephsmithpapers.org/paperSummary /history-1838-1856-volume-a-1-23-december-1805-30-august-1834?p=318; see also D&C 70:8, 10; 85:3.

16. *Journal*, 31 Dec. 1834.

that they designed for themselves a highly regulated society. Wages and prices were set, production quotas assigned, commerce carefully managed, interest rates controlled."[17]

Among the early Latter-day Saints, property or holdings or responsibility was deeded back to the individual, based on family size, circumstances, needs, just wants, and abilities (D&C 51:3–4; 82:17). The Lord's system made room for those whose talents or abilities or assignments were not strictly temporal. The Saints were instructed, therefore, that "he who is appointed to administer spiritual things, the same is worthy of his hire, even as those who are appointed to a stewardship to administer in temporal things" (D&C 70:12; compare 72:14).[18] It might be, therefore, that after consultation with the bishop, a person would be issued a stewardship that consisted of essentially the same holdings he or she had consecrated. Or, depending on the decision after consultation with the bishop, the person might receive more or less than consecrated. Joseph explained: "The matter of consecration must be done by mutual consent of both parties; for to give the Bishop power to say how much every man shall have, and he be obliged to comply with the Bishop's judgment, is giving to the Bishop more power than a king has; and, upon the other hand, to let every man say how much he needs and the Bishop be obliged to comply with his judgment, is to throw Zion into confusion and make a slave of the Bishop. The fact is, there must be a balance or equilibrium of power, between the Bishop and the people; and thus harmony and good will may be preserved among you."[19]

---

17. Bedell, Sandon, and Wellborn, *Religion in America,* 295.

18. The reference here is to the work done by Joseph Smith, Martin Harris, Oliver Cowdery, John Whitmer, Sidney Rigdon, and William W. Phelps as the Literary Firm. Their specific assignment (stewardship) was the care and preparation of the revelations for publication (D&C 70).

19. History, 1838–1856, volume A-1 [23 December 1805–30 August 1834], The Joseph Smith Papers, accessed 15 Mar. 2016, http://josephsmithpapers.org/paperSummary/history-1838-1856-volume-a-1-23-december-1805-30-august-1834?p=319.

The Saints were to manage their stewardships as though they were their own property. A man, for all intents and purposes, had total control over how his farm or dairy or market or teaching assignment was handled. His stewardship represented both his responsibility or job, as well as his contribution to the community. Joseph F. Smith explained: "Each holder of a stewardship—which might be the same farm, workshop, store, or factory that this same person had 'consecrated'—was expected to manage it thereafter in the interest of the whole community; all his gains reverting to a common fund, from which he would derive a sufficient support for himself and those dependent upon him."[20] In reality, and as the scriptures affirmed, God owned the property, and the citizens of Zion were expected to serve as profitable agents of God in managing the Lord's business. "Behold, all these properties are mine," the Savior declared, "and *if the properties are mine, then ye are stewards*" (D&C 104:55–56; emphasis added; see also 42:32).

Each steward was charged to operate according to the principles taught in the parable of the talents (Matthew 25:14–30) to improve upon and expand his stewardship, which would include making his goods or services available on the open market. Many years ago noted historian Leonard Arrington pointed out that "each member was free to work as he pleased within the limitations of his stewardship. The profit system, the forces of supply and demand, and the price system presumably would continue to allocate resources, guide production decisions, and distribute primary or earned income. Some of the institutions of capitalism were thus retained and a considerable amount of economic freedom was permitted."[21] Professor Hyrum Andrus offered a similar opinion: "The system of economics under the Law of Consecration is that of Christian free

---

20. "The Truth about 'Mormonism,'" *Millennial Star* 67, no. 40 (Oct. 1905): 628.

21. "Early Mormon Communitarianism," 344; see also Geddes, *United Order among the Mormons*, 32, 163–64.

enterprise. Under the Law, the saints produce for the open market, not for the Common Storehouse which is merely to house the surplus profits of each steward. Since the saints produce for the free market, there is no reason the finished products cannot be sold outside the circle of the Mormon community and compete with other commodities produced by others. Reciprocally, foreign goods could compete on local markets among the saints."[22]

Because the principles of consecration and stewardship were not given to encourage communal living, individuals were expected to "pay for that which thou shalt receive of thy brother" (D&C 42:54). Even though the social and spiritual union intended in Zion would certainly lead to the trading or swapping of goods and services, it would appear that the system was established as a money-based order, wherein payment for receipt of goods or services was the rule of society (also 72:11).

MANAGING THE STEWARDSHIP

Though the details are wanting as to exactly how equality was to be maintained after stewardships had been granted, one matter was certain: *surplus consecration* (the amount above and beyond what a steward needed after the initial consecration) and *surplus production* (any excess beyond personal and family needs resulting from proper and successful management of the stewardship) were not to be kept by the steward; they became a part of the community *storehouse*. The storehouse was the center of economic interests in the community. Funds from the storehouse (from surplus consecration or surplus production) were to be used for a number of purposes: community improvements (D&C 42:34–35), expansion of stewardships (D&C 104:6, 77), and the creation of new stewardships (D&C 83:5). Further, widows, orphans and other dependent

---

22. Andrus, correspondence with author, 21 Sept. 1982.

children, and young adults (for example, newly married couples) were to be assisted through the funds in the storehouse (D&C 83).

Thus another means by which individuals were made equal was through their right to draw upon the resources of the common storehouse. "And you are to be equal," the members were instructed, "or in other words, you are to have equal claims on the properties, for the benefit of managing the concerns of your stewardships, every man according to his wants and his needs, inasmuch as his wants are just" (D&C 82:17). Hence having "all things in common" meant two things to the Latter-day Saints: a *common storehouse* upon which to draw, and *common consent* as to how the moneys were to be expended in the community (D&C 104:71–75).

Each steward was expected to be wise in the management of the Lord's properties. Accountability was exacted, presumably by means of a system of audits and interviews. "It is required of the Lord, at the hand of every steward, to render an account of his stewardship, both in time and in eternity" (D&C 72:3; compare 104:11–13). To render an account of the stewardship in time probably had reference to a regular audit and an interview in which the bishop is apprised of the productivity of the steward. To render an account in eternity implies one's responsibility to answer to God concerning the stewardship. Any member of the order found guilty of the violation of the standards of the Church and the pattern established for Zion, and who was excommunicated from the fellowship of the Saints, had no claim on the surplus of the original consecration; such a person could, however, retain the stewardship he had received. That is, "he that sinneth and repenteth not shall be cast out of the church, and shall not receive again that which he has consecrated unto the poor and the needy of my church, or in other words, unto me" (D&C 42:37; see also 32; 51:5). Speaking of the transgressor, the Prophet explained that "if he is found a transgressor and should be cut off, out of the church, his inheritance is his still. . . . But the property which he consecrated to the poor, for their benefit and inheritance and stewardship [the surplus consecration], he cannot obtain again by the law of the Lord. Thus you see the propriety of this law, that rich men cannot have power to disinherit the poor by obtaining again that which they have consecrated."[23]

CONCLUSION

No person lives to himself or herself, and Zion is only established by a people whose concerns reach beyond themselves. "The greatest temporal and spiritual blessings," Joseph Smith explained, "which always flow from faithfulness and concerted effort, never attended individual exertion or enterprise. The history of all past ages abundantly attests this fact."[24] The Latter-day Saints' initial attempt to live the law of consecration was relatively short lived. "This resulted mostly," Lyndon Cook wrote, "from inexperience but partly because of human selfishness. . . . In the spring of 1833 a law suit resulted in the failure of the first phase of the Mormon economic law in Missouri. On Friday, the 1st of March, 1833, a member of the Church, named Bates, from New London, Ohio, brought a suit against Edward Partridge for return of his consecrated properties. While contractually Bates had relinquished his rights to the properties, the court in Independence went beyond the deed of gift and its stewardship agreement in its review of the case." The court "rescinded the contract because it determined that it was contrary to standards of fairness for the Mormon Church to require its members to deed over all of their possessions to remain in good standing."

Cook indicates that the initial failure of the system is not surprising, since requiring those who entered the order to "transfer all of their property to the bishop and to re-consecrate their annual

---

23. Joseph Smith to Edward Partridge, 2 May 1833, in Orson F. Whitney, "The Aaronic Priesthood," *Contributor* 6, no. 1 (Oct. 1884): 7.

24. *Joseph Smith* [manual], 278.

surpluses threatened the incentive motive and prompted members to withhold possessions from consecration [compare Acts 5:1–11] or pursue private investments outside of the system." Second, the system failed because "the members were by and large poor before they entered the consecration system. Redistribution of property thus resulted in a leveling down rather than a leveling up of the stewards' living standard."[25]

From the Lord's perspective, the Saints' efforts to succeed in consecration and stewardship failed because the people had not "learned to be obedient to the things which I required at their hands, but are full of all manner of evil, and do not impart of their substance, as becometh saints, to the poor and afflicted among them" (D&C 105:3). Elder Orson Pratt suggested that the Saints "had been so accustomed to holding property individually, that it was very difficult to get them to comply with this law of the Lord."[26] The selfishness of the Saints seemed to manifest itself in a refusal to recognize and surrender one's surplus. Again from Elder Pratt: "Go around among the Saints, among the immigrants who have gathered up from time to time, and there has been only now and then a man who had any surplus property [if we] let him be the judge."[27]

President Brigham Young, with characteristic directness, graphically described the problem of selfishness among the early Latter-day Saints: "Some were disposed to do right with their surplus property, and once in a while you would find a man who had a cow which he considered surplus, but generally she was of the class that would kick a person's hat off, or the wolves had eaten off her teats. You would once in a while find a man who had a horse that he considered surplus, but at the same time he had the ringbone, was

25. *Joseph Smith and the Law of Consecration*, 20–21.
26. In *Journal of Discourses*, 17:108.
27. In *Journal of Discourses*, 17:110.

broken-winded, spavined in both legs, had the pole evil at the end of the neck and a fistula at the other, and both knees sprung."[28]

During the lifetime of Joseph Smith the Saints were later given a slightly different order of consecration, in which members were instructed to consecrate their surplus each year and, in addition, to pay a tithing on their interest, or income (D&C 119:1–4). And later, as the members of the Church settled in Nauvoo, Illinois, the Lord delivered to them, through his Prophet, the temple endowment, which we receive in temples in our own day. In a very real sense, the consecration to which the Saints are called in holy temples is higher and grander, deeper and more comprehensive than that which the Saints in Ohio and Missouri had been expected to live. While members today do not give all of their funds and properties to the local bishop, endowed Saints are called upon to consecrate *themselves*—to give themselves wholly and completely to the work of the Lord and the establishment of the kingdom of God on earth. Truly, "a religion that does not require the sacrifice of all things never has power to produce the faith necessary unto life and salvation."[29]

It is not merely our wallets but also our *wills* that Christ requires of those who would inherit the highest degree of the celestial kingdom. Elder Neal A. Maxwell put it beautifully: "In striving for ultimate submission, our wills constitute all we really have to give God anyway. The usual gifts and their derivatives we give to Him could be stamped justifiably 'Return to Sender,' with a capital *S*. Even when God receives this one gift in return, the fully faithful will receive 'all that [He] hath' (D&C 84:38). What an exchange rate!"[30]

---

28. In *Journal of Discourses*, 2:307.

29. *Lectures on Faith*, 69.

30. "Consecrate Thy Performance," *Ensign*, May 2002, 38.

Chapter 10

MORE HEAVENS THAN ONE

Hyrum, Ohio, February 1832. Joseph Smith's translation of the Bible not only made known remarkable truths concerning the ancients but also prompted the Prophet to find and recognize special meaning and perspective, patterns and underlying themes in holy scripture, even to be so bold as to ask difficult questions about how certain doctrines had been understood and taught for generations. Joseph Smith and Sidney Rigdon began to wonder, for example, about the views of heaven and hell that had been promulgated by Roman Catholic and Protestant divines and philosophers for hundreds of years. It was during the translation of the fifth chapter of John, particularly verse 29, that the vision of the glories burst upon the translator and his scribe.

L et not your heart be troubled: ye believe in God, believe also in me. In my Father's house are many mansions: if it were not so, I would have told you. I go to prepare a place for you" (John 14:1–2). Christ seems to be teaching the Twelve during the Last Supper that life hereafter consists of more than merely a heaven and a hell; if it were not so, he would have told us otherwise. Reason suggests that not all people are equally good and thus not all good people deserve the same reward hereafter. Likewise, not all bad people are equally bad, and surely some are so bad they deserve to sink to the lowest pit in hell. Something so fundamental, so central to salvation as this principle of justice, would surely be a part of what God would make known during the times of restitution.

BACKGROUND TO THE VISION

We recall from our discussion in chapter 7 that in June 1830 the Prophet Joseph Smith began an inspired translation of the King James Version of the Bible, a labor to which he was divinely appointed (D&C 42:56; 76:15) and a work he considered to be a "branch of [his] calling."[1] The Prophet and his scribes progressed through the book of Genesis until 7 March 1831, when the Lord commanded the Prophet to turn his attention to the New Testament (D&C 45:60–61). On 12 September 1831, to escape persecution, the Smiths relocated to Hiram, Ohio, to live with the John Johnson family.

By 16 February 1832 the Prophet and Sidney Rigdon had translated much of the fifth chapter of John. In verses 28 and 29 the Savior indicates that the time will come when the dead will hear the voice of the Son of God and come forth from the grave, "they that have done good, unto the resurrection of life; and they that have done evil, unto the resurrection of damnation." The translator felt impressed to alter the text as follows: "And shall come forth; they who have done good, in the resurrection of *the just*; and they who have done evil, in the resurrection of *the unjust*" (Joseph Smith Translation, John 5:29; D&C 76:17; emphasis added). "Now this caused us to marvel," Joseph stated, "for it was given unto us of the Spirit. And while we meditated upon these things, the Lord touched the eyes of our understandings and they were opened, and the glory of the Lord shone round about" (D&C 76:18–19). The

---

1. *Joseph Smith* [manual], 207.

alteration in the text, though interesting, is not earthshaking or overwhelming. Truly, however, "out of small things proceedeth that which is great" (D&C 64:33).

"The scripture [John 5:29] raised the question," historian Richard Bushman observed, "of how God could divide people into stark categories of saved and damned when individuals were so obviously a mix in ordinary life." In commenting further on the theological significance of this very question, Bushman continues: "The question Joseph posed was a classic post-Calvinist puzzle. For over a century Anglo-American culture had struggled to explain the arbitrary judgments of the Calvinist God who saved and damned according to his own good pleasure with little regard for human effort. . . . . During the preceding century, the Calvinist notion of arbitrary sovereignty had come to seem incongruous and offensive. . . . Calvinism still flourished in sophisticated forms in theological circles, but people were asking questions much like Smith's. Is God's judgment of humanity consistent with His benevolent character?"[2]

There came to Joseph Smith and his scribe on this occasion one of the most remarkable oracles ever given to men and women on earth, one we have come to know simply as the vision, or the vision of the glories, as recorded in Doctrine and Covenants 76. This revelation is an interpretive commentary on the Savior's words concerning "many mansions" in the world to come (John 14:2) and provides a priceless insight into Paul's otherwise cryptic comment about various types of bodies in the resurrection (1 Corinthians 15:40–42).

Philo Dibble, one who was present at the Johnson home when the vision was received, recorded the following fascinating account: "The vision of the three degrees of glory which is recorded in the

2. *Rough Stone Rolling,* 196–97.

Doctrine and Covenants was given at the house of 'Father Johnson,' in Hiram, Ohio, and during the time that Joseph and Sidney were in the Spirit and saw the heavens open there were other men in the room, perhaps twelve, among whom I was one during a part of the time—probably two-thirds of the time. I saw the glory and felt the power, but did not see the vision.

"Joseph wore black clothes, but at this time seemed to be dressed in an element of glorious white, and his face shone as if it were transparent, but I did not see the same glory attending Sidney. . . .

"Joseph would, at intervals, say: 'What do I see?' as one might say while looking out the window and beholding what all in the room could not see. Then he would relate what he had seen or what he was looking at.

"Then Sidney replied, 'I see the same.'

"Presently Sidney would say, 'What do I see?' and would repeat what he had seen or was seeing.

"And Joseph would reply, 'I see the same.'

"This manner of conversation was repeated at short intervals to the end of the vision, and during the whole time not a word was spoken by any other person. Not a sound or motion was made by anyone but Joseph and Sidney, and it seemed to me that they never moved a joint or limb during the time I was there, which I think was over an hour, and to the end of the vision.

"Joseph sat firmly and calmly all the time in the midst of a magnificent glory, but Sidney sat limp and pale, apparently as limber as a rag, observing which, Joseph remarked, smilingly, 'Sidney is not used to it as I am.'"[3]

---

3. In Andrus and Andrus, *They Knew the Prophet*, 67–68; see also McConkie, *Remembering Joseph*, 252–53.

VISION OF THE GLORIES

In a sense, the vision of the glories consists of six visions, each of which we will consider briefly.

Vision I: The Glory of the Son

The first vision briefly sets the stage for what follows by placing things in perspective with regard to the work of redemption and salvation—namely, that salvation is in Christ and comes through the shedding of his own blood and his glorious rise to newness of life in resurrection. The translators thus saw in vision "the glory of the Son, on the right hand of the Father, and received of his fulness; and saw the holy angels, and them who are sanctified before his throne, worshipping God, and the Lamb, who worship him forever and ever" (D&C 76:20–21). Similarly, John the Revelator had recorded concerning the Redeemer, "Ten thousand times ten thousand, and thousands of thousands; saying with a loud voice, Worthy is the Lamb that was slain to receive power, and riches, and wisdom, and strength, and honour, and glory, and blessing" (Revelation 5:11–12).

The Prophet and his scribe bore witness of the Redeemer in powerful language: "And now, after the many testimonies which have been given of him, this is the testimony, last of all, which we give of him: That he lives! For we saw him, even on the right hand of God; and we heard the voice bearing record that he is the Only Begotten of the Father—That by him, and through him, and of him, the worlds are and were created, and the inhabitants thereof are begotten sons and daughters unto God" (D&C 76:22–24). Truly, the testimony of Jesus is the spirit of prophecy (Revelation 19:10), and all the holy prophets, from the beginning, have testified of the One who called and sent them (Acts 10:43; Jacob 4:4; 7:11; Mosiah 13:33).

In addition, Sidney and Joseph's witness contains significant doctrine. For one thing, their testimony affirms the burden of scripture—that Jehovah, who is Christ, was and is the Creator of worlds without number (Moses 1:33; 7:30; Ephesians 3:9; Hebrews 1:1–2). It confirms also the infinite and eternal nature of the Atonement. Whatsoever our Lord and Master creates, he redeems. That is to say, his redemptive labors reach beyond the bounds of our earth (Moses 1:32–35). In 1843 the Prophet Joseph Smith wrote in poetry an account of this vision. Verses 22 through 24 of Doctrine and Covenants 76 were rendered as follows:

> And now after all of the proofs made of him,
> By witnesses truly, by whom he was known,
> This is mine, last of all, that he lives; yea he lives!
> And sits at the right hand of God, on his throne.
>
> And I heard a great voice, bearing record from heav'n,
> He's the Savior, and only begotten of God—
> By him, of him, and through him, the worlds were all made,
> Even all that career in the heavens so broad,
>
> Whose inhabitants, too, from the first to the last,
> Are sav'd by the very same Savior of ours;
> And, of course, are begotten God's daughters and sons,
> By the very same truths, and the very same pow'rs.[4]

Or, as a later apostle, President Russell M. Nelson, pointed out, "the mercy of the Atonement extends not only to an infinite number of people, but also to an infinite number of worlds created by Him."[5]

Vision II: The Fall of Lucifer

The Prophet Joseph and his scribe received an affirmation of a vital element of the plan of salvation—the nature of opposition through Satan and satanic influences. Lucifer is described in the

---

4. "The Answer," *Times and Seasons* 4, no. 6 (Feb. 1843): 82–83, stanzas 18–20.
5. *Perfection Pending,* 167; see also McConkie, *New Witness for the Articles of Faith,* 131.

vision as one "who was in authority in the presence of God" (D&C 76:25), who rebelled against the Father and the Son in the premortal council in heaven, thus becoming known as *perdition,* meaning "ruin" or "destruction." Because he was indeed a spirit son of God, "a son of the morning" (D&C 76:26), the heavens wept over his defection. He coveted the throne of the Father and proposed to save all the sons and daughters of God in a way contrary to the plan of the Father (Moses 4:1–4). "The contention in heaven was—Jesus said there would be certain souls that would not be saved; and the devil said he could save them all, and laid his plans before the grand council, who gave their vote in favor of Jesus Christ. So the devil rose up in rebellion against God, and was cast down, with all who put up their heads for him."[6] Lucifer became thereby an enemy to God and to all righteousness: "Wherefore, he maketh war with the saints of God, and encompasseth them round about" (D&C 76:29).

Vision III: The Sons of Perdition

Joseph and Sidney were permitted to view those who receive light and truth and the revelations of heaven and who then choose knowingly to deny the light and defy God and his work. These are the sons of perdition, "vessels of wrath, doomed to suffer the wrath of God, with the devil and his angels in eternity" (D&C 76:33). Truly, "it is impossible for those who were once enlightened, and have tasted of the heavenly gift, and were made partakers of the Holy Ghost, and have tasted the good word of God, and the powers of the world to come, if they shall fall away, to renew them again unto repentance" (Hebrews 6:4–6; compare 10:26–29).

"What must a man do to commit the unpardonable sin?" Joseph the Seer asked in the King Follett sermon. "He must receive the Holy Ghost, have the heavens opened unto him, and know God, and then sin against Him. After a man has sinned against

---

6. *Joseph Smith* [manual], 209.

the Holy Ghost, there is no repentance for him. He has got to say that the sun does not shine while he sees it; he has got to deny Jesus Christ when the heavens have been opened unto him, and to deny the plan of salvation with his eyes open to the truth of it; and from that time he begins to be an enemy. . . . You cannot save such persons; you cannot bring them to repentance; they make open war, like the devil, and awful is the consequence."[7]

All of the sons and daughters of Adam and Eve will rise from the grave in the resurrection, including sons of perdition (D&C 88:32). The sons of perdition are guilty of the unpardonable sin (Alma 39:6), a sin not covered by the atonement of Christ, a sin for which no amount of personal suffering will right the wrongs done. There is no forgiveness for them, neither here nor hereafter, for, "having denied the Holy Spirit after having received it, and having denied the Only Begotten Son of the Father, having crucified him unto themselves and put him to an open shame" (D&C 76:34–35), they are guilty of shedding innocent blood, meaning the innocent blood of Christ. "The blasphemy against the Holy Ghost," a later revelation attests, "which shall not be forgiven in the world nor out of the world, is in that *ye commit murder wherein ye shed innocent blood, and assent unto my death,* after ye have received my new and everlasting covenant, saith the Lord God" (D&C 132:27; emphasis added). The sons of perdition are the only ones who will be subject to the second spiritual death, the final expulsion from the presence of God. They, after being resurrected and standing before God to be judged (2 Nephi 9:15), will be consigned to a kingdom of no glory.

In the midst of this gloomy scene the Lord provides one of the most beautiful definitions of the gospel of Jesus Christ: the "glad tidings" that "he came into the world, even Jesus, to be crucified for the world, and to bear the sins of the world, and to sanctify the

---

7. *Words of Joseph Smith,* 347.

world, and to cleanse it from all unrighteousness; that through him all might be saved whom the Father had put into his power and made by him; who glorifies the Father, and saves all the works of his hands, except those sons of perdition who deny the Son after the Father has revealed him" (D&C 76:40–43).

This third vision ends with a sobering reminder that the particulars of the fate of the sons of perdition have not been revealed (D&C 76:45–48). In 1833 the Prophet Joseph explained that "the Lord never authorized [certain individuals] to say that the devil, his angels, or the sons of perdition, should ever be restored; for their state of destiny was not revealed to man, is not revealed, nor shall be revealed, save to those who are made partakers thereof: consequently those who teach this doctrine have not received it of the Spirit of the Lord. Truly Brother Oliver declared it to be the doctrine of devils."[8]

Vision IV: The Celestial Glory

The Prophet and Sidney next studied and learned by contrast: Their attention shifted from those who will inherit no glory to those who inherit the highest. They beheld the glories of the celestial kingdom and provided broad descriptions of those who inhabit the same. They witnessed the inhabitants of the "resurrection of the just" (D&C 76:50), what we call the first resurrection (Mosiah 15:21–25), the resurrection of celestial and terrestrial persons. Celestial persons are those who receive the testimony of Jesus and accept the terms and conditions of the gospel covenant. They are "baptized after the manner of his burial" and receive the gift of the Holy Ghost, thereby becoming "cleansed from all their sins" (D&C 76:51–52).

---

8. History, 1838–1856, volume A-1 [23 December 1805–30 August 1834], The Joseph Smith Papers, accessed 15 Mar. 2016, http://josephsmithpapers.org/paperSummary /history-1838-1856-volume-a-1-23-december-1805-30-august-1834?p=320.

Those who inherit a celestial glory are they who "overcome by faith" (D&C 76:53), who have learned to "withstand every temptation of the devil, with their faith on the Lord Jesus Christ" (Alma 37:33). They overcome the world in forsaking worldliness and carnal attractions and give themselves to the Lord and his work. These are "sealed by the Holy Spirit of promise, which the Father sheds forth upon all those who are just and true" (D&C 76:53). The Holy Spirit of Promise is the Holy Ghost, the Holy Spirit promised to the Saints. Because "the Comforter knoweth all things" (D&C 42:17; Moses 6:61), the Holy Ghost is able to search the souls of individuals and to ascertain the degree to which they have truly yielded their hearts unto God, the degree to which they are "just and true" (D&C 76:53). Thus to be sealed by the Holy Spirit of Promise is to have the ratifying approval of the Holy Ghost upon our lives and upon the ordinances and covenants into which we have entered. It is to have passed the tests of mortality, to have qualified for celestial glory hereafter. The poem continues:

> For these overcome, by their faith and their works,
> Being tried in their life-time, as purified gold,
> And seal'd by the spirit of promise, to life,
> By men called of God, as was Aaron of old.[9]

Celestial men and women are "the Church of the Firstborn" (D&C 76:54). The Church of the Firstborn is composed of faithful Saints who have proven true and faithful to their covenants. As the covenant of baptism is the gate to membership in the Church of Jesus Christ on earth, so the covenant of celestial marriage opens the door to membership in the heavenly church.[10] The Church of

---

9. "The Answer," *Times and Seasons* 4, no. 6 (Feb. 1843): 84, stanza 43.
10. See Smith, *Doctrines of Salvation*, 2:42; *Man: His Origin and Destiny*, 272; *Way to Perfection*, 208; McConkie, *Promised Messiah*, 47; *New Witness for the Articles of Faith*, 337.

the Firstborn is the Church beyond the veil, the organized body of Saints who inherit exaltation. It is made up of those who qualify for the blessings of the Firstborn. Jesus is the Firstborn of the Father and as such is entitled to the birthright. As an act of consummate mercy and grace, our blessed Savior makes it possible for us to inherit, receive, and possess the same blessings he receives, *as though each of us were the Firstborn*. Those who come into the Church and live worthy of the companionship of the Holy Ghost are born again; they become the sons and daughters of Jesus Christ by adoption (Mosiah 5:1–7). If they continue faithful, receive thereafter the covenants and ordinances of the temple, including the endowment and celestial marriage, and are true to those higher covenants, they will eventually become the sons and daughters of God, meaning the Father.[11] They become heirs of God and joint-heirs, or co-inheritors, with Jesus Christ to all that the Father has, including eternal life. "Wherefore, as it is written, they are gods, even the sons of God" (D&C 76:58). President Brigham Young therefore stated that "the ordinances of the house of God are expressly for the Church of the Firstborn."[12]

"They are they who are priests and kings, who have received of his fulness, and of his glory" (D&C 76:56). That is, they are kings and queens, priests and priestesses, individuals who through their steadfastness and immovability in keeping their covenants have received what the prophets call the "fulness of the priesthood" (D&C 124:28). These are they who will accompany the Master when he returns in glory, those who, if they have already passed through the veil of death, will come forth from the grave in glorious immortality. The first resurrection, which began at the time of Christ's resurrection, will thus resume. These are they whose names are written in heaven, in the Lamb's book of life (D&C 88:2), "where God and Christ are the judge of all" (D&C 76:68).

---

11. See McConkie, *Doctrinal New Testament Commentary*, 2:472, 475, 491.
12. In *Journal of Discourses*, 8:154.

And then, lest we should conclude that such persons have attained to this highest degree of glory on their own, through their own merits and moral accomplishments or without divine assistance, the holy word attests: "These are they who are just men *made perfect through Jesus the mediator of the new covenant, who wrought out this perfect atonement through the shedding of his own blood*" (D&C 76:69; emphasis added). They are made perfect—whole, complete, fully formed, spiritually mature—through their covenant union with the Redeemer.

Vision V: The Terrestrial Glory

The vision of the first resurrection or resurrection of the just continues. The Prophet and his scribe witnessed the final state of those who chose to abide by goodness and equity and decency in their second estate but also chose not to receive and incorporate the fulness of that light and power that derive from receiving the everlasting gospel. The terrestrial glory is made up of those who in this life did not receive the testimony of Jesus—the testimony that he is the Savior and Redeemer of mankind—but afterward received it; that is, they received that witness in the postmortal spirit world (D&C 76:73–74). The terrestrial world is also inhabited by those who knew in this life that Jesus was the Christ but who were not valiant enough in that witness to receive the fulness of the gospel when it was presented to them. Or, as the Prophet rendered it poetically:

> Not valiant for truth, they obtain'd not the crown,
> But are of that glory that's typ'd by the moon:
> They are they, that come into the presence of Christ,
> But not to the fulness of God, on his throne.[13]

For that matter, those who received the fulness of the gospel of Jesus Christ—in our day, those who join The Church of Jesus

---

13. "The Answer," *Times and Seasons* 4, no. 6 (Feb. 1843): 84, stanza 57.

Christ of Latter-day Saints—and then do not prove valiant in their testimony. These are candidates for the terrestrial degree of glory hereafter.

Vision VI: The Telestial Glory

Remembering that celestial persons receive the testimony of Jesus and also the gospel covenant and that terrestrial persons receive the testimony of Jesus but not the gospel covenant, we now learn concerning the inhabitants of the telestial world: "These are they who received not the gospel of Christ, neither the testimony of Jesus" (D&C 76:82; see also 101). They "deny not the Holy Spirit" (D&C 76:83). That is, their wickedness is not such as to lead to complete perdition; they have not committed the unpardonable sin, but they are "thrust down to hell" (D&C 76:84); at the time of their mortal death, they enter into that realm of the postmortal sphere we know as hell, or spirit prison, and are confronted with their sinfulness (2 Nephi 9:10–12; Alma 40:13–14). These do not come from the grave until the last resurrection, until the end of the Millennium, "until the Lord, even Christ the Lamb, shall have finished his work" (D&C 76:85).

As is the case with the other kingdoms of glory, there are broad classifications of telestial people. These are they "who are of Paul, and of Apollos, and of Cephas. These are they who say they are some of one and some of another—some of Christ and some of John, and some of Moses, and some of Elias, and some of Esaias, and some of Isaiah, and some of Enoch; but received not the gospel, neither the testimony of Jesus, neither the prophets, neither the everlasting covenant" (D&C 76:99–101). Further, the telestial kingdom is the final abode of liars, sorcerers, adulterers and whoremongers, and, as John the Revelator learned, of murderers (D&C 76:103; Revelation 21:8; 22:15).

Finally, this portion of the vision adds the sobering detail that the inhabitants of the telestial world will be "as innumerable as the stars in the firmament of heaven, or as the sand upon the seashore" and that the inhabitants will be "servants of the Most High; but where God and Christ dwell they cannot come, worlds without end" (D&C 76:109, 112).

Although the telestial kingdom is the lowest of the kingdoms of glory, the inhabitants of that glory will be "heirs of salvation" in a world that "surpasses all understanding" (D&C 76:88–89). Generally, the word *salvation* means in scripture exactly the same thing as *exaltation* or *eternal life* (D&C 6:13; 14:7; Alma 11:40). There are a few times in scripture, however, when *salvation* refers to something less than exaltation and this is one of those times (see also, for example, D&C 132:17). In this expansive sense, our Lord seeks to save all of his children with an everlasting salvation. And he does so, in that all but the sons of perdition eventually inherit a kingdom of glory (D&C 76:43). In fact, Elder Charles W. Penrose observed about the telestial kingdom: "While there is one soul of this race, willing and able to accept and obey the laws of redemption, no matter where or in what condition it may be found, Christ's work will be incomplete until that being is brought up from death and hell, and placed in a position of progress, upward and onward, in such glory as is possible for its enjoyment and the service of the great God.

"The punishment inflicted will be adequate to the wrongs performed. In one sense the sinner will always suffer its effects. When the debt is paid and justice satisfied; when obedience is learned through the lessons of sad experience; when the grateful and subdued soul comes forth from the everlasting punishment, thoroughly willing to comply with the laws once rejected; there will be an abiding sense of loss. The fullness of celestial glory in the presence and society of God and the Lamb are beyond the reach of that saved but not perfected soul, forever. The power of increase, wherein are dominion and exaltation and crowns of immeasurable glory, is not for the class of beings who have been thrust down to hell and endured the wrath of God for the period allotted by eternal judgment. . . .

"They cannot go up into the society of the Father nor receive of the presence of the Son, but will have ministrations of messengers from the terrestrial world, and have joy beyond all expectations and the conception of uninspired mortal minds. They will all bow the knee to Christ and serve God the Father, and have an eternity of usefulness and happiness in harmony with the higher powers. They receive the telestial glory."[14]

It is not uncommon to have a person not of our faith challenge the idea of "more heavens than one" as being odd or unbiblical or unnecessary. But just how odd is it? Just how strange, how unusual is this belief in varying degrees of reward hereafter? St. Augustine, who has exerted perhaps the most significant influence on both Roman Catholic and Protestant theology, wrote: "But who can conceive, not to say describe, *what degrees of honor and glory shall be awarded to the various degrees of merit? Yet it cannot be doubted that there shall be degrees.* And in that blessed city there shall be this great blessing, that no inferior shall envy any superior, as now the archangels are not envied by the angels, because *no one will wish to be what he has not received.*"[15]

During the First Great Awakening, the early American theologian Jonathan Edwards stated: "There are many mansions in God's house because heaven is intended for various degrees of honor and blessedness. Some are designed to sit in higher places there than others; some are designed to be advanced to higher degrees of honor

---

14. *"Mormon" Doctrine*, 72, 74–75.
15. *The City of God*, 865; emphasis added.

and glory than others are."[16] Similarly, John Wesley, essentially the father of Methodism, spoke of some persons enjoying "higher degrees of glory" hereafter: "There is an inconceivable variety in the degrees of reward in the other world. . . . In worldly things men are ambitious to get as high as they can. Christians have a far more noble ambition. The difference between the very highest and the lowest state in the world is nothing to the smallest difference between the degrees of glory."[17]

The vision is a remarkable oracle. "Nothing could be more pleasing to the Saints upon the order of the Kingdom of the Lord," Joseph Smith stated, "than the light which burst upon the world through the foregoing vision." The Prophet described it as "a transcript from the records of the eternal world. The sublimity of the ideas; the purity of the language; the scope for action . . . are so much beyond the narrow-mindedness of men, that every man is constrained to exclaim: 'It came from God.'"[18]

CONCLUSION

The Prophet Joseph Smith and Sidney Rigdon received the vision of the glories in February of 1832. God continued to reveal himself, his plan, and the doctrines of salvation, precept upon precept, during the next twelve years of the Prophet's mortal ministry and subsequently to his successors. Sometime after the coming of Elijah and the restoration of the sealing powers and fulness of the priesthood in April 1836, the Prophet introduced the doctrine and practice of celestial marriage to the Saints. He taught that "in the celestial glory there are three heavens or degrees; and in order to

16. In Wilkinson, *A Life God Rewards,* 119. Edwards's use of the word *designed* indicates his Reformed or Calvinistic perspective on predestination.

17. "Notes on the Revelation of Jesus Christ," chapter 7, note 9, in Wilkinson, *A Life God Rewards,* 120–21; emphasis added.

18. *Joseph Smith* [manual], 219.

obtain the highest, a man must enter into this order of the priesthood [meaning the new and everlasting covenant of marriage]; and if he does not, he cannot obtain it. He may enter into the other, but that is the end of his kingdom; he cannot have an increase" (D&C 131:1–4). Or, as the Prophet stated another way, "except a man and his wife enter into an everlasting covenant and be married for eternity, while in this probation, by the power and authority of the Holy Priesthood, they will cease to increase when they die; that is, they will not have any children after the resurrection. But those who are married by the power and authority of the priesthood in this life, and continue without committing the sin against the Holy Ghost, will continue to increase and have children in the celestial glory."[19]

Truly there are many mansions of the Father (John 14:1–2), and the Holy One of Israel has made provision for his people to attain to that level of glory hereafter that they are willing to receive. In describing the revolutionary nature of the vision, Richard Bushman pointed out that "the most radical departure of 'the Vision' was not the tripartite heaven but the contraction of hell. . . . The doctrine recast life after death." In the vision, "a permanent hell threatened very few [the sons of perdition]. The question was not escape from hell but closeness to God. God scaled the rewards to each person's capacity."[20]

Here is a message of hope, a breath of fresh air amid the fiery winds of sectarian theology, a doctrine that manifests the mercy and wisdom of our Divine Redeemer.

---

19. *Joseph Smith* [manual], 479.
20. *Rough Stone Rolling,* 199.

Chapter 11

MAN—IN THE
BEGINNING WITH GOD

Kirtland, Ohio, May 1833. Between June and October 1830 while translating the Bible, Joseph Smith and his scribe discovered a doctrine that would in time prove to be one of the most distinctive teachings in Mormonism—namely, that humankind and all things on earth were created spiritually before they were naturally upon the face of the earth. It would be three years, however, before this monumental truth would be expanded upon by additional revelation (D&C 93) and another eleven years after that before it would reach the theological summit it achieved in the King Follett discourse.

During my undergraduate years as a student at Brigham Young University, one of my favorite religion instructors began our Doctrine and Covenants class with words something like this: "Today we will discuss one of the greatest revelations ever given to the human family." I was a bit surprised by his comment, given that we had already studied the vision of the glories (D&C 76) and the revelation known as the Olive Leaf (D&C 88). The teacher added: "If I were told that I was being abandoned on a desert island and that I would be allowed only one religious document, I think I would choose the revelation we are about to study." We turned as a class to Doctrine and Covenants 93 and began what was for me an exploration of some of the most profound doctrinal insights of the Restoration. Although there is no way in a book of this size that we could even begin to delve into each of the revelations given to the Prophet Joseph Smith, I have chosen to devote this chapter to one revelation, for it is truly a pearl of great price. Though our principal emphasis will be on the doctrine of premortal existence, we will first attend to other magnificent theological concepts in Doctrine and Covenants 93.

GOD MAY BE KNOWN AND SEEN

For centuries upon centuries theologians and religionists had yielded to the philosophical notion of God as the distant deity, the wholly other, the unknowable, unreachable, and certainly unseeable One. They had succumbed to the idea that because God is infinite and eternal and perfect, and because we are finite and mortal and imperfect, any concept that humans might devise about God would obviously be deficient at best and perverse at worst. That is, since we cannot explain what and who God is, we can only speak in terms of what he (or she or it) *is not*. And further, because God is immaterial, because he does not have form or does not have substance, he can certainly never be seen by the human eye. Thus I suppose it is neither coincidental nor unimportant that section 93 begins with this remarkable verse: "Verily, thus saith the Lord: It shall come to pass that every soul who forsaketh his sins and cometh unto me, and calleth on my name, and obeyeth my voice, and keepeth my commandments, shall see my face and know that I am" (D&C 93:1). This is a restatement of the promise given earlier to the School of the Prophets: "And if your eye be single to my glory, your whole bodies shall be filled with light, and there shall be no darkness in you; and that body which is filled with light comprehendeth all things."

Now note the divine charge given to the Lord's children: "Therefore, sanctify yourselves that your minds become single to God, and *the days will come that you shall see him; for he will unveil his face unto you,* and it shall be in his own time, and in his own way, and according to his own will" (D&C 88:67–68; emphasis added).

There it is: what for the larger Christian world would have been unthinkable is spelled out to the Saints. We may know God. We may be filled with his light. We may be sanctified and cleansed from the blood and sins of this world. We may so live as to be able, in the Lord's own time and according to his omniscient will, to see his face and have our faith and hope transformed into perfect knowledge. The theological chasm that had been put in place by learned religious thinkers was bridged by means of a revelation to an unlearned seeker after truth.

THE LIGHT OF CHRIST

One day, whether in this life or the next, faithful persons whose lives qualify them to see their Master will appreciate more than ever that he is "the true light that lighteth every man that cometh into the world" (D&C 93:2). Because Jehovah was the foreordained Redeemer and Savior of worlds (D&C 76:22–24; Moses 1:32–35), the Lamb slain from the foundation of the world (Revelation 5:6; 13:8; Moses 7:47), the Father's plan became his by adoption. The gospel of God (Romans 1:1–3) thus became known as the gospel of Jesus Christ. Because Elohim has invested his Beloved Son with his own attributes and powers (Mosiah 15:3; D&C 93:4) and because the "Father of lights" (James 1:17) has ordained that Christ is the Light of lights and the Light of the world, those powers of life and light that we know as the power of God have come to be known as the Light of Christ or the Spirit of Jesus Christ.

The Light of Christ has both natural and redemptive functions.

Elder Parley P. Pratt, an attentive student of the Prophet Joseph Smith, explained: "It is, in its less refined existence, the physical light that reflects from the sun, moon, and stars, and other substances, and, by reflection on the eye, makes visible the truths of the outward world. It is also in its higher degrees the intellectual light of our inward and spiritual organs, by which we reason, discern, judge, compare, comprehend, and remember the subjects within our reach. Its inspiration constitutes instinct in animal life, reason in man, and vision in the prophets, and is continually flowing from the Godhead throughout all his creations."[1] The Holy Ghost, who is a male personage of spirit, draws upon the Light of Christ to communicate sacred truths and to dispense spiritual gifts to a myriad of beings separated in time and space (Moroni 10:17).[2]

The same power that makes it possible for us to see with our physical eyes also makes it possible for us to see with our spiritual eyes (D&C 88:6–13). Discernment, the innate capacity to distinguish good from evil and the relevant from the irrelevant, also comes through this Spirit of Jesus Christ (Moroni 7:12–19). Further, those who are true to this Spirit within them—which includes their conscience and thus the canons of right and wrong and decency in society—will be led, whether in this life or the next, to the higher light of the Holy Ghost that comes through the gospel covenant (D&C 84:44–53).

Elder Bruce R. McConkie wrote: "The light of Christ (also called the Spirit of Christ and the Spirit of the Lord) is a light, a power, and an influence that proceeds forth from the presence of God to fill the immensity of space. . . . It is the agency of God's power and the law by which all things are governed. It is also the agency used by the Holy Ghost to manifest truth and dispense

---

1. *Key to the Science of Theology*, 25.
2. See Smith, *Doctrines of Salvation*, 1:54; McConkie, *New Witness for the Articles of Faith*, 258.

spiritual gifts to many people at one and the same time. . . . It is in this way that the person of the Holy Ghost makes his influence felt in the heart of every righteous person at one and the same time."[3]

The Savior goes on to explain in this amazing revelation that those who see his face will know and understand that "I am in the Father, and the Father in me, and the Father and I are one." A modern apostle, Elder Jeffrey R. Holland, spoke of the Latter-day Saint concept of the oneness of the Father, Son, and Holy Ghost: "We believe these three divine persons constituting a single Godhead are united in purpose, in manner, in testimony, in mission. We believe Them to be filled with the same godly sense of mercy and love, justice and grace, patience, forgiveness, and redemption. I think it is accurate to say we believe They are one in every significant and eternal aspect imaginable *except* believing Them to be three persons combined in one substance, a Trinitarian notion never set forth in the scriptures because it is not true."[4]

The revelation then continues with language reminiscent of the words of Abinadi in which he spoke of Jesus Christ as both the Father and the Son (Mosiah 15:1–4). Christ is the Father because God the Father "gave me of his fulness" (D&C 93:4)—the fulness of his powers, attributes, glory, and even his name.[5] Christ is the Son "because I was in the world and made flesh my tabernacle, and dwelt among the sons of men" (D&C 93:4).

The revelation then speaks in language similar to that found in the forepart of the Gospel of John, which is generally believed to be taken from the writings of John the Baptist (D&C 93:6, 18).[6] John

3. *New Witness for the Articles of Faith*, 70.

4. "The Only True God and Jesus Christ Whom He Hath Sent," *Ensign*, Nov. 2007, 40.

5. See "The Father and the Son: A Doctrinal Exposition of the First Presidency and the Council of the Twelve Apostles," 30 June 1916, in Talmage, *Articles of Faith*, 465–73; see also Clark, *Messages of the First Presidency*, 5:26–34.

6. See Orson Pratt, in *Journal of Discourses*, 16:58; Taylor, *Mediation and Atonement*, 55; McConkie, *Doctrinal New Testament Commentary*, 1:70–71.

"bore record, saying: I saw his glory, that he was in the beginning, before the world was; therefore in the beginning the Word was, for he was the Word, even the messenger of salvation—the light and the Redeemer of the world; the Spirit of truth, who came into the world, because the world was made by him, and in him was the life of men and the light of men" (D&C 93:7–9). We will speak more of Christ's premortal existence shortly.

OUR LORD'S PATHWAY TO GODHOOD

With divine assistance, people are in a position to grow into the attributes and powers of the Spirit through repentance and subsequent faithfulness: they may receive what this marvelous oracle calls "grace for grace." Of the Savior, the revelation states that he "received not of the fulness [of the glory and power of the Father] at the first, but received grace for grace" (D&C 93:12). To receive *grace for grace* is to receive of the Father as we give to others. One writer put it this way: "Grace may be defined as an unearned gift or endowment given as a manifestation of divine love and compassion, for which the recipient does not pay an equivalent price. But though grace is unearned, it need not be unmerited. When Jesus received the attributes and powers of his Father's glory, He received grace for grace; that is, He received the divine endowments of the Father's glory as He gave grace to others. Service and dedication to the welfare of others, in doing the will of the Father, therefore were keystone principles in Christ's spiritual development. Jesus had also covenanted with the Father that He would consecrate the glory which He would receive and develop in others to the Man of Holiness [Moses 4:2]. Here, too, He promised to give grace in order to receive grace."[7]

The revelation continues: "And he [Jesus] received not of the

_____

7. Andrus, *God, Man and the Universe,* 206.

fulness at first, but continued from grace to grace, until he received a fulness" (D&C 93:13). To grow *from grace to grace* implies a developmental process, a progression from one level of spiritual attainment to a higher. Joseph Smith, in the King Follett sermon, provided a definition of eternal life as that of knowing "the only wise and true God." He further taught: "You have got to learn how to be gods yourselves, and to be kings and priests to God, the same as all Gods have done before you, namely, by going from one small degree to another, and from a small capacity to a great one; from grace to grace, from exaltation to exaltation, until you attain to the resurrection of the dead, and are able to dwell in everlasting burnings."[8]

The revelation then sets forth the true meaning of worship: "I give unto you these sayings"—concerning how and in what manner Christ received grace for grace and grew from grace to grace— *"that you may understand and know how to worship, and know what* [Whom] *you worship,* that you may come unto the Father in my name, and in due time receive of his fulness. For if you keep my commandments *you shall receive of his fulness, and be glorified in me as I am in the Father; therefore, I say unto you, you shall receive grace for grace"* (D&C 93:19–20; emphasis added). We worship God as did our Master, Jesus Christ, by participating in what James called "pure religion"—namely, visiting "the fatherless and widows in their affliction, and [keeping ourselves] unspotted from the vices of the world" (JST, James 1:27). We worship God by following the example of him who went about doing good (Acts 10:38). Thus perfect worship is emulation, or what Thomas à Kempis called the "Imitation of Christ." It is to be holy as Jehovah is holy. It is to be pure as Christ is pure. It is to do the things that enable us to become more and more like our blessed Lord.

---

8. *Joseph Smith* [manual], 221.

In the Beginning

Clearly one of the most distinctive doctrines of The Church of Jesus Christ of Latter-day Saints is the doctrine of the premortal existence of all humankind, the concept that every human being lived as a spirit before he or she was born into this sphere of existence. The larger Christian world has always believed in a premortal existence, insofar as God the Father and Christ the Son are concerned; that truth is clearly stated in John 1:1–2. The doctrine of the premortal existence of all human beings was in fact expounded principally by Origen, a man considered by many to be the first significant Christian theologian. This belief was, however, officially condemned by the Church in A.D. 543 and slipped from the stage of Christian doctrine.[9]

So where and when did this doctrine originate within the restored Church? We certainly believe that it is alluded to in the Bible (Job 38:4, 7; Jeremiah 1:5–6; John 9:1–3; Revelation 12:7–11). It appears, however, that the first mention of such an idea within the restored gospel is to be found in the Book of Mormon, in Alma 13. Here we read of men being prepared and ordained (today we would say foreordained) to the priesthood "from the foundation of the world," an expression that we have come to equate with our first estate. We are told, for example, that these were foreordained "on account of their exceeding faith and good works; in the first place [in that premortal existence] being left to choose good or evil; therefore they having chosen good, and exercising exceedingly great faith, are called with a holy calling. . . . And thus they have been called to this holy calling on account of their faith, while others would reject the Spirit of God on account of the hardness of their hearts

---

9. For a comprehensive discussion of the doctrine throughout religious and literary history, see Givens, *When Souls Had Wings*. For a brief consideration of the Latter-day Saint understanding of premortal existence, see Givens, *Wrestling the Angel*, 147–75; see also Top, *The Life Before*.

and blindness of their minds, while, if it had not been for this [their lack of faith in this world] they might have had as great privilege as their [faithful] brethren" (Alma 13:3–4).[10] And of course the Book of Mormon prophet-writers speak repeatedly of the plan of salvation, the atonement of Jesus Christ, and blessings of the gospel and priesthood that were prepared from the foundation of the world (1 Nephi 10:18; 2 Nephi 9:18; Mosiah 4:6–7; 15:19; 18:13; Alma 12:25, 30; 13:5, 7; 18:39; 22:13; 42:26; 3 Nephi 1:14; Ether 3:14; Moroni 8:12).

In speaking of the doctrine of the premortal existence of the children of God, Elder Orson Pratt pointed out that this doctrine "is inculcated in some small degree in the Book of Mormon. However, I do not think that I should have ever discerned it in that book had it not been for the new translation of the Scriptures, that throwing so much light and information on the subject, I [later] searched the Book of Mormon to see if there were indications in it that related to the preexistence of man." Elder Pratt then spoke of rediscovering the appearance of the premortal Christ to the brother of Jared (Ether 3) and adds: "I think there are one or two other passages in which it is just referred to."[11] For all we know, what was true of Brother Orson may also have been true of Brother Joseph— he may not have grasped the rather cryptic allusions to premortal existence in the Book of Mormon; he certainly does not seem to have referred to these Book of Mormon passages in sermons or writings in which premortal existence was the topic of conversation.

---

10. President Harold B. Lee provided a fascinating commentary on the scriptural phrase "many are called, but few are chosen" (Matthew 22:14): "This suggests that even though we have our free agency here, there are many who were foreordained before the world was, to a greater state than they have prepared themselves for here. Even though they might have been among the noble and great, from among whom the Father declared he would make his chosen leaders, they may fail of that calling here in mortality" ("Understanding Who We Are Brings Self-Respect," *Ensign*, Jan. 1974, 5).

11. In *Journal of Discourses*, 15:249.

As Elder Pratt stated, this doctrine begins to make its way onto the grand stage of restored truth in a more visible manner through the Prophet's inspired translation of the King James Bible, the "new translation of the Scriptures." This sacred labor began with the translation of the opening chapters of Genesis in June 1830. Between June and October the translators made their way deliberately through those early chapters of the Bible until they came to the end of the creation of the heavens and the earth. Then these words appear in the New Translation: "And now, behold, I say unto you, that these are the generations of the heaven and of the earth, when they were created, in the day that I, the Lord God, made the heaven and the earth, and every plant of the field before it was in the earth, and every herb of the field before it grew. For *I, the Lord God, created all things, of which I have spoken, spiritually, before they were naturally upon the face of the earth.* For I, the Lord God, had not caused it to rain upon the face of the earth. And *I, the Lord God, had created all the children of men; and not yet a man to till the ground; for in heaven created I them;* and there was not yet flesh upon the earth, neither in the water, neither in the air" (JST, Genesis 2:4–6; Moses 3:4–5; emphasis added).

Soon thereafter we read in the inspired translation about the council in heaven in which Jehovah was chosen to be the Savior and Redeemer, the chief proponent and advocate of the Father's plan of salvation, whereas Lucifer's nefarious amendatory offer was refused, and he and his minions were cast down to earth (JST, Genesis 3:1–5; Moses 4:1–4).[12] Given within a matter of weeks, another revelation spoke of a much larger group in the council: *"A third part of the hosts of heaven turned away from me because of their agency; and they were thrust down, and thus came the devil and his angels"* (D&C

---

12. It is noteworthy that there is no mention in this account of any of the children of God being in attendance at this council other than Jehovah and Lucifer. We learn that detail from the account in Abraham 3:22–28.

29:36–37; emphasis added). Then within three months Joseph and the Saints learned via the Bible translation that God "called upon our father Adam by his own voice, saying: I am God; I made the world, and *men before they were in the flesh*" (JST, Genesis 6:52; Moses 6:51; emphasis added).

"We know that we had our agency before this world was," President Thomas S. Monson observed, "and that Lucifer attempted to take it from us. He had no confidence in the principle of agency or in us and argued for imposed salvation. He insisted that with his plan none would be lost, but he seemed not to recognize—or perhaps, not to care—that in addition, none would be any wiser, any stronger, any more compassionate, or any more grateful if his plan were followed."[13]

Now, returning to Doctrine and Covenants 93 (6 May 1833), we read the following: "And now, verily I say unto you, *I was in the beginning with the Father, and am the Firstborn*; and all those who are begotten through me are partakers of the glory of the same, and are the church of the Firstborn" (D&C 93:21–22; emphasis added). Herein is the scriptural basis for the Latter-day Saint concept that Jehovah was the firstborn spirit child of the Father, a teaching mentioned in the New Testament as well (Romans 8:29; Colossians 1:15). An official proclamation by the First Presidency of the Church affirmed: "Jesus . . . is the firstborn among all the sons of God—the first begotten in the spirit, and the only begotten in the flesh. He is our elder brother, and we, like Him, are in the image of God."[14]

Section 93 continues: "Ye were also in the beginning with the Father; that which is Spirit, even the Spirit of truth. . . . Man was also in the beginning with God. Intelligence, or the light of truth, was not created or made, neither indeed can be. All truth

13. *Teachings of Thomas S. Monson*, 14.
14. "The Origin of Man," Nov. 1909, in Clark, *Messages of the First Presidency*, 4:203.

is independent in that sphere in which God has placed it, to act for itself, as all intelligence also; otherwise there is no existence" (D&C 93:23–30).[15] When one reflects on just how early in the Restoration this revelation was given, it is rather astonishing to contemplate what the God of heaven was willing to communicate to his children: that there is something within the human being—call it intelligence or ego or some primal essence—that has always lived, indeed had no beginning. Most of us can wrap our minds around the truth that we will continue to live after this mortal life comes to an end, that there is in fact an immortality of the soul. Christians in particular look to the atonement and resurrection of Jesus Christ with gratitude and awe for his victory over the grave and the promise that because he rose from the tomb, so will each and every one of us (1 Corinthians 15:21–22).

This revelation to Joseph Smith provides a unique and profound insight into the concept of immortality, a perspective that is singularly Latter-day Saint—namely, that we have been, are, and will forevermore be immortal persons. What Jesus Christ made possible for each of earth's inhabitants is the inseparable union of body and spirit that comes with the resurrection. As Latter-day Saint philosopher Truman Madsen put it, "Man as a self had a beginningless beginning. He has never been identified wholly with any other being. Nor is he a product of nothing."[16]

As to exactly what intelligence is, President Joseph Fielding Smith wrote: "The Latter-day Saints believe that man is a spirit clothed with a tabernacle of flesh and bones, the intelligent part of which was never created or made, but existed eternally. This belief is based upon a revelation given to the Church, May 6, 1833, at

---

15. Truman G. Madsen commented on the phrase "otherwise there is no existence": "I interpolate cautiously that the meaning here is 'Otherwise there is no existence of selves' distinct from inanimate reality" (*Eternal Man*, 25n6).

16. *Eternal Man*, 24.

Kirtland, Ohio [D&C 93]. . . . Some of our writers have endeavored to explain what an intelligence is, but to do so is futile, for we have never been given any insight into this matter beyond what the Lord has fragmentarily revealed. We know, however, that there is something called intelligence which always existed. It is the real eternal part of man, which was not created or made. This intelligence combined with the spirit constitutes a spiritual identity or individual."[17]

One other doctrinal matter associated with man's first estate taught in this supernal revelation is worthy of at least a brief comment. The Lord declared: "*Every spirit of man was innocent in the beginning;* and God having redeemed man from the fall, *men became again, in their infant state, innocent before God*" (D&C 93:38; emphasis added). We know that one of the unconditional benefits and blessings deriving from the matchless atonement of Christ is that little children will live; that they are redeemed from the foundation of the world; that they are freed from what the Christian world has come to know as the "original sin"; that those who die before the age of accountability are saved in the celestial kingdom. In short, "little children are whole, for they are not capable of committing sin; wherefore the curse of Adam is taken from them in me; that it hath no power over them" (Moroni 8:8; see also Mosiah 3:16; 15:25; D&C 29:46; 74:7; 137:10; Moses 6:53–54; JST, Matthew 19:13).

What, then, would the scriptural verse mean when it states that persons become *again,* "in their infant state, innocent before God"? Could this phrase not be a faithful witness of the infinite scope

---

17. *Progress of Man,* 10–11. At least two schools of thought have arisen to explain what intelligence is: One school proposes that "an intelligence" or "intelligences" existed as conscious, agency-equipped, identities forever; the second suggests that while intelligence is eternal, such attributes as consciousness, agency, and identity come into being at the time of spirit birth. For a thorough discussion of this issue, see Top, *The Life Before,* 39–51.

of the Atonement, in this case, the timeless nature of our Lord's atoning sacrifice? As discussed in Chapter 6, Restoration scripture and prophetic pronouncements are consistent in declaring that Christian prophets have declared Christian doctrine and officiated in Christian ordinances since the days of Adam and Eve. Truly, "as many as would believe and be baptized in his holy name, and endure in faith to the end, should be saved—not only those who believed after he came in the meridian of time, in the flesh, but all those from the beginning, even as many as were before he came, who believed in the words of the holy prophets, . . . who truly testified of him in all things, should have eternal life, as well as those who should come after" (D&C 20:25–27; compare Alma 39:17–19).

Let us now take this conversation a step further. What did Enoch and John the Revelator mean when they referred to the Savior as "the Lamb . . . slain from the foundation of the world"? (Moses 7:47; Revelation 13:8). Knowing as we do that there was a gradation of spirits in the premortal world, that following their spirit birth no two spirits remained the same,[18] that there were spirits who chose to follow Lucifer and rebel against the Father and his Beloved Son, and thus that sin existed in the first estate as it exists in our second estate—knowing these things, were Enoch and John teaching that the means whereby remission of sins could be obtained there, in the premortal state, came in the same way that it comes to us here, through faith and repentance in the name of Jesus Christ and by virtue of the Atonement that he would make in the meridian of time?

Elder Orson Pratt taught: "We see no impropriety in Jesus offering Himself as an acceptable offering and sacrifice before the Father to atone for the sins of His brethren, committed, not only in the second, but also in the first estate. Certain it was, that the work

---

18. See McConkie, *Mortal Messiah*, 1:23.

which Jesus was to accomplish, was known in the Grand Council where the rebellion broke out. . . . Why was the Lamb considered as 'slain from the foundation of the world'? If there were no persons who had sinned in their first estate, that could be benefited by the sufferings of their elder brother, then we can see no reason for considering Him at that early period, as already slain: the very fact, that the atonement which was to be made in a future world, was considered as already having been made, seems to show that there were those who had sinned, and who stood in need of the atonement. The nature of the sufferings of Christ was such that it could redeem the spirits of men as well as their bodies."[19]

Additional Insights from Abraham

On 1 March 1842 Joseph the Prophet began publishing excerpts in the *Times and Seasons* from his translation of the book of Abraham. A few matters from that translation pertain specifically to the premortal existence. Abraham was permitted to see God face to face and was then granted a vision of the nature and order of the cosmos. But his recitation of detail concerning the planets and the stars was intended to do more than make him a proficient astronomer; rather, Abraham was given to understand that these physical realities were in fact pointing to greater and grander spiritual realities. Abraham's was a lesson in priesthood government, for just as there is one star above another, moving gradually closer to the highest star, Kolob, the one "set nigh unto the throne of God" (Abraham 3:9), so there is one spirit above another, moving

---

19. "The Pre-Existence of Man," *Seer* 1, no. 4 (Apr. 1853): 54. My friend and late colleague Robert J. Matthews mentioned to me once that after a long meeting of the Scriptures Publications Committee, he turned to Elder Bruce R. McConkie and inquired whether he might ask a doctrinal question. Elder McConkie replied, "Please do." Bob then asked the apostle if he felt that Doctrine and Covenants 93:38 was a reference to Christ's atonement covering all time, including sins committed in the first estate. Elder McConkie responded, "Well, what else could it mean?"

gradually to the greatest of all spirits, Jehovah, who is "like unto God." "And the Lord said unto me: These two facts do exist, that there are two spirits, one being more intelligent than the other; there shall be another more intelligent than they; I am the Lord thy God, I am more intelligent than they all" (Abraham 3:19).[20]

The vision continues, and Abraham is allowed to witness "the intelligences that were organized before the world was; and among all these there were many of the noble and great ones; and God saw these souls that they were good, and he stood in the midst of them, and he said: These I will make my rulers; for he stood among those that were spirits, and he saw that they were good; and he said unto me: Abraham, thou art one of them; thou wast chosen before thou wast born" (Abraham 3:22–23).

From that account we learn that spirits are "organized intelligences." Abraham then sees that the noble and great spirits were called upon to "go down, for there is space there, and . . . take of these materials, and . . . make an earth whereon these [the assembled spirit children of God] may dwell; and we will prove them herewith, to see if they will do all things whatsoever the Lord their God shall command them; and they who keep their first estate shall be added upon; . . . and they who keep their second estate shall have glory added upon their heads for ever and ever."

Then follows a two-verse summary of the fact that God the Father accepted the offer of Jehovah, the one "like unto God," to uphold the Father's plan for the salvation of his children, and rejected the selfish and destructive proposal of Lucifer. "The second was angry, and kept not his first estate; and, at that day, many followed after him" (Abraham 3:24–28).

---

20. Elder B. H. Roberts wrote of this verse: "I believe that this means more than that God is more intelligent than any other one of the intelligences. It means that *he is more intelligent than all of the other intelligences combined.* His intelligence is greater than that of the mass" (in *Teachings of the Prophet Joseph Smith,* 353n8; emphasis added).

Other vital and important truths set forth by the Prophet Joseph Smith concerning the eternal nature of God's children came precept upon precept in his King Follett discourse, delivered on 7 April 1844. In speaking of "the mind of man—the immortal spirit," the Prophet said: "Where did it come from? All learned men and doctors of divinity say that God created it in the beginning; but it is not so: the very idea lessens man in my estimation. . . . We say that God himself is a self-existent being. Who told you so? It is correct enough; but how did it get into your heads? Who told you that man did not exist in like manner upon the same principles? Man does exist upon the same principles. . . . I am dwelling on the immortality of the spirit of man. Is it logical to say that the intelligence of spirits is immortal, and yet that it had a beginning? The intelligence of spirits had no beginning, neither will it have an end. That is good logic. That which has a beginning may have an end. There never was a time when there were not spirits; for they are co-equal[21] with our Father in heaven."[22] In short, this property, called by philosophers *aseity* or necessary self-existence, is a characteristic of both Deity and humanity.

A Stranger Here

The great Christian apologist C. S. Lewis spoke often of those significant moments when individuals sense in their heart of hearts that there is much, much more to the universe than they had ever supposed; that we as human beings are part of something larger than our own family or community; that we seem occasionally to

---

21. Elder B. H. Roberts commented on this idea: "Undoubtedly the proper word here would be 'co-eternal,' not 'co-equal'" (*Teachings of the Prophet Joseph Smith*, 353n8). Another Latter-day Saint writer observed similarly: "Latter-day revelation declares that man existed as a conscious entity before his birth into mortality, and that the fundamental elements of life within man are coeval [coeternal] with God" (Andrus, *God, Man and the Universe*, 170).

22. *Joseph Smith* [manual], 209–10.

bump up against something eternal; and that in a vague and rather odd sort of way we are strangers to mortality, that we were made of the stuff of eternity. Lewis observed: "If I find in myself a desire which no experience in this world can satisfy, the most probable explanation is that I was made for another world. . . . Probably earthly pleasures were never meant to satisfy it, but only to arouse it, to suggest the real thing. . . . I must keep alive in myself the desire for my true country, which I shall not find until after death; I must never let it get snowed under or turned aside; I must make it the main object of life to press on to that other country and to help others to do the same."[23] Terryl and Fiona Givens observed that from a Restoration perspective, "It is more than the recurrent intimations of a different sphere, a different domain of existence only dimly perceived, that haunt us. It is the familiarity we cannot shake."[24]

The choice seer, Joseph Smith, was fearless in introducing theological concepts to a religious world that was anything but open to novelty. And his views were certainly novel, for they struck at the core of the Christian theological foundation and boldly called upon the religionists of his time to consider their ways. There is no small crowd of critics eager to attack the notion that the souls of mortal men and women are as immortal as an infinite and omnipotent God. They suppose that this idea inevitably demotes or in some way diminishes Deity, when in fact it elevates the human personality and provides a grand perspective on the purpose of life and the joys and delights, as well as the disappointments and tragedies, associated with this second estate. Terryl and Fiona Givens wrote, "Our profoundly felt frailty and dependence dispel any illusion that co-eternity means co-equality. Our perennial longing for Home affirms a relationship rooted in the love of a child for a tender parent."[25]

---

23. *Mere Christianity*, 121.
24. *The God Who Weeps*, 39.
25. *The God Who Weeps*, 54.

Prophets, seers, and revelators of the Church in an earlier day stated: "The doctrine of the preexistence, revealed so plainly, particularly in latter days, pours a wonderful flood of light upon the otherwise mysterious problem of man's origin. It shows that man, as a spirit, was begotten and born of heavenly parents, and reared to maturity in the heavenly mansions of the Father, prior to coming upon the earth in a temporal body to undergo an experience in mortality. It teaches that all men existed in the spirit before any man existed in the flesh, and that all who have inhabited the earth since Adam have taken bodies and become souls in like manner."[26]

And in our own time the First Presidency and Council of the Twelve Apostles affirmed that "all human beings—male and female—are created in the image of God. Each is a beloved son or daughter of heavenly parents, and, as such, each has a divine nature and destiny. Gender is an essential characteristic of individual premortal, mortal, and eternal identity and purpose. In the premortal realm, spirit sons and daughters knew and worshipped God as their Eternal Father and accepted His plan by which each of His children could obtain a physical body and gain earthly experience to progress toward perfection and ultimately realize his or her divine destiny as an heir of eternal life."[27]

"Important as is the body," President Russell M. Nelson pointed out, "it serves as a tabernacle for one's eternal spirit. Our spirits existed in the premortal realm, and will continue to live after the body dies. *The spirit provides the body with animation and personality.* In this life and in the next, spirit and body, when joined together, become a living soul of supernal worth."[28]

Another modern apostle, President Boyd K. Packer, observed: "I do not think the Lord is quite so hopeless about what's going on

---

26. "The Origin of Man," Nov. 1909, in Clark, *Messages of the First Presidency,* 4:205.
27. "The Family: A Proclamation to the World," *Ensign,* Nov. 2010, 129.
28. *Accomplishing the Impossible,* 41; emphasis added.

in the world as we are. He could put a stop to all of it any moment. But He will not! Not until every player has a chance to meet the test for which we were preparing before the world was, before we came into mortality." President Packer also observed: "This doctrine of premortal life was known to ancient Christians. For nearly five hundred years the doctrine was taught, but it was then rejected as a heresy. . . . Once they rejected this doctrine, the doctrine of pre-mortal life, . . . they could never unravel the mystery of life."[29]

CONCLUSION

Early in this dispensation Sidney Rigdon was informed that the Lord had "given unto him [the Prophet Joseph] the keys of the mystery of those things which have been sealed, even things which were from the foundation of the world, and the things which shall come from this time until the time of my coming" (D&C 35:18; compare 28:7; 64:5). And surely one of the greatest and grandest and most profound of those mysteries—sacred matters that the world cannot comprehend or appreciate—is the doctrine of the eternal existence of the children of God. And what a glorious truth it is! "I am a child of God with a spirit lineage to heavenly parents," Elder Dallin H. Oaks testified. "Knowledge of that parentage defines our eternal potential. That powerful idea is a potent antidepressant. It can strengthen each of us to make righteous choices and to seek the best that is within us."[30]

President Dieter F. Uchtdorf spoke tenderly to the Saints when he affirmed: "While we may look at the vast expanse of the universe and say, 'What is man in comparison to the glory of creation?' God Himself said we are the reason He created the universe! His work and glory—the purpose for this magnificent universe—is to save and exalt mankind. In other words, the vast expanse of eternity, the

---

29. "The Mystery of Life," *Ensign*, Nov. 1983, 16–18.
30. *With Full Purpose of Heart*, 46.

glories and mysteries of infinite space and time are all built for the benefit of ordinary mortals like you and me. Our Heavenly Father created the universe that we might reach our potential as His sons and daughters.

"This is a paradox of man," President Uchtdorf continued. *"Compared to God, man is nothing; yet we are everything to God.* While against the backdrop of infinite creation we may appear to be nothing, we have a spark of eternal fire burning within our breast. We have the incomprehensible promise of exaltation—worlds without end—within our grasp. And it is God's great desire to help us reach it."[31]

Philosopher Truman Madsen put it so beautifully: "One begins mortality with the veil drawn, but slowly he is moved to penetrate the veil within himself. He is, in time, led to seek the 'holy of holies' within the temple of his own being."[32] Elder Neal A. Maxwell commented on those poignant encounters: "Brothers and sisters, in some of those precious and personal moments of deep discovery, there will be a sudden surge of recognition of an immortal insight, a doctrinal déjà vu. We will sometimes experience a flash from the mirror of memory that beckons us forward toward a far horizon."[33]

These things are true. They matter. They are not merely the product of clever or whimsical theological explorations. They mark the path to understanding the God we worship and the Redeemer we seek to emulate, which is the path to life eternal (John 17:3). When received humbly and gratefully, these teachings are liberating and exhilarating. They point us to an infinite past and a never-ending future. In understanding and accepting them, we begin to turn the pages of our book of eternal possibilities.

---

31. "You Matter to Him," *Ensign,* Nov. 2011, 20; emphasis added.
32. *Eternal Man,* 20.
33. "Meeting the Challenges of Today," 156.

Chapter 12

FAITH UNTO LIFE
AND SALVATION

Kirtland, Ohio, Winter 1834–1835. In the revelation known to the Saints as the Olive Leaf (D&C 88), the Lord called upon the leading elders to establish a program of instruction, a training forum that would especially benefit those who would soon be called to the ministry. The School of the Prophets was established in January 1833. Journal and diary accounts describe the supernal spiritual experiences enjoyed by this group of men and also some of the curriculum, which included such things as grammar, biblical languages, and, of course, doctrine. By the winter of 1835–36 a formal series of lectures was begun, delivered by the leading Brethren to the elders of the Church.

The School of the Prophets proved to be a type of early missionary training center, so that those sent throughout the world to spread the news of the restored gospel might be "prepared in all things when I shall send you again to magnify the calling whereunto I have called you, and the mission with which I have commissioned you" (D&C 88:80). The Kirtland School was begun in February 1833. Of those days, the Prophet reports that they "had many glorious seasons of refreshing." Further, "great joy and satisfaction continually beamed in the countenances of the School of the Prophets, and the Saints, on account of the things revealed, and our progress of the knowledge of God."[1]

The School was interrupted as a result of the expulsion of the Saints from Missouri in 1833, but in November 1834 preparations were under way to continue the instruction. "It now being the last of the month," Joseph explained, "and the Elders beginning to come in, it was necessary to make preparations for the school for the Elders, wherein they might be more perfectly instructed in the great things of God, during the coming winter. A building for a printing office [in Kirtland] was nearly finished, and the lower story of this building was set apart for that purpose [the school] when it was completed. So the Lord opened the way according to our faith and works, and blessed be His name."[2]

During that winter of 1834–35, the Prophet Joseph Smith and his brethren in the Church's leadership prepared and delivered a series of lectures to the School of the Elders. These lectures came to be known as the Lectures on Faith. This collection of addresses is a systematic study of faith—what it is, the objects on which it rests, and the fruits that flow from it.[3] These seven lectures contain some of the most profound and mind-expanding teachings in our literature and are more than worthy of serious and sober reflection on the part of Latter-day Saints who desire to grow in faith and come unto Christ. President Joseph Fielding Smith expressed sorrow that the lectures were so little known among the Saints of the twentieth century: "I suppose that the rising generation knows little about the Lectures on Faith. . . . In my own judgment, these Lectures

1. History, 1838–1856, volume A-1 [23 December 1805–30 August 1834], The Joseph Smith Papers, accessed 15 Mar. 2016, http://josephsmithpapers.org/paperSummary /history-1838-1856-volume-a-1-23-december-1805-30-august-1834?p=287.

2. History, 1838–1856, volume B-1 [1 September 1834–2 November 1838], The Joseph Smith Papers, accessed 15 Mar. 2016, http://josephsmithpapers.org/paperSummary /history-1838-1856-volume-b-1-1-september-1834-2-november-1838?p=11.

3. See Lectures on Faith, 38–39.

are of great value. . . . They were not taken out of the Doctrine and Covenants [in 1921] because they contained false doctrine, and I consider them to be of extreme value in the study of the gospel of Jesus Christ." President Smith added that the Prophet Joseph compiled and "prepared them. There may have been some suggestions in them that came from some other brethren, but the Prophet himself revised and prepared these Lectures on Faith for publication."[4]

The Lectures on Faith were included in the first edition (1835) of the Doctrine and Covenants. That edition was made up of two parts: Part I was called "doctrine" and consisted of the Lectures on Faith; Part II was called "covenants" and consisted of many of the revelations received to that point in time. The Lectures on Faith remained in the Doctrine and Covenants until 1921.

LECTURE ONE

Lecture One is a discussion of the nature of faith. The lecture describes faith as "the first principle in revealed religion, and the foundation of all righteousness" (1:1). It shows from scripture that faith is not only the underlying principle behind all action but also "a principle of power." The lecture observes that, as taught in Hebrews 11:3, "the principle of power which existed in the bosom of God, by which the worlds were framed, was faith; and . . . it is by reason of this principle of power existing in the Deity, that all created things exist; so that all things in heaven, on earth, or under the earth exist by reason of faith as it existed in Him. . . . It is the principle by which Jehovah works, and through which he exercises power over all temporal as well as eternal things."[5]

The equation of faith as a principle of power is an important

---

4. *Seek Ye Earnestly*, 194.

5. *Lectures on Faith*, 3. Elder Bruce R. McConkie stated that the Light of Christ "is the power of God who sitteth upon his throne. *It may be that it is also priesthood and faith and omnipotence, for these too are the power of God*" (*New Witness for the Articles of Faith*, 257; emphasis added).

one. Faith thereby becomes more than a passive wish or even a strong longing or yearning for some eventuality to occur. It helps us to understand the Savior's statement, "If ye have faith, and doubt not, ye shall not only do this which is done to the fig tree [that is, wither it], but also if ye shall say unto this mountain, Be thou removed, and be thou cast into the sea; it shall be done. And all things, whatsoever ye shall ask in prayer, believing, ye shall receive" (Matthew 21:21–22).

The concept that it was by faith that God framed the worlds (Hebrews 11:3) and the subsequent discussion of that principle introduce us to a notion that is quite novel for most Saints—namely, that *God operates by faith.* In Lecture One we learn that "the principle of power which existed in the bosom of God, by which the worlds were framed, was faith; and that it is by reason of this principle of power existing in the Deity, that all created things exist; so that all things in heaven, on earth, or under the earth exist by reason of faith as it existed in Him. . . . It is the principle by which Jehovah works, and through which he exercises power over all temporal as well as eternal things. Take this principle or attribute—for it is an attribute—from the Deity, and he would cease to exist."[6]

---

6. *Lectures on Faith,* 3. Elder McConkie commented on this grand principle: "It is with faith or power as it is with knowledge. God himself is the very embodiment of this attribute. His infinite knowledge gives him infinite power. None can stay his hand. . . . Unless men know that God has all power (which power is itself faith), it is impossible for them to exercise faith in him unto life and salvation." Also, "in the eternal sense, because faith is the power of God himself, it embraces within its fold a knowledge of all things. This measure of faith, the faith by which the worlds are and were created and which sustains and upholds all things, is found only among resurrected persons. It is the faith of saved beings. But mortals are in process, through faith, of gaining eternal salvation. Their faith is based on a knowledge of the truth, within the meaning of Alma's statement that 'faith is not to have a perfect knowledge of things,' but that men have faith when they 'hope for things which are not seen, which are true.' In this sense faith is both preceded and supplanted by knowledge, and when any person gains a perfect knowledge on any given matter, then, as pertaining to that thing, he has faith no longer; or, rather, his faith is dormant; it has been supplanted by pure knowledge (Alma 32:21–34)" (*New Witness for the Articles of Faith,* 176–77, 209–10).

LECTURE TWO

Lecture Two is a statement of how faith comes—namely, by the power of human testimony. The brethren in the School of the Elders were taught (from Joseph's inspired translation of the first chapters of Genesis, what we have now as the book of Moses) that after Adam and Eve were cast from the Garden of Eden, they did not lose the knowledge they had gained in Eden. Although the knowledge of their premortal existence was veiled from memory, Adam's "transgression did not deprive him of the previous knowledge with which he was endowed, relative to the existence and glory of his Creator." That is, Adam and Eve "retained a knowledge of [God's] existence, and that sufficiently to move them to call upon him."[7]

Further, after the expulsion from Eden, God continued to reveal himself to our first parents. They in turn taught their children about the Almighty and the plan of salvation. "And the evidences which these men had of the existence of a God, was the testimony of their fathers in the first instance." This knowledge was transmitted from generation to generation, "as a matter of tradition at least; for we cannot suppose that a knowledge of this important fact could have existed in the mind of any of the before-mentioned individuals, without their having made it known to their posterity." And then, after a lengthy discussion of how old each of the patriarchs was when he died—an effort to demonstrate how the power of human testimony was transmitted and was thus the means by which men and women could have faith in the existence of God—comes this remarkable conclusion to the lecture: "We have seen that it was human testimony, and human testimony only, that excited this inquiry, in the first instance, in their minds. It was the credence they gave to the testimony of their fathers, this testimony having aroused their minds to inquire after the knowledge of God; the

---

7. *Lectures on Faith*, 14–15.

inquiry frequently terminated"—and note this profound truth—"indeed always terminated when rightly pursued, in the most glorious discoveries and eternal certainty."[8]

LECTURES THREE AND FOUR

Lecture Three gives prerequisites for the exercise of faith in God unto life and salvation:

"1. The idea that God actually exists;

"2. A correct idea of his character, perfections, and attributes; and,

"3. An actual knowledge that the course in life one is pursuing is according to the will of God."[9]

Both Lectures Three and Four deal with the character and attributes of God, establishing that God possesses all virtues, traits, and ennobling qualities in their perfection. That is what it means to be God. Thus God is all-wise, all-caring, all-truthful, all-benevolent, all-patient, and forevermore consistent, constant, and dependable. Further, in order to exercise faith in him, one must know that God embodies all of these attributes and qualities. How, for example, can one call upon the Almighty with confidence if there were any question about God's judgment, his sense of justice, or his approachability? How could one dare to call upon God for forgiveness if there were any doubt of God's willingness to forgive? "Such is the weakness of man," the brethren were taught, "and such his frailties, that he is liable to sin continually, and if God were not long-suffering, and full of compassion, gracious and merciful, and of a forgiving disposition, man would be cut off from before him, in consequence of which he would be in continual doubt and could not exercise faith; for where doubt is, there faith has no power."[10]

---

8. *Lectures on Faith,* 17, 23, 24.

9. *Lectures on Faith,* 38–39.

10. *Lectures on Faith,* 46.

In the same vein, consider our plight if there were any question in the mind of man about God having all power or knowing all things. "Without the knowledge of all things, God would not be able to save any portion of his creatures; for it is by reason of the knowledge which he has of all things, from the beginning to the end, that enables him to give that understanding to his creatures by which they are made partakers of eternal life; and if it were not for the idea existing in the minds of men that God had all knowledge it would be impossible for them to exercise faith in him." Anyone, therefore, who doubts God's power, knowledge, or ability will never acquire the kind and quality of faith that leads unto life and salvation. Truly, as stated in an earlier lecture, "God is the only supreme governor and independent being in whom all fullness and perfection dwell; who is omnipotent, omnipresent and omniscient; without beginning of days or end of life; and . . . in him every good gift and every good principle dwell."[11]

LECTURE FIVE

Lecture Five continues a discussion of the nature of God, focusing primarily on the perfections of Deity and the relationship of God the Father to God the Son. This lecture is particularly deep and penetrating and requires prayerful and serious reflection to grasp its message. Of Lecture Five, Elder Bruce R. McConkie wrote: "Using the holy scriptures as the recorded source of the knowledge of God, knowing what the Lord has revealed to them of old in visions and by the power of the Spirit, and writing as guided by that same Spirit, Joseph Smith and the early brethren of this dispensation prepared a creedal statement on the Godhead. It is without question the most excellent summary of revealed and eternal truth relative to the Godhead that is now extant in mortal

---

11. *Lectures on Faith*, 51–52, 10.

language. In it is set forth the mystery of Godliness; that is, it sets forth the personalities, missions, and ministries of those holy beings who comprise the supreme presidency of the universe. To spiritually illiterate persons, it may seem hard and confusing; to those whose souls are aflame with heavenly light, it is a nearly perfect summary of those things which must be believed to gain salvation."[12] Earlier he had stated: "In my judgment, it is the most comprehensive, intelligent, inspired utterance that now exists . . . in one place defining, interpreting, expounding, announcing, and testifying what kind of being God is. It was written by the power of the Holy Ghost, by the spirit of inspiration. It is, in effect, eternal scripture; it is true."[13]

As Latter-day Saints, we go to great lengths to establish that the Father and the Son are separate and distinct personages, separate Beings, that they are not somehow fused magically and intertwined, not merely two manifestations of the same Being. And yet, our Heavenly Father and his Beloved Son are infinitely more one than they are separate: They are separate in person and being, but they are one in glory, one in purpose, one in focus and mission, and one in the sense that they both possess all of the attributes of godliness in perfection. The brethren in the School of the Elders were also taught that they are one *in mind,* and that that oneness of mind is assured and maintained through the indwelling presence of the Holy Spirit. The Father and the Son possess "the same mind, the same wisdom, glory, power, and fullness—filling all in all; the Son being filled with the fullness of the mind, glory, and power; or, in other words, the spirit, glory, and power, of the Father."[14]

What may be a somewhat perplexing statement in Lecture Five is the following: "There are two personages who constitute the great, matchless, governing, and supreme power over all things, by whom

12. *New Witness for the Articles of Faith,* 72.
13. *The Lord God of Joseph Smith,* 4.
14. *Lectures on Faith,* 60.

all things were created and made. . . . They are the Father and the Son—*the Father being a personage of spirit, glory, and power*, possessing all perfection and fullness, *the Son*, who was in the bosom of the Father, *a personage of tabernacle* . . . possessing all the fullness of the Father, or the same fullness with the Father."[15] The puzzling part of this statement, of course, is "the Father being *a personage of spirit*." One possibility for understanding this passage is that Joseph Smith did not yet understand the corporeal or physical nature of God the Father. He might not have gained that understanding as a result of the First Vision in 1820, and, of course, he might not yet have understood it even in the winter of 1834–35, when the Lectures on Faith were delivered. His knowledge—like that of all mortals—was often gained incrementally, and his development in doctrinal understanding was thereby accomplished precept upon precept. The First Vision, in 1820, taught Joseph that the heavens were no longer sealed; that Satan was more than myth or metaphor; and that the Father and Son were separate and distinct Beings.

As we pointed out in Chapter 2, there is no mention in any of his known accounts of the First Vision that God has a physical body. The earliest reference we have to a sermon by Joseph Smith on the corporeality of God seems to be 5 January 1841. On that occasion William Clayton recorded the Prophet as saying: "That which is without body or parts is nothing. There is no other God in heaven but that God who has flesh and bones."[16] Six weeks later "Joseph said concerning the Godhead [that] it was not as many imagined—three heads and but one body; he said the three were separate bodies."[17] On 9 March 1841 he declared that "the Son had a tabernacle and so had the Father."[18] Finally, on 2 April 1843 in

---

15. *Lectures on Faith*, 60; emphasis added.
16. *Words of Joseph Smith*, 60.
17. *Words of Joseph Smith*, 63.
18. *Words of Joseph Smith*, 64.

Ramus, Illinois, Brother Joseph delivered instructions that are the basis for Doctrine and Covenants 130:22–23: "The Father has a body of flesh and bones as tangible as man's; the Son also; but the Holy Ghost . . . is a personage of Spirit."[19]

Another possibility for understanding this passage in Lecture Five is that Joseph Smith did understand that God has a body but that the *passage* has been misunderstood. If so, what could the phrase mean? To begin with, the complete expression is not that God the Father is "a personage of spirit" but "a personage of spirit, glory, and power." This expression may well be more a description of God's divine nature—a statement regarding his glorified and exalted status—than of his physical being. The word *spirit* as used, for example, in Moses 1, is a synonym for *glory* or *power:* His Spirit is his glory (Moses 1:9, 20). In the words of Elder McConkie, the phrase "a personage of spirit" refers to God's *spiritual* nature (compare 1 Corinthians 15:44; Alma 11:45; D&C 88:27; Moses 3:9)—that he is a resurrected and immortal being and as such is not subject to death; that is, God's is a *spiritual* body. "They are the two personages who came to Joseph Smith in the spring of 1820," Elder McConkie also wrote. "They are exalted men. Each is a personage of spirit; each is a personage of tabernacle. Both of them have bodies, tangible bodies of flesh and bones. They are resurrected beings. . . . A personage of tabernacle, as here used, is one whose body and spirit are inseparably connected and for whom there can be no death. A personage of spirit, as here used, . . . is a resurrected personage."[20]

One final thought on this matter. Professor Milton V. Backman brought to light many years ago a description of Mormonism by a Protestant clergyman in Ohio. Truman Coe, a Presbyterian minister who had for four years lived among the Saints in Kirtland,

---

19. *Words of Joseph Smith,* 173.
20. *New Witness for the Articles of Faith,* 226.

published the following regarding the beliefs of the Latter-day Saints in the 11 August 1836 *Ohio Observer:* "They contend that the God worshipped by the Presbyterians and all other sectarians is no better than a wooden god. *They believe that the true God is a material being, composed of body and parts;* and that when the Creator formed Adam in his own image, he made him about the size and shape of God himself."[21] If a minister of another faith had observed as early as 1836 that the Latter-day Saints were teaching that God has a body, it is not inconceivable that such things were known by Joseph Smith a year or so earlier at the time the School of the Elders were engaged in their study of the Lectures on Faith.

Lecture Five goes on to state how mortal man—frail and weak and in constant need of divine intervention—may grow and develop into a spiritual union with the Gods. The Holy Spirit, which conveys the mind of God, "is shed forth upon all who believe on his name and keep his commandments; and all those who keep his commandments shall grow up from grace to grace, and become heirs of the heavenly kingdom, and joint heirs with Jesus Christ; possessing the same mind, being transformed into the same image or likeness, even the express image of him who fills all in all; being filled with the fullness of his glory, and become one in him, even as the Father, Son and Holy Spirit are one."[22] We will pursue the implications of these statements in Chapter 20 when we look more closely at the doctrine of deification.

LECTURE SIX

Lecture Six discusses the third criterion for faith—a knowledge that the course in life we are pursuing is according to the divine will. This may well be the greatest challenge of all. The first two prerequisites require us to learn and understand something *about*

---

21. "Truman Coe's 1836 Description of Mormonism," 347, 354; emphasis added.
22. *Lectures on Faith*, 60.

God. The third requires that we know something *about ourselves.* That is to say, faith unto life and salvation is dependent on *confidence*—a word the Prophet uses interchangeably with *faith.*[23] We must have confidence that there is a God, confidence that he is who he says he is and that he has all power. And then, we must have some degree of confidence in ourselves, a quiet assurance that the Lord is pleased with us. Individuals who doubt their standing before God, who constantly question their own goodness and impugn their own righteousness, who are always and forever feeling inadequate and inferior—such persons cannot develop faith unto life and salvation. Though a certain measure of humility is typical of those who approach the Lord (2 Nephi 4:17–18; Ether 3:2), yet there must also be that hope in Christ—that anticipation of divine acceptance because of him, assurance of eternal life through him, and expectation of glory with him—if one is to chart a course and follow it to salvation:

"An actual knowledge to any person that the course of life which he pursues is according to the will of God, is essentially necessary to enable him to have that confidence in God without which no person can obtain eternal life. It was this that enabled the ancient saints to endure all their afflictions and persecutions, and to take joyfully the spoiling of their goods, knowing (not believing merely) that they had a more enduring substance." Indeed, "such was, and always will be, the situation of the saints of God, that unless they have an actual knowledge that the course they are pursuing is according to the will of God they will grow weary in their minds and faint."[24]

Stated another way, the people of God need to know that the Lord is pleased with them and that their acts and faith are acceptable to him if they are to have the moral courage and the faith to

---

23. *Lectures on Faith,* 68–69, 71.
24. *Lectures on Faith,* 67–68.

overcome the world. "For a man to lay down his all, his character and reputation, his honor, and applause, his good name among men, his houses, his lands, his brothers and sisters, his wife and children, and even his own life also—counting all things but filth and dross for the excellency of the knowledge of Jesus Christ [compare Philippians 3:7–10]—requires more than mere belief or supposition that he is doing the will of God; but actual knowledge, realizing that, when these sufferings are ended, he will enter into eternal rest, and be a partaker of the glory of God."[25]

And how do we gain such knowledge? How do we come to know that we are on course, that our lives are in order and thus approved of the heavens? The members of the School of the Elders were taught—and this is one of the transcendent truths of the Restoration—that we must be willing to *sacrifice* all things for the gospel cause. If we would become inheritors of all that the Father has, we must be willing to give up all that we have. With us, it must be the kingdom of God or nothing. "Let us here observe," the brethren learned, "that a religion that does not require the sacrifice of all things never has power sufficient to produce the faith necessary unto life and salvation."[26] Only a church that asks everything of its members—everything!—is in a position to produce in its members the faith that will lead them to the riches of eternity. Total surrender to God is always prerequisite to total victory. Only those who reach the point in their spiritual development where they are at last able to fully consecrate themselves to the Lord and his Church and kingdom, and to do so without let or hindrance, can gain that confidence before God of which the scriptures speak (D&C 121:45), a confidence that results in the promise of eternal life. In speaking of the ancients, the elders were instructed that "through the knowledge thus obtained [that their course in life

---

25. *Lectures on Faith*, 68.
26. *Lectures on Faith*, 69.

was in harmony with the divine will] their faith became sufficiently strong to lay hold upon the promise of eternal life, . . . and obtain the end of their faith, even the salvation of their souls."[27]

LECTURE SEVEN

In Lecture Seven is a most fascinating commentary on a passage from the apostle Paul, namely, "Without faith it is impossible to please [God]: for he that cometh to God must believe that he is, and that he is a rewarder of them that diligently seek him" (Hebrews 11:6). "Why is it impossible to please God without faith? The answer would be—Because without faith it is impossible for men to be saved; and as God desires the salvation of men, he must, of course, desire that they should have faith; and he could not be pleased unless they had, or else he could be pleased with their destruction."[28]

The Prophet and his associates taught of the fruits of faith, namely spiritual gifts enjoyed by the faithful and ultimately complete salvation granted to the fully consecrated. Further, we learn that one of the benefits of true faith is that it develops in us a Christlike character, leading us onward toward becoming ever more like Christ our Master. Jesus is indeed the Prototype of all saved beings. "Salvation consists in the glory, authority, majesty, power and dominion which Jehovah possesses and in nothing else; and no being can possess it but himself or one like him." The plan of salvation is in fact "a system of faith—it begins with faith, and continues by faith; and every blessing which is obtained in relation to it is the effect of faith, whether it pertains to this life or that which is to come."[29]

Having established what faith is, what underlies that faith, and

---

27. *Lectures on Faith,* 70.

28. *Lectures on Faith,* 74.

29. *Lectures on Faith,* 74–76, 80.

what is required of us to be counted among the favored of heaven, Lecture Seven continues: "We understand that *when a man works by faith he works by mental exertion instead of physical force. It is by words, instead of exerting his physical powers, with which every being works when he works by faith.*"[30] We are not to understand from this statement, however, that exercising faith is merely an intellectual exercise or that those with unusual mental capacities necessarily have more faith. Rather, the mental exertion of which the Prophet spoke seems to be the rigor and strenuous labor of soul searching and personal denial associated with coming to know the mind and will of God and then acting upon it.

It is sometimes surprising to observe how some of us use the word *faith* in our daily walk and talk. A missionary in Vienna says to his companion or to his district: "Come on, where's your faith? Why, if we had the faith, we could baptize this whole city!" Occasionally well-meaning but insensitive souls may explain to a sorrowing mother and father that if the family had sufficient faith, their daughter who has struggled with multiple sclerosis for five years would not be forced to suffer longer. Faith is not the power of positive thinking, although it is certainly better to be optimistic than cynical. Faith is not the personal resolve that enables us to will some difficult situation out of existence. Faith is not always the capacity to turn tragedy into celebration. We do not generate faith on our own, for it is the gift of God, a gift of the Spirit (1 Corinthians 12:9; Ephesians 2:8; Moroni 10:11). We do not act ourselves into faith, for faith is given by God to suit his purposes and bless the body of Christ, the Church.[31]

---

30. *Lectures on Faith,* 72; emphasis added.

31. Faith is both a gift of the Spirit and a choice. It is an endowment that must be bestowed upon us, but it is also, as Elder Neil L. Andersen pointed out, a decision, a choice. It is a decision or choice to be faithful, to follow the Lord and keep one's covenants, on the basis of testimony which has been planted in the heart (see "It's True, Isn't It? Then What Else Matters?" *Ensign,* May 2007, 74; "Faith Is Not by Chance, but by Choice," *Ensign,* Nov. 2015, 65).

People act in faith when they act according to the will of God. To say that another way, I have sufficient faith to move Mount Everest to the middle of Lake Michigan only when I know that the Lord wants it moved! I have faith or power to touch the hearts of others with my testimony of the truth only when they are prepared and ready for the word. That is, faith cannot override individual moral agency. Even the Master could not perform miracles in the midst of a people steeped in spiritual indifference. Jesus said in speaking of his own reception in Nazareth, "A prophet is not without honour, but in his own country, and among his own kin, and in his own house. And *he could there do no mighty work,* save that he laid his hands upon a few sick folk, and healed them" (Mark 6:4–5; emphasis added). Similarly, the prophet-leader Mormon loved his people and poured out his soul in prayer in their behalf; "nevertheless, *it was without faith,* because of the hardness of their hearts" (Mormon 3:12; emphasis added). Someone watching from the sidelines, unaware of what faith really is, might have cried out: "Come on, Mormon, where's your faith?"

Allow me to share a personal experience that illustrates this point. I remember very well one warm June evening in Louisiana, only a few months after I had returned from a mission, sitting with my mom and dad, watching television. The phone rang, and my father was quickly summoned to the hospital to give a priesthood blessing to someone. A sixteen-year-old boy, a friend of my younger sister, had suddenly collapsed on the softball field and been rushed to the hospital. My dad was told that the boy had been diagnosed with some strange degenerative nerve disease and that if something didn't happen soon, he would die. Dad and I rushed to the hospital, took the elevator to the fifth floor, and hurried into the waiting room. We were greeted with the news that the young man had passed away. We did our best to console the mourners and then made our way home.

As we walked in the back door, my sister asked, "How is he?"

I answered that her friend had died.

She came right back with, "Well, why didn't you raise him from the dead?"

Being the seasoned and experienced returned missionary that I was and having most all the answers to life's questions, I stuttered for a second and then turned to my father. "Yeah, why didn't we raise him from the dead?"

Dad's answer was kind but firm. It was also instructive. "Because the Spirit of the Lord didn't prompt us to do so," he said.

I have to admit that at that moment such a reply seemed like a kind of spiritual cop-out. But in the years that have followed, I came to know something about my dad's faith. He had been with his own father many years before when in fact the Spirit had prompted and the dead had been raised to life again. My dad knew when to move and when not to move. He had faith.

Now an illustration from the history of the Church. In 1838 Wilford Woodruff was traveling to Zion to assume his new assignment in the Quorum of the Twelve Apostles. On the journey, his wife, Phoebe, was overcome with a high fever. "I alighted at a house," Brother Woodruff wrote, "and carried my wife and her bed into it, with a determination to tarry there until she either recovered her health, or passed away. This was on Sunday morning, December 2nd.

"After getting my wife and things into the house and wood provided to keep up a fire, I employed my time in taking care of her. It looked as though she had but a short time to live.

"She called me to her bedside in the evening and said she felt as though a few moments more would end her existence in this life. She manifested great confidence in the cause she had embraced, and exhorted me to have confidence in God and keep his commandments.

"To all appearances, she was dying. I laid hands upon her . . . , and she soon revived and slept some during the night.

"December 3rd found my wife very low. I spent the day taking care of her. . . . She seemed to be gradually sinking, and in the evening her spirit apparently left her body, and she was dead.

"The sisters gathered around her body, weeping, while I stood looking at her in sorrow. The spirit and power of God began to rest upon me until, for the first time during her sickness, faith filled my soul, although she lay before me as one dead.

"I had some oil that was consecrated for my anointing while in Kirtland. . . . I then bowed down before the Lord and prayed for the life of my companion, and I anointed her body with the oil in the name of the Lord. I laid my hands upon her, and in the name of Jesus Christ, I rebuked the power of death and the destroyer, and commanded the same to depart from her, and the spirit of life to enter her body.

"Her spirit returned to her body, and from that hour she was made whole; and we all felt to praise the name of God, and to trust in Him and to keep His commandments.

"While this operation was going on with me (as my wife related afterwards) her spirit left her body, and she saw her body lying upon the bed, and the sisters weeping. She looked at them and at me, and upon her babe, and while gazing upon this scene, two personages came into the room . . . , and told her they had come for her. . . . One of these messengers informed her that she could have her choice: she might go to rest in the spirit world, or, on one condition she could have the privilege of returning to her tabernacle and continuing her labors upon the earth. The condition was, if she felt that she could stand by her husband, and with him pass through all the cares, trials, tribulations and afflictions of life which he would be called to pass through for the gospel's sake unto the end. When she looked at the situation of her husband and child she said: 'Yes, I will do it!'

"At the moment that decision was made the power of faith rested upon me, and when I administered unto her, her spirit entered her tabernacle, and she saw the messengers [go out] the door."[32]

Although the brethren in the School of the Elders were taught that working by faith is working by the power of "mental exertion," we need to understand that this does not mean that the higher the IQ the greater the faith. Not at all. "There may be those," Elder McConkie observed, "whose mental powers and thought processes are greater than any of the saints, but only persons who are in tune with the Infinite can exercise the spiritual forces and powers that come from him. . . . He . . . *must approve the use of his power in the case at hand. Faith cannot be exercised contrary to the order of heaven or contrary to the will and purposes of him whose power it is.* Men work by faith when they are in tune with the Spirit and when what they seek to do by mental exertion and by the spoken word is the mind and will of the Lord."[33]

The brethren were taught in the Lectures on Faith that "where doubt and uncertainty are there faith is not, nor can it be. For doubt and faith do not exist in the same person at the same time; so that persons whose minds are under doubts and fears cannot have unshaken confidence, and where unshaken confidence is not there faith is weak."[34] "Remember," President Thomas S. Monson declared, "that faith and doubt cannot exist in the same mind at the same time, for one will dispel the other. Cast out doubt. Cultivate faith. . . . My beloved brothers and sisters, fear not. Be of good cheer. The future is as bright as your faith."[35]

---

32. *String of Pearls,* 85; emphasis added.
33. *New Witness for the Articles of Faith,* 192; emphasis added.
34. *Lectures on Faith,* 71.
35. *Teachings of Thomas S. Monson,* 108.

CONCLUSION

Approximately half a century ago I found myself sitting in a religion class at Brigham Young University. It was my first experience involving a serious study of the restored gospel, beyond my missionary study, inasmuch as there had been no seminary or institute programs during the years of my youth in Louisiana. My BYU class was Religion 325, the second half of the Doctrine and Covenants. Often the instructor either quoted or read from the Lectures on Faith, which intrigued me, because I had never come across them before. One day after class I spoke to him about them.

He inquired, "Would you like to really understand the Lectures on Faith?"

I answered that I would.

His response startled me. "First, read them twenty times, and then start to study them."

Through the years since then I have taken my teacher's counsel seriously, and the results have been stunningly sweet. I do not know what parts of the Lectures were written by Joseph Smith himself, or what parts may have been prepared by Sidney Rigdon or William W. Phelps or any of the other early brethren. What I do know is that Brother Joseph compiled them, prepared them for publication, and included them in the first edition of the Doctrine and Covenants. That's a strong enough recommendation for me.

The Lectures on Faith, while not on the same level of canonical respectability as the revelations and translations of the Prophet, are nevertheless worthy of rigorous study. In the preface to the first edition of the Doctrine and Covenants (1835) are these words: "The first part of the book [the Lectures on Faith] will be found to contain a series of Lectures as delivered before a Theological class in this place, and in consequence of their embracing the important doctrine of salvation, we have arranged them into the following work."

It is my feeling that anyone who desires to know and understand something about the breadth and depth of the mind of Joseph Smith would be foolish to ignore or treat lightly the Lectures on Faith. They point us to the truth that the plan of salvation is in essence a "system of faith—it begins with faith, and continues by faith; and every blessing which is obtained in relation to it is the effect of faith, whether it pertains to this life or that which is to come."[36] Truly, when Jesus the Messiah offered to save the human family, he essentially proposed to "make them like unto himself, and he was like the Father, the great prototype of all saved beings; and for any portion of the human family to be assimilated into their likeness is to be saved."[37] My prayer for all of us is what the members of the Twelve in the meridian of time uttered in a moment when the Savior had charged them to undertake a difficult endeavor. They said to him simply, "Increase our faith" (Luke 17:3–5).

---

36. *Lectures on Faith*, 80.
37. *Lectures on Faith*, 79.

Chapter 13

THE PROMISES MADE
TO THE FATHERS

Kirtland, Ohio, March and April 1836. Joseph Smith stated on 30 March 1836: "I . . . observed to the quorums, that I had now completed the organization of the church, and we had passed through all the necessary ceremonies; that I had given them all the instruction they needed [to] go forth and build up the kingdom of God."[1] To be sure, the First Presidency, Quorum of the Twelve, and Quorum of the Seventy had been organized and put in place, as had the offices and quorums of the Aaronic and Melchizedek Priesthoods. Then, as a result of what took place on 3 April 1836 in the Kirtland Temple, nothing would ever be the same in the restored Church.

Much inspiration and insight may be gained through a simple reading of the book of Genesis. Timely and timeless lessons are to be found on almost every page—painful and joyous lessons from the lives of men and women of the past. Moses the Lawgiver, the author of the Pentateuch, leads the reader quickly through the Creation, the Fall, the Flood, and the scattering of the nations

---

1. History, 1838–1856, volume B-1 [1 September 1834–2 November 1838], The Joseph Smith Papers, accessed 15 Mar. 2016, http://josephsmithpapers.org/paperSummary /history-1838-1856-volume-b-1-1-september-1834-2-november-1838?p=179.

through the confounding of tongues. By the time we have read ten chapters in Genesis—fifteen pages in the Latter-day Saint edition of the King James Version of the Bible—we discover that more than two thousand years have passed since the Fall. It is as though Moses were eager to move the reader without delay to a certain point in history. That point in time is the life of the patriarchs—Abraham, Isaac, Jacob, and Joseph.

THE PATRIARCHS

There is sufficient information in our present Old Testament to understand to some degree the lives of the patriarchs—their upbringing, strengths and talents, and, of course, their tests and trials. One could certainly come away from a reading of Genesis understanding why Abraham became known as the "father of the faithful" and feeling deep gratitude and admiration for his goodness and integrity. When we study the lives of the patriarchs by the lamp of modern revelation, however, we recognize clearly that plain and precious truths and many covenants of the Lord have indeed been taken from the Bible (1 Nephi 13:20–29; Moses 1:40–41). Though we treasure the timeless lessons of the Bible and know of its essential truthfulness, the heart of the gospel message is missing from the Old Testament. The degree to which the gospel of Jesus Christ was known from Adam to Malachi is largely a mystery.

Let us remember that—

1. Adam and Eve were taught the gospel by God and angels. They were married in the Garden of Eden, baptized, and born again (Moses 5:1–12; 6:51–68).[2] "Adam held the priesthood," President Russell M. Nelson explained, "and Eve served in matriarchal partnership with the patriarchal priesthood."[3]

2. Redemption through the Holy Messiah has been declared

---

2. *Joseph Smith* [manual], 482; see also Smith, *Doctrines of Salvation*, 2:69–70.
3. *Power within Us*, 109.

by prophets since the days of Adam (Jacob 4:4; 7:11; Mosiah 13:33; Alma 39:17–19; D&C 20:21–29). The gospel was preached "from the beginning, being declared by holy angels sent forth from the presence of God, and by his own voice, and by the gift of the Holy Ghost" (Moses 5:58; see also D&C 20:35).

3. The fulness of the gospel is the "new and everlasting covenant" (D&C 1:22; 39:11; 45:9; 49:9; 66:2; 133:57). It is *new* in the sense that it is restored anew, generally after periods of apostasy. It is *everlasting* because it is timeless.

4. The principles and ordinances of salvation are forever the same. That is, in the beginning and whenever the fulness of the gospel has been on earth, individuals have exercised faith in the Lord Jesus Christ, have repented of their sins, have been baptized by water and by the Spirit, and have been endowed and sealed in holy places.[4] God's people have always been commanded to build temples and officiate in sacred ordinances therein (D&C 124:39). The Lord explained through the Prophet Joseph that "in all ages of the world, whenever the Lord has given a dispensation of the priesthood to any man by actual revelation, or any set of men, this [sealing] power has always been given" (D&C 128:9).

5. Abraham sought for the "blessings of the fathers" and the right to administer the same (Abraham 1:1–3). His father, Terah, was an idolater, and so Abraham's blessings could not be received from him in father-to-son fashion. Abraham looked instead to Melchizedek, the great high priest of that day, for counsel, direction, and authority. In his discussion of the ancients who entered the rest of the Lord, Alma chose Melchizedek to illustrate his doctrine. "And now, my brethren," he said, "I would that ye should humble yourselves before God, and bring forth fruit meet for

---

4. See, for example, McConkie, *Promised Messiah*, 4–5; *Joseph Smith* [manual], 48–49, 93, 107; see Smith, "Baptism," *Times and Seasons* 3, no. 21 (Sept. 1842): 904; Smith, *Doctrines of Salvation*, 1:156. See also scriptures and other sources cited in Chapter 6.

repentance, that ye may also enter into that rest. Yea, humble yourselves even as the people in the days of Melchizedek, who was also
a high priest after this same order [the holy order of God] which
I have spoken, who also took upon him the high priesthood forever" (Alma 13:13–14).

The Saints of God who lived at that time, "the church in ancient days," called the Holy Priesthood after Melchizedek (D&C
107:2–4). Alma noted that Abraham paid tithing to Melchizedek
(Alma 13:15). A modern revelation informs us that "Esaias . . . lived
in the days of Abraham, and was blessed of him—which Abraham
received the priesthood from Melchizedek, who received it through
the lineage of his fathers, even till Noah" (D&C 84:13–14). It appears that Abraham sought for the same power and authority as
Melchizedek, the power to administer endless lives, the fulness
of the powers of the priesthood. According to Elder Franklin D.
Richards, the Prophet Joseph Smith explained that the power of
Melchizedek was "not the power of a prophet, nor apostle, nor patriarch only, but of a king and priest to God, to open the win-
dows of heaven and pour out the peace and law of endless life to
man. And no man can attain to the joint heirship with Jesus Christ
without being administered to by one having the same power and
authority of Melchizedek."[5] In summary, the Prophet explained,
"Abraham says to Melchizedek, I believe all that [thou] hast taught
me concerning the Priesthood, and the coming of the Son of Man;
so Melchizedec ordained Abraham and sent him away. Abraham
rejoiced, saying, now I have a Priesthood."[6]

6. God established the patriarchal order, a system of family

---

5. *Words of Joseph Smith*, 245.

6. See History, 1838–1856, volume E-1 [1 July 1843–30 April 1844], The Joseph Smith
Papers, accessed 15 Mar. 2016, http://josephsmithpapers.org/paperSummary/history
-1838-1856-volume-e-1-1-july-1843-30-april-1844&p=80; compare *Words of Joseph
Smith*, 244.

government presided over by a father and mother, patterned after what existed in heaven. It is, as President Ezra Taft Benson observed, "an order of family government where a man and woman enter into a covenant with God—just as did Adam and Eve—to be sealed for eternity, to have posterity, and to do the will and work of God throughout their mortality."[7] The patriarchal order, established in the days of Adam (D&C 107:40–42), was and is an order of the Melchizedek Priesthood. It is, in fact, what we know as the new and everlasting covenant of marriage (D&C 131:2).[8] The patriarchal order continued through Abraham and his righteous descendants until Moses was translated, when the keys of the Melchizedek Priesthood were taken from the people (D&C 84:19–27).

7. Abraham saw the days of the coming of the Son of Man and rejoiced. He learned by revelation of the atoning sacrifice of the Son of God and of the power of Christ's resurrection to raise all humankind from the grave (JST, Genesis 15:9–12; John 8:56; Helaman 8:17).

8. Although the Lord's promises to Abraham of an endless posterity and a chosen land are given in Genesis (13:14–17; 15:1–6; 17:1–8), it is the book of Abraham in the Pearl of Great Price that explains more fully the Abrahamic covenant. God called upon Abraham and his posterity to be a peculiar people, to set themselves apart forevermore from worldliness, to live godly and upright lives—to be a covenant and chosen people. In return, the Lord promised Abraham and his posterity that they would be entitled to the blessings of the gospel, the priesthood, and eternal life (Abraham 2:8–11). Further, we learn that "in addition to Abraham's direct descendants, all who should receive the Gospel from that time forth, should also become of Abraham's seed by adoption, and

---

7. "What I Hope You Will Teach Your Children about the Temple," *Ensign*, Aug. 1985, 9.
8. See McConkie, "The Ten Blessings of the Priesthood," *Ensign*, Nov. 1977, 34.

his blood should be mixed among the nations to leaven them with the privileges of the Gospel."[9]

9. The covenant was renewed with Isaac, Abraham's son (Genesis 26:1–4), and then with Jacob, his grandson (Genesis 28; 35:9–13; 48:3–4). Abraham, Isaac, and Jacob lived true to their trust and faithful to their covenants. "And because they did none other things than that which they were commanded, they have entered into their exaltation, according to the promises, and sit upon thrones, and are not angels but are gods" (D&C 132:37).

10. "Under the patriarchal order, the right or inheritance of the firstborn is known as the birthright. This generally included a land inheritance as well as the authority to preside."[10] We would assume that the patriarchs who held the birthright were those who also held the keys of the priesthood, the right of presidency (D&C 107:8), or directing power.[11] Because Reuben, the eldest of the twelve sons of Jacob, lost the birthright through disobedience (Genesis 35:22; 1 Chronicles 5:1–2), the privilege and responsibility of presiding among the tribes of Israel fell to Joseph and his descendants. Why not to Simeon, Leah's second born? Because Joseph was the firstborn of the second wife, Rachel. The birthright belonged to the firstborn.

11. We know from the Bible something of Joseph's spiritual gifts (Genesis 37:1–11; 40:1–23; 41:38), as well as his nobility, as manifested in his refusal to yield to evil (Genesis 39:7–12). Joseph was also a seer and a revelator; Joseph "truly prophesied concerning all his seed. And the prophecies which he wrote, there are not many greater" (2 Nephi 4:2). He spoke of Moses the deliverer and lawgiver, as well as Aaron, Moses's brother and spokesman; of the coming of Shiloh, or the Redeemer; and of the call of a "choice

---

9. Smith, *Way to Perfection*, 88.

10. "Birthright," LDS Bible Dictionary.

11. Smith, *Way to Perfection*, 72–73.

seer" in the last days who would—as a descendant of Joseph (and one called after his name)—gather latter-day Israel to their God and restore the ancient covenants among the people (JST, Genesis 50; 2 Nephi 3).

THE ANCIENT KEYS RESTORED

Jesus of Nazareth came to earth in the meridian of time to save us from sin and death. Our Lord came among men also as a restorer, one sent by the Father to bring again to earth knowledge and keys and authorities that had been lost during the centuries of apostasy. Because the Melchizedek Priesthood had not been available generally to the people for a millennium and a half—since Moses and the keys of the priesthood were taken from Israel as a body (D&C 84:19–27; JST, Exodus 34:1–2; JST, Deuteronomy 10:1–2)—Jesus restored this holy order. "Christ came according to the words of John, and He was greater than John, because He held the keys of the Melchizedek Priesthood and kingdom of God."[12] He organized a church among men, ordained chosen disciples to the holy apostleship, and oversaw the conferral of sacred keys (Matthew 16:16–19; 17:1–9; 18:17–18). The Prophet Joseph Smith explained simply that "Jesus was then the legal administrator, and ordained His Apostles."[13]

"I say also unto thee," the Savior stated at Caesarea Philippi, "that thou art Peter, and upon this rock I will build my church; and the gates of hell shall not prevail against it. And I will give unto thee the keys of the kingdom of heaven: and whatsoever thou shalt bind on earth shall be bound in heaven: and whatsoever thou shalt loose on earth shall be loosed in heaven" (Matthew 16:13–19). Within a week the Lord's promise was fulfilled: Jesus took with him Peter, James, and John—the chief apostles and First Presidency of

---

12. *Joseph Smith* [manual], 83.
13. *Words of Joseph Smith*, 235.

the meridian Church—to a high mountain to pray. While there, these four were transfigured—lifted spiritually to a higher plane— and thus prepared for a transcendent experience. In addition, Moses and Elijah appeared and bestowed sacred priesthood keys on the meridian First Presidency (Matthew 17:8–9).[14] These directing powers would allow the apostles to govern and direct the Church in the absence of the Savior and make available to the members of the Church all the blessings of the everlasting gospel. Peter, James, and John had received the Melchizedek Priesthood earlier and been given apostolic power and commission at the time of their appointment to the Twelve. As a result of their experience on the Mount of Transfiguration, they were granted the right to bind and seal on earth with the full confidence that their actions would receive sealing validity in the heavens.

The restoration of the gospel in this final dispensation entailed the restoration of the Abrahamic covenant, the renewal of God's promises to Abraham, Isaac, Jacob, Joseph, and their innumerable posterity. The early missionaries were thus "called to bring to pass the gathering of mine elect; for mine elect hear my voice and harden not their hearts" (D&C 29:7). "And verily, verily, I say unto you, that this church have I established and called forth out of the wilderness. And even so will I gather mine elect from the four quarters of the earth, even as many as will believe in me, and hearken unto my voice" (D&C 33:5–6). The Saints were instructed to keep the commandments and covenants by which they were bound, "And Israel shall be saved in mine own due time; and by the keys which I have given shall they be led, and no more be confounded at all" (D&C 35:24–25). James Covel, a Methodist minister, was likewise directed to be baptized and cleansed of his sins and then to proclaim the restored gospel: "Thou shalt preach the fulness of

---

14. *Joseph Smith* [manual], 105.

my gospel, which I have sent forth in these last days, the covenant which I have sent forth to recover my people, which are of the house of Israel" (D&C 39:10–11).

MOSES, ELIAS, AND ELIJAH

What had taken place on the holy mount some six months before the Savior's death serves as a pattern for what needed to occur in our own day. On Sunday, 3 April 1836, one week after the dedicatory service of the Kirtland Temple, the Saints again assembled in the house of the Lord. In the morning Thomas B. Marsh, then president of the Council of the Twelve Apostles, and David W. Patten were called upon to speak. In the afternoon the First Presidency and the Twelve participated in a sacrament service, after which Joseph Smith and Oliver Cowdery knelt in prayer behind drawn curtains adjacent to the large pulpits on the west side of the main floor of the temple. After rising from prayer, a wondrous vision burst upon them.

Jesus the Christ appeared. He came to his temple, the first to be authorized by him for centuries. There he accepted the offering of his Saints, this temple built at great sacrifice, and then expanded their vision in regard to the importance of what they had accomplished: "Yea the hearts of thousands and tens of thousands shall greatly rejoice in consequence of the blessings which shall be poured out, and the endowment with which my servants have been endowed in this house" (D&C 110:9).

"After this vision [of Christ] closed, the heavens were again opened unto us; and Moses appeared before us, and committed unto us the keys of the gathering of Israel from the four parts of the earth, and the leading of the ten tribes from the land of the north" (D&C 110:11). The keys restored by the ancient Lawgiver formalized the work of gathering people into the fold. The President of The Church of Jesus Christ of Latter-day Saints, the man appointed "to preside over the whole church, and to be like unto Moses" (D&C 107:91), was given keys to gather modern Israel. Even as Moses led ancient Israel out of Egyptian bondage, so Joseph Smith as President of the Church was given keys to gather latter-day Israel into Zion.

"After this, Elias appeared, and committed the dispensation of the gospel of Abraham, saying that in us and our seed all generations after us should be blessed" (D&C 110:12). The identity of Elias is not given in the revelation.[15] This heavenly messenger restored the keys necessary to establish the Abrahamic covenant, making Joseph Smith and the faithful Saints who receive celestial marriage heirs to the blessings and "promises made to the fathers"—Abraham, Isaac, and Jacob (D&C 27:10; 98:32). Elias thus restored the patriarchal order, the power by which eternal families are organized through the new and everlasting covenant of marriage. "As the crowning cause for wonderment, that God who is no respecter of persons has given a like promise [to that of Abraham and Joseph Smith] to every [member] in the kingdom who has gone to the holy temple and entered into the blessed order of matrimony there performed. Every person married in the temple for time and for all eternity has sealed upon him, conditioned upon his faithfulness, all of the blessings of the ancient patriarchs, including the crowning promise and assurance of eternal increase, which means, literally, a posterity as numerous as the dust particles of the earth."[16]

---

15. President Joseph Fielding Smith offered his opinion that the Elias of the Kirtland Temple was Noah. President Smith seems to have reached that conclusion through understanding that it was the angel Gabriel who appeared to Zacharias (Luke 1:19), that Gabriel is Noah (*Joseph Smith* [manual], 104) and that Elias visited Zacharias (D&C 27:7). See also Joseph Fielding Smith, in Conference Report, Apr. 1960, 72; *Answers to Gospel Questions*, 3:138–41. President John Taylor expressed the view that the Elias of the Kirtland Temple was Abraham (in *Journal of Discourses*, 18:326). Elder Bruce R. McConkie suggested that it was either Abraham or someone from Abraham's dispensation (*Millennial Messiah*, 103, 268).

16. McConkie, *Millennial Messiah*, 264.

"After this vision had closed, another great and glorious vision burst upon us; for Elijah the prophet, who was taken to heaven without tasting death, stood before us, and said: Behold, the time has fully come, which was spoken of by the mouth of Malachi— testifying that he [Elijah] should be sent, before the great and dreadful day of the Lord come—to turn the hearts of the fathers to the children, and the children to the fathers, lest the whole earth be smitten with a curse" (D&C 110:13–15). Precisely on the day that Elijah's appearance took place, Jews throughout the world were engaged in the celebration of the Passover. Since the time of Malachi, Jews worldwide have awaited Elijah's coming with anxious anticipation. Elijah did come but not to Jewish homes; he came, rather, to a sanctuary of the Saints and to the Savior's legal administrators on earth. There he bestowed keys of inestimable worth.

In his first appearance to Joseph Smith in 1823, Moroni quoted numerous passages from the Old and New Testaments and rendered Malachi 4:5–6 concerning the coming of Elijah in a somewhat different way from the way that passage is recorded in the King James Version. The prophecy began: "Behold, I will reveal unto you the Priesthood, by the hand of Elijah the prophet, before the coming of the great and dreadful day of the Lord" (D&C 2:1; Joseph Smith–History 1:38). Joseph and Oliver had been ordained to the Melchizedek Priesthood and been given apostolic power and commission as early as 1829. How was it, then, that Elijah would reveal the priesthood? Elijah was sent in 1836 to reveal keys of the priesthood and sealing powers that had not yet been fully understood or were not fully operational in this dispensation. Elijah restored the keys whereby families (organized in the patriarchal order through the powers delivered by Elias) could be bound and sealed for eternity. "The spirit, power, and calling of Elijah is, that ye have power to hold the key of the revelation, ordinances, oracles, powers and endowments of the fullness of the Melchizedek Priesthood and of the kingdom of God on the earth."[17]

Elijah came to "plant in the hearts of the children the promises made to the fathers" whereby the "hearts of the children [would] turn to their fathers" (D&C 2:2; Joseph Smith–History 1:39). The Spirit of the Lord witnesses to faithful Latter-day Saints of the central place of eternal marriage and of the sublime joys associated with the everlasting continuation of the family. Through temples, God's promises to the fathers—the promises pertaining to the gospel, the priesthood, and eternal increase (Abraham 2:8–11)—are extended to all faithful Saints in all ages. The hearts of the children turn to the ancient fathers because the children are now participants in and recipients of the blessings of the fathers. Being profoundly grateful for such privileges, members of the Church, motivated by the spirit of Elijah, also find their hearts turning to their more immediate fathers, and do all within their power (through family history research and attendant temple work) to ensure that the blessings of Abraham, Isaac, Jacob, and Joseph are enjoyed by ancestors as well as posterity. "If it were not so [that is, if Elijah had not come], the whole earth would be utterly wasted at [Christ's] coming" (D&C 2:3; Joseph Smith–History 1:39).

Why? Because the earth would not have accomplished its foreordained purpose—to establish on its face a family system patterned after the order of heaven. If there were no sealing powers whereby families could be bound together, the earth would never "answer the end of its creation" (D&C 49:16). It would be wasted and cursed, for all individuals would be forever without root or branch, without ancestry or posterity. Because Elijah came, however, all ordinances for the living and the dead (baptisms, confirmations,

---

17. *Joseph Smith* [manual], 311.

ordinations, washings, anointings, endowments, sealings) have real meaning and are of efficacy, virtue, and force in eternity.[18]

The ordinances associated with the ministry and bestowal of keys by Moses, Elias, and Elijah (culminating in temples of the Lord) are the capstone blessings of the gospel of Jesus Christ and the consummation of the Father's work: they provide purpose and perspective for all other gospel principles and ordinances. More than any other work in this Church, these keys and powers and covenants and ordinances link us with the ancient Saints; we thereby have sealed upon us the blessings of Abraham, Isaac, Jacob, and Joseph.

DESCENDANTS OF THE PATRIARCHS

In speaking of the angel Moroni, the Prophet Joseph Smith stated: "This messenger proclaimed himself to be an angel of God, sent to bring the joyful tidings that the covenant which God made with ancient Israel was at hand to be fulfilled, that the preparatory work for the second coming of the Messiah was speedily to commence; that the time was at hand for the Gospel in all its fulness to be preached in power, unto all nations that a people might be prepared for the Millennial reign. I was informed that I was chosen to be an instrument in the hands of God to bring about some of His purposes in this glorious dispensation."[19]

Joseph of old prophesied that his latter-day namesake would be raised up by God to bring the people of the last days to the knowledge of the covenants that God had made with the ancient fathers (2 Nephi 3:7; compare 1 Nephi 13:26). The name *Joseph* is a blessed and significant name. Whether taken from the Hebrew word *Yasaf,* which means "to add," or the Hebrew word *Asaph,* meaning "to gather," one senses that the latter-day Seer was destined to perform

---

18. *Joseph Smith* [manual], 310; see also Smith, *Doctrines of Salvation,* 2:115–28.
19. *Joseph Smith* [manual], 439.

a monumental labor in regard to the fulfillment of the Abrahamic covenant in the final dispensation. Truly, the tribe of Joseph has been foreordained to "push the people together from the ends of the earth" (D&C 58:45; see also Deuteronomy 33:17).

Joseph Smith was a descendant of Abraham, a "pure Ephraimite."[20] By lineage he had a right to the priesthood, the gospel, and eternal life (Abraham 2:8–11). In a revelation received on 6 December 1832, the Savior said: "Thus saith the Lord unto you, with whom the priesthood hath continued through the lineage of your fathers—for ye are lawful heirs, according to the flesh, and have been hid from the world with Christ in God—therefore your life and the priesthood have remained, and must needs remain through you and your lineage until the restoration of all things spoken by the mouths of all the holy prophets since the world began" (D&C 86:8–10).

The Lord spoke of his Latter-day Saints as "a remnant of Jacob, and those who are heirs according to the covenant" (D&C 52:2). "Awake, awake; put on thy strength, O Zion," Isaiah recorded; "put on thy beautiful garments, O Jerusalem, the holy city" (Isaiah 52:1). A modern revelation provides our finest commentary on this passage and explains that Jehovah "had reference to those whom God should call in the last days, who should hold the power of priesthood to bring again Zion, and the redemption of Israel; and to put on her strength is to put on the authority of the priesthood, which she, Zion, has a right to by lineage; and to return to that power which she had lost" (D&C 113:8). The Lord also encouraged Israel through Isaiah to shake herself from the dust and loose herself from the bands about her neck (Isaiah 52:2). That is, "the scattered remnants are exhorted to return to the Lord from whence they have fallen; which if they do, the promise of the Lord is that he will

---

20. Brigham Young, in *Journal of Discourses,* 2:269.

speak to them, or give them revelation." In so doing, Israel rids herself of "the curses of God upon her," that is, her "scattered condition among the Gentiles" (D&C 113:10).

Joseph Smith became a father of the faithful to those of this final dispensation, the means by which the chosen lineage could be identified, gathered, organized as family units, and sealed forevermore in the house of Israel to their God. The Patriarch in the days of the early Church, Joseph Smith Sr., blessed his son Joseph as follows: "A marvelous work and a wonder has the Lord wrought by thy hand, even that which shall prepare the way for the remnants of his people to come in among the Gentiles, with their fulness, as the tribes of Israel are restored. I bless thee with the blessings of thy Fathers Abraham, Isaac and Jacob; and even the blessings of thy father Joseph, the son of Jacob. Behold, he looked after his posterity in the last days, when they should be scattered and driven by the Gentiles."[21] Or, as God declared, "As I said unto Abraham concerning the kindreds of the earth, *even so I say unto my servant Joseph: In thee and in thy seed shall the kindred of the earth be blessed*" (D&C 124:58; emphasis added). Further, "Abraham received promises concerning his seed, and of the fruit of his loins—from whose loins ye are, namely, my servant Joseph—which were to continue so long as they were in the world; and as touching Abraham and his seed, out of the world they should continue; both in the world and out of the world should they continue as innumerable as the stars; or, if ye were to count the sand upon the seashore ye could not number them. *This promise is yours also, because ye are of Abraham*" (D&C 132:30–31; emphasis added).

Through Joseph Smith the blessings of Abraham, Isaac, and Jacob are available to all who will join the Church and prove

---

21. Blessing from Joseph Smith Sr., 9 December 1834, The Joseph Smith Papers, accessed 18 Apr. 2016, http://josephsmithpapers.org/paperSummary/blessing-from-joseph -smith-sr-9-december-1834.

themselves worthy of the blessings of the temple. Jehovah's plea through Isaiah that the people of the covenant become a light to the nations, that they might be his "salvation unto the end of the earth" (Isaiah 49:6), is thus realized through the restoration of the gospel. Thereby, as the Choice Seer himself declared, "the election of the promised seed still continues, and in the last days they shall have the priesthood restored unto them, and they shall be 'saviors on Mount Zion.'"[22] Our patriarchal blessings mean what they say—we are entitled, either by direct lineage or through adoption, to the promises made to the fathers. Those who are not directly descended from Israel who join the Church should in no way feel disadvantaged or less than chosen. Chosenness is a status based on the choice to follow the Lord and associate with his people, and entrance into the true Church qualifies one for the blessings of Abraham. "For . . . as many of the Gentiles as will repent are the covenant people of the Lord; . . . for the Lord covenanteth with none save it be with them that repent and believe in his Son, who is the Holy One of Israel" (2 Nephi 30:2).

"We are . . . children of the covenant," President Russell M. Nelson explained. "We have received, as did they of old, the holy priesthood and the everlasting gospel. Abraham, Isaac, and Jacob are our ancestors. We are of Israel. We have the right to receive the gospel, blessings of the priesthood, and eternal life. Nations of the earth will be blessed by our efforts and by the labors of our posterity. The literal seed of Abraham and those who are gathered into his family by adoption receive these promised blessings— predicated upon acceptance of the Lord and obedience to his commandments."[23]

---

22. *Words of Joseph Smith*, 73–74.
23. "Children of the Covenant," *Ensign*, May 1995, 33.

CONCLUSION

"We are a covenant people," President Gordon B. Hinckley explained, "and that is a very serious matter. When this work was restored and the Lord set forth the purposes for that Restoration, He said that one reason for the Restoration was that His everlasting covenant might be established, or reestablished."[24] Latter-day Saints should therefore read the Old Testament with a careful eye, for we know that God's covenant with the descendants of Abraham, Isaac, Jacob, and Joseph—the "promises made to the fathers"—was not completely fulfilled as the Old Testament was closed or even with the coming of the Messiah to earth in the meridian of time (D&C 27:10; 98:32).

The Prophet Joseph Smith taught: "The time has at last arrived when the God of Abraham, of Isaac, and of Jacob, has set his hand again the second time to recover the remnants of his people. . . . Christ, in the days of His flesh, proposed to make a covenant with [Israel], but they rejected Him and His proposals, and in consequence thereof, they were broken off, and no covenant was made with them at that time. But their unbelief has not rendered the promise of God of none effect."[25] Indeed, Nephi declared that all the kindreds of the earth could not be blessed, as promised to the ancient patriarchs, unless God "shall make bare his arm," or reveal his power, in the last days. "Wherefore, the Lord God will proceed to make bare his arm in the eyes of all the nations, in bringing about his covenants and his gospel" unto those who live in the final dispensation (1 Nephi 22:8–11). God has done just that in our dispensation, and the keys and powers and blessings have come to us precept upon precept.

---

24. "Inspirational Thoughts," *Ensign*, Aug. 1997, 3.

25. History, 1838–1856, volume A-1 [23 December 1805–30 August 1834], The Joseph Smith Papers, accessed 15 Mar. 2016, http://josephsmithpapers.org/paperSummary /history-1838-1856-volume-a-1-23-december-1805-30-august-1834?p=264.

As the people of the covenant, we have been called as heralds of salvation—called to deliver glad tidings, to take the message of the restored gospel to all nations, to provide "salvation unto the end of the earth" (Isaiah 49:6; 2 Nephi 21:6). As the people of the covenant, we are expected to walk with fidelity and devotion, to hold up the ensign, or standard, of truth to a world that desperately needs direction. Such is our challenge, our glory or our condemnation.

Chapter 14

THOSE WHO NEVER
HEARD THE GOSPEL

Kirtland, Ohio, January 1836. Joseph Smith and other early leaders of the Church had begun to meet in the Kirtland Temple before its completion and participated in washings, anointings, and blessings. On Thursday evening, 21 January 1836, the Prophet and a number of Church leaders from Kirtland and Missouri gathered on the third, or attic, floor of the Kirtland Temple in the translating room, or the President's Room. After a "blessing meeting," in which the men present blessed both Father Smith and Joseph Jr. with the laying on of hands, a vision was given to the Prophet, a divine communication that addresses itself to one of the most vexing, perplexing problems in Christian history.

One difficult question for people in our day to answer is the problem of evil and suffering. In essence, it is as follows: If our God is all-loving, all-knowing, and all-powerful, why is there so much evil and suffering in the world? If God knows of the pain on this planet (because he is omniscient), if he has the power to change things (because he is omnipotent), then how can he be all-loving if he does not bring such evil and suffering to an end? The doctrines and perspective of the Restoration provide significant insight into this difficult matter, particularly as we consider Restoration teachings on the nature of God, the purposes of life, and the vital place of human agency. For now, however, let us turn our attention to another but related problem, which has been called the soteriological problem of evil. *Soteriology* is the study of salvation—what it is and how it comes to the children of God. The soteriological problem of evil and suffering may be stated this way: If Jesus Christ is the only name, the only means, by which salvation is to come to the human family (Acts 4:12), then what do we make of the fact that most of humankind will go to their graves without even hearing the name of Christ, much less the message of Christianity?

One Evangelical Christian writer asked: "What is the fate of those who die never hearing of the gospel of Christ? Are all the 'heathen' lost? Is there an opportunity for those who have never heard of Jesus to be saved?

"These questions raise one of the most perplexing, provocative and perennial issues facing Christians. It has been considered by philosophers and farmers, Christians and non-Christians. . . . Far and away, this is the most-asked apologetic question on U.S. College campuses. . . .

"Although there is no way of knowing exactly how many people died without ever hearing about Israel or the church, it seems safe to conclude that the vast majority of human beings who have ever lived fall into this category.

"In terms of sheer numbers, then, an inquiry into the salvation of the unevangelized is of immense interest. What may be said about the destiny of countless billions who have lived and died apart from any understanding of the divine grace manifested in Jesus?"[1]

---

1. Sanders, *What about Those Who Have Never Heard?* 7–8, 9; see also Pinnock and Brown, *Theological Crossfire*, 227.

PRECEPT UPON PRECEPT

We cannot help but appreciate that when the Prophet Joseph Smith learned the gospel, he learned it first and foremost from the Book of Mormon. Later there would be revealed through him, both in his translation of the Bible and through the revelations of the Restoration, ancillary doctrines that would expand his mind and broaden the Saints' understanding of the plan of salvation.

What did he learn from the Book of Mormon about salvation for all people? He learned that baptism is an essential ordinance, one that must be properly performed to admit a person into the kingdom of God (2 Nephi 31; Mosiah 18). He learned that "this life is the time for men to prepare to meet God; yea, behold the day of this life is the day for men to perform their labors" and that "after this day of life, which is given us to prepare for eternity, behold, if we do not improve our time while in this life, then cometh the night of darkness wherein there can be no labor performed" (Alma 34:32–33). That is to say, in the formative years of his ministry, the Prophet was tutored largely by the Book of Mormon—a scriptural record that, like Deuteronomy, essentially sets forth the doctrine of the two ways: things are either black or white, good or evil, and our choices lead to either blessing or cursing.

Some time between 16 February 1832 and 2 February 1833, Joseph Smith and Sidney Rigdon were involved in translating the epistle to the Hebrews.[2] The Prophet rendered verses 39 and 40 of chapter 11 as follows: "And these all, having obtained a good report through faith, received not the promises; God having provided some better things for them through their sufferings, for without sufferings they could not be made perfect." The importance of this change—which reflects the context of the chapter on the challenges

---

2. See Matthews, *"Plainer Translation,"* 96.

and trials and sufferings associated with gaining faith unto salvation—is in what it *does not* seem to convey.

The King James Version renders the passage thus: "God having provided some better thing for us, that they without us should not be made perfect." The Prophet's alteration of the King James text, an important contribution in its own right, may suggest that at this early date, Joseph Smith had not yet grasped the concept of salvation for the dead. If he did, there is no public record of any teachings on the matter at that time.

One of the earliest accounts we have of teachings related to salvation for the dead is found in an experience of Lydia Goldthwait, who later became the wife of Newel Knight. She grew up in Massachusetts and New York and at the age of sixteen married Calvin Bailey. Calvin had a serious drinking problem and eventually left Lydia and their child. At the time, Lydia was also expecting another baby. The baby died at birth, and within months her first child died also. When she was twenty years old, Lydia moved to Canada to stay with the Freeman Nickerson family. There she was introduced to the restored gospel and became acquainted with the Prophet Joseph Smith. On 24 October 1833 the family sat around the table and listened to the Prophet. The Spirit was poured out upon the group in a remarkable manner, and Lydia even spoke in tongues.

The next day, as Joseph's company prepared to return to Kirtland, the Prophet "paced back and forth in the sitting room in deep study. Finally he said: 'I have been pondering on Sister Lydia's lonely condition, and wondering why it is that she has passed through so much sorrow and affliction and is thus separated from all her relatives. I now understand it. The Lord has suffered it even as he allowed Joseph of old to be afflicted, who was sold by his brethren as a slave into a far country, and through that became a savior to his father's house and country. Even so shall it be with her;

the hand of the Lord will overrule it for good to her and her father's family.'

"Turning to the young woman he continued: 'Sister Lydia, great are your blessings. The Lord, your Savior, loves you, and will overrule all your past sorrows and afflictions for good unto you. Let your heart be comforted. You are of the blood of Israel descended through the loins of Ephraim. You shall yet be a savior to your father's house. Therefore be comforted, and let your heart rejoice, for the Lord has a great work for you to do. Be faithful and endure unto the end and all will be well.'"[3]

This statement represents one of the earliest declarations of lineage, as well as one of the first references in this dispensation to individuals becoming what the Old Testament prophet Obadiah called saviors on mount Zion (see Obadiah 1:21). Later in her life, Lydia participated in the ordinance work for some seven hundred of her deceased relatives in the St. George Temple, thus fulfilling Joseph Smith's prophecy.[4]

A VISION OF THE CELESTIAL KINGDOM

The Prophet recorded that on 21 January 1836, "at early candle-light I met with the Presidency at the west school room, in the Temple, to attend to the ordinance of anointing our heads with holy oil; also the [High] Councils of Kirtland and Zion met in the two adjoining rooms, and waited in prayer while we attended to the ordinance. I took the oil in my left hand, Father Smith being seated before me, and the remainder of the Presidency encircled him round about. We then stretched our right hands towards heaven, and blessed the oil, and consecrated it in the name of Jesus Christ.

"We then laid our hands upon our aged Father Smith, and invoked the blessings of heaven. . . . The Presidency then . . . received

---

3. "Lydia Knight's History," 21–23, in Journal History, 19 Oct. 1833.
4. See *Church History in the Fulness of Times*, 117.

their anointing and blessing under the hands of Father Smith. And in turn, my father anointed my head, and sealed upon me the blessings of Moses, to lead Israel in the latter days, even as Moses led him in days of old; also the blessings of Abraham, Isaac, and Jacob. All of the Presidency laid their hands upon me, and pronounced upon my head many prophecies and blessings, many of which I shall not notice at this time. But as Paul said, so say I, let us come to visions and revelations."[5]

Joseph the Prophet had learned by vision in February 1832 the nature of those who would inherit the highest heaven, or the celestial kingdom. These persons are they who "overcome by faith, and are sealed by the Holy Spirit of promise," they "into whose hands the Father has given all things" (D&C 76:53, 55). In the vision given to Joseph Smith in the Kirtland Temple in 1836, "the heavens were opened upon us, and I beheld the celestial kingdom of God, and the glory thereof, whether in the body or out I cannot tell. I saw the transcendent beauty of the gate through which the heirs of that kingdom will enter, which was like unto circling flames of fire; also the blazing throne of God, whereon was seated the Father and the Son. I saw the beautiful streets of that kingdom, which had the appearance of being paved with gold" (D&C 137:1–4).

Joseph Smith's vision of the celestial kingdom was not unlike the vision given to John the Revelator of the holy city, the earth in its sanctified and celestial state: "The foundations of the wall of the city," wrote John, "were garnished with all manner of precious stones." Further, "the street of the city was pure gold, as it were transparent glass" (Revelation 21:19, 21).

---

5. History, 1838–1856, volume B-1 [1 September 1834–2 November 1838], The Joseph Smith Papers, accessed 15 Mar. 2016, http://josephsmithpapers.org/paperSummary /history-1838-1856-volume-b-1-1-september-1834-2-november-1838?p=149; referring to 2 Corinthians 12:1–5.

ALVIN SMITH: THE SCRIPTURAL PROTOTYPE

Joseph's account of the vision continues: "I saw Father Adam and Abraham; and my father and my mother; my brother Alvin, that has long since slept; and marveled how it was that he had obtained an inheritance in that kingdom, seeing that he had departed this life before the Lord had set his hand to gather Israel the second time, and had not been baptized for the remission of sins" (D&C 137:5–6).

Joseph's vision was a glimpse into the future celestial realm, for he saw his parents in the kingdom of the just, when in fact both were still living in mortality in 1836. Joseph Sr. would not die until 1840, and Mother Smith would live as a widow thereafter for sixteen years. Father Smith was, as we mentioned earlier, in the same room with his son at the time the vision was received.

The Prophet also saw his brother Alvin, who was the eldest child of Joseph Sr. and Lucy Mack Smith. He was born on 11 February 1798 in Tunbridge, Vermont. His was a pleasant and loving disposition, and he constantly sought opportunities to aid the family in their financial struggles. Lucy Mack Smith described Alvin as "a youth of singular goodness of disposition" and spoke of how he had proven a blessing "every hour of his existence."[6]

Lucy Mack Smith wrote that on the morning of 15 November 1823, "Alvin was taken very sick with the bilious colic," probably appendicitis. A physician hurried to the Smith home and administered calomel, an experimental drug, to Alvin. The dose of calomel "lodged in his stomach," and on the third day of sickness Alvin recognized that he was going to die. He asked that each of the Smith children come to his bedside for his parting counsel and final expression of love. According to Mother Smith's record, "When he came to Joseph, he said, 'I am now going to die, the distress which

---

6. *Joseph Smith* [manual], 401.

I suffer, and the feelings that I have, tell me my time is very short. I·want you to be a good boy, and do everything that lies in your power to obtain the Record. [Joseph had been visited by Moroni less than three months before this time.] Be faithful in receiving instruction, and in keeping every commandment that is given you.'"[7]

Alvin died on 19 November 1823. Mother Smith wrote of the pall of grief surrounding his passing and how "lamentation and mourning filled the whole neighborhood in which he resided."[8] Joseph wrote many years later: "I remember well the pangs of sorrow that swelled my youthful bosom and almost burst my tender heart when he died. He was the oldest and noblest of my father's family. . . . He lived without spot from the time he was a child. . . . He was one of the soberest of men, and when he died the angel of the Lord visited him in his last moments."[9]

Because Alvin had died seven years before the organization of the Church and had not been baptized by proper authority, Joseph wondered during his vision how it was possible for his brother to have attained the highest heaven. Alvin's family had been shocked and saddened at his funeral by the remarks of a Presbyterian minister. William Smith, Alvin's younger brother, recalled: "Hyrum, Samuel, Katherine, and mother were members of the Presbyterian Church. My father would not join. He did not like it because Rev. Stockton had preached at my brother's funeral sermon and intimated very strongly that he had gone to hell, for Alvin was not a church member, but he was a good boy, and my father did not like it."[10] What joy and excitement must have filled the souls of both Joseph Smith Junior and Senior when they heard the voice of an

---

7. *History of Joseph Smith by His Mother*, 87; *Joseph Smith* [manual], 401.

8. *History of Joseph Smith by His Mother*, 88.

9. *Joseph Smith* [manual], 485.

10. Briggs and Peterson, Interview with William Smith, *Deseret News*, 20 Jan. 1894, 11; see also Walker, *William B. Smith*, 50; *Joseph Smith* [manual], 401, 403.

omniscient and omniloving God saying: "All who have died without a knowledge of this gospel, who would have received it if they had been permitted to tarry, shall be heirs of the celestial kingdom of God; also all that shall die henceforth without a knowledge of it, who would have received it with all their hearts, shall be heirs of that kingdom; for I, the Lord, will judge all men according to their works, according to the desire of their hearts" (D&C 137:7–9).[11]

God does not hold anyone accountable for a gospel law of which he or she was ignorant. Joseph the Prophet learned that every person will have an opportunity, whether here or hereafter, to accept and apply the principles of the gospel of Jesus Christ. Only God is capable of perfect judgment, and thus only he can discern completely the hearts and minds of mortal men and women. He alone knows when a person has received sufficient knowledge or impressions of the Spirit to constitute a valid opportunity to receive the message of salvation. This vision reaffirmed that the Lord will judge men not only by their actions but also by their attitudes—the desires of their hearts (see Alma 41:3).

THE SALVATION OF CHILDREN

Another profoundly beautiful doctrine enunciated in the vision of the celestial kingdom deals with the status of children who die. "And I also beheld that all children who die before they arrive at the years of accountability are saved in the celestial kingdom of heaven" (D&C 137:10). This part of the vision affirmed what earlier

---

11. Having encountered this principle of the gospel—that God will judge us not only by our works but also by the desires of our hearts—one might ask: "Then why the necessity of baptism for the dead?" The answer is quite simple: The sooner that vicarious ordinances have been performed in behalf of an individual in the postmortal spirit world who has there heard and accepted the fullness of the gospel, the sooner he or she can progress and move forward on the path that leads to eternal life. The Prophet Joseph noted specifically that *"as soon as the law of the Gospel is obeyed here by their friends who act as proxy for them, the Lord has administrators there to set them free"* (*Joseph Smith* [manual], 474; emphasis added).

prophets had taught. King Benjamin had learned from an angel that "the infant perisheth not that dieth in his infancy" (Mosiah 3:18). After having described the nature of those who will come forth in the first resurrection, Abinadi said simply, "Little children also have eternal life" (Mosiah 15:25). A revelation given to Joseph Smith in September 1830 had specified that "little children are redeemed from the foundation of the world through mine Only Begotten" (D&C 29:46; compare JST, Matthew 19:13–15; D&C 74:7). Joseph Smith later taught that "the Lord takes many away, even in infancy, that they may escape the envy of man, and the sorrows and evils of this present world; they were too pure, too lovely, to live on earth; therefore, if rightly considered, instead of mourning we have reason to rejoice as they are delivered from evil, and we shall soon have them again."[12] By virtue of his infinite understanding of the human family, "we must assume that the Lord knows and arranges beforehand who shall be taken in infancy and who shall remain on earth to undergo whatever tests are needed in their cases."[13]

Will children who die before the age of accountability be subject to temptation and testing? Amulek informed us that our disposition here will be our disposition in the hereafter (Alma 34:32–35). Such is the case with little children. They were pure in this mortal existence, will be pure in the world of spirits, and will come forth in the resurrection of the pure in heart at the appropriate time. At the time of the second coming of Christ, wickedness will be cleansed from the face of the earth. The Millennium will be ushered in with great power, and then Satan and his hosts will be bound by the righteousness of the people (1 Nephi 22:26). During this glorious time, the earth will be given to the righteous "for an inheritance;

---

12. *Joseph Smith* [manual], 176.
13. Joseph Fielding Smith, in Bruce R. McConkie, "The Salvation of Little Children," *Ensign*, Apr. 1977, 6.

and they shall multiply and wax strong, and their children shall grow up without sin unto salvation" (D&C 45:58).

Some may ask, Won't the devil be loosed at the end of the Millennium? Could not those who left mortality without trial be tested during that "little season"? No, for these children will already have come forth from the grave as resurrected and immortal beings. How could such persons, whose salvation is already assured, ever be tested? President Joseph Fielding Smith observed that "Satan will be loosed to gather his forces after the millennium. The people who will be tempted, will be people living on this earth [mortals], and they will have every opportunity to accept the gospel or reject it. Satan will have nothing to do whatever with little children, or grown people who have received their resurrection and entered into the celestial kingdom. Satan cannot tempt little children in this life, nor in the spirit world, nor after the resurrection. Little children who die before reaching the years of accountability will not be tempted."[14]

The vision of the celestial kingdom unlocks one of the mysteries of eternity: the blessed concept that the work of the salvation of souls continues after this life is over, well beyond the grave. The work of the Lord goes forward, here and hereafter. We did not first begin to exercise faith in the plan of redemption in this second estate; here and now is but a continuation of there and then. Hereafter we will continue to labor for ourselves and for our brothers and sisters. Truly, "the course of the Lord is one eternal round" (1 Nephi 10:19).

UNFOLDING THE DOCTRINE

On the afternoon of Tuesday, 8 May 1838, the Prophet Joseph answered a series of questions about the faith and practices of the

---

14. *Doctrines of Salvation,* 2:56–57; see also McConkie, "The Salvation of Little Children," *Ensign,* Apr. 1977, 6.

Latter-day Saints. One question was, "If the Mormon doctrine is true what has become of all those who died since the days of the apostles?" The Prophet responded, "All those who have not had an opportunity of hearing the gospel, and being administered to by an inspired man in the flesh, must have it hereafter, before they can be finally judged."[15] We cannot help but conclude that the Prophet must have spoken of this doctrinal matter since the time of his vision of Alvin more than two years earlier, but we have no record of such a conversation.

The first public discourse by the Prophet on this sweet and sacred doctrine and practice was delivered on 15 August 1840 at the funeral of Seymour Brunson, a member of the Nauvoo High Council.[16] Simon Baker described the occasion: "I was present at a discourse that the prophet Joseph delivered on baptism for the dead 15 August 1840. He read the greater part of the 15th chapter of Corinthians and remarked that the Gospel of Jesus Christ brought glad tidings of great joy, and then remarked that he saw a widow in that congregation that had a son who died without being baptized, and this widow in reading the sayings of Jesus 'except a man be born of water and of the spirit he cannot enter the kingdom of heaven,' and that not one jot nor tittle of the Savior's words should pass away, but all should be fulfilled. He then said that this widow should have glad tidings in that thing. He also said the apostle [Paul] was talking to a people who understood baptism for the dead, for it was practiced among them. He went on to say that people could now act for their friends who had departed this life, and that the plan of salvation was calculated to save all who were willing to obey the requirements of the law of God. He went on and made a very beautiful discourse."[17]

---

15. *Elders' Journal* 1, no. 3 (July 1838): 43.
16. *Joseph Smith* [manual], 472.
17. *Words of Joseph Smith*, 49.

After the meeting, the widow, Jane Nyman, was baptized for her son by Harvey Olmstead in the Mississippi River.[18] Just one month later, on 14 September 1840, on his deathbed the Patriarch, Joseph Smith Sr., made a final request of his family that someone be baptized in behalf of his eldest son, Alvin. Hyrum complied with that wish and was baptized for his elder brother in 1840 and again in 1841.[19]

In an epistle to the Twelve dated 19 October 1840, the Prophet Joseph Smith stated: "I presume the doctrine of 'baptism for the dead' has ere this reached your ears, and may have raised some inquiries in your minds respecting the same. I cannot in this letter give you all the information you may desire on the subject; but aside from knowledge independent of the Bible, I would say that it was certainly practiced by the ancient churches." The Prophet then quoted from 1 Corinthians 15:29 and continued: "I first mentioned the doctrine in public when preaching the funeral sermon of Brother Seymour Brunson: and have since then given general instructions in the Church on the subject. The Saints have the privilege of being baptized for those of their relatives who are dead, whom they believe would have embraced the Gospel, if they had been privileged with hearing it, and who have received the Gospel in the spirit, through the instrumentality of those who have been commissioned to preach to them while in prison."[20]

On 19 January 1841 the revelation now recorded in Doctrine and Covenants 124 was given. In this remarkable oracle the Lord gives a stern warning concerning the need to complete a temple in Nauvoo so that baptisms for the dead may be acceptable before

---

18. See Baugh, "Practice of Baptism for the Dead Outside of Temples," 3–6.

19. "Nauvoo Baptisms for the Dead," 145, 149. Presumably the first baptism was in the Mississippi River; later baptisms were performed in a font in the unfinished Nauvoo Temple.

20. *Joseph Smith* [manual], 472.

him (D&C 124:29–36). Further, Joseph learned that the ordinance of baptism for the dead was "instituted from before the foundation of the world" (D&C 124:33; compare D&C 128:5, 22). On 3 October 1841 the Prophet declared that baptism for the dead was "the only way that men can appear as saviors on Mount Zion."[21]

On 20 March 1842 the Prophet stated that if we have the authority to perform valid baptisms for the living, it is our responsibility to make those same blessings available to those who have passed through death.[22] On 15 April 1842, in an editorial in the *Times and Seasons,* Joseph the Prophet called upon the Saints to expand their vision beyond the narrow views of unenlightened humankind. "While one portion of the human race are judging and condemning the other without mercy," he said, "the great parent of the universe looks upon the whole of the human family with a fatherly care, and paternal regard; He views them as His offspring, and without any of those contracted feelings that influence the children of men." He observed that "it is an opinion which is generally received, that the destiny of man is irretrievably fixed at his death; and that he is made either eternally happy, or eternally miserable; that if a man dies without a knowledge of God, he must be eternally damned. . . . [O]ur Saviour says that all manner of sin, and blasphemy shall be forgiven men wherewith they shall blaspheme; but the blasphemy against the Holy Ghost shall not be forgiven, neither in *this world,* nor in the *world to come,* evidently showing that there are sins which may be forgiven in the *world to come.*" To this doctrinal statement the Prophet added: "The great Jehovah contemplated the whole of the events connected with the earth, [and] the past, present and the future, were and are with him, one eternal 'now.'" Moreover, Brother Joseph stated, "Chrysostum [A.D. 349–407] says that the Marcionites practiced baptism for the dead.

---

21. *Words of Joseph Smith,* 77; compare *Joseph Smith* [manual], 474.
22. *Joseph Smith* [manual], 472.

. . . The church of course at that time was degenerate, and the particular form might be incorrect, but the thing is sufficiently plain in the scriptures." He again quoted 1 Corinthians 15:29 and concluded by referring to the restoration of this vital dimension of the "ancient order of things" as the fulfillment of the words of Obadiah concerning saviors on Mount Zion (Obadiah 1:21). "A view of these things reconciles the scriptures of truth, justifies the ways of God to man; places the human family upon an equal footing, and harmonizes with every principle of righteousness, justice, and truth."[23]

The two epistles of the Church preserved in Doctrine and Covenants 127 and 128 were written in early September 1842. They contain practical counsel concerning the recording of sacred ordinances (127:5–7; 128:3–4) and also a profound doctrinal foundation upon which those ordinances rest. Salvation for the dead is a central aspect of the larger work of gathering together all things in one—people as well as principles and precepts—in the dispensation of the fulness of times (D&C 128:15–18). In Doctrine and Covenants 128 the Prophet masterfully blended several scriptural passages in unfolding the doctrinal drama of the Restoration. He stated: "These are principles in relation to the dead and the living that cannot be lightly passed over, as pertaining to our salvation." And then, standing in the full light of revealed knowledge concerning these matters, knowledge that he may not yet have possessed at the time of his work on the Bible, he added: "For their salvation is necessary and essential to our salvation, as Paul says concerning the fathers [in Hebrews 11:40]—that they without us cannot be made perfect—neither can we without our dead be made perfect" (D&C 128:15).

On 11 June 1843, while discoursing on the gathering of Israel, Joseph Smith explained that the doctrine of baptism for the dead

---

23. "Baptism for the Dead," *Times and Seasons* 3, no. 12 (Apr. 1842): 761; emphasis added.

"was the reason why Jesus said unto the Jews, 'How oft would I have gathered thy children together, even as a hen gathereth her chickens under her wings, and ye would not!'—that they might attend to the ordinances of baptism for the dead as well as other ordinances of the priesthood, and receive revelations from heaven, and be perfected in the things of the kingdom of God—but they would not. This was the case on the day of Pentecost: those blessings were poured out on the disciples on that occasion. God ordained that He would save the dead, and would do it by gathering His people together."[24]

On 7 April 1844, as a part of the King Follett sermon, Joseph the Seer stated: "I will open your eyes in relation to your dead. All things, whatsoever God in his infinite reason has seen fit to reveal to us in our mortal state in regard to our mortal bodies, are revealed to us as if we had no bodies. And those revelations, which will save our dead, will save our bodies. . . . Hence the awful responsibility that rests upon us for our dead, for all the spirits must either obey the gospel or be damned. Solemn thought! Dreadful thought!"[25]

According to William Clayton's report, the Prophet also said: "When [God's] commandments teach us, it is in view of eternity. The greatest responsibility in this world is to seek after our dead."[26] One day later the Prophet taught that there must be a house where "men may receive the endowment to make [of them] kings and priests unto the Most High God. . . . When we want to save our dead we go through all the ordinances, the same as for ourselves, from baptism to ordination to endowment."[27]

And then on 2 May 1844 he taught: "In regard to the law of the Priesthood, there should be a place where all nations shall come up

---

24. *Words of Joseph Smith*, 213.
25. *Words of Joseph Smith*, 352.
26. *Words of Joseph Smith*, 360.
27. *Words of Joseph Smith*, 362.

from time to time to receive their endowments; and the Lord has said this shall be the place for the baptisms for the dead. *Every man that has been baptized and belongs to the kingdom has a right to be baptized for those who have gone before; and as soon as the law of the Gospel is obeyed here by their friends who act as proxy for them, the Lord has administrators there to set them free.*"[28] Truly, as we can clearly see, in Joseph's own words, the subject of baptism for the dead seemed "to occupy my mind, and press itself upon my feelings the strongest, since I have been pursued by my enemies" (D&C 128:1).

Precept upon precept, here a little and there a little, the Lord made known significant truths relative to work in behalf of the dead. In time the Saints came to understand, for example, that men should receive the ordinances in behalf of men, women in behalf of women.[29] In Nauvoo a practice evolved among Church members of being "sealed" or "adopted" to prominent Church leaders. And yet there was an unrest, an anxiety among some of the leaders, a quiet realization that the complete mind and will of God had not been made known on the matter. Some fifty years after the death of the Prophet Joseph Smith, President Wilford Woodruff wrote, "When I went before the Lord to know who I should be adopted to (we were then being adopted to prophets and apostles), the Spirit of God said to me, *'Have you not a father, who begot you?'* 'Yes, I have.' *'Then why not honor him? Why not be adopted to him?'* 'Yes,' says I, 'that is right.' I was adopted to my father, and should have had my father sealed to his father, and so back; and the duty that I want every man who presides over a Temple to see performed from this day henceforth and forever, unless the Lord Almighty commands otherwise, is, let every man be adopted to his father." President Woodruff further instructed the Saints: "*We want the Latter-day Saints from this time to trace their genealogies as far as they can, and to be sealed*

---

28. *Joseph Smith* [manual], 474; emphasis added.
29. See Brigham Young, in *Journal of Discourses,* 16:165–66.

to their fathers and mothers. Have children sealed to their parents, and run this chain through as far as you can get it. . . . This is the will of the Lord to his people, and I think when you come to reflect upon it you will find it to be true."[30] This divine directive was, of course, fundamental to the establishment of the Genealogical Society and to what we now know as family history associated with the labor of redeeming the dead in temples.

CONCLUSION

When one contemplates Joseph Smith's most significant contributions to the world of religious thought—as well as the billions of persons who would eventually be affected by this doctrine—then surely the redemption of the dead ranks high on the list. Brother Joseph once remarked that "we are frequently asked the question, what has become of our fathers? Will they all be damned for not obeying the Gospel, when they never heard it? Certainly not. But they will possess the same privilege that we here enjoy, through the medium of the everlasting priesthood, which not only administers on earth, but also in heaven, and the wise dispensations of the great Jehovah."[31]

The good news, or glad tidings, of salvation in Christ is intended to lift our sights and bring hope to our souls, to "bind up the brokenhearted, to proclaim liberty to the captives, and the opening of the prison to them that are bound" (Isaiah 61:1). That hope in Christ is hope in the infinite capacity of an infinite Being to save all humankind from ignorance as well as from sin and death. The God of Abraham, Isaac, and Jacob is indeed the God of the living (Matthew 22:32), and his influence and redemptive mercies span the veil of death. The apostle Paul wrote that "if in this life

---

30. Clark, *Messages of the First Presidency,* 3:256–57; emphasis added; also in Packer, *Holy Temple,* 201–2.
31. *Joseph Smith* [manual], 408.

only we have hope in Christ, we are of all men most miserable" (1 Corinthians 15:19).

So what of those who never have the opportunity in this life to know of Christ and his gospel, who never have the opportunity to be baptized for a remission of sins and for entrance into the kingdom of God, who never have the privilege of being bound in marriage and sealed in the family unit? In a society gripped by cynicism, strangled by hopelessness, and spiritually rudderless in a world where there has been a waning of belonging, the scriptures and revelations of the Restoration bear witness of a God of mercy and vision, of an omnipotent One whose reach to his children is neither blocked by distance nor dimmed by death. Truly, "all those who have not had an opportunity of hearing the Gospel, and being administered unto by an inspired man in the flesh, *must have it hereafter, before they can be finally judged*."[32]

And so, after the doctrinal foundation had been laid, God made known through the Prophet of the Restoration those ennobling truths that pertain to life and salvation, both here and hereafter. Truly, as Joseph explained, "It is no more incredible that God should *save* the dead, than that he should *raise* the dead."[33] Surely no work could represent a more noble cause, a more valiant enterprise. And no labor in time could have more eternal implications.

---

32. *Joseph Smith* [manual], 471; emphasis added.
33. *Joseph Smith* [manual], 471.

Chapter 15

"WE BELIEVE"

Nauvoo, Illinois, March 1842. The Prophet Joseph received the Egyptian papyri in the summer of 1835 and began to translate them within a short time. That work of translation was interrupted and delayed as Joseph dealt with such matters as the construction and dedication of the Kirtland Temple, sending missionaries to Great Britain, apostasy in Kirtland, persecution in Missouri, and leading a growing Church. By March of 1842 the papyri had been translated, and the writings of Abraham and the accompanying facsimiles were being prepared for publication in the Times and Seasons. *During this same time John Wentworth requested information from the Prophet on the rise and progress of The Church of Jesus Christ of Latter-day Saints. Joseph's letter to Wentworth contained a brief history and then thirteen unnumbered statements of belief and practice.*

Few teachings are better known to the Saints than the statements we call the Articles of Faith, which were written by Joseph Smith to set forth a fairly comprehensive summary of our beliefs and practices. Young children memorize them in Primary, missionaries make them available to persons investigating the Church, and millions of members far and wide refer to them when asked what we believe. They are, in many ways, a handy guide to our faith, a systematic treatment of the major doctrines of the restored gospel.

The Articles of Faith were the concluding part of what the Saints for decades have called the Wentworth Letter. John Wentworth, editor of the popular newspaper the *Chicago Democrat,* was approached by an acquaintance named George Barstow who was seeking information on the Mormons, presumably for a history of New Hampshire that he was writing. Wentworth approached the Prophet and received from him a brief but beautifully written history of the rise and progress of the Church. Appended to this history were thirteen unnumbered statements of belief.[1] The Wentworth Letter first appeared in print on 1 March 1842 in the *Times and Seasons.*[2] These thirteen statements of religious belief were canonized by vote of the Church as a part of the Pearl of Great Price at the October 1880 general conference.[3]

Regarding the Articles of Faith, Elder B. H. Roberts penned the following: "These Articles of Faith were not produced by the labored efforts and harmonized contentions of scholastics, but were struck off by one inspired mind at a single effort to make a declaration of that which is most assuredly believed by the Church, for one making earnest inquiry about the truth. The combined directness, perspicuity [sharpness, penetrating insight], simplicity and comprehensiveness of this statement of the principles of our religion may be relied upon as strong evidence of a divine inspiration resting upon the Prophet, Joseph Smith."[4]

---

1. For a consideration of various documents that such persons as Oliver Cowdery, Joseph Young, Orson Pratt, and Orson Hyde prepared on the basic beliefs of the Church, see Welch and Whittaker, "'We Believe. . . . ': Development of the Articles of Faith," *Ensign,* Sept. 1979, 51–55; see also Brandt, "Origin and Importance of the Articles of Faith," 411–20.
2. Joseph Smith, "Church History," *Times and Seasons* 3, no. 9 (Mar. 1842): 706–10.
3. See Peterson, *Pearl of Great Price,* 22–23.
4. *History of the Church,* 4:535n.

DOCTRINAL SIGNIFICANCE

Each of the Articles of Faith is a clear and straightforward expression of doctrine or practice. In some cases, these statements are also an indication of some of the theologically distinctive beliefs of the Restoration, that is, how the restored gospel and The Church of Jesus Christ of Latter-day Saints differ from other established churches or denominations.

ARTICLE OF FAITH 1

We believe in God the Eternal Father, and in His Son, Jesus Christ, and in the Holy Ghost.

The First Vision was, as we discussed in Chapter 2, the beginning of the revelation of God to man in these last days. In that supernal theophany, the boy prophet became a firsthand witness that the Father and Son were separate Persons and distinct Beings. "I have always declared God to be a distinct personage," Joseph Smith taught only eleven days before his death, "Jesus Christ a separate and distinct personage from God the Father, and that the Holy Ghost was a distinctive personage and a Spirit; and *these three constitute three distinct personages and three Gods.*"[5] Such a statement would have clearly been at variance with the teachings of Jews, traditional Christians, and Muslims. To be monotheistic is to believe in one God. From a Jewish perspective, that one God is Yahweh, or Jehovah. For Muslims it is Allah. For traditional Christians, it is a God who is manifest in plurality and unity, a Trinity made up of three distinct persons but one being—Father, Son, and Holy Spirit—of one essence or one substance.

Joseph Smith and the Latter-day Saints believe themselves to be monotheistic. We are not deistic or polytheistic. "In the

---

5. *Joseph Smith* [manual], 41–42; emphasis added.

ultimate and final sense of the word," Elder Bruce R. McConkie wrote, "there is only one true and living God. He is the Father, the Almighty Elohim, the Supreme Being, the Creator and Ruler of the universe. . . . Christ is God; he alone is the Savior. The Holy Ghost is God; he is one with the Father and the Son. But these two are the second and third members of the Godhead. The Father is God above all, and is, in fact, the God of the Son."[6] Joseph Smith taught that it is "the province of the Father to preside as the Chief or President, Jesus as the Mediator, and the Holy Ghost as a Testator or Witness. The Son [has] a tabernacle and so [does] the Father, but the Holy Ghost is a personage of spirit without tabernacle."[7] We balance this understanding with the fact that to love the Father is to love the Son, to have faith in the Father is to have faith in the Son, to serve the Father is to serve the Son, and to worship the Father is to worship the Son. We do not specialize in members of the Godhead. We know they are separate identities, separate Persons, and separate Beings, but we neither divide our loyalties nor dissect our devotion. We believe in God.

We believe in one God in that we believe in one Godhead, one Divine Presidency of the universe. Restoration scripture affirms that these three Gods, three Beings, are one (2 Nephi 31:21; Alma 11:44; Mormon 7:7; D&C 20:28). How so? As the brethren in the School of the Elders learned, "These three constitute the great, matchless, governing and supreme power over all things; by whom all things were created and made that were created and made, and these three constitute the Godhead, and are one; the Father and the Son possessing the same mind, the same wisdom, glory, power, and fullness."[8] Further, the Father, Son, and Holy Ghost are infinitely more one than they are separate, but they happen to be, from

6. *New Witness for the Articles of Faith*, 51.

7. *Joseph Smith* [manual], 42.

8. *Lectures on Faith*, 59.

a Latter-day Saint perspective, separate Beings, separate Gods. In the words of Elder Jeffrey R. Holland: "We believe these three divine persons constituting a single Godhead are united in purpose, in manner, in testimony, in mission. We believe Them to be filled with the same godly sense of mercy and love, justice and grace, patience, forgiveness, and redemption. I think it is accurate to say we believe They are in every significant and eternal aspect imaginable *except* believing Them to be three persons combined in one substance, a Trinitarian notion not set forth in scriptures because it is not true." He added, "Our view of the Godhead breaks with post-New Testament Christian history and returns to the doctrine taught by Jesus Himself."[9]

ARTICLE OF FAITH 2

We believe that men will be punished for their own sins, and not for Adam's transgression.

Dating from the early centuries of the Christian Church, the doctrine of human depravity—the notion that the human soul is bent, warped, tainted by the "original sin" of our first parents—held full sway in the hearts and minds of most all Christian religionists and believers throughout the world. Onto the stage of faith came the weak and simple Prophet of the Restoration, and his teachings were as a refreshing breeze upon a people who had been scorched by the flames of high Calvinism. Joseph translated these simple words in the Book of Mormon, words that would have profound implications: "And now, behold, *if Adam had not transgressed he would not have fallen, but he would have remained in the garden of Eden. . . .* And *they would have had no children*; wherefore they would have remained in a state of innocence, having no joy, for they knew no misery; doing no good, for they knew no sin. But behold, *all things*

---

9. "The Only True God and Jesus Christ Whom He Hath Sent," *Ensign,* Nov. 2007, 40.

have been done in the wisdom of him who knoweth all things. Adam fell that men might be; and men are, that they might have joy. And the Messiah cometh in the fulness of time, that he may redeem the children of men from the fall" (2 Nephi 2:22–25; emphasis added).

In a letter to his son Moroni, Mormon offered a doctrinal corrective to a heresy that had crept into Nephite culture. Quoting the Savior, Mormon wrote: "Little children are whole, for they are not capable of committing sin; wherefore the curse of Adam is taken from them in me, that it hath no power over them." Mormon added that "little children are alive in Christ, even from the foundation of the world" (Moroni 8:8, 12). "The doctrine of baptizing children," Brother Joseph emphatically declared, "or sprinkling them, or they must welter in hell, is a doctrine not true, not supported in Holy Writ, and is not consistent with the character of God. All children are redeemed by the blood of Jesus Christ, and the moment that children leave this world, they are taken to the bosom of Abraham."[10]

In his inspired translation of Genesis, the Prophet recorded the following words of God to Adam: "I have forgiven thee thy transgression in the Garden of Eden." Enoch then wrote: "Hence came the saying abroad among the people, that the Son of God hath atoned for original guilt, wherein the sins of the parents cannot be answered upon the heads of the children, for they are whole from the foundation of the world" (JST, Genesis 6:55–56; Moses 6:53–54). These marvelous truths were echoed again and again in modern revelations (D&C 29:46–47; 74:7; 137:10). In February 1841 the Prophet Joseph is reported to have said: *"Adam did not commit sin in eating the fruit, for God had decreed that he should eat and fall. . . . Therefore the Lord appointed us to fall and also redeemed us, for where sin abounded grace did much more abound."*[11]

---

10. *Joseph Smith* [manual], 95.
11. *Words of Joseph Smith,* 63; emphasis added.

James Burgess recorded that he heard the Prophet say the following about the Creation and the Fall: "In the image of the Gods created they them, male and female, innocent, harmless, and spotless, bearing the same character and image as the Gods. And *when man fell he did not lose his image, but his character still retained the image of his Maker.* Christ, who is in the image of man, is also the express image of his Father's person. . . . Through the Atonement of Christ and the resurrection, and obedience to the gospel, we shall again be conformed to the image of his Son, Jesus Christ; then we shall have attained to the image, glory, and character of God."[12]

Deeply significant messages are contained in those short passages: Adam and Eve needed to fall; theirs was a "fortunate fall"; if they had not fallen, they would have remained spiritually stagnant; if they had not fallen, they would have had no children; because they fell, they gained a knowledge of good and evil and could thereby acquire experience and joy. The Fall opened the door to the Atonement. Christ's atonement cancels out the effect of the transgression of our first parents. By implication, Christ came to do far more than fix the books, far more than balance justice and mercy, as important as that was; he came to reclaim and redeem humanity, for redeemed humanity will rise to grander spiritual heights than unfallen humanity.[13]

Elder Dallin H. Oaks explained in general conference that "it was Eve who first transgressed the limits of Eden in order to initiate the conditions of mortality. Her act, whatever its nature, was formally a transgression but eternally a glorious necessity to open the doorway to eternal life. Adam showed his wisdom by doing the same. . . .

"Some Christians condemn Eve for her act, concluding that she and her daughters are somehow flawed by it. But Latter-day Saints,

---

12. *Joseph Smith* [manual], 52; emphasis added.
13. See Lewis, *Miracles*, 162.

informed by revelation, celebrate Eve's act and honor her wisdom and courage in the great episode called the Fall."[14]

ARTICLE OF FAITH 3

We believe that through the Atonement of Christ, all mankind may be saved, by obedience to the laws and ordinances of the Gospel.

In contrast to beliefs held by many Christians in the nineteenth century, particularly those who subscribed to the teachings of John Calvin, the message of the restored gospel was that no human being comes to the earth who is outside the reach of redemption and salvation. All who breathe the breath of life are capable of hearing the word of truth (here or hereafter), being touched by that word, coming unto Christ by covenant, being born again into a newness of life, contributing to the establishment of the kingdom of God on earth, and eventually enjoying life everlasting in the highest heaven.

Elder D. Todd Christofferson reminded us of the sober reality that "by virtue of the Fall and our own disobedience, the law condemns us to temporal and spiritual death. Law, or justice, is not a pleasant concept when one is condemned by it and 'miserable forever.' Worldly philosophies attempt to resolve this misery and guilt by endeavoring to erase divine law or define it out of existence. . . . [I]f we could get rid of the law, there would be no such thing as sin and thus no misery. With Corianton, there are many today who 'try to suppose that it is injustice that the sinner should be consigned to a state of misery' (Alma 42:1). This approach, however, if it could succeed, would also eliminate our potential for happiness. We need to preserve justice for our own sakes, for our own potential happiness.

"There is a better way. That better way is not to deny the law,

---

14. *With Full Purpose of Heart,* 30.

but to come out from under its condemnation. The righteous are supported by law, a pleasant position to be in. But to achieve that status, we need more than the law alone. We need a Savior. We need a Mediator."[15]

Jesus of Nazareth chose, because of his infinite love, to offer himself as a ransom for our sins and make available thereby forgiveness and spiritual renewal to the whole of humankind. It is all made possible by the gift of Jesus Christ, but it is a gift that must be received (D&C 88:33). It comes by grace, by his unearned divine assistance, his enabling power, but we must exercise faith and participate in the works that evidence our faith.[16]

The scriptures of the Restoration reveal the mind-expanding doctrine that Christ's is an "infinite atonement" (2 Nephi 9:7; 25:16; Alma 34:14; D&C 76:22–24). President Russell M. Nelson stated that the Savior's Atonement "is infinite—without an end. It was also infinite in that all of humankind would be saved from never-ending death. It was infinite in terms of his immense suffering. It was infinite in time, putting an end to the preceding prototype of animal sacrifice. It was infinite in scope—it was to be done once for all. And the mercy of the Atonement extends not only to an infinite number of people, but also to an infinite number of worlds created by Him. It was infinite beyond any human scale of measurement or mortal comprehension."[17]

ARTICLE OF FAITH 4

We believe that the first principles and ordinances of the Gospel are: first, Faith in the Lord Jesus Christ; second, Repentance; third, Baptism by immersion for the remission of sins; fourth, Laying on of hands for the gift of the Holy Ghost.

---

15. "Justification and Sanctification," *Ensign,* June 2001, 20.

16. See Uchtdorf, "The Gift of Grace," *Ensign,* May 2015, 107.

17. *Perfection Pending,* 167.

The gospel of Jesus Christ is the good news, the glad tidings of redemption from sin and death and hell and endless torment. "Behold I have given unto you my gospel," the risen Lord said to his American Hebrews, "and this is the gospel which I have given unto you—that I came into the world to do the will of my Father, because my Father sent me. And my Father sent me that I might be lifted up upon the cross" (3 Nephi 27:13–14). In Restoration scripture, the Prophet Joseph and Sidney Rigdon gave a similar definition of the gospel: "And this is the gospel, the glad tidings, . . . that he came into the world, even Jesus, to be crucified for the world, and to bear the sins of the world, and to sanctify the world, and to cleanse it from all unrighteousness; that through him all might be saved whom the Father had put into his power and made by him" (D&C 76:40–42). In short, the gospel is the Atonement, the glad tidings that there is hope for spiritual recovery, hope for renewal and re-creation, hope for the immortality of the soul. And yet the scriptures also testify that the gospel is the good news that there is a path, a way, a specific course to follow to appropriate the powers and blessings of the Atonement. And that path is what we call the first principles and ordinances of the gospel (3 Nephi 27:19–21; D&C 33:11–12; 39:5–6). These are what the Prophet called the "articles of adoption,"[18] the means by which we are adopted into the family of the Lord Jesus Christ.

With the Protestant Reformation, beginning in the sixteenth century, and with the introduction of the notion of a "priesthood of all believers," there came by necessity a change in attitude toward the ordinances, or sacraments, of the Church. The Savior's counsel to Nicodemus that a man *must* be born of water and of the Spirit, *must* be properly baptized (John 3:3–5)—a requirement from the Son of God himself—came to be viewed in figurative terms and to

---

18. *Words of Joseph Smith,* 256.

be taken somewhat lightly. Baptism could not be *required* for salvation, the theologians reasoned, since that would mean that something must be added to what they called the "finished work of Jesus Christ." To suggest, as the Christian Church had done for fourteen centuries, that one must be baptized was to make of baptism a supplementary work, and as all good Christians know, we are not saved by our works. And so it was that ordinances slid into the ranks of the recommended and perhaps even the expected but certainly not the required. I once asked a Protestant minister, "Is baptism essential for salvation?" He paused for a moment and replied: "Well, it is *necessary* but not *essential*." Teasing apart those two words is no easy task.

The Restoration sounded the charge loud and clear: Jesus Christ is the only way by which humankind may be saved. His atonement makes available forgiveness of sins, transformation of human nature, and deliverance from the pulls of the natural man into the realm of divine experience. And the message is further extended: The ordinances of salvation are required, and they must be performed properly and in order and by the power of restored priesthood authority. "Behold, I say unto you that all old covenants have I caused to be done away in this thing; and this is a new and an everlasting covenant, even that which was from the beginning. Wherefore, although a man should be baptized [without authority] an hundred times it availeth him nothing, for you cannot enter in at the strait gate by the law of Moses, neither by your dead works. For it is because of your dead works that I have caused this last covenant and this church to be built up unto me, even as in days of old. Wherefore, enter ye in at the gate, as I have commanded, and seek not to counsel your God. Amen" (D&C 22:1–4).

ARTICLE OF FAITH 5

We believe that a man must be called of God, by prophecy, and by the laying on of hands by those who are in authority, to preach the Gospel and administer in the ordinances thereof.

We need not belabor the point we have already made, namely, that divine authority may well be the greatest dividing point between The Church of Jesus Christ of Latter-day Saints and all other religious denominations (see Chapter 4). Joseph Smith was called to serve as a revealer of doctrine, to be sure, and most of our discussion in this book is taken up with demonstrating that what he learned by revelation and what he taught to the Saints is perhaps the greatest fruit, or evidence, of his prophetic call. But he was also called to be a legal administrator, one through whom priesthood, keys, authorities, and a correct understanding of quorums and councils were restored to earth. Joseph knew, and his followers today acknowledge, that one is not ordained by receiving a ministerial degree or certificate of graduation; rather, ordination comes by the laying on of hands by those who have been previously and properly ordained.

ARTICLE OF FAITH 6

We believe in the same organization that existed in the Primitive Church, namely, apostles, prophets, pastors, teachers, evangelists, and so forth.

The sixth article of faith highlights the need for a church, a gathering of Saints, a body of believers, what the early apostles called the "body of Christ." Christianity entails more than prayer, fasting, and searching the scriptures—more than an individual effort to live the principles of the gospel of Jesus Christ. As vital as personal devotion and individual effort are, Christianity is fully lived out only *in community*. In our day, millions of persons throughout the world claim to be spiritual but not religious, wanting mystical experience without affiliating with a religious organization. We learn through the restored doctrine and practices revealed through Joseph Smith that without the Church, one cannot receive the requisite ordinances of salvation or exaltation; cannot develop those Christlike qualities and attributes that come only through association and affiliation with other individuals who are striving for basically the same things; cannot participate in the ongoing service and organized sacrifice that can come only through working with others. Without the Church and Church affiliation and involvement, one simply cannot cultivate the gospel light that emanates freely and enticingly from striving and stretching members of the Church.

President Henry B. Eyring spoke of one person's attempt to go it on his own. "I have heard the boast of a man who walked away from the Church slowly, at first just ceasing to teach his Sunday School class and then staying away from church and then forgetting tithing now and then. Along the way he would say to me: 'I feel just as spiritual as I did before I stopped those things and just as much at peace. Besides, I enjoy Sundays more than I did; it's more a day of rest.' Or, 'I think I've been blessed temporally as much or more as I was when I was paying tithing.' *He could not sense the difference, but I could. The light in his eyes and even the shine in his countenance were dimming.* He could not tell, since one of the effects of disobeying God seems to be the creation of just enough spiritual anesthetic to block any sensation as the ties to God are being cut. Not only did the testimony of truth slowly erode, but even the memories of what it was like to be in the light began to seem to him like a delusion."[19]

The Church of Jesus Christ is and forevermore will be built

---

19. *Because He First Loved Us*, 7–8; emphasis added.

upon the foundation of apostles and prophets (Ephesians 2:20). These are the chief officers within the household of faith, the presiding legal administrators, the ones charged to stand as special witnesses of the name of Christ in all the world, the ones commissioned to build up the Church and regulate all its affairs throughout the earth (D&C 107:23, 34). They are the prophets, the seers, and the revelators, the ones called to see things "afar off" (D&C 101:54), to be watchmen on the tower of Israel, the stewards of the household of God. Like Enoch, they see "things which [are] not visible to the natural eye" (Moses 6:36).

As to the other offices and callings that make up the Church, there will, of course, always be a need for teachers and preachers and pastors (bishops and stake presidents) and patriarchs. But the names and functions of callings and assignments may change as needed, for ours is not only a true Church but also a *living* one (D&C 1:30). Elder Neal A. Maxwell, a modern apostle, put it this way: "When the word *living* is used, it carries a divinely deliberate connotation. The Church is neither dead nor dying. Nor is it even wounded. The Church, like the living God who established it, is alive, aware, and functioning. It is not a museum that houses a fossilized faith; rather, it is a kinetic kingdom characterized by living faith in living disciples."[20]

Thus we need not believe there were in the Primitive Church, the Church established by Christ in the first century, Regional Representatives, Assistants to the Twelve, a Presiding Bishopric, regional welfare agents, or Single Adult representatives in order to stand by our sixth article of faith. Rather, the Lord's Church will always have some organization in place, but the particular organization may and will differ according to needs, circumstances, and ongoing divine direction. What will not change is that it will always

---

20. *Things As They Really Are*, 46.

be led by properly ordained prophets and seers who make known the current mind and will of the Almighty.

On 11 March 1844 Joseph Smith gave a most unusual assignment to a group of brethren. He asked them to prepare a kind of constitution for the kingdom of God. Later in the week, John Taylor, as a representative of that group of three, responded that no progress had been made toward the accomplishment of that assignment. Joseph acknowledged their failure by stating that he knew that such a thing could not be done. He had gone before the Lord, seeking that such a constitution be made known by revelation. The answer had come in a most interesting way: "*Ye are my constitution* and I am your God and ye are my spokesmen, therefore from henceforth keep my commandments."[21] The leaders of Zion are to govern by revelation—modern, current, even daily revelation—and not by written documents alone. All of God's purposes and designs for his children cannot and should not be codified (Moroni 6:9; D&C 20:45; 46:2), at least not in a living Church.

ARTICLE OF FAITH 7

We believe in the gift of tongues, prophecy, revelation, visions, healings, interpretation of tongues, and so forth.

The Gospel of Mark contains a record of the resurrected Savior's final instructions before his ascension, which has come to be known as the great commission: "And he said unto them, Go ye into all the world, and preach the gospel to every creature. He that believeth and is baptized shall be saved; but he that believeth not shall be damned. And these signs shall follow them that believe; in my name shall they cast out devils; they shall speak with new tongues; they shall take up serpents; and if they drink any deadly thing, it

---

21. Joseph F. Smith Minutes of the Council of Fifty, 21 Apr. 1880, as cited in Ehat, "'It Seems like Heaven Began on Earth,'" 259; emphasis added.

shall not hurt them: they shall lay hands on the sick, and they shall recover" (Mark 16:15–18).

As we have mentioned, in the nineteenth century opinions on the matter of spiritual gifts were mixed. Some like Sidney Rigdon believed that they ought to be found among those professing Christ, while persons like John Wesley (the "reasonable enthusiast") and Alexander Campbell (a rational religionist) were more skeptical, or at least nervous and uncomfortable about such gifts. Even in today's Christian world there are those individuals and denominations known as continuationists, who hold that the gifts of the Spirit have continued from the time of the first-century Church. There are others, known as cessationists, who believe that all such gifts and spiritual outpourings ceased with the first-century Church and are not to be practiced or enjoyed today. There are Pentecostals in our time who speak in tongues and prophesy, just as there are theologians and preachers who condemn such as "charismatic chaos."[22]

The Church of Jesus Christ of Latter-day Saints is a living, breathing manifestation of the truth that God speaks, that angels appear, that visions are received, that prophets prophesy, that healings and tongues are alive and well in the restored Church. Indeed, as Jesus said, if these manifestations of the workings of the Spirit are not present, then the Church of Jesus Christ is not on earth. Mormon taught that if miracles have ceased or angels no longer appear, it is because faith has ceased among the children of men (Moroni 7:37–38).

Contemplate for a moment such scenes as the First Vision; the coming of Moroni; the translation of the golden plates; the visits of John the Baptist as well as Peter, James, and John; the spiritual outpourings in Kirtland; the ministry of Moses, Elias, Elijah, Michael, Raphael, and "divers angels . . . all declaring their dispensation,

---

22. Rack, *Reasonable Enthusiast;* MacArthur, *Charismatic Chaos.*

their rights, their keys, their honors, their majesty and glory, and the power of their priesthood; giving line upon line, precept upon precept; here a little, and there a little; giving us consolation by holding forth that which is to come, confirming our hope!" (D&C 128:21). Reflect on the marvelous day of the Lord's power when scores of persons were healed miraculously in Nauvoo, Illinois, and in Montrose, Iowa. Meditate for a moment on the thousands upon thousands of journal entries by Latter-day Saints that record miracles and wonders and signs abounding, from Palmyra to Paris and from Salt Lake City to São Paulo. Indeed, if the people of God live to receive them, the gifts of the Spirit are frequent and ongoing and invigorating; they remind us that this is the work of Almighty God, and that while "faith cometh not by signs," signs do indeed "follow those that believe" (D&C 63:9).

ARTICLE OF FAITH 8

We believe the Bible to be the word of God as far as it is translated correctly; we also believe the Book of Mormon to be the word of God.

Elder M. Russell Ballard stated in general conference: "The Holy Bible is well named. It is holy because it teaches truth, holy because it warms us with its spirit, holy because it teaches us to know God and understand His dealings with men, and holy because it testifies throughout its pages of the Lord Jesus Christ. . . . Honest, diligent study of the Bible does make us better and better. . . . Brothers and sisters, I am sure many of you have had the experience of hearing people say that 'Mormons are not Christians because they have their own Bible, the Book of Mormon.' To anyone harboring this misconception, we say that we believe in the Lord Jesus Christ as our Savior and the author of our salvation and that we believe, revere, and love the Holy Bible. We do have additional sacred scripture, including the

Book of Mormon, but it supports the Bible, never substituting for it." Finally, Elder Ballard testified that the Bible "is one of the pillars of our faith, a powerful witness of the Savior and of Christ's ongoing influence in the lives of those who worship and follow Him. The more we read and study the Bible and its teachings, the more clearly we see the doctrinal underpinnings of the restored gospel of Jesus Christ. We tend to love the scriptures that we spend time with. We may need to balance our study in order to love and understand all scripture."[23]

Elder Dallin H. Oaks referred to the standard works and the Joseph Smith Translation of the Bible as the "royal family of scripture."[24] And we do not love one child in our family more than we love another.

The removal of precious truths from the Bible took place in the process of the translation of the text, as well as through the process of transmission through the generations. To be sure, translation, or the transition from one language to another, is a potentially serious barrier to the communication of sacred truths. Elder Bruce R. McConkie wrote that as the words of scripture "fell from seeric lips and flowed from prophetic pens," they made known the mind and will of God. "Since then there have been additions and deletions, editorial and other changes, and translations into tongues that oftentimes have no equivalent words or phrases to convey the original and precise meaning" of the Spirit-breathed word. He explained that "aside from the sorry state of the text due to scholastic incompetence, there was a far more serious problem, namely, the theological bias of the translators. This caused them to change the meaning or paraphrase texts that were either unclear or embarrassing to them."[25] Thus the understanding of doctrines was influenced by the process of translation.

---

23. "The Miracle of the Holy Bible," *Ensign*, May 2007, 80–82.
24. In Millet and Matthews, *Plain and Precious Truths Restored*, 13.
25. *New Witness for the Articles of Faith*, 401, 403.

As truths were either taken away or kept back (1 Nephi 13:26, 28, 32, 34), lacunae, or holes, gaps in the manuscript, would affect what was remaining, leading to more confusion and misunderstanding. One can only translate what is there, can only render an honest translation with what remains. The question is not whether there have been scribal errors through the centuries—there have been. The question is not whether the Bible is the word of God—it is. "The question is not whether the Bible can be relied upon with confidence if in fact there have been errors—it can."[26]

Latter-day Saints do not believe the Bible has to have come down in perfectly untampered fashion to be spiritually normative and eternally valuable. Errors in the Bible do not tarnish its image for us. For that matter, while Latter-day Saints accept the Book of Mormon, Doctrine and Covenants, and Pearl of Great Price as holy scripture, we would not rush to proclaim their inerrancy. The greater marvel is that an infinite and perfect Being can work through finite and imperfect humans to deliver his word to his children.

Joseph Smith believed, to be sure, that the message of the Bible was true and from God. We could say that he believed the Bible was "God's word." I am not so certain that he or modern Church leaders would be convinced that every sentence recorded in the Testaments necessarily contains "God's words," meaning a direct quotation or a transcription of divine direction. Rowan Williams, the former Archbishop of Canterbury, wrote: "Even on the most conservative estimate of [the four Gospels] accounts, there must have been episodes imperfectly seen or understood, episodes where direct eyewitness evidence was lacking, along with partially conflicting testimonies. To grant this is simply to allow that the inspiration of the Gospel narratives is not the gift to the writers of a miraculous God's-eye view. If Jesus' life is a truly human one, the

---

26. See Ballard, "The Miracle of the Holy Bible," *Ensign*, May 2007, 80–82.

witness to his life must be human as well, and human witness is seldom straightforward or comprehensive."[27]

We need not say more about the correctness of the Book of Mormon or its doctrinal soundness beyond what we have already discussed (see Chapter 3). We need only be reminded that while the *truthfulness* of a spiritual matter can be known only by the power of the Spirit of God (1 Corinthians 2:11–14), its spiritual *significance* can often be discerned by the kind of opposition it engenders. If I did not know, for example, by the power of the Holy Spirit, that temples are in very deed the house of the Lord and that sacred, exalting ordinances are performed there, I might reasonably suspect that to be the case as I witness the vicious venom with which otherwise sane and sophisticated human beings stand in line to rail and protest against the building of such houses of worship. Now, the Book of Mormon has certainly had its enemies, those who with rabid ferocity rush to denounce it as false, even devilish. One has to wonder what it is that causes such attitudes and behavior, especially in regard to a book that encourages people to love God and do good. We are reminded of Nephi's chilling words: "Yea, wo be unto him that sayeth: We have received, and we need no more! And in fine, wo unto all those who tremble, and are angry because of the truth of God! For behold, he that is built upon the rock receiveth it with gladness" (2 Nephi 28:27–28).

ARTICLE OF FAITH 9

We believe all that God has revealed, all that He does now reveal, and we believe that He will yet reveal many great and important things pertaining to the Kingdom of God.

On a number of occasions through the years I have had an opportunity to speak with persons who have chosen to leave The

27. *Christ on Trial*, xv.

Church of Jesus Christ of Latter-day Saints and join another religious denomination. I have often asked if they miss anything in particular, now that they have formally separated themselves from the faith of the Latter-day Saints. Many of them comment that they miss the culture—the people, the brotherhood and sisterhood, the activities, the service projects, the worship services, or the temple. A surprising number have expressed to me that what they miss most is hearing about revelation, both general and personal. Depending on the kind of church they have joined, they express that they seldom hear of the leaders of that particular tradition seeking for or receiving divine direction, nor do they receive much if any encouragement to seek for personal revelation when they have family challenges, spiritual questions, or decisions to make. It isn't that churches, particularly Christian churches, do not believe that the children of God can receive what they might call illumination or direction from heaven, for they do. What they seldom talk about, however, is revelation, at least revelation beyond the holy scriptures. From their perspective, if in fact the Bible is the final, complete, and infallible word of God, why would a person need to look elsewhere?

Joseph Smith received revelation directly from God, and he stood as the prophet and revelator, the head of the dispensation. But he also encouraged every member of the Church to seek for and expect the Lord's guidance. Membership in the restored Church entailed the reception of the Holy Spirit, and, as Joseph taught, no man can receive the Holy Ghost and not receive revelation, because the Holy Ghost is a revelator.[28] It is not just that the Saints have an *opportunity* to come to know the things of God; rather, they have a *responsibility* to qualify for and seek after such things. It comes with membership in the Lord's Church. The strength of this latter-day work is to be found in the witness, conviction, and personal

---

28. *Joseph Smith* [manual], 132.

revelation acquired by the weak and simple, the boys and girls, the men and women who know in their heart of hearts that they can approach God and receive heavenly help in the form of comfort, guidance, and ongoing direction.

Elder Jeffrey R. Holland emphasized the vital point that "the scriptures are *not* the ultimate source of knowledge for Latter-day Saints. They are manifestations of the ultimate source. The ultimate source of knowledge and authority for a Latter-day Saint is the living God. The communication of those gifts comes from God as living, vibrant, divine revelation. . . . I express the deepest *personal* thanks that [God's] works never end and His 'words . . . never cease.' I bear witness of such divine loving attention and the recording of it."[29]

ARTICLE OF FAITH 10

We believe in the literal gathering of Israel and in the restoration of the Ten Tribes; that Zion (the New Jerusalem) will be built upon the American continent; that Christ will reign personally upon the earth; and that the earth will be renewed and receive its paradisiacal glory.

Joseph's mention of "the literal gathering of Israel" is by itself a significant deviation from the beliefs of most nineteenth-century Christians in America. By the time of the Restoration, Americans spoke often symbolically of Christians as "modern Israel" wandering in the wilderness in search of the promised land. But it was only symbolic, for very few took seriously the truth that the covenant God had made with Father Abraham would be fulfilled through the work of his "literal descendants." Onto the scene came Joseph Smith and the Latter-day Saints, a people who read the Old Testament, the New Testament, the Book of Mormon, and the Doctrine and Covenants, and they came away from their study of holy writ

---

29. "My Words . . . Never Cease," *Ensign*, May 2008, 93–94.

convinced that the prophetic word was to be taken literally, that they were in fact a part of a chosen people. From their study of the Book of Mormon alone they would come to understand that modern-day Jews were not the only descendants of Jacob of old.

In a revelation given through Joseph Smith at the time of a Church conference where the first ordinations to the office of high priest took place, the Lord said: "I, the Lord, will make known unto you what I will that ye shall do from this time until the next conference, which shall be held in Missouri, upon the land which I will consecrate unto *my people, which are a remnant of Jacob, and those who are heirs according to the covenant*" (D&C 52:2; emphasis added).

"Now do you see the importance of your patriarchal blessing?" President Russell M. Nelson asked. "I hope each of you has obtained one. It is precious. It is personal scripture to you. It declares your special lineage. It reminds you of your linkage with the past. And it will help you realize your future potential. Literally, you can lay claim upon the Lord for fulfillment of those blessings through your faithfulness."[30]

As we touched upon lightly in Chapter 8, the Latter-day Saints came to know that the prophecies of Isaiah and Jeremiah and Ezekiel concerning the establishment of Zion, the city of God, were to have their grand fulfillment in the dispensation of the fulness of times; that Zion was not limited to the Holy Mount in Jerusalem; that Zion was anywhere the pure in heart dwelt in the stakes throughout the world (D&C 97:21); that eventually the center place was to be in Independence, Jackson County, Missouri (D&C 57:1–3; 101:17–21). It was to this center place that the King of kings would come to his temple and to the priesthood council at Adam-ondi-Ahman (Malachi 3:1; D&C 84:2–5; 116).[31] The Saints rejoiced in

---

30. *Perfection Pending*, 205.

31. The Savior's preliminary appearances, as well as his coming in glory, are discussed in Chapter 19.

the knowledge that their trials and vicissitudes were temporary and that the millennial Messiah would one day cleanse the earth of all wickedness and dwell in peace for a thousand years on a paradisiacal earth with his covenant people.

ARTICLE OF FAITH 11

We claim the privilege of worshipping Almighty God according to the dictates of our own conscience, and allow all men the same privilege, let them worship how, where, or what they may.

Joseph Smith the Prophet loved the United States of America. He believed with all his heart that the founding fathers had been raised up by God (D&C 98:4–10; 101:76–80) to put in place a system of government that would ensure the kind of religious liberty that would permit and welcome a new order of religion—a restored order, based largely upon the teachings of Primitive Christianity. He observed that "the Constitution of the United States is a glorious standard; it is founded in the wisdom of God. It is a heavenly banner; it is to all those who are privileged with the sweets of liberty, like the cooling shades and refreshing waters of a great rock in a thirsty and weary land. It is like a great tree under whose branches men from every clime can be shielded from the burning rays of the sun."[32]

The Prophet said on another occasion: "We deem it a just principle, and it is one the force of which we believe ought to be duly considered by every individual, that all men are created equal, and that all have the privilege of thinking for themselves upon all matters relative to conscience. Consequently, then, we are not disposed, had we the power, to deprive any one of exercising that free

---

32. History, 1838–1856, volume C-1 [2 November 1838–31 July 1842], The Joseph Smith Papers, accessed 15 Mar. 2016, http://josephsmithpapers.org/paperSummary/history-1838-1856-volume-c-1-2-november-1838-31-july-1842?p=94.

independence of mind which heaven has so graciously bestowed upon the human family as one of its choicest gifts."[33]

An openness of mind and breadth of spirit characterized the Prophet of the Restoration, a genuine respect for noble men and women of various stripes and a compelling quest for truth wherever it could be found. Joseph identified the "first and fundamental principle of our holy religion" as a belief that "we have a right to embrace all, and every item of truth, without limitation or without being circumscribed or prohibited by the creeds or superstitious notions of men, or by the dominations of one another, when that truth is clearly demonstrated to our minds, and we have the highest degree of evidence of the same."[34]

ARTICLE OF FAITH 12

We believe in being subject to kings, presidents, rulers, and magistrates, in obeying, honoring, and sustaining the law.

In September of 1830 the Lord revealed a principle that would provide a distinctive perspective on life for the Prophet Joseph Smith and members of the restored Church. The Savior declared: "Wherefore, verily I say unto you that all things unto me are spiritual, and not at any time have I given unto you a law that was temporal" (D&C 29:34). Because God's work and glory, his highest priority, is to "bring to pass the immortality and eternal life of man" (Moses 1:39), everything he does—and everything we do—has eternal implications. This would include our civic and political responsibilities as citizens of a nation or principality.

The Savior himself established the principle that ought to guide how we carry out our responsibilities as citizens of a country. The

---

33. *Joseph Smith* [manual], 344–45.
34. "Copy of a Letter from J. Smith Jr. to Mr. Galland," *Times and Seasons* 1, no. 4 (Feb. 1840): 54; *Joseph Smith* [manual], 264.

Pharisees and Herodians sought to ensnare Jesus when they asked, "Is it lawful to give tribute unto Caesar, or not?" They of course hoped that the Master, the rightful King of the Jews, would prove by his reply to be disloyal to the emperor or in general to their Roman overlords. But, once again, Jesus spoiled their plans by replying, "Render . . . unto Caesar the things which are Caesar's; and unto God the things that are God's" (Matthew 22:15–21). Similarly, the apostle Paul counseled the Corinthian Saints to "be subject unto the higher powers. For there is no power but of God." Now note this significant comment: "*The powers that be are ordained of God.* Whosoever resisteth the power, resisteth the ordinance of God" (Romans 13:1–2; emphasis added).

On 17 August 1835 the first edition of the Doctrine and Covenants was being prepared to go to the Saints and the world. On that day, a document on governments and laws in general (presumably prepared by Oliver Cowdery but certainly approved by the Prophet) was accepted for inclusion in that first edition and has come down to us as section 134.

Members of The Church of Jesus Christ of Latter-day Saints have been charged by the Lord to be loyal citizens in the lands where they reside; to support and uphold the laws of the land; and if change is called for, to work for it through legal and appropriate means. A successor of Joseph Smith, President Howard W. Hunter, reminded us that "if executive officials have been elected by the vote of the people, after that vote is complete and the majority has spoken, we have the obligation to support and sustain those who have been elected by the majority. . . . In the legislative branches of our government, there may be laws enacted that we may find difficult to sustain as individuals, yet while they remain law, we have the obligation to abide by and support those laws. It may be that we think the law should be different, but while the statutes stand and until revoked by the people or by legislative or judicial action, we should sustain those laws. . . . I would hope that as members of the Church we can stand fast on these principles by supporting and sustaining our governments wherever we may live and by sustaining the officers of those governments with our prayers as well."[35]

President Hunter's immediate successor, President Gordon B. Hinckley, called for decency, respect, tolerance, and civility in political matters. "It's a wholesome and wonderful system that we have," he pointed out, "under which people are free to express themselves in electing those who shall represent them in the councils of government. I would hope that those concerned would address themselves to issues and not to personalities. The issues ought to be discussed freely, openly, candidly, and forcefully. But, I repeat, I would hope that there would be an avoidance of demeaning personalities."[36]

Because "the Lord God worketh not in darkness" (2 Nephi 26:23), leaders of the Church, charged by that same Lord and God to take the message of the Restoration to all nations (D&C 68:8–9), have nonetheless sought to do so openly, respectfully, and in harmony with local governments and policies. Official permission is always sought when the Brethren feel moved upon to enter a country. In short, the Church always enters through the front door to seek official status or for permission to have Latter-day Saint missionaries enter that land.

ARTICLE OF FAITH 13

We believe in being honest, true, chaste, benevolent, virtuous, and in doing good to all men; indeed, we may say that we follow the admonition of Paul—We believe all things, we hope all things, we have endured many things, and hope to be able

---

35. *Teachings of Howard W. Hunter,* 167–68.
36. *Teachings of Gordon B. Hinckley,* 455.

to endure all things. If there is anything virtuous, lovely, or of good report or praiseworthy, we seek after these things.

It is not insignificant that the Choice Seer reserved for last the subject of the thirteenth article of faith, nor did he exhaust what might have been mentioned about the beliefs of The Church of Jesus Christ of Latter-day Saints. Rather, this article is a powerful statement that the proclamation of sound doctrine must and should always precede, and lay the foundation for, the good life, the Christian life, the life that ought to characterize the followers of our Master. As Alma taught, God gave the commandments anciently to his people *after* he had made known unto them the plan of redemption (Alma 12:32). Rules and guidelines and regulations have purpose and value—and accomplish the Lord's desired ends—only as they are built upon the foundation of gospel doctrine. This is why President Boyd K. Packer in our own day declared that "true doctrine, understood, changes attitudes and behavior. The study of the doctrines of the gospel will improve behavior quicker than a study of behavior will improve behavior. . . . That is why we stress so forcefully the study of the doctrines of the gospel."[37]

"The thirteenth Article of Faith is in effect an addendum to all the others," Elder McConkie wrote. This particular article "does provide the ideal occasion to show the relationship between the great doctrines of the preceding articles and the ethical principles set forth in this concluding formal statement of belief.

"It is one thing to teach ethical principles, quite another to proclaim the great doctrinal verities, which are the foundation of true Christianity and out of which eternal salvation comes. True it is that salvation is limited to those in whose souls the ethical principles abound, but true it is also that Christian ethics, in the

---

37. "Little Children," *Ensign*, Nov. 1986, 17.

full and saving sense, automatically become a part of the lives of those who first believe Christian doctrines."[38]

CONCLUSION

The Articles of Faith are more than a handy guide to Latter-day Saint beliefs, though they are certainly that. They are a pattern for understanding what concepts and teachings are foundational and fundamental to our faith and way of life; they set forth an order, a significant order, that is highly instructive in what matters are of greatest importance. There is clearly a purpose to the order in which the articles are written.

Obviously, Joseph Smith did not address every Latter-day Saint belief. He might well also have taught that we believe in the Sacrament of the Lord's Supper, the premortal existence of all humankind, the redemption of the dead in the postmortal spirit world, eternal marriage and family, the degrees of glory hereafter, and other doctrinal tenets that fill out the glorious fabric of the restored gospel. What he did include, however, are vital and important features of our way of life, supernal verities that make us who and what we are. What a blessing it is to have a believing heart, and what a consummate privilege it is to have the truth—the truth that can awaken distant memories from a premortal past, the truth that places things in proper order and assists us to make sense of life, the truth that makes us free and saves our eternal souls.

---

38. *New Witness for the Articles of Faith,* 699.

Chapter 16

ENDOWMENT, CONSOLATION, AND INSTRUCTION

Kirtland, Ohio, 1836, and Nauvoo, Illinois, 1842–1843. The early Saints were informed that in Ohio, "I will give unto you my law; and there you shall be endowed with power from on high" (D&C 38:32). Two months later they were charged to "sanctify yourselves and ye shall be endowed with power" (D&C 43:16). Indeed, the Savior later promised that he had prepared "a great endowment and blessing to be poured out upon them" (D&C 105:12). The fulfillment of those prophecies came with the construction of the Kirtland Temple. There, during a pentecostal season of spiritual gifts and manifestations (from January to May of 1836), the God of Abraham, Isaac, and Jacob poured out his Spirit in a most unusual manner and also delivered a partial endowment to his chosen people. In May 1842 a more complete endowment was given to the Lord's people in the beautiful city of Nauvoo, and in 1843 the fulness of the blessings of the temple were administered.

The unfolding of divine truth and priesthood authority, including temple rites and ordinances, came gradually, precept upon precept. John the Baptist, the prophet about whom the Savior stated that there were none greater (Luke 7:28), appeared to Joseph Smith and Oliver Cowdery on 15 May 1829 (see Chapter 4). John, the man who connected two dispensations—ending the Mosaic dispensation and initiating the messianic—ordained Joseph and Oliver and conferred upon them the keys of the Aaronic Priesthood, thus strengthening our link to the past (D&C 13). Peter, James, and John, who were tutored and trained and ordained by the Lord Jesus and who also received keys at the hands of the ancient prophets Moses and Elijah on the Mount of Transfiguration (Matthew 17:1–9),[1] appeared a few weeks later to restore apostolic authority and the keys of the priesthood of Melchizedek (D&C 18:9; 20:3; 27:12; 128:20). The Church was organized on 6 April 1830 with Joseph and Oliver as its first and second elders. The first high priests were ordained in June 1831, the First Presidency was established in 1832, and the Quorum of the Twelve Apostles and the First Quorum of the Seventy were put in place in February 1835.

ENDOWED FROM ON HIGH

The Saints were instructed very early that "ye are to be taught from on high. Sanctify yourselves and ye shall be endowed with power, that ye may give even as I have spoken" (D&C 43:16). Further, in the revelation we know as the Olive Leaf (D&C 88), the Lord provided instructions for the School of the Prophets, directives that anticipated temple worship: "Sanctify yourselves; yea, purify your hearts, and cleanse your hands and your feet before me, that I may make you clean." In addition, the early leaders were told to "organize yourselves; prepare every needful thing; and establish a house, even a house of prayer, a house of fasting, a house of faith, a house of learning, a house of glory, a house of order, a house of God" (D&C 88:74, 119; compare 109:14–16).

On 12 November 1835 the Prophet Joseph met with the Twelve. He told them: "The house of the Lord must be prepared, and the

---

1. *Joseph Smith* [manual], 105.

solemn assembly called and organized in it, according to the order of the house of God. . . .

"The order of the house of God has been, and ever will be, the same, even after Christ comes; and after the termination of the thousand years it will be the same; and we shall finally enter into the celestial kingdom of God, and enjoy it forever." He added, "You need an endowment, brethren, in order that you may be prepared and able to overcome all things."[2]

The endowment promised to the Latter-day Saints was like the endowment promised to the Former-day Saints. Just before his ascent into heaven, Jesus said to his meridian Twelve: "I send the promise of my Father upon you: but tarry ye in the city of Jerusalem, until ye be endued [clothed, or invested] with power from on high" (Luke 24:49; see also Acts 1:4). In our day that same Lord declared: "I gave unto you a commandment that you should build a house, in the which house I design to endow those whom I have chosen with power from on high; for this is the promise of the Father unto you; therefore I command you to tarry, even as mine apostles at Jerusalem" (D&C 95:8–9). The endowment in the first-century Christian Church, like the endowment in the restored Church, was two-fold: an unusual outpouring of the Spirit of God, and participation in sacred temple covenants and ordinances.

We are told by Luke that Jesus "shewed himself alive after his passion [suffering] by many infallible proofs, being seen of them forty days, and speaking of the things pertaining to the kingdom of God" (Acts 1:3). Robert J. Matthews has suggested that it may have been during the Savior's forty-day ministry, after his resurrection but before his final ascension, that the full-fledged church organization (later spoken of by Paul in Ephesians 4:11–14) came into being.[3] Further, it is fascinating to discover such ordinances as

---

2. *Joseph Smith* [manual], 419.
3. *Unto All Nations*, 1–2.

washings, anointings, sacred clothing, new names, and sacred marriage ceremonies mentioned in what is known as the apocryphal Forty-day Literature.[4]

The day of Pentecost stands as the scriptural reminder of the baptism by fire that came to the early Christians. On that occasion they preached, prophesied, and spoke in tongues, inspired and divinely empowered in a way that they had not hitherto known or experienced (Acts 2). This outpouring, combined with their encounter with the resurrected Lord, transformed a group of simple and fearful disciples into powerful, indefatigable witnesses of the work. In addition, according to Willard Richards, Joseph the Prophet taught that "at one time God obtained a house where Peter washed and anointed, etc., on the day of Pentecost."[5]

A similar outpouring of the Spirit took place among the Latter-day Saints. Milton Backman wrote: "During a fifteen-week period, extending from January 21 to May 1, 1836, probably more Latter-day Saints beheld visions and witnessed other unusual spiritual manifestations than during any other era in the history of the Church. There were reports of Saints' beholding heavenly beings at ten different meetings held during that time. At eight of these meetings, many reported seeing angels; and at five of the services, individuals testified that Jesus, the Savior, appeared. While the Saints were thus communing with heavenly hosts, many prophesied, some spoke in tongues, and others received the gift of interpretation of tongues."[6]

The second part of the Lord's promise, the ordinance of the endowment as now administered in Latter-day Saint temples, came to us incrementally, as did all of the truths of the Restoration.

---

4. See Nibley, *Mormonism and Early Christianity*, 10–44.

5. *Words of Joseph Smith*, 211.

6. *Heavens Resound*, 285. An excellent treatment of the many appearances of Jesus Christ in Kirtland is Anderson, *Savior in Kirtland*.

Beginning in January of 1833, the Saints in Kirtland participated in what we have come to know as a "partial endowment," which consisted of washings, anointings, sealing of anointings, and washing of feet.[7] Further, Joseph Smith's vision of the celestial kingdom (D&C 137), received on 21 January 1836 (see Chapter 14), unlocked one of the mysteries of eternity—the blessed concept that the work for the salvation of souls continues after this life is over: The work of the Lord goes forward, here and hereafter.

This vision prepared the Saints to receive the doctrine of the redemption of the dead. As we indicated earlier, it would be another four years before the Prophet spoke of baptism for the dead in a public sermon, at the funeral of Seymour Brunson on 15 August 1840, but the foundation had been laid. Further, Moses, Elias, and Elijah came in April 1836 (D&C 110) to restore essential keys associated with the formation and sealing of eternal family units. Moses restored the keys of the gathering of Israel. Elias restored the keys associated with establishing eternal families through the blessings of celestial marriage, the new and everlasting covenant of marriage. And Elijah restored the fulness of the priesthood, power and keys sufficient to seal individuals and families together forever.

ENDOWED IN NAUVOO

The Prophet's confinement in Liberty Jail in the winter of 1838–39, though hellish in terms of hunger, privation, and alienation, proved a great blessing to the Saints through its spiritual impact on Joseph Smith. The months of solitude in what Elder B. H. Roberts called the "prison temple"[8] were also months of sacred surrender and deep and prayerful reflection on things of eternal worth, a type of spiritual gestation period. The relatively peaceful years in Nauvoo resulted in tremendous outpourings of light

---

7. Backman, *Heavens Resound*, 285–87.

8. *Comprehensive History of the Church*, 1:521.

and truth, in great doctrinal development, in both formal revelatory settings as well as public discourses. Elder Neal A. Maxwell pointed out that "earlier, Joseph had Oliver Cowdery and Sidney Rigdon to be not only his aides-de-camp but also in a measure as his spokesmen. After the Liberty Jail experience, however, Joseph was clearly his own spokesman. From that time forward, we begin to receive Joseph's stretching sermons, involving some of the gospel's most powerful doctrines."[9] And of course among the most profound of his teachings and revelations was the expanded temple endowment in Nauvoo.

In a revelation received on 19 January 1841, the Lord gave instructions to build a temple in Nauvoo. The Saints were to "build a house to my name, for the Most High to dwell therein. For there is not a place found on earth that he may come to and restore again that which was lost unto you, or which he hath taken away, even the fulness of the priesthood" (D&C 124:27–28). The Lord went on to say that the ordinance of baptism for the dead belongs "to my house, and cannot be acceptable to me, only in the days of your poverty, wherein ye are not able to build a house unto me. But I command you, all ye my saints, to build a house unto me; and I grant unto you a sufficient time to build a house unto me; and during this time your baptisms [performed in the Mississippi River or in a portable font] shall be acceptable unto me" (D&C 124:30–31). It would thus be through the blessings of the temple that the people of the covenant would come to know "things which have been kept hid from before the foundation of the world, things that pertain to the dispensation of the fulness of times" (D&C 124:41).

In 1884 Lucius Scoville recalled the following: "I can testify that on the 3rd of May, 1842, Joseph Smith the Prophet called upon five or six, viz.: Shadrach Roundy, Noah Rogers, Dimick B.

---

9. *"But for a Small Moment,"* 17.

Huntington, Daniel Cairns, and myself (I am not certain but that Hosea Stout was there also) to meet with him (the Prophet) in his business office (the upper part of his brick store). He told us that his object he had was for us to go to work and fit up that room preparatory to giving endowments to a few Elders that he might give unto them all the keys of power pertaining to the Aaronic and Melchizedek Priesthoods.

"We therefore went to work making the necessary preparations, and everything was arranged representing the interior of a temple as much as the circumstances would permit, he being with us dictating everything. . . . Some weeks previous to the dedication he told us we should have the privilege of receiving the whole of the ordinances in due time. The history of Joseph Smith speaks for itself. But I can and do testify that I know of a surety that room was fitted up by his order which we finished in the forenoon of the said 4th of May 1842. And he gave us to understand that he intended to have everything done by him that was in his power while he remained with us. He said his work was nearly done and he should roll the burden of the kingdom upon the shoulders of the Twelve. I am the only one living that I know of, who helped to fit up that room, except Hosea Stout, [who] was there."[10]

The following is from the journal of the Prophet Joseph Smith under date of 4 May 1842: "I spent the day in the upper part of the store, that is in my private office . . . in council with General James Adams, of Springfield, Patriarch Hyrum Smith, Bishops Newel K. Whitney and George Miller, and President Brigham Young and Elders Heber C. Kimball and Willard Richards, instructing them in the principles and order of the Priesthood, attending to washings, anointings, endowments and the communication of keys pertaining to the Aaronic Priesthood, and so on to the highest order

---

10. "Higher Ordinances," 2.

of the Melchizedek Priesthood, setting forth the order pertaining to the Ancient of Days, and all those plans and principles by which any one is enabled to secure the fullness of those blessings which have been prepared for the Church of the Firstborn, and come up and abide in the presence of the Eloheim in the eternal worlds. In this council was instituted the ancient order of things for the first time in these last days. . . . [T]herefore let the Saints be diligent in building the Temple, and all houses which they have been, or shall hereafter be, commanded of God to build."[11]

President Brigham Young taught us that "your endowment is, to receive all those ordinances in the house of the Lord, which are necessary for you, after you have departed this life, to enable you to walk back to the presence of the Father, passing the angels who stand as sentinels, . . . and gain your eternal exaltation."[12]

As we know, Joseph the Seer never lived to see the Nauvoo Temple completed and dedicated. The duty of administering the endowment to thousands of Saints before the exodus to the Great Basin devolved upon President Brigham Young and the Quorum of the Twelve Apostles.

A YEAR OF DOCTRINAL EXPANSION

The year 1843 was an extremely important year in terms of doctrinal growth and development. It was a year filled with instructions on sacred things. The following are but illustrations of what God taught His people through the instrumentality of Joseph Smith.

Angels and Ministering Spirits

Elder Parley P. Pratt had been away on a mission and missed some of the instruction the Twelve received during that time. Thus on 9 February 1843 Joseph spent time conversing with Elder Pratt

---

11. *Joseph Smith* [manual], 414.
12. *Discourses of Brigham Young*, 416.

on how to discern spirits and angels (resurrected beings), which we now have as Doctrine and Covenants 129.[13]

When the Savior Appears

On 2 April 1843 the Prophet went to a meeting in Ramus, Illinois, in which Orson Hyde spoke of Christ appearing at the time of His second coming as a warrior riding on a horse and how each of us can have the Father and the Son dwelling in our hearts. "We dined with my sister Sophronia McCleary," the Prophet said, "when I told Elder Hyde that I was going to offer some corrections to his sermon this morning. He replied, 'They shall be thankfully received.'" Joseph then delivered what we now have as the first seventeen verses of Doctrine and Covenants 130. He explained, among other things, that when the Savior appears he will appear as a man and that the idea of the Father and Son dwelling in our hearts is an old sectarian notion and is false. Later that day instructions that constitute verses 18–23 of section 130 were given.[14]

Calling and Election

Early in his ministry Joseph Smith taught that as individuals live in such a way as to cultivate the gift and gifts of the Holy Ghost, they eventually receive the assurance of eternal life—they make their calling and election sure. "After a person has faith in Christ," the Prophet taught, "repents of his sins, and is baptized for the remission of his sins and receives the Holy Ghost (by the laying on of hands), which is the first Comforter, then let him continue to humble himself before God, and the Lord will soon say unto him, Son, thou shalt be exalted. When the Lord has thoroughly proved him, and finds that the man is willing to serve him at all hazards,

---

13. History, 1838–1856, volume D-1 [1 August 1842–1 July 1843], The Joseph Smith Papers, accessed 15 Mar. 2016, http://josephsmithpapers.org/paperSummary/history-1838-1856-volume-d-1-1-august-1842-1-july-1843&p=108.
14. *Words of Joseph Smith*, 168–73.

then the man will find his calling and his election made sure."[15] That is, the Lord seals an exaltation upon him, which means He seals him up unto eternal life. The individual has thereby passed the tests of mortality and qualified for exaltation and glory hereafter.

On 14 May 1843 Wilford Woodruff recorded a sermon by Brother Joseph explaining Peter's words in his second epistle regarding a significant moment on the Mount of Transfiguration. The Savior and his apostles were transfigured, keys of the priesthood were conferred, and the voice of God the Father was heard bearing record of Christ's divine Sonship. Peter added that the apostles had also a "more sure word of prophecy." How could one's assurance be "more sure" than hearing the very voice of Almighty God? "Though they might hear the voice of God and know that Jesus was the Son of God," the Prophet clarified, "this would be no evidence that their election and calling was made sure, that they had part with Christ, and were joint heirs with Him. They then would want that more sure word of prophecy [the knowledge that they had been sealed up unto eternal life; D&C 131:5–6], that they were sealed in the heavens and had the promise of eternal life in the kingdom of God. Then, having this promise sealed unto them, it was an anchor to the soul, sure and steadfast." Joseph Smith then issued this sobering injunction: "I would exhort you to go on and continue to call upon God, until you make your calling and election sure for yourselves,[16] by obtaining this more sure word of prophecy, and wait patiently for the promise until you [receive] it."[17]

---

15. *Words of Joseph Smith,* 4–5.

16. Clearly the people of God do not make their calling and election sure "for themselves" in the sense of doing it on their own. Rather, this supernal blessing comes "by revelation and the spirit of prophecy, *through the power of the Holy Priesthood*" (D&C 131:5; emphasis added), that is, under the direction of those who hold the keys.

17. History, 1838–1856, volume D-1 [1 August 1842–1 July 1843], The Joseph Smith Papers, accessed 15 Mar. 2016, http://josephsmithpapers.org/paperSummary/history -1838-1856-volume-d-1-1-august-1842-1-july-1843?p=193.

"As our understanding grows," Elder Robert D. Hales explained, "we are forever changed, until we have 'no more disposition to do evil, but to do good continually' (Mosiah 5:2). In this way, our lifelong learning in us develops 'an eye single to the glory of God' (D&C 82:19), and *our calling* to return with honor to Him and His Son, Jesus Christ, *is made sure*."[18]

The Fulness of the Priesthood

In the fall of 1843 Joseph Smith began to confer upon men and women the fulness of the blessings of the priesthood. "Those holding the fullness of the Melchizedek Priesthood are kings and priests of the Most High God," Joseph explained, "holding the keys of power and blessings. In fact, that priesthood is a perfect law of theocracy, and stands as God to give laws to the people, administering endless lives to the sons and daughters of Adam. Abraham says to Melchizedek, I believe all that thou hast taught me concerning the priesthood and the coming of the Son of Man; so Melchizedek ordained Abraham and sent him away. Abraham rejoiced, saying, Now I have a priesthood."[19] James Burgess's record of this sermon is as follows: "Abraham gave a tenth part of all his spoils and then received a blessing under the hands of Melchizedek, even the last law or a fullness of the law or priesthood, which constituted him [Abraham] a king and priest after the order of Melchizedek or an endless life."[20]

In recent years, Elder Dallin H. Oaks offered valuable clarification on the doctrine of the priesthood, in terms of the responsibilities and blessings flowing to both women and men. He taught that "the Church work done by women or men, whether in the temple or in the wards or branches, is done under the direction of those

---

18. *Return*, 374; emphasis added.
19. *Joseph Smith* [manual], 109.
20. *Words of Joseph Smith*, 246.

who hold priesthood keys." Later in the address he offered this significant insight: "We are not accustomed to speaking of women having the authority of the priesthood in their Church callings, but what other authority can it be? When a woman—young or old—is set apart to preach the gospel as a full-time missionary, she is given priesthood authority to perform a priesthood function. The same is true when a woman is set apart to function as an officer or teacher in a Church organization under the direction of one who holds the keys of the priesthood. Whoever functions in an office or calling received from one who holds priesthood keys exercises priesthood authority in performing her or his assigned duties."[21]

The highest blessings of the temple come to a husband and wife together. President Charles W. Penrose stated that "when a woman is sealed to a man holding the Priesthood, she becomes one with him. . . . The glory and power and dominion that he will exercise when he has the fulness of the Priesthood and becomes a 'king and a priest unto God,' she will share with him."[22]

Securing Children through the Covenant

The power of the everlasting covenant transcends our finite capacity to fully understand an infinite God's willingness and eternal plan to save all of those who choose to be saved. We know so little. In a world that presses for fairness, we too often close our eyes to the tender mercies and endless grace of a loving Savior. The Master demonstrates his infinite mercy, for example, by refusing to condemn those who were ignorant of the gospel message and its requirements (2 Nephi 9:25–26; Mosiah 3:11; Moroni 8:22; D&C 137:7–9), including little children who died before the age

---

21. "The Keys and Authority of the Priesthood," *Ensign*, May 2014, 51; emphasis added; see also Ballard, "Men and Women in the Work of the Lord," *New Era*, Apr. 2014, 4.

22. In Conference Report, Apr. 1921, 198; see also Joseph Fielding Smith, in Conference Report, Apr. 1970, 58.

of accountability (Mosiah 3:16; 15:25; Moroni 8:8–12, 22; D&C 29:46–47; 74:7; 137:10). He offers the sublime gift—eternal life—to those laborers who join the work in the vineyard in the eleventh hour, the same gift he offers to those who have labored the entire day (Matthew 20:1–16).[23]

In speaking at funeral services for Judge Elias Higbee on 13 August 1843, the Prophet stated: "Had I inspiration, revelation, and lungs to communicate what my soul has contemplated in times past, there is not a soul in this congregation but would go to their homes and shut their mouths in everlasting silence on religion till they had learned something."[24] Later in the sermon he referred to the four angels mentioned in Revelation 7. "Four destroying angels holding power over the four quarters of the earth until the servants of God are sealed in their foreheads."[25] This sealing in the forehead "means to seal the blessing upon their heads, meaning the everlasting covenant, thereby making their calling and election sure. *When a seal is put upon the father and mother, it secures their posterity, so that they cannot be lost, but will be saved by virtue of the covenant of their father and mother.*"[26]

We believe that those who are faithful in their first estate come to the earth with certain predispositions to receive and embrace the truth. The Prophet himself declared that those of the house of Israel who come into the Church do so with quiet receptivity to the

---

23. Two insightful apostolic commentaries on this unusual parable are Oaks, "The Challenge to Become," *Ensign*, Nov. 2000, 43–44; Holland, "The Laborers in the Vineyard," *Ensign*, May 2012, 31–33.

24. *Words of Joseph Smith*, 238.

25. *Words of Joseph Smith*, 239. These angels are described in modern revelation as "four angels sent forth from God, to whom is given power over the four parts of the earth, to save life and to destroy; these are they who have the everlasting gospel to commit to every nation, kindred, tongue, and people; having power to shut up the heavens, *to seal up unto life,* or to cast down to the regions of darkness" (D&C 77:8; emphasis added).

26. *Words of Joseph Smith*, 242.

Spirit of the Lord and an openness to pure intelligence.[27] Similarly, we have no difficulty speaking of the "spirit of Elijah" reaching out, touching, directing, and impelling individuals to search out their dead and perform the saving ordinances. Why should we have difficulty accepting the truth that the power of the covenant could reach out, touch, redirect, and impel wandering sheep? Could it be that that power is indeed the same spirit of Elijah, the Spirit that turns the hearts of the children to the covenant made with their fathers?[28]

Elder Orson F. Whitney, a member of the Quorum of the Twelve Apostles in the early twentieth century, offered the following powerful commentary on Joseph Smith's words: "The Prophet Joseph Smith declared—and he never taught more comforting doctrine—that the eternal sealings of faithful parents and the divine promises made to them for valiant service in the Cause of Truth, would save not only themselves, but likewise their posterity. Though some of the sheep may wander, the eye of the Shepherd is upon them, and sooner or later they will feel the tentacles of Divine Providence reaching out after them and drawing them back to the fold. Either in this life or in the life to come, they will return. They will have to pay their debt to justice; they will suffer for their sins; and may tread a thorny path; but if it leads them at last, like the penitent Prodigal, to a loving and forgiving father's heart and home, the painful experience will not have been in vain. Pray for your careless and disobedient children; hold on to them with your faith. Hope on, trust on, till you see the salvation of God. . . .

"You parents of the willful and the wayward: Don't give them up. Don't cast them off. *They are not utterly lost. The Shepherd will*

---

27. *Words of Joseph Smith*, 4.
28. President Russell M. Nelson explained that the "spirit of Elijah" is "a manifestation of the Holy Ghost bearing witness of the divine nature of the family" ("A New Harvest Time," *Ensign*, May 1998, 34).

find his sheep. They were his before they were yours—long before he entrusted them to your care; and you cannot begin to love them as he loves them. *They have but strayed in ignorance from the Path of Right, and God is merciful to ignorance. Only the fulness of knowledge brings the fulness of accountability.* Our Heavenly Father is far more merciful, infinitely more charitable, than even the best of his servants, and the Everlasting Gospel is mightier in power to save than our narrow finite minds can comprehend."[29]

Elder Robert D. Hales offered the following comforting assurance: "Parents are never failures when they do their best. Their faith, prayers, and efforts will be consecrated to the good of them and their children now and in the eternities." Further, "as parents of struggling children, we should be careful that our hope does not falter and our faith does not waver. The choices of our children should never weaken our own commitment to the Savior. Our worthiness will not be measured according to their righteousness."[30] Perhaps only those who have become participants in the painful drama of witnessing a loved one drift from the gospel and from most of what they were taught can fully appreciate the beauty and hope that flow from this magnificent teaching.

CONCLUSION

All aspects of the restored gospel, made known through Joseph Smith the Prophet, were put in place in a proper manner, in correct order, precept upon precept. From the time the naïve boy prophet beheld God the Father and Jesus Christ the Son in the grove in

---

29. In Conference Report, Apr. 1929, 110; emphasis added. More recently, President Boyd K. Packer addressed this topic and offered profound comfort to troubled parents ("Our Moral Environment," *Ensign,* May 1992, 66–68); see also Faust, "Dear Are the Sheep That Have Wandered," *Ensign,* May 2003, 61–68; Bednar, "Faithful Parents and Wayward Children: Sustaining Hope While Overcoming Misunderstanding," *Ensign,* Mar. 2014, 28–33.

30. *Return,* 320.

Palmyra, New York, until that same mature prophet suffered martyrdom in Carthage, Illinois, the Lord God opened the heavens and made known precious truths and delivered consummate powers, one truth and power building upon another, until the Saints were in a position to be bound and united as families forevermore. Placing all things in perspective, the purpose "of all activity in the Church is to see that a man and a woman with their children are happy at home, sealed together for time and for all eternity."[31] "Rewards for obedience to the commandments," President Russell M. Nelson reminded us, "are almost beyond mortal comprehension. Here, children of the covenant become a strain of sin-resistant souls. And hereafter . . . 'each generation would be linked to the one which went on before.'"[32]

A prophet is first and foremost a witness of God. His competence as a witness is predicated on knowledge, that is, the extent to which he unveils the heavens and reveals the mind and will of the Almighty. He is then a revelator and a teacher; he makes known and clarifies the principles of salvation. The message is not his own but that of the Father, who sent him. The prophet must be a pure vessel in order that the message not be soiled. Of that which he taught, Joseph Smith said: "This is good doctrine. It tastes good. I can taste the principles of eternal life, and so can you. They are given to me by the revelations of Jesus Christ; and I know that when I tell you these words of eternal life as they are given to me, you taste them, and I know that you believe them. You say honey is sweet, and so do I. I can also taste the spirit of eternal life. I know it is good; and when I tell you of these things which were given me

---

31. Packer, "The Plan of Happiness," *Ensign*, May 2015, 26.
32. "Children of the Covenant," *Ensign*, May 1995, 33. President Nelson quoted President Joseph Fielding Smith, in Conference Report, Apr. 1965, 10.

by inspiration of the Holy Spirit, you are bound to receive them as sweet, and rejoice more and more."[33]

We rejoice in those teachings. As we study them, and teach them, and write about them, we find ourselves rejoicing "more and more." Their taste *is* sweet. They *are* light and truth. They lift the soul and expand the mind. They provide peace and perspective in the midst of turmoil. They carry within them, as all truth does, the evidence of their own truthfulness. Separately and collectively, they testify that Joseph Smith was an authorized prophet of God.

---

33. *Joseph Smith* [manual], 525.

Chapter 17

A NEW AND
EVERLASTING COVENANT

Nauvoo, Illinois, July 1843. The promise of Malachi that Elijah the prophet would be sent to "turn the heart of the fathers to the children, and the heart of the children to their fathers" (Malachi 4:6)—the eternal decree that binding and sealing powers of heaven would come once again—would have its ultimate fulfillment in the dispensation of the fulness of times. And fundamental to the realization of that prophetic promise, central to its implementation, was the revelation of the eternal marriage covenant, the formal beginning of a new eternal family unit. Joseph Smith and some of the leading brethren had already entered into polygamous marriages, but on 12 July 1843 Joseph dictated the revelation on eternal and plural marriage to William Clayton, who wrote it as the Prophet delivered it.

The profound truths contained in Doctrine and Covenants 132 (when read in conjunction with other revelations, particularly section 131) constitute the scriptural authority for the unique and exalted concept of marriage and family among the Latter-day Saints. In a day when iniquity abounds and the love of many has begun to wax cold (D&C 45:27), the revelations of God through his prophets provide an anchor to the troubled soul. Doctrine and

Covenants 132 is a message that is both peaceful and penetrating, a divine oracle that can bring order and organization to things on earth, as well as point men and women toward their infinite possibilities in the worlds to come. The revelations of the Restoration stress powerfully that marriage is only incidentally a civil ceremony; it is principally a religious ordinance. "Marriage [is] an institution of heaven," Joseph Smith taught, "instituted in the garden of Eden."[1]

The covenant of eternal marriage is a vital part of the "new and everlasting covenant," which is the fulness of the gospel of Jesus Christ (D&C 39:11; 45:9; 66:2; 133:57).[2] Some four to five centuries before the birth of Christ, Jehovah spoke through Malachi: "Behold, I will send my messenger, and he shall prepare the way before me: and the Lord, whom ye seek, shall suddenly come to his temple, even the messenger of the covenant, whom ye delight in: behold, he shall come, saith the Lord of hosts" (Malachi 3:1). This prophecy was surely fulfilled in the meridian of time in the coming of John the Baptist as an Elias, a forerunner before his Master, Jesus Christ. Its latter-day fulfillment, however, would await the final dispensation, a time wherein God would gather together in one all things in Christ (Ephesians 1:10). In our day the Lord made known through the Prophet Joseph that the restored gospel was itself a "messenger" sent to prepare the people of the earth for the Second Coming. "I came unto mine own," the Savior said, "and mine own received me not; but unto as many as received me gave I power to do many miracles, and to become the sons of God; and even unto them that believed on my name gave I power to obtain eternal life. And even so *have I sent mine everlasting covenant into the world, to be a light to the world, and to be a standard for my people, and for the Gentiles to seek to it, and to be a messenger before my face to prepare the way before me*" (D&C 45:8–9; emphasis added).

---

1. *Joseph Smith* [manual], 482.
2. See Smith, *Doctrines of Salvation*, 1:156–59.

HISTORICAL SETTING

Eternal marriage, the ordinance by which couples enter into the patriarchal order (D&C 131:1–4), is called in verse 2 of section 132 a "new and everlasting covenant." It is *a* new and everlasting covenant within *the* new and everlasting covenant of the gospel or fulness of the gospel. It is a crucial element in the restitution of all things in our day (D&C 132:40, 45). Eternal marriage is that covenant and ordinance that leads to the consummate blessings of the gospel; it is that order of the priesthood which, when entered into worthily, will bind ancestry to posterity and thus prevent the earth from being utterly wasted at the time of the Savior's return in glory (D&C 2; Joseph Smith–History 1:39).

It appears that Joseph Smith learned of the doctrine of eternal marriage—as he did in so many other matters—in a gradual way, precept upon precept. Joseph Noble, a close associate of the Prophet, observed that the revelation on eternal marriage was given to Joseph "while he was engaged in the work of the translation of the Scriptures [the Joseph Smith Translation]."[3] More specifically, it seems evident that the first inklings of understanding concerning *plural* marriage[4] came as early as 1831, while the Prophet was engaged in his study of Genesis.[5] The opening verse of section 132 suggests strongly that Joseph had inquired concerning Old Testament personalities and their participation in plural marriage.

It is difficult to know exactly at what point in the history of the Church Joseph Smith began to understand and teach the principles associated with *eternal* marriage. William W. Phelps indicates that

3. See minutes of the Davis Stake conference, published under "Plural Marriage," *Millennial Star* 45, no. 29 (July 1883): 454, in Bachman, "New Light on an Old Hypothesis," 22.

4. The most comprehensive treatment of Joseph Smith's involvement in plural marriage is Hales, *Joseph Smith's Polygamy,* 3 vols.

5. See Matthews, *"Plainer Translation,"* 96, 257; see also note by B. H. Roberts in *History of the Church,* 5:xxix–xxx.

he learned some things pertaining to the eternity of the marriage covenant as early as 1835. He wrote: "New light is occasionally bursting in to our minds of the sacred scriptures, for which I am truly thankful. We shall by and bye learn that we were with God in another world, before the foundation of the world, and had our agency: that we came into this world and have our agency, in order *that we may prepare ourselves for a kingdom of glory; become* arch-angels; even *the sons of God where the man is neither without the woman, nor the woman without the man in the Lord:* A consumma-tion of glory, and happiness, and perfection so greatly to be wished, that I would not miss of it for the fame of ten worlds."[6]

In 1839–40 Joseph explained similar truths to Parley P. Pratt. "In Philadelphia," Parley writes, "I had the happiness of once more meeting with President Smith, and of spending several days with him and others, and with the saints in that city and vicin-ity. During these interviews he taught me many great and glori-ous principles concerning God and the heavenly order of eternity."[7] Parley explained particulars concerning the beauty and boundless-ness of this transcendent ordinance, to which we will return in the conclusion of this chapter.

The Prophet shared details of the revelation concerning *plural* marriage with various intimate associates when he felt that each could be trusted to preserve a sacred confidence. Between 1831 and 1843 a number of the leaders of the Church were instructed con-cerning the plurality of wives and were told that eventually many of the faithful would be called upon to comply with the will of the Lord. In speaking to a gathering of the Reorganized Church of Jesus Christ of Latter Day Saints in Plano, Illinois, in 1878, Orson Pratt "explained the circumstances connected with the coming

---

6. William W. Phelps, "Letter no. 8," *Messenger and Advocate* 1, no. 9 (June 1835): 130; emphasis added.

7. *Autobiography of Parley P. Pratt,* 297; see also Givens and Grow, *Parley P. Pratt,* 174–75.

forth of the revelation on plural marriage. Refuted the statement and belief of those present that Brigham Young was the author of the revelation; showed that Joseph Smith the Prophet had not only commenced the practice of that principle himself, and taught it to others, before President Young and the Twelve had returned from their mission to Europe, in 1841, but that Joseph actually received revelations upon that principle as early as 1831."[8]

Most of those who became Latter-day Saints during the nineteenth century had been associated with other religious societies before their conversion and had been reared in traditional, monogamous homes. The idea of husbands having more than one wife thus came into sharp contrast with all they had been brought up to believe. Therefore plural marriage was at first extremely difficult for many Saints to accept, including Church Presidents Joseph Smith, Brigham Young, and John Taylor. President Taylor remarked that "it was one of the greatest crosses that ever was taken up by any set of men since the world stood."[9] President Young declared: "It was the first time in my life that I had desired the grave, and I could hardly get over it for a long time. When I saw a funeral I felt to envy the corpse its situation, and to regret that I was not in the coffin."[10]

One of those for whom the principle of plural marriage was especially difficult was Emma Smith, wife of the Prophet. It appears, therefore, that one of the principal reasons for the formal recording of the revelation in 1843 was to assist Emma in recognizing the divine source of this difficult doctrine. William Clayton, private secretary to Brother Joseph, recorded the following: "On the morning of the 12th of July, 1843, Joseph and Hyrum Smith came into the office of the upper story of the 'Brick-store,' on the bank

---

8. "Report of Elders Orson Pratt and Joseph F. Smith," *Millennial Star* 40, no. 50 (Dec. 1878): 788; see also Matthews, *"Plainer Translation,"* 258.

9. In *Journal of Discourses,* 11:221.

10. In *Journal of Discourses,* 3:266.

of the Mississippi River. They were talking of the subject of plural marriage, [and] Hyrum said to Joseph, 'If you will write the revelation on celestial marriage, I will take and read it to Emma, and I believe I can convince her of its truth, and you will hereafter have peace.' Joseph smiled and remarked, 'You do not know Emma as well as I do.' Hyrum repeated his opinion, and further remarked, 'The doctrine is so plain, I can convince any reasonable man or woman of its truth, purity, and heavenly origin,' or words to that effect. . . . Joseph and Hyrum then sat down, and Joseph then commenced to dictate the Revelation on Celestial Marriage, and I wrote it, sentence by sentence, as he dictated. After the whole was written, Joseph asked me to read it through slowly and carefully, which I did, and he pronounced it correct."[11]

Brother Clayton recorded in his diary that same day: "This A.M. I wrote a revelation consisting of 10 pages on the order of the priesthood, showing the designs in Moses, Abraham, David and Solomon having many wives and concubines, &c. After it was wrote Prests. Joseph & Hyrum presented it and read it to E[mma] who said she did not believe a word of it and appeared very rebellious."[12]

THE JUSTIFICATION

Doctrine and Covenants 132 is a revelation dealing with eternal marriage. It also contains information and explanations concerning the practice of plural marriage, which is a small subset of eternal marriage. Latter-day Saint historian Danel Bachman suggested that section 132 consists largely of the Lord's answers to three critical questions posed by the Prophet Joseph Smith.[13]

Question 1. The first question asked by Joseph seems to be why the polygamous actions of notable Old Testament prophet-leaders

---

11. Smith, *Intimate Chronicle,* 110.
12. Smith, *Intimate Chronicle,* 110, in Hales and Hales, *Joseph Smith's Polygamy,* 78.
13. See "New Light on an Old Hypothesis," 19–32.

had received divine approval. Why was it, the Prophet wanted to know, that prophets, patriarchs, and kings could have many wives and concubines?[14] In the Lord's response, Joseph was told to prepare his heart for the instructions about to be given (D&C 132:3). In this instance, the explanation for the ancient phenomenon was accompanied by a commandment to eventually institute the practice in modern times. Seeking further light and knowledge had led the Prophet into further and greater obligations; much was about to be given, and much was about to be required (D&C 82:3).

Question 2. The second question posed by the Prophet Joseph Smith seems to be associated with a cryptic statement by Jesus in response to the Sadducean trap: "Ye do err, not knowing the scriptures, nor the power of God. For in the resurrection they neither marry, nor are given in marriage, but are as the angels of God in heaven" (Matthew 22:29–30; compare Luke 20:34–36). This expression, little understood in the days of the Prophet Joseph, is repeatedly given today as scriptural evidence against the Latter-day Saint doctrine of eternal marriage. Joseph Smith's query concerning its meaning led to a modern revealed commentary on the biblical passage and points us to the reality that Jesus Christ seems to have taught the doctrine of eternal marriage during his mortal ministry.[15]

To properly understand the disputed scriptural passage, we ask, To whom was the statement of the Savior directed? Clearly he was addressing himself to the Sadducees, a Jewish sect that denied life

---

14. Generally speaking, a concubine was a wife who came from a lower social standing and thus did not enjoy the same status as one of higher birth. In ancient times, when caste systems were much more widespread than at present, a man could take a slave or noncitizen as a legal wife, but it was understood that she was of a lower status. This was the case with Hagar, the servant of Sarah who became a concubine of Abraham. In the Book of Mormon, however, the word *concubine* takes on a different meaning, more like a paramour, a mistress, a kept woman (Jacob 2–3).
15. See McConkie, *Doctrinal New Testament Commentary,* 3:374–81.

after death, the resurrection of the body, angels, or spirits. In addition, they obviously rejected Jesus the Messiah and his gospel and considered the Lord to be a threat to their influence among the people. In a broader sense, the text applies to all others who reject the gospel and the power and authority to act in the name of God. None such can claim a sealing bond between marriage partners beyond the grave.

The modern equivalent would be for a woman who does not accept the restored gospel or our belief in resurrection or the afterlife to ask the President of the Church which of the seven men she had been married to in civil ceremonies would be her husband in the world to come. The answer, of course, is none of them. Because one unbeliever has been told that her civil marriages are not binding in eternity and thus that her husbands and children cannot be secured hereafter, is not to say that this is true for everyone else, especially for those whose marriages are solemnized in holy temples by proper authority. "And for that matter," Elder Bruce R. McConkie taught, "there is no revelation, either ancient or modern, which says there is neither marrying nor giving in marriage in heaven itself for righteous people. All that the revelations set forth is that such is denied to the Sadducees and other worldly and ungodly people."[16] Nor does it constitute a doctrinal justification for the idea that no resurrected beings can be married or that other gospel ordinances cannot be performed for people after they have been resurrected.

From Doctrine and Covenants 132 we learn that they who "neither marry nor are given in marriage" in eternity are they who choose not to enter in at the strait gate and partake of the new and everlasting covenant of marriage. Even persons who qualify in every other way for the glories of the celestial kingdom but who reject opportunities for celestial marriage cannot attain unto the highest degree of the

---

16. *Doctrinal New Testament Commentary*, 1:607.

celestial glory (compare D&C 131:1–4). Such persons are "appointed angels in heaven, which angels are ministering servants, to minister for those who are worthy of a far more, and an exceeding, and an eternal weight of glory." Because they did not abide by the Lord's law, "they cannot be enlarged, but remain separately and singly, without exaltation, in their saved condition, to all eternity; and from henceforth are not gods, but are angels of God forever and ever" (D&C 132:16–17). In commenting on the status of angels, Joseph said: "Gods have an ascendency over the angels. Angels remain angels, [while] some are resurrected to become god."[17]

The Holy Spirit of Promise is the Holy Ghost, the Holy Spirit promised to the faithful. The Holy Ghost is a member of the Godhead with vital and important roles in the salvation of the children of God. He is a revelator, a witness and a testifier, the means by which a spiritual conviction of the truth is obtained. He is a sanctifier, the means by which filth and dross are burned out of the human soul as though by fire. One of the highest functions the Holy Ghost serves is as a sealer, as the Holy Spirit of Promise. In this capacity he searches the heart, certifies that a person is justified before God, and thereafter seals an exaltation upon that person. In commenting on Doctrine and Covenants 132:7 (regarding all contracts, covenants, etc. having the seal of the Holy Spirit of Promise), Elder McConkie observed: "By way of illustration, this means that baptism, partaking of the sacrament, administering to the sick, marriage, and every covenant that man ever makes with the Lord . . . must be performed in righteousness by and for people who are worthy to receive whatever blessing is involved, otherwise whatever is done has no binding and sealing effect in eternity. . . .

"When the Holy Spirit of Promise places his ratifying seal upon a baptism, or a marriage, or any covenant, . . . the seal is a

---

17. *Words of Joseph Smith,* 212.

conditional approval or ratification; it is binding in eternity only in the event of subsequent obedience to the terms and conditions of whatever covenant is involved.

"But when the ratifying seal of approval is placed upon someone whose calling and election is thereby made sure—because there are no more conditions to be met by the obedient person—this act of being sealed up unto eternal life is of such transcendent import that of itself it is called being sealed by the Holy Spirit of Promise, which means that in this crowning sense, being so sealed is the same as having one's calling and election made sure."[18]

As a type of follow-up to the first questions, Joseph was given additional insights into requirements made of individuals in ancient times. The patriarch Abraham was instructed to take Hagar, the servant of Sarah, as a second wife, as a part of fulfilling the promises made earlier to the Father of the Faithful that his posterity would be as numerous as the stars in the heavens or the sands on the seashore (Genesis 13:14–16; 15:5; 22:17; Abraham 3:14). Thus modern revelation helps to clarify the Old Testament story considerably (Genesis 16), and shows that the decision to take an additional wife was a God-inspired directive and not simply a desperate or resourceful move on the part of Sarah to ensure mortal posterity for her grieving husband. Joseph Smith was told that because of Abraham's perfect obedience he was granted the privilege of eternal increase. The Lord then said to Joseph: "This promise is yours also, because ye are of Abraham, and the promise was made unto Abraham" (D&C 132:31). Then came the command to Joseph Smith, who had in 1836 received the keys necessary to become a modern father of the faithful (D&C 110:12): "Go ye, therefore, and do the works of Abraham; enter ye into my law and ye shall be saved" (D&C 132:32; compare 124:58).

---

18. *Doctrinal New Testament Commentary*, 3:335–36.

The Lord further explained that Abraham, Isaac, and Jacob had attained godhood because of their obedience. More specifically, because they took additional wives only as those wives were given to them by God, they have entered into their exaltation. David and Solomon were also given direction through the legal administrators of their day to take additional wives, and they enjoyed the approbation of heaven while they stayed within the bounds the Lord had set. When they moved outside those bounds, however, and began to acquire wives and concubines for selfish or lustful reasons (for example, David in the case of Bathsheba, 2 Samuel 11; Solomon in taking "strange women" as wives who "turned away his heart from the things of righteousness," 1 Kings 11), they offended God and forfeited the eternal rewards that might have been theirs. Jacob, son of Lehi in the Book of Mormon, warned his people: "Behold, David and Solomon truly had many wives and concubines, which thing was abominable before me, saith the Lord" (Jacob 2:24).

When both scriptural passages (Jacob 2 and D&C 132) are read together, it becomes clear that the Lord was condemning— in no uncertain terms—*unauthorized* plural marriages and not the principle of plurality of wives per se. Later in Jacob 2 the word of the Lord came: "For if I will, saith the Lord of Hosts, raise up seed unto me, I will command my people; otherwise they shall hearken unto these things" (Jacob 2:30). The instruction of the Lord to the Saints of our own day is also to "go . . . and do the works of Abraham" (D&C 132:32), not through the practice of plural marriage—for such has been discontinued by divine command—but by entering into holy temples and participating in the new and everlasting covenant of marriage.

Question 3. Doctrine and Covenants 132:41 suggests the third question that Joseph Smith seems to have asked of the Lord. In essence, the question of the Prophet was, "Why were such polygamous relationships not violations of the law of chastity? Why was this not considered adultery?" The Lord's answer was simple and forthright, although considerable space is devoted to the issue in the revelation: any action inspired, authorized, or commanded of God is moral and good. More specifically, marriages approved of the Almighty are recognized and acknowledged as sacred. Joseph wrote in 1839: "How much more dignified and noble are the thoughts of God, than the vain imaginations of the human heart!"[19] Doctrine and Covenants 132:36 sheds light on the principle that whatever God requires is right: "Abraham was commanded to offer his son Isaac; nevertheless, it was written: Thou shalt not kill. Abraham, however, did not refuse, and it was accounted unto him for righteousness."

In a letter written in 1842 to Nancy Rigdon, daughter of Sidney, Joseph sought to explain (albeit in veiled language) the appropriateness of plural marriage when divinely sanctioned: "Happiness is the object and design of our existence, and will be the end thereof if we pursue the path that leads to it; and this path is virtue, uprightness, faithfulness, holiness, and keeping all the commandments of God. But we cannot keep all the commandments without first knowing them, and we cannot expect to know all, or more than we now know, unless we comply with or keep those we have already received. That which is wrong under one circumstance, may be and often is, right under another. God said thou shalt not kill,—at another time he said thou shalt utterly destroy. *This is the principle on which the government of heaven is conducted—by revelation adapted to the circumstances in which the children of the kingdom are placed.* Whatever God requires is right, no matter what it is, although we may not see the reason thereof till long after the events transpire. If we seek first the kingdom of God, all good things will be added."[20]

---

19. *Joseph Smith* [manual], 267.
20. Jessee, *Personal Writings of Joseph Smith,* 538; emphasis added. Nancy Rigdon declined the Prophet's proposal of marriage (Hales and Hales, *Joseph Smith's Polygamy,* 55–56).

QUESTIONS THAT ARISE

Plural marriage is a difficult subject, even for the most committed believer. It raises a number of questions, such as the following:

1. Why did Joseph Smith institute this practice? The following have been suggested as reasons for Joseph Smith instituting the practice of plural marriage: (1) He was commanded by God to do so; (2) the practice was instituted as a part of the "restitution of all things" (Acts 3:21); (3) the practice was to serve as a significant trial to the faith of many of the Saints[21]; (4) the practice was to provide a means for multiplying and replenishing the earth; and (5) the practice was to provide opportunity for more than one worthy woman to be sealed to a righteous man in the new and everlasting covenant of marriage.[22] Indeed, one simply cannot begin to understand this practice unless he or she realizes that once the Prophet Joseph

---

21. Elder Bruce R. McConkie pointed out that a "testing and sifting process has ever been part of the Lord's system." He observed: "In this dispensation, the promulgation of the law of eternal marriage had an effect similar to the presentation of the doctrine of the Bread of Life in the meridian dispensation [John 6]. Opposition from without the Church increased, while some unstable members of the kingdom itself found themselves unable to accept the fullness of the revealed program of the Lord. There were many important reasons why the Lord revealed the doctrine of plurality of wives. But if plural marriage had served no other purpose than to sift the chaff from the wheat, than to keep the unstable and semi-faithful people from the fullness of gospel blessings, it would have been more than justified" (*Doctrinal New Testament Commentary,* 1:361–62).

22. Suggested reasons 2, 3, and 4 are discussed at some length in Hales and Hales, *Joseph Smith's Polygamy,* 1–14. There are many who for the foreseeable future cannot enjoy the full blessings of eternal marriage and family, such as those who are single, who are married to someone who is not a member of the Church, or one who experiences same-gender attraction. To such persons, Elder Dallin H. Oaks offers this consolation: "The Lord has promised that in the eternities no blessing will be denied His sons and daughters who keep the commandments, are true to their covenants, and desire what is right. Many of the most important deprivations of mortality will be set right in the Millennium, which is the time for fulfilling all that is incomplete in the great plan of happiness for all of our Father's worthy children. We know that will be true of temple ordinances. I believe it will also be true of family relationships and experiences" (*With Full Purpose of Heart,* 35). See also Nash, "The New and Everlasting Covenant," *Ensign,* Dec. 2015, 41–47.

Smith was able to glimpse the significance of such matters as sealing powers, celestial marriage, and eternal families, the effort to make these blessings available to as many of the sons and daughters of God as possible became a pressing obligation. Why? Because, as the Prophet stated, "Those who keep no eternal Law in this life or make no eternal contract are single & alone in the eternal world."[23]

2. Isn't plural marriage forbidden by the Bible? There is scriptural precedent for plural marriage in the lives of noble and faithful men and women in the Old Testament. For example, Abraham, Jacob, and Moses took additional wives (Genesis 16:1–11; 29:28; 30:4, 9, 26; Exodus 2:21; Numbers 12:1), and there is no indication that God disapproved of their actions. God did condemn King David's unauthorized relationship with Bathsheba (2 Samuel 11–12) and King Solomon's marriages to foreign women who turned his heart away from the worship of Jehovah (1 Kings 11). Further, evidence suggests that authorized plural marriages took place in the days of Jesus.[24]

3. Were all Latter-day Saint households involved in the practice? No. The only members of the Church who were authorized to enter into this order of matrimony were those who did so under the direction of the presiding authorities of the Church. Elder Orson Pratt, one of the early Latter-day Saint apostles who was at first opposed to the principle, stated later: "How are these things to be conducted? Are they to be left at random? Is every servant of God at liberty to run here and there, seeking out the daughters of men as wives unto themselves without any restrictions, law, or condition? No. We find these things were restricted in ancient times. Do you not recollect the circumstances of the Prophet Nathan's coming to David? He came to reprove him for certain disobedience. . . . Nathan the Prophet, in relation to David, was the man that held

---

23. *Words of Joseph Smith*, 232.
24. See Pagels, *Adam, Eve, and the Serpent*, 11.

the keys concerning this matter in ancient days [see D&C 132:39]; and it was governed by the strictest laws.

"So in these last days . . . there is but one man in all the world, at the same time, who can hold the keys of this matter, but one man has power to turn the key to enquire of the Lord, and to say whether I, or these my brethren, or any of the rest of this congregation, or the Saints upon the face of the whole earth, may have this blessing of Abraham conferred upon them; he holds the keys of these matters now, the same as Nathan, in his day."[25]

4. *Why were some of the women who were asked to become plural wives so young?* It is tempting for us in the twenty-first century to apply present-day customs and standards to an earlier day, to judge behavior in an earlier time by what is or is not considered appropriate today. In the nineteenth century it was not uncommon for women to be married as young teenagers. We must keep in mind that this was a day before the existence of the sociological phenomenon we know as adolescence. In writing specifically about Joseph Smith's marriage proposal to Helen Mar Kimball, age fourteen, Latter-day Saint historian J. Spencer Fluhman explained that "nineteenth-century women married on average earlier than today; early American legal understandings of youthful marriage might baffle modern readers. Borrowing from English common law traditions, American law during the 1840s set the legal age for marriage at twelve for females and fourteen for males. Similarly, pre-Civil War 'age of consent' laws set a low standard; not until the 1880s did states begin raising the age of female consent from ten or twelve to sixteen. In rural communities where marriageable women could be scarce, marriage age could dip well below modern conventions—for

---

25. In *Journal of Discourses,* 1:63–64.

instance, Martin Harris married his wife Lucy in 1808 when she was fifteen."[26]

5. *Is it true that Joseph Smith was married to a number of women who were already married?* It is important to know that during this time "Latter-day Saints distinguished between sealings for time and eternity and sealings for eternity only. Sealings for time and eternity included commitments and relationships during this life, generally including the possibility of sexual relations. Eternity only sealings indicated relationships in the next life alone.

"Evidence indicates that Joseph Smith participated in both types of sealings. . . . Some of the women who were sealed to Joseph Smith testified that their marriages were for time and eternity, while others indicated that their relationships were for eternity alone. . . .

"There are several possible explanations for this practice. These sealings may have provided a way to create an eternal bond or link between Joseph's family and other families within the Church. These ties extended both vertically, from parent to child, and horizontally, from one family to another. Today such eternal bonds are achieved through the temple marriages of individuals who are also sealed to their own birth families, in this way linking families together. Joseph Smith's sealings to women already married may have been an early version of linking one family to another. In Nauvoo, most if not all of the first husbands seemed to have continued living in the same household with their wives during Joseph's lifetime, and complaints about these sealings with Joseph Smith are virtually absent from the documentary record. . . .

"Several of these women were married either to non-Mormons or former Mormons, and more than one of the women later expressed unhappiness in their present marriages. Living in a time

---

26. Fluhman, "'A Subject That Can Bear Investigation,'" 106–7; see also Grossberg, *Governing the Hearth*, 105–6; Odem, *Delinquent Daughters*, 9.

when divorce was difficult to obtain, these women may have be-lieved a sealing to Joseph Smith would give them blessings they might not otherwise receive in the next life."[27]

6. How did Latter-day Saint women in the nineteenth century feel about the practice? There were, of course, women who chose not to enter into the practice, or who, having entered it, chose to leave the marriage.[28] For the most part, however, the women who sought divine guidance and a testimony of the truthfulness of the prin-ciple received a confirming witness that the practice was approved of God. Decades after the principle was introduced and faced with a national antipolygamy campaign, Latter-day Saint women startled their eastern sisters (who had equated plural marriage with the op-pression of women) by publicly demonstrating in favor of their right to live plural marriage as a religious principle. For example, in January 1870 thousands of women met in the Salt Lake Tabernacle in what they called the "Great Indignation Meeting"; these women gathered to manifest their indignation and protest against antipoly-gamy laws.

7. How long did the practice of plural marriage continue? Why did it cease? Public opposition in the United States to the practice of plu-ral marriage grew during the last quarter of the nineteenth century. Several Church officials were incarcerated, and the government threatened to confiscate Church property, including the temples. In the wake of oppressive laws, President Wilford Woodruff, President of the Church from 1887 to 1898, after seeking revelation from the Lord, issued what has come to be known as the Manifesto. This document called for the discontinuance of plural marriage, and a constituent assembly of the Latter-day Saints in general confer-ence accepted it in October 1890. The Manifesto brought about a

---

27. lds.org/topics, "Plural Marriage in Kirtland and Nauvoo."
28. See Hales and Hales, *Joseph Smith's Polygamy,* 39, 51–53, 55–56, 77–86.

noticeable change in public attitudes toward the Church, and by 1896 Utah was granted statehood. Some persons continued in the practice until a second manifesto (1904) was issued.

8. *What about those who, since the start of the twentieth century and even today, continue to practice and advocate plural marriage?* President Gordon B. Hinckley explained: "I wish to state categorically that this Church has nothing whatever to do with those practicing polygamy. They are not members of this Church. Most of them have never been members. . . . If any of our members are found to be practicing plural marriage, they are excommunicated, the most serious penalty the Church can impose. . . . More than a century ago God clearly revealed . . . that the practice of plural marriage should be discontinued, which means that it is now against the law of God."[29]

9. *What does the Church do today to bring to account those who practice plural marriage?* Latter-day Saints believe in "obeying, honoring, and sustaining the law" (Articles of Faith 1:12). While they stand firmly against the practice of plural marriage today, they leave to local magistrates the enforcement of the civil law. President Hinckley said of those who continue to practice plural marriage: "They are in violation of the civil law. They know they are in violation of the law. They are subject to its penalties. The Church, of course, has no jurisdiction whatever in this matter."[30]

10. *How do modern Latter-day Saints deal with this nineteenth-century practice as a part of the Church's history? Doesn't it shake their faith?* I can speak only for myself. As with many other aspects of the restored gospel, coming to terms with plural marriage is a matter of faith. Just as the First Vision must be accepted on faith, a faith that is accompanied by a solid witness of the Spirit, so it is with the other miraculous and supernatural events of the Restoration—the

---

29. "What Are People Asking about Us?" *Ensign,* Nov. 1998, 71–72.
30. "What Are People Asking about Us?" *Ensign,* Nov. 1998, 71.

coming forth and translation of the Book of Mormon, ordinations under the hands of heavenly messengers, the vision granted to the witnesses of the Book of Mormon, the vision of the glories (D&C 76) as well as the vision of the celestial kingdom (D&C 137), appearances of Jesus Christ himself, and the myriad of revelations and translations given to the Prophet Joseph Smith and his successors. They are all fundamental to a belief in the truthfulness of the claims of The Church of Jesus Christ of Latter-day Saints. But they are matters of faith, and they include events that we did not witness personally but of which the Holy Spirit of the Living God has testified and affirmed to millions of Latter-day Saints. If I do not know all the details, if I do not now have in my possession all of the pieces of the puzzle, I can wait and anticipate; I can trust and believe; I can move forward with faith. I do not do so ignorantly or naïvely, for, once again, I do so after decades of study and hundreds of hours of searching contemplation and fervent prayer. I choose to exercise faith in the whole matter, to "hope for things which are not seen, which are true" (Alma 32:21).

Neither Joseph Smith nor his prophetic successors have asked us to believe that they are perfect men; we do not believe in apostolic or prophetic infallibility. President Gordon B. Hinckley said: "I have worked with seven Presidents of this Church. I have recognized that all have been human. But I have never been concerned over this. They may have had some weaknesses. But this has never troubled me. I know that the God of heaven has used mortal men throughout history to accomplish His divine purposes."[31] On another occasion President Hinckley pleaded with the Saints that "as we continue our search for truth . . . we look for strength and goodness rather than weakness and foibles in those who did so great a work in their time. We recognize that our forebears were human.

31. "Believe His Prophets," *Ensign,* May 1992, 53.

They doubtless made mistakes. . . . There was only one perfect man who ever walked the earth. The Lord has used imperfect people in the process of building his perfect society. If some of them occasionally stumbled, or if their characters may have been slightly flawed in one way or another, the wonder is the greater that they accomplished so much."[32]

CONCLUSION

Let us remember that plural marriage is the exception, a subset of the more comprehensive doctrine and practice—*eternal marriage.* As Latter-day Saints we may not always take the time to reflect seriously on what a treasure, a pearl of great price, we have been given in the restored doctrine and practice of eternal marriage. Consider this statement by a respected Christian leader, a point of view that would be generally accepted by most Christian pastors and theologians but would be at odds with what we know as Latter-day Saints:

"The question I'm most often asked about heaven is, 'Will I be married to the same spouse in heaven?' . . .

"Marriage and other business of this life can sometimes intrude on more important matters of eternal concern. . . . So if you can remain single, do. Concentrate on the things of the Lord, because marriage is only a temporary provision. . . .

"While married couples are heirs together of the grace of *this* life (compare 1 Peter 3:7), *the institution of marriage is passing away.* There are higher eternal values. . . .

"But what of those of us who are happily married supposed to think of this? I love my wife. She's my best friend and my dearest companion in every area of life. If those are your thoughts about your spouse as well, don't despair! You will enjoy an eternal companionship in heaven that is more perfect than any earthly

---

32. "The Continuous Pursuit of Truth," *Ensign,* Apr. 1986, 5.

partnership. The difference is that you will have such a perfect relationship with every other person in heaven as well. If having such a deep relationship with your spouse here is so wonderful, imagine how glorious it will be to enjoy a perfect relationship with every human in the whole expanse of heaven—forever!"[33]

Joseph Smith placed all things in proper perspective. He helped us see that some things really do matter more than others, that family life, family associations, and family love matter more than fame and fortune, more than intellectual acclaim, more than the acquisition of this world's goods. Elder Parley P. Pratt wrote: "It was at this time [in Philadelphia in 1839–40] that I received from [Joseph Smith] the first idea of eternal family organization, and the eternal union of the sexes in those inexpressibly endearing relationships which none but the highly intellectual, the refined and pure in heart, know how to prize, and which are at the very foundation of everything worthy to be called happiness.

"Till then I had learned to esteem kindred affections and sympathies as appertaining solely to this transitory state, as something from which the heart must be entirely weaned, in order to be fitted for its heavenly state.

"It was Joseph Smith who taught me how to prize the endearing relationships of father and mother, husband and wife; of brother and sister, son and daughter.

"It was from him that I learned that the wife of my bosom might be secured to me for time and all eternity; and that the refined sympathies and affections which endeared us to each other emanated from the fountain of divine eternal love. It was from him that I learned that we might cultivate these affections, and grow and increase in the same to all eternity. . . .

"*I had loved before, but I knew not why. But now I loved—with*

---

33. MacArthur, *Glory of Heaven*, 134–38; emphasis added.

a pureness—an intensity of elevated, exalted feeling, which would lift my soul from the transitory things of this groveling sphere and expand it as the ocean. I felt that God was my heavenly Father indeed; that Jesus was my brother, and that the wife of my bosom was an immortal, eternal companion; a kind ministering angel, given to me as a comfort, and a crown of glory for ever and ever. In short, *I could now love with the spirit and with the understanding also.*"[34]

More recently President Russell M. Nelson wrote: "But what of the many mature members of the Church who are not married? Through no failing of their own, they deal with the trials of life alone. Be we all reminded that, in the Lord's own way and time, no blessings will be withheld from His faithful Saints. The Lord will judge and reward each individual according to heartfelt desire as well as deed."[35]

Years ago I was sitting in my office at Brigham Young University when a knock came at my door. It was a very devout member of another faith with whom I had developed a cordial relationship. We chatted for a bit, and he said, essentially, "Bob, I've been thinking a good bit about some of our conversations, and to be honest with you, there is one matter with which I am particularly uncomfortable—your teaching about temples, about marriage and family in the life to come. I just don't see it in scripture. I cannot see why it is necessary."

I responded, "Let me ask you this. Do you love your wife?"

He replied, "Of course I love my wife. You know that. I'm crazy about her, and for some strange reason she seems to feel the same way about me!"

I smiled. "Well, let me take this a little further. Do you love your children?"

---

34. *Autobiography of Parley P. Pratt,* 297–98; emphasis added.
35. *Hope in Our Hearts,* 37–38; see also Smith, *Doctrines of Salvation,* 2:76–77; *Teachings of Lorenzo Snow,* 137–38.

He gave me a funny look and said, "Yes, I love my children. You have been in our home. You know what they mean to me, don't you?"

I nodded affirmatively. "Then do I understand you that you really do love your family? How much do you love them?"

He said in a very sober voice, "Bob, other than my love for God and my Savior, I love my family more than anything in this world."

I looked at him for a moment. Here was a wonderful, God-fearing, Christ-affirming man, one deeply focused on things that matter most. I asked him if he would be willing to put on a shelf what he had been taught all his life in church, just for a minute or two. I asked him if he could simply be a spiritually minded seeker of religious truth.

He chuckled. "Whatever would make you happy."

I looked deep into his eyes. "You really do believe that you and your family will be together in heaven, don't you?"

He looked back at me as tears filled his eyes and he replied, "Yes, I do."

I then said, "All the Latter-day Saints are doing in temples is formalizing and institutionalizing what you know in your heart of hearts to be true. Do you understand what I mean?"

He nodded.

One has only to attend a few Christian funerals and listen closely to what the pastor or priest says by way of consolation to the bereaved to grasp the profound truth that eternal marriages and forever families is a doctrine that lies deep in the marrow of our bones and even deeper in our very souls. How often do we hear those of other faiths offer sweet consolation in such words as, "You and your sweet husband will be together again one day" or "Rest assured that because Jesus Christ rose from the dead, you and your beloved child will live together again as a family." It's much, much more than wishful thinking; it is the kind of thinking that comes naturally from the lips of religious leaders because such notions come naturally to the human heart.

President Russell M. Nelson stated that "while salvation is an individual matter, exaltation is a family matter. Only those who are married in the temple and whose marriage is sealed by the Holy Spirit of Promise will continue as spouses after death and receive the highest degree of celestial glory, or exaltation. . . . The noblest yearning of the human heart is for a marriage that can endure beyond death. Fidelity to a temple marriage does that. It allows families to be together forever."[36]

God is our Father, Jesus is our Lord and Savior, and they are the object of our worship. We devote ourselves to their work and strive, through the power of the Holy Spirit, to grow in spiritual graces and divine attributes so that one day we may qualify to be with them and, to some degree at least, be like them (1 John 3:1–3). Indeed, the work and glory of the Father and the Son is to bring to pass the immortality and eternal life of the children of God (Moses 1:39). That eternal life is intended to include, as a vital and sacred dimension of the world to come, the union and fulfillment and joy that we develop and with which we are endowed through living the law of eternal marriage.

"The family must hold its preeminent place in our way of life," President Thomas S. Monson warned, "because it is the only possible base upon which a society of responsible human beings has ever found it practicable to build for the future and maintain the values they cherish in the present."[37] President Monson's first counselor, President Henry B. Eyring, also counseled the Saints: "We can understand why our Heavenly Father commands us to reverence life and to cherish the powers that produce it as sacred. If we

36. *Hope in Our Hearts*, 34.
37. *Teachings of Thomas S. Monson*, 112.

do not have those feelings in this life, how could our Father give them to us in the eternities? Family life here is the schoolroom in which we prepare for family life there. And to give us the opportunity for family life there was and is the purpose of creation."[38] And surely heaven could never be heaven without our family.

---

38. *To Draw Closer to God,* 165.

Chapter 18

LIFE BEYOND THE GRAVE

Nauvoo, Illinois, 1843–1844. While elements of the Latter-day Saint doctrine of death and the afterlife were revealed precept upon precept, an insight here and a principle there, it was in Nauvoo, during a time of relative peace, that the Prophet began to unfold in surprising detail the final piece of the puzzle of man's eternal existence and the answer to such age-old questions as "If a man die, shall he live again?" (Job 14:14). Where do we go when we die and what do we do? Many of the answers to such questions came during the Nauvoo period, especially in the Prophet Joseph's remarks at funeral services for such men as Ephraim Marks (9 April 1842), Lorenzo Barnes (16 April 1843), Judge Elias Higbee (13 August 1843), James Adams (9 October 1843), and King Follett (7 April 1844).

Nothing is more sobering than death. It is a topic that most of us prefer to avoid. We are uncomfortable with having to face up to our own mortality—we may be eager for the glories that await us after the resurrection but extremely nervous about what it takes to get there. Why do we fear death? For some of us, it is because of our ignorance of the unknown, the anxiety associated with going to a place we do not understand. Others stew over unfinished earthly business. Even the faithful are hesitant to let go, to surrender themselves to the powers of eternity and release their grip on mortality and those they love. Surely a God who has power over all things, even death, would be merciful enough to his children to reveal sufficient truth to prepare us and comfort us concerning what lies ahead. And so he has.

Joseph Smith learned very early in his ministry about life beyond the grave. As we discussed in chapter 2, God the Eternal Father and his Son Jesus Christ appeared to the boy prophet in the Sacred Grove in the spring of 1820. The very presence of those two holy personages attested to the reality of the life beyond. Holy messengers from the Old and New Testaments sent to bestow knowledge, keys, and powers testified to the Latter-day Saints that death is not the end. "All men know they must die," Joseph explained to the Latter-day Saints in Nauvoo. "And it is important that we should understand the reasons and causes of our exposure to the vicissitudes of life and of death, and the designs and purposes of God in our coming into the world, our sufferings here, and our departure hence. . . . It is but reasonable to suppose that God would reveal something in reference to the matter, and it is a subject we ought to study more than any other."[1] Joseph Smith himself made known the basic tenets concerning life after death, and further knowledge and understanding of this rather mysterious topic continued to come precept upon precept through those who were his apostolic and prophetic successors.

FACING THE INEVITABLE

There is nothing more common to this life than death; it is the common lot of all who come into this life to leave it. All are born as helpless infants, and all depart this sphere equally helpless in the

---

1. *Joseph Smith* [manual], 211.

face of death. President Thomas S. Monson asked: "What mortal being, faced with the loss of a loved one or, indeed, standing himself or herself on the threshold of infinity, has not pondered beyond the veil which separates the seen from the unseen?"[2] On another occasion he stated: "Frequently death comes as an intruder. It is an enemy that suddenly appears in the midst of life's feast, putting out its lights and gaiety. . . . Death lays its heavy hand upon those dear to us and at times leaves us baffled and wondering. In certain situations, as in great suffering and illness, death comes as an angel of mercy. But for the most part, we think of it as the enemy of human happiness."[3]

Even among those who read by the lamp of gospel understanding, death is frequently viewed with fear and trembling. Wilford Woodruff "referred to a saying of Joseph Smith, which he heard him utter (like this), That if the people knew what was behind the veil, they would try by every means to . . . get there. But *the Lord in his wisdom had implanted the fear of death in every person that they might cling to life and thus accomplish the designs of their Creator.*"[4] And that fear of death makes such partings particularly painful. "Irrespective of age," President Russell M. Nelson explained, "we mourn for those loved and lost. Mourning is one of the deepest expressions of pure love. . . . Moreover, we can't fully appreciate joyful reunions later without tearful separations now. *The only way to take sorrow out of death is to take love out of life.*"[5]

Strictly speaking, there is no death and there are no dead. When persons die, they do not cease to be; they merely cease to be in this world. Life goes on. Death is a transition, a change in assignment, a transfer to another realm. When we die, our spirit

---

2. *Teachings of Thomas S. Monson*, 19.
3. *Teachings of Thomas S. Monson*, 78–79.
4. *Diary of Charles L. Walker*, 1:595–96; emphasis added.
5. *Perfection Pending*, 136–37; emphasis added.

continues to see and act and feel and associate; it is only the physical body that becomes inactive and lifeless for a season. And so it is that we use the term *death* to describe what seems to be from our limited perspective. From an eternal perspective, however, there is only life.

We often speak of a person's untimely death. Generally we mean that it is untimely for us who remain behind. Though it is true that individuals may hasten their death and thus shorten their day of probation,[6] for the faithful there is nothing untimely about death. President Joseph Fielding Smith, grandnephew to Joseph the Seer, stated at the funeral of Elder Richard L. Evans: "May I say for the consolation of those who mourn, and for the comfort and guidance of all of us, that no righteous man is ever taken before his time. In the case of the faithful saints, they are simply transferred to other fields of labor. The Lord's work goes on in this life, in the world of spirits, and in the kingdoms of glory where men go after their resurrection."[7]

Truly, death passes upon all mortals "to fulfil the merciful plan of the great Creator" (2 Nephi 9:6). Death is merciful in that it delivers us from the toils and agonies of this life. "When men are prepared," the Prophet observed, "they are better off to go hence."[8]

Death is merciful too because it opens us to a new phase of life, a time wherein the restrictions of this mortal coil are gone and the mind or spirit can soar. "How do we know," asked Elder Orson Pratt, "when this spirit is freed from this mortal tabernacle, but that all [our] senses will be greatly enlarged? . . . I believe we shall be freed, in the next world, in a great measure, from these narrow, contracted methods of thinking. Instead of thinking in one channel, and following up one certain course of reasoning to find a certain

---

6. See Kimball, *Faith Precedes the Miracle,* 103, 105.
7. Funeral of Elder Richard L. Evans, 4 Nov. 1971, 2.
8. *Joseph Smith* [manual], 179.

truth, knowledge will rush in from all quarters . . . , informing the spirit, and giving understanding concerning ten thousand things at the same time; and the mind will be capable of receiving and retaining all."[9]

Losing family members to death is particularly painful, and those of the household of faith are not spared such feelings. "Thou shalt live together in love, insomuch that thou shalt weep for the loss of them that die" (D&C 42:45). We weep and we long for a reassociation, but we do not grieve as do those who have no hope (1 Thessalonians 4:13), for to do so is to express a lack of faith in the purposes and plan of God and to ignore the promise of reunion and restoration. Thus in the process of time we move on, seeking always to view things as God views them. "Precious in the sight of the Lord," the revealed word declares, "is the death of his saints" (Psalm 116:15). We have the assurance from modern revelation that "those that die shall rest from all their labors, and their works shall follow them; and they shall receive a crown in the mansions of my Father, which I have prepared for them" (D&C 59:2).

The cycle of life continues everlastingly. If there were no death, there would be no life. If there were no death, the growth and development and expansion that lie ahead would be forever withheld from us. There is purpose in life, and there is purpose in death. He who knows all things knows what is best for us and orchestrates the events of our existence.

A POSTMORTAL WORLD

Modern prophets attest that the transition from time into eternity is immediate. As we breathe our last breath, our spirit leaves the body and passes directly into the postmortal spirit world. Joseph Smith taught: "The spirits of the just are exalted to a greater and

9. In *Journal of Discourses,* 2:243, 246.

more glorious work; hence they are blessed in departing hence. Enveloped in flaming fire, *they are not far from us,* and know and understand our thoughts, feelings, and motions, and are often pained therewith."[10] "Is the spirit world here?" President Brigham Young asked. "It is not beyond the sun, but is on this earth that was organized for the people that have lived and that do and will live upon it."[11] Elder Parley P. Pratt similarly explained that the spirit world "is here on the very planet where we were born."[12]

At the time of one's entrance into the spirit world, the individual experiences what President Joseph F. Smith, Joseph's nephew, called a "partial judgment."[13] He or she goes either to paradise or to hell or outer darkness (see also 1 Nephi 15:29; 2 Nephi 9:12). Paradise is the abode of the faithful, a state of happiness, "a state of rest, a state of peace, where they shall rest from all their troubles and from all care, and sorrow" (Alma 40:12). Paradise is a place where spirits "expand in wisdom, where they have respite from all their troubles, and where care and sorrow do not annoy."[14] On the other hand, the spirits of the wicked "shall be cast out into outer darkness; there shall be weeping, and wailing, and gnashing of teeth, and this because of their own iniquity, being led captive by the will of the devil" (Alma 40:13).

Modern revelation also makes clear that the entire spirit world, not just that part known as hell or outer darkness, is, in a sense, a spirit prison. Though there are divisions of some kind between the righteous and the wicked, all the postmortal spirits are in one world, just as they are in the flesh. In the postmortal spirit world, the disembodied long for deliverance from their present condition;

---

10. *Words of Joseph Smith,* 253–54.
11. In *Journal of Discourses,* 3:372.
12. *Key to the Science of Theology,* 80.
13. *Gospel Doctrine,* 448–49.
14. *Gospel Doctrine,* 448.

they look upon the absence of their spirits from their bodies as a bondage (D&C 45:17; 138:50; see also 138:15–18, 23). "When our spirits leave these bodies, will they be happy?" Elder Orson Pratt asked. "Not perfectly so," he responded. "Why? Because the spirit is absent from the body; it cannot be perfectly happy while a part of the man is lying in the earth. . . . You will be happy, you will be at ease in paradise; but still you will be looking for a house where your spirit can enter and act as you did in former times."[15]

President Brigham Young asked: "Where are the spirits of the ungodly? They are in prison. Where are the spirits of the righteous, the Prophets, and the Apostles? They are in prison, brethren; that is where they are." He continued: "I know it is a startling idea to say that the Prophet and the persecutor of the Prophet, all go to prison together . . . , but *they have not got their bodies yet, consequently they are in prison.*"[16] The Prophet Joseph taught: "Hades, the Greek, or Sheol, the Hebrew, these two significations mean a world of spirits. Hades, Sheol, paradise, spirits in prison, are all one: it is a world of spirits."[17] Thus for the apostle Peter to declare that Jesus went, after his mortal death, to preach to the "spirits in prison" (1 Peter 3:18–20)—and knowing from modern scripture that the Master did not minister in person to the wicked (D&C 138:20–22, 29, 37)—we conclude that he preached to the spirits in prison in the sense that "from among the righteous, he organized his forces and appointed messengers, clothed with power and authority, and commissioned them to go forth and carry the light of the gospel to them that were in darkness, even to all the spirits of men" (D&C 138:30).

It was quite common in the nineteenth century, and is today, for most Christians to envision hell as a place where wicked and unredeemed individuals go after their death and where they will remain

15. In *Journal of Discourses,* 1:289–90.
16. In *Journal of Discourses,* 3:94–95; emphasis added.
17. *Words of Joseph Smith,* 213.

in the fiery flames forever. In June 1843 Joseph Smith offered invaluable insight on this matter: "The great misery of departed spirits in the world of spirits, where they go after death, is to know that they come short of the glory that others enjoy and that they might have enjoyed themselves, and they are their own accusers."[18] Or, as he put it ten months later, "A man is his own tormentor and his own condemner. Hence the saying, They shall go into the lake that burns with fire and brimstone [see Revelation 21:8]. *The torment of disappointment in the mind of man is as exquisite as a lake burning with fire and brimstone.* I say, so is the torment of man."[19]

Just as there are variations among the godly in paradise, so also there must be differences among those in hell. There are the very wicked who, as Alma explained, are subject to confrontation, suffering, and sore repentance. There are others—good people, on the whole—who have not enjoyed the blessings of the fulness of the gospel because such were unavailable to them. These work and grow and learn and develop. Many of them open their hearts to the gospel message and are taught. Modern prophets have further clarified that once the gospel message is delivered and accepted by individuals in the spirit world, and once the appropriate ordinances have been performed by those in the flesh who act as proxy for the departed, "the Lord has administrators there to set them free."[20] That is, once a person has received the gospel and its saving ordinances, he or she is permitted to cross that gulf that separates hell from paradise and thereafter enjoy sweet association with the faithful (Luke 16:26; see also 1 Nephi 15:28–30).[21]

Any number of factors can affect a person's capacity to see and feel and hear and receive the truth. Some of those factors bear upon

18. *Joseph Smith* [manual], 224.
19. *Joseph Smith* [manual], 224; emphasis added.
20. *Joseph Smith* [manual], 474.
21. See Smith, *Doctrines of Salvation,* 2:158, 230.

all of us, and some of them are beyond our power to control. As we move closer to the great millennial day, wickedness will widen and malevolence will multiply. The index of moral pollution will rise, thus making it more and more difficult to remain unscathed and unwounded in the war against evil. "It is my conviction," Elder Boyd K. Packer testified, "that those wicked influences one day will be overruled."[22]

"In this space between death and the resurrection of the body, the two classes of souls remain, in happiness or in misery, until the time which is appointed of God that the dead shall come forth and be reunited both spirit and body."[23] And so the postmortal spirit world is an intermediate stop for all humankind. It is a place of waiting, of repentance and suffering, of peace and rest, and of instruction and preparation. Those who receive and enjoy the blessings of the gospel (celestial), or at least who receive the testimony of Jesus (terrestrial), will come forth from the spirit world at the time of the first resurrection, or resurrection of the just (D&C 76:51, 74, 82). Those who continue to assert their own will and refuse the Savior's offer of enlightenment and renewal will remain in the spirit world until the thousand years are ended. Then in that second, or last resurrection, they will come forth either to a telestial glory or to a kingdom of no glory (as sons of perdition—see D&C 76:32, 88:24).

"This Day . . . in Paradise"

On Golgotha Jesus hung on the cross between two thieves. One of them "railed on him, saying, If thou be Christ, save thyself and us. But the other answering rebuked him, saying, Dost not thou fear God, seeing thou art in the same condemnation? And we indeed justly; for we receive the due reward of our deeds: but this man hath done nothing amiss. And he said unto Jesus, Lord,

---

22. "Our Moral Environment," *Ensign*, May 1992, 68.
23. Smith, *Gospel Doctrine*, 448.

remember me when thou comest into thy kingdom. And Jesus said unto him, Verily I say unto thee, To day shalt thou be with me in paradise" (Luke 23:39–43).

As we might expect, this passage has given rise to a whole host of interpretations, perhaps the most prevalent being a belief in a type of deathbed repentance. To be sure, it is good to repent, no matter when we do it. That is, it is better to repent than to remain in our sins. The Prophet Joseph taught that "there is never a time when the spirit is too old to approach God. All are within the reach of pardoning mercy, who have not committed the unpardonable sin."[24] Thus, although we would never denigrate the value of sincere repentance—no matter how late in one's mortal probation (Matthew 20:1–16)—we acknowledge the divine word that "he that repents and does the commandments of the Lord shall be forgiven" (D&C 1:32). The Savior affirmed: "Not every one that saith unto me, Lord, Lord, shall enter into the kingdom of heaven; but he that doeth the will of my Father which is in heaven" (Matthew 7:21).

On the other hand, the Prophet Joseph taught on one occasion: "The infidel will grasp at every straw for help until death stares him in the face, and then his infidelity takes its flight, for the realities of the eternal world are resting upon him in mighty power; and when every earthly support and prop fails him, he then sensibly feels the eternal truths of the immortality of the soul. We should take warning and not wait for the death-bed to repent. . . . Let this, then, prove as a warning to all not to procrastinate repentance, or wait till a death-bed, for it is the will of God that man should repent and serve him in health, and in the strength and power of his mind, in order to secure his blessing, and not wait until he is called to die."[25]

Furthermore, we must look a little deeper into this matter to understand what the Savior really said on this occasion. Did the

---

24. *Joseph Smith* [manual], 76, 471.
25. *Joseph Smith* [manual], 73.

Master actually promise the thief on the cross that he would at the time of death enter into paradise, the abode of the righteous? Would all his sins be overlooked? Joseph Smith stated: "I will say something about the spirits in prison. There has been much said by modern divines about the words of Jesus (when on the cross) to the thief, saying, 'This day shalt thou be with me in paradise.' King James' translators make it out to say paradise. But what is paradise? It is a modern word; it does not answer at all to the original word that Jesus made use of. Find the original of the word *paradise*. You might as easily find a needle in a haymow. Here is a chance for battle, ye learned men. There is nothing in the original word in Greek from which this was taken that signifies paradise; but it was—This day thou shalt be with me *in the world of spirits*."[26]

Josiah Quincy, a man who later became the mayor of Boston, visited the Prophet Joseph Smith in Nauvoo and wrote of an occasion wherein Joseph spoke on the necessity of baptism for salvation. A minister in the audience contended as follows with the Prophet: "*Minister.* Stop! What do you say to the case of the penitent thief? *Prophet.* What do you mean by that? *Minister.* You know our Saviour said to the thief, 'This day shalt thou be with me in Paradise,' which shows he could not have been baptized before his admission. *Prophet.* How do you know he wasn't baptized before he became a thief? At this retort the sort of laugh that is provoked by an unexpected hit ran through the audience; but this demonstration of sympathy was rebuked by a severe look from Smith, who went on to say: 'But that is not the true answer. In the original Greek, as this gentleman [turning to me] will inform you, the word

---

26. History, 1838–1856, volume D-1 [1 August 1842–1 July 1843]. The Joseph Smith Papers, accessed 28 July 2016, http://www.josephsmithpapers.org/paperSummary /history-1838-1856-volume-d-1-1-august-1842-1-july-1843?p=218&highlight =find%20the%20original%20of%20the%20word%20paradise; see also *Words of Joseph Smith*, 213.

that has been translated paradise means simply a place of departed spirits. To that place the penitent thief was conveyed.'"[27]

The prophets of this dispensation have borne repeated testimony of the love and light to be known by those who have lived faithfully and then passed through the veil of death into the postmortal spirit world. "I testify of the extraordinary peace and tranquility that await those beyond the veil who have followed the light and knowledge they have received in this life," said Elder Robert D. Hales. "If we could experience, only momentarily, the scene that awaits the righteous there, we would find it difficult to return to mortality. I know this from experience."[28]

RESURRECTION AND JUDGMENT

If Jesus' greatest accomplishments consisted of his kindness, his generosity, and his sage advice, then our hope for happiness hereafter is unfounded (1 Corinthians 15:19). Like Paul, the Book of Mormon prophet Jacob declared that if Christ did not rise from the dead (as it was prophesied that he would do), then we would one and all, at the time of death, be consigned to spiritual ruin and destruction; we would be forevermore subject to the father of lies. Why? Because if Jesus did not have the power to rise from the dead and thus redeem the body from the grave, then he surely did not have the power to forgive sins and thereby redeem the spirit from hell (2 Nephi 9:7–9; compare 1 Corinthians 15:12–17). Truly, "the most glorious, comforting, and reassuring of all events of human history had taken place—the victory over death. The pain and agony of Gethsemane and Calvary had been wiped away. The salvation of mankind had been secured. The Fall of Adam had been reclaimed."[29]

---

27. *Figures of the Past*, 391–92.
28. *Return*, 404.
29. *Teachings of Thomas S. Monson*, 21–22.

The Prophet emphasized that if Christ has not risen from the dead, "the bands of the temporal death are broken that the grave has no victory. If then, the grave has no victory, those who keep the sayings of Jesus and obey His teachings have not only a promise of a resurrection from the dead, but an assurance of being admitted into His glorious kingdom."[30] Because Jesus Christ has risen from the dead, we also will rise from the dead. Because he lives, we also will live, beyond the grave.

Joseph Smith and the early Brethren taught that certain keys of the priesthood—keys we do not now possess but will be conferred upon those who are exalted—include the keys of resurrection. The Prophet Joseph spoke longingly of his great desire to be buried near his family, so that they "may hear the sound of the trump that shall call them forth to behold [the Savior], that in the morn of the resurrection they may come forth in a body and come right up out of their graves and strike hands immediately in eternal glory and felicity."[31]

In the Manchester England Area Conference, Church President Spencer W. Kimball explained to holders of the priesthood: "Your wife is your counterpart, and together you use the God-given powers that are given to you . . . to create this great person that is born of yourselves [your children]. Now you become the servant of the Lord, with his power. What you have now is a miniature power. I mean there is no one in this room, perhaps, who is enjoying his power to its great limit. . . . You have the power over the elements. You will have many other powers that you never thought or dreamed of yet. You will have the power of the resurrection some day. Did you realize that?

"Today you or I could not stand here and call to life a dead

---

30. *Joseph Smith* [manual], 51.

31. *Words of Joseph Smith*, 194–95; see also Brigham Young, in *Journal of Discourses*, 6:275; 9:139–40; 15:137–39; Erastus Snow, in *Journal of Discourses*, 25:33–34.

person, but the day will come when I can take my wife by the hand and raise her up out of the grave in the resurrection. The day will come when you can bring each of your family who has preceded you in death back into a resurrected being to live forever."[32]

Less than a year later, President Kimball spoke similarly in a general priesthood meeting: "You and I—what helpless creatures are we! Such limited power we have, and how little can we control the wind and the waves and the storms! We remember the numerous scriptures which, concentrated in a single line, were said by a former prophet, Lorenzo Snow: 'As man is, God once was; and as God is, man may become.' This is a power available to us as we reach perfection and receive the experience and power."[33]

President Russell M. Nelson taught that "at the time of our resurrection, we shall take up our immortal tabernacles. Bodies that now age, deteriorate, and decay will no longer be subject to processes of degeneration. . . .

"The great priesthood power of resurrection is vested in the Lord of this world. He taught, 'All power is given unto me in heaven and in earth' (Matthew 28:18). Though he supplicated his Father for aid at the eleventh hour, the final victory over death was earned by the Son. . . . The keys of the resurrection repose securely with our Lord and Master."[34] In summary, Elder Dallin H. Oaks explained, "the priesthood is the power by which we will be resurrected and proceed to eternal life."[35]

The resurrected body is a spiritual body, meaning that it is immortal, not subject to death (1 Corinthians 15:44; Alma 11:45; D&C 88:27). The scriptural promise is that we rise from the grave with a resurrected body suited to the respective kingdom we will

---

32. In Manchester England Area Conference Report, 21 June 1976, 34.
33. "Our Great Potential," *Ensign*, May 1977, 49.
34. *Power within Us*, 147–48.
35. "The Keys and Authority of the Priesthood," *Ensign*, May 2014, 49.

inherit: "They who are of a celestial spirit shall receive the same body which was a natural body; even ye shall receive your bodies, and your glory shall be that glory by which your bodies are quickened. Ye who are quickened by a portion of the celestial glory [in mortality] shall then [in the resurrection] receive of the same, even a fulness. And they who are quickened by a portion of the terrestrial glory shall then receive of the same, even a fulness. And also they who are quickened by a portion of the telestial glory shall then receive of the same, even a fulness. And they who remain [the sons of perdition] shall also be quickened; nevertheless, they shall return again to their own place, to enjoy that which they are willing to receive, because they were not willing to enjoy that which they might have received" (D&C 88:28–32).

The scriptures of the Restoration also clarify the nature of the resurrected body. "The soul [meaning, in this instance, the spirit] shall be restored to the body," Alma explained, "and the body to the soul; yea, and every limb and joint shall be restored to its body; yea, even a hair of the head shall not be lost; but all things shall be restored to their proper and perfect frame" (Alma 40:23; see also 11:43). In speaking of the righteous who waited anxiously for the Savior's entrance into paradise, President Joseph F. Smith wrote: "Their sleeping dust was to be restored unto its perfect frame, bone to his bone, and the sinews and the flesh upon them, the spirit and the body to be united never again to be divided, that they might receive a fulness of joy" (D&C 138:17; compare 93:33).

On one occasion Elder Orson Pratt pointed out that a person's mortal body is constantly changing—old cells being replaced by new ones, etc. The Prophet Joseph responded: "There is no fundamental principle belonging to a human system that ever goes into another in this world or in the world to come; I care not what the theories of men are. . . . We have the testimony that God will raise us up, and he has the power to do it. If any one supposes that any part of our bodies, that is, the fundamental parts thereof, ever goes into another body, he is mistaken."[36] Indeed, the revelation states with clarity that "ye shall receive *your bodies,* and your glory shall be that glory by which your bodies are quickened" (D&C 88:28; emphasis added). President Russell M. Nelson added: "The Lord who created us in the first place surely has power to do it again. The same necessary elements now in our bodies will still be available— at His command. The same unique genetic code now embedded in each of our living cells will still be available to format new ones then."[37]

We have the comforting assurance that even though men and women are refined, renewed, and perfected body and soul in the resurrection, they will maintain their identity. We will know friends and loved ones in and after the resurrection, even as we know them now. In speaking of meeting a departed loved one in the future, President Joseph F. Smith taught: "I expect to be able to recognize her, just as I could recognize her tomorrow, if she were living . . . because her identity is fixed and indestructible, just as fixed and indestructible as the identity of God the Father and Jesus Christ the Son. They cannot be any other than themselves. They cannot be changed; they are from everlasting to everlasting, eternally the same; so it will be with us. We will progress and develop and grow in wisdom and understanding, but our identity can never change."[38]

In the Book of Mormon, resurrection and eternal judgment are companion doctrines, just as are the Fall and the Atonement. The Prophet therefore instructed the Saints that "the doctrines of the resurrection of the dead and the eternal judgment are necessary to preach among the first principles of the Gospel of Jesus Christ."[39]

---

36. *Words of Joseph Smith,* 182.
37. *Perfection Pending,* 140–41.
38. *Gospel Doctrine,* 25.
39. *Words of Joseph Smith,* 4.

One of the great acts of mercy and grace is that all who took a physical body, including the sons of perdition, will be resurrected and thereafter brought to stand before God to be judged of their works. In a sense, therefore, the Atonement overcomes spiritual death for all, at least for a short season in which all persons stand once again in the divine presence. Jacob wrote: "And it shall come to pass that when all men shall have passed from this first death unto life, insomuch as they have become immortal, they must appear before the judgment-seat of the Holy One of Israel; and then cometh the judgment, and then must they be judged according to the holy judgment of God" (2 Nephi 9:15; see also Helaman 14:15; 3 Nephi 27:13–16). Finally, Moroni bore witness that "because of Jesus Christ came the redemption of man. And because of the redemption of man, which came by Jesus Christ, they are brought back into the presence of the Lord; yea, *this is wherein all men are redeemed*" (Mormon 9:12–13; emphasis added).

CONCLUSION

"More painful to me are the thoughts of annihilation than death," Joseph Smith once declared.[40] With the restoration of divine truths concerning God's plan of salvation, we know where we came from. We know why we are here. And we know where we are going when death calls each of us to pass through the veil that separates time and eternity. There are no wrongs that will not be righted in time or eternity, no burdens that will not be lifted, no stories left untold. Through the power of the Lamb of God, slain from before the foundation of the world, we have the sweet assurance that death will have been defeated, the grave will have been robbed of its captive, and all the toils of mortality will have passed away. "And God shall wipe away all tears from their eyes; and there shall be no more

---

40. *Joseph Smith* [manual], 176.

death, neither sorrow, nor crying, neither shall there be any more pain: for the former things are passed away" (Revelation 21:4; see also 7:17). And what mortal who possesses even a sliver of hope in the plan of our Eternal Father does not look with sweet anticipation to that day?

From Palmyra to Nauvoo, September 1830-June 1844. The restored Church had been formally organized only six months when the Lord began to open to the Latter-day Saints the prophetic picture, including the signs that would precede the second advent of the Savior, as well as the nature of life on the millennial earth. Prophetic particulars came occasionally in revelations dealing almost exclusively with future events and also as small but significant revelations that covered a wide range of topics (D&C 29; 43; 63; 77; 84; 88; 133).

I t just may be that Joseph Smith made known to us more about the past than he did about the future. Having said that, I hasten to add that he and his successors have certainly provided a stunning and remarkably thorough picture of what lies ahead.[1] The Prophet declared quite early in his ministry: "When I contemplate the rapidity with which the great and glorious day of the coming

---

1. Obviously, whole books have been written on this subject, and so we must be painfully brief and confine ourselves in this chapter to some of the fundamental teachings. See, for example, Smith, *Signs of the Times;* Lund, *Coming of the Lord;* McConkie, *Millennial Messiah;* Ostler, *Refuge from the Storm;* Millet, *Living in the Eleventh Hour; Living in the Millennium.*

of the Son of Man advances, when He shall come to receive His Saints unto Himself, where they shall dwell in His presence, and be crowned with glory and immortality; when I consider that soon the heavens are to be shaken, and the earth tremble and reel to and fro; and that the heavens are to be unfolded as a scroll when it is rolled up; and that every mountain and island are to flee away, I cry out in my heart, What manner of persons ought we to be in all holy conversation and godliness!"[2]

LOOKING AHEAD TO HIS COMING

Christians throughout the nation in the nineteenth century were divided as to how and when and in what manner the King of kings would come to earth and take charge. Some believed that much of the responsibility rested with the people and that their task was to build up God's kingdom, establish righteousness throughout the earth, spread Christianity to all walks of life, and in general work to transform society and prepare the world for the Second Advent. From this perspective (known as postmillennialism), the Millennium would be brought in by the gradual spread of righteousness. Others (premillennialists) held that God would soon and dramatically step into history, destroy the wicked, bind Satan, and welcome in a thousand years of peace and rest and worldwide goodness. The Millennium would be brought in by power, divine power.

While Joseph Smith and his followers seem to fit best into the category of premillennialists, they also felt driven to extend their religious fervor beyond church meetings and out into the workaday world. The members of the restored Church were charged by their leaders to build the kingdom of God in preparation for the coming kingdom of heaven (D&C 65:5–6). One eminent historian

---

2. *Joseph Smith* [manual], 255; compare 2 Peter 3:10–11.

described the situation: "The Mormons did not passively await Christ's millennial kingdom but worked to prepare for it. Their brand of premillennialism was as activist as any postmillennialism, and even more certain of a special role for America."[3]

"I was once praying very earnestly," Joseph Smith stated in August 1843, "to know the time of the coming of the Son of Man, when I heard a voice repeat the following: Joseph, my son, if thou livest until thou art eighty-five years old, thou shalt see the face of the Son of Man; therefore let this suffice, and trouble me no more on this matter." The Prophet's assessment of the Lord's rather vague response was: "I was left thus, without being able to decide whether this coming referred to the beginning of the millennium or to some previous appearing, or whether I should die and thus see his face. I believe the coming of the Son of Man will not be any sooner than that time" (D&C 130:14–17). Some seven months later, the Prophet declared: "Jesus Christ never did reveal to any man the precise time that He would come. Go and read the Scriptures, and you cannot find anything that specifies the exact hour He would come; and all that say so are false teachers."[4]

---

3. Howe, *What Hath God Wrought*, 316.

4. *Joseph Smith* [manual], 253. James Burgess recorded a sermon delivered by Joseph Smith on 6 April 1843: "Christ says no man knoweth the day or the hour when the Son of Man cometh. . . . Did Christ speak this as a general principle throughout all generations? O no. He spoke in the present tense. No man then living upon the footstool of God knew the day or the hour. But he did not say that there was no man throughout all generations that should not know the day or the hour. No, for this would be in flat contradiction with other scripture, for the prophet says that God will do nothing but what he will reveal unto his servants the prophets [Amos 3:7]. Consequently, if it is not made known unto the prophets, it will not come to pass." Joseph then employed the Pauline analogy (1 Thessalonians 5:2–6) of a pregnant woman recognizing the signs within her body concerning the imminent birth of her child (*Words of Joseph Smith*, 180–81). A modern revelation explains that "the coming of the Lord draweth nigh, and *it overtaketh the world as a thief in the night*—therefore, gird up your loins, *that you may be the children of light, and that day shall not overtake you as a thief*" (D&C 106:4–5; emphasis added).

FROM THE NEW TRANSLATION OF THE BIBLE

The Prophet's translation of Matthew 24 is what we now call Joseph Smith–Matthew in the Pearl of Great Price. Verse 34 of Matthew 24 in the King James Version of the Bible has been a problematic verse for a long time. It reads: "Verily I say unto you, This generation shall not pass, till all these things shall be fulfilled." "All these things" includes the destruction of the temple, false Christs, wars and rumors of wars, famines, pestilences, earthquakes, false prophets, iniquity abounding, the gospel being preached to all the world,[5] the gathering of Israel, and the sign of the Son of Man. Clearly "all these things" did *not* take place before the end of the Savior's generation, causing many scholars through the centuries to conclude either (1) Jesus did not know what lay ahead; or (2) Jesus simply missed it. His prophecy did not come to pass.

But notice how the Prophet's translation of verse 34 assists us: "Verily, I say unto you, this generation *in which these things shall be shown forth* [that is, the generation in which the signs actually take place], shall not pass away until all I have told you shall be fulfilled" (emphasis added).

The inspired translation of Matthew 24 also clarifies another matter: the meaning of the phrase "end of the world" and the difference between the end of the world and the "end of the earth."

---

5. The Joseph Smith Translation reads as follows: "And again, this Gospel of the kingdom shall be preached in all the world, for a witness unto all nations, and then shall the end come, or the destruction of the wicked" (Joseph Smith–Matthew 1:31). Less than two months before his death, Joseph rendered this passage in a most unusual manner: "I shall read the 24th chapter of Matthew, and give it a literal rendering and reading; and when it is rightly understood, it will be edifying. . . . 'And it will be preached, the Gospel of the kingdom, in the whole world, to a witness over all people: and then will the end come.'" The Prophet then said: "The Savior said when these tribulations should take place, it [the gospel of the kingdom] should be committed to a man who should be a witness over the whole world: the keys of knowledge, power and revelations should be revealed to a witness who should hold the testimony to the world" (*Words of Joseph Smith*, 366; see also 370).

We learn herein that the end of the world is "the destruction of the wicked," or the destruction of worldliness that comes at the time of the Savior's second coming in glory (vv. 4, 31). Further, in the very last verse of Joseph Smith–Matthew we read: "And thus cometh *the end of the wicked,* according to the prophecy of Moses, saying: They shall be cut off from among the people [Acts 3:22–23; 3 Nephi 20:23; 21:11; D&C 1:38]; but *the end of the earth is not yet,* but by and by" (emphasis added). The end of the earth is the end of the Millennium (D&C 38:5; 43:31; 88:101).

Many students of the New Testament have concluded that the early Christian apostles and the Saints in general felt that the Savior's second coming was imminent and that they would surely live to see it. They often give as a second illustration some of the writings of the apostle Paul. It seems that the Saints in Thessalonica, for example, were particularly troubled about when the Lord would return and what would become of their righteous dead. From the King James Version: "For this we say unto you by the word of the Lord, that *we which are alive and remain unto the coming of the Lord* shall not prevent [precede, have preference over] them which are asleep. For the Lord himself shall descend from heaven with a shout, with the voice of the archangel, and with the trump of God: and the dead in Christ shall rise first: Then *we which are alive and remain* shall be caught up together with them in the clouds, to meet the Lord in the air: and so shall we ever be with the Lord. Wherefore comfort one another with these words" (1 Thessalonians 4:15–18; emphasis added). One can recognize how easy it would be to conclude that the great apostle to the Gentiles didn't have his theological chronology down pat. In point of fact, Joseph Smith's translation of Matthew 24 simply changes "we which are alive and remain" to "they who are alive."

In the history of the Church under the date of March 1832 are found these words: "In connection with the translation of the

Scriptures, I received the following explanation of the Revelation of St. John."[6] Then follows Doctrine and Covenants 77, a most unusual revelation. It is essentially a question-and-answer session between the Lord and his prophet. Some of the matters it addresses include the earth as a sea of glass (vv. 1–2); the four beasts seen by John in Revelation 4 (vv. 2–4); the twenty-four elders surrounding the throne of God (v. 5); the seven seals with which the history of humankind is sealed (vv. 6–7); the various angels described in Revelation 7 (vv. 8–9); the 144,000 high priests mentioned in Revelation 7 and 14 (v. 11); and the two witnesses who are sent to prophesy during the time of the battle of Armageddon (v. 15). The answers to the questions found in section 77 are instructive.

Jesus taught: "Blessed are those servants, whom the Lord when he cometh shall find watching: verily I say unto you, that he shall gird himself, and make them to sit down to meat, and will come forth and serve them. For, behold, he cometh in the first watch of the night, and he shall also come in the second watch, and again he shall come in the third watch. And verily I say unto you, *He hath already come,* as it is written of him" (JST, Luke 12:40–42; emphasis added).

What a strange statement! How is it that our Lord comes in the first watch of the night and also in the second and third watches? In addition, how has he come already? Elder Bruce R. McConkie offered the following helpful commentary: "One of the great incentives which encourages and entices men to live lives of personal righteousness, is the doctrine of the Second Coming of the Messiah. . . .

"All of the Lord's ministers, all of the members of the Church, and for that matter all men everywhere ('What I say unto one, I say unto all'), are counseled to await with righteousness the coming of the Lord. However, most men will die before he comes, and

---

6. Heading to Doctrine and Covenants 77.

only those then living will rejoice or tremble, as the case may be, at his personal presence. But all who did prepare will be rewarded *as though they had lived when he came,* while the wicked will be 'cut asunder' and appointed their 'portion with the hypocrites' *as surely as though they lived in the very day of dread and vengeance.* Thus, in effect, the Lord comes in every watch of the night, on every occasion when men are called to face death and judgment."[7]

THE LORD'S PRIVATE APPEARANCES

Joseph Smith gave us to understand that there would be several appearances of the Savior, some of which would be private and the last of which would be very public; all will know when he comes in glory (D&C 49:23; 133:19–22). First, the Lord will make a preliminary appearance at his temple in Independence, Jackson County, Missouri (Malachi 3:1; see also D&C 36:8; 42:36). This seems to be a private appearance to those holding the keys of power in the earthly kingdom. Elder Orson Pratt, in speaking of this appearance, said: "All of them who are pure in heart will behold the face of the Lord and that too before he comes in his glory in the clouds of heaven, for he will suddenly come to his Temple, and he will purify the sons of Moses and of Aaron, until they shall be prepared to offer in that Temple an offering that shall be acceptable in the sight of the Lord [see Malachi 3:3; D&C 13; 84:31]. In doing this, he will purify not only the minds of the Priesthood in that Temple, but he will purify their bodies until they shall be quickened, renewed and strengthened, and they will be partially changed, not to immortality, but changed in part that they can be filled with the power of God, and they can stand in the presence of Jesus, and behold his face in the midst of that Temple."[8]

---

7. *Doctrinal New Testament Commentary,* 1:674–75, 676–77; emphasis added.

8. In *Journal of Discourses,* 15:365–66.

Second, the Lord will make an appearance at Adam-ondi-Ahman, "the place where Adam shall come to visit his people, or the Ancient of Days shall sit" (D&C 116). This grand council will be the occasion for a large sacrament meeting, a time when the Son of Man will partake of the fruit of the vine once more with his earthly friends. And who will be in attendance? The revelations specify Moroni, Elias, John the Baptist, Elijah, Abraham, Isaac, Jacob, Joseph, Adam, Peter, James, John, "and also," the Savior clarifies, "all those whom my Father hath given me out of the world" (D&C 27:5–14), multitudes of faithful Saints from the beginning of time to the end. This will be a private appearance in that it will be unknown to the world. It will be a leadership meeting, a time of accounting for priesthood stewardships. The Prophet Joseph Smith explained that Adam, the Ancient of Days, "will call his children together and hold a council with them to prepare them for the coming of the Son of Man. He (Adam) is the father of the human family, and presides over the spirits of all men, and all that have had the keys must stand before him in this grand council. . . . The Son of Man stands before him, and there is given him [Christ] glory and dominion. Adam delivers up his stewardship to Christ, that which was delivered to him as holding the keys of the universe, but retains his standing as head of the human family."[9]

President Joseph Fielding Smith observed: "This gathering of the children of Adam, where the thousands, and the tens of thousands are assembled in the judgment, will be one of the greatest events this troubled earth has ever seen. At this conference, or council, all who have held keys of dispensations will render a report for their stewardship. Adam will do likewise, and then he will surrender to Christ all authority. Then Adam will be confirmed in his calling as the prince over his posterity and will be officially installed

---

9. *Joseph Smith* [manual], 104.

and crowned eternally in this presiding calling. Then Christ will be received as King of kings, and Lord of lords. We do not know how long a time this gathering will be in session, or how many sessions will be held at this grand council. . . . Judgment will be rendered unto them for this is a gathering of the righteous. . . . It is not to be the judgment of the wicked. . . . This will precede the great day of destruction of the wicked and will be the preparation for the Millennial Reign."[10] How this is to be accomplished, how all these priesthood holders and legal administrators are to be in attendance, has not been revealed, but given what we are able to do even in our own time in terms of satellite communication, it is not impossible to conceive of such a gathering.

Third, the Savior will appear to the Jews on the Mount of Olives. It will be at the time of the battle of Armageddon, a day when his people will find themselves with their backs against the wall. At about this time, the Savior will come to the rescue of his covenant people: "Then shall the Lord go forth, and fight against those nations, as when he fought in the day of battle. And his feet shall stand in that day upon the mount of Olives, which is before Jerusalem on the east, and the mount of Olives shall cleave in the midst thereof toward the east and toward the west, and there shall be a very great valley; and half of the mountain shall remove toward the north, and half of it toward the south" (Zechariah 14:3–4).

Then will come to pass the conversion of a nation in a day, the acceptance by the Jews of their Messiah. "And then shall the Jews look upon me and say: What are these wounds in thine hands and in thy feet? Then shall they know that I am the Lord; for I will say unto them: These wounds are the wounds with which I was wounded in the house of my friends. I am he who was lifted up. I am Jesus that was crucified. I am the Son of God. And then shall they weep

---

10. *Progress of Man*, 481–82; see also Smith, *Way to Perfection*, 288–91; McConkie, *Millennial Messiah*, 582–84; Orson Pratt, in *Journal of Discourses*, 17:185–86.

because of their iniquities; then shall they lament because they persecuted their king" (D&C 45:51–53; see also Zechariah 12:10; 13:6).

THE RETURN OF ENOCH

In a revelation to the Church given in March of 1831, the "God of Enoch" spoke of the ancient Zion as having been "separated from the earth, and . . . received unto myself—a city reserved until a day of righteousness shall come" (D&C 45:11–12). We know from the Prophet Joseph's inspired translation of the Bible that Enoch, the seventh from Adam, was true to his charge and preached the gospel with unusual spiritual power, being the means of preparing a people (over a period of 365 years; D&C 107:49) to become Zion, the City of Holiness, a holy commonwealth in which the people "were of one heart and one mind, and dwelt in righteousness; and there was no poor among them" (Moses 7:18).

Elder Joseph Young, brother of Brigham Young, recalled hearing the Prophet Joseph Smith explain that "the people and the city, and the foundations of the earth on which it stood, had partaken of so much of the immortal elements, bestowed upon them by God through the teachings of Enoch, that it became philosophically impossible for them to remain any longer upon the earth."[11] "And all the days of Zion, in the days of Enoch, were three hundred and sixty-five years. And Enoch and all his people walked with God, and he dwelt in the midst of Zion; and it came to pass that Zion was not, for God received it up into his own bosom; and from thence went forth the saying, Zion is Fled" (Moses 7:68–69).

We learn from the portion of Joseph Smith's translation of the scriptures that we know as the book of Moses that in the last days righteousness would be sent down out of heaven and that truth would be sent forth out of the earth, paving the way for the

---

11. *History of the Organization of the Seventies*, 11.

establishment of a latter-day Zion, a New Jerusalem. The glorious scriptural account then speaks of a grand reunion, a uniting of the peoples who are pure in heart, a true communion of the Saints: "And the Lord said unto Enoch: Then shall thou and all thy city meet them there [in the New Jerusalem on earth], and we will receive them into our bosom, and they shall see us; and we will fall upon their necks, and they shall fall upon our necks, and we will kiss each other; and there shall be mine abode, and it shall be Zion" (Moses 7:63–64). Clearly, Enoch's city will return. Zion from above will join Zion from beneath.

As a part of his inspired translation, the Prophet came to understand something more about the rainbow, the token of the covenant with Enoch (confirmed with Noah; Moses 7:50–51; Genesis 9:11–17) that the earth would never again be destroyed by water. Reflect on the following profound truths spoken by Jehovah to Noah: "The bow shall be in the cloud; and I will look upon it, that I may remember the everlasting covenant, which I made unto thy father Enoch; that, when [in the last days] men shall keep all my commandments, Zion should again come on the earth, the city of Enoch which I have caught up unto myself.

"And this is mine everlasting covenant, that when thy posterity shall embrace the truth, and look upward, then shall Zion [from above, Enoch's Zion] look downward, and all the heavens shall shake with gladness, and the earth shall tremble with joy;

"And the general assembly of the church of the firstborn shall come down out of heaven, and possess the earth, and shall have place until the end come. And this is mine everlasting covenant, which I made with thy father Enoch" (JST, Genesis 9:21–23).

THE CLEANSING OF PLANET EARTH

"The presence of the Lord shall be as the melting fire that burneth, and as the fire which causeth the waters to boil. . . . And so great shall be the glory of his presence that the sun shall hide his face in shame, and the moon shall withhold its light, and the stars shall be hurled from their places" (D&C 133:41–49). It will be a selective burning, for those who are of a celestial or a terrestrial state or order will abide the day; all else will be cleansed from the surface of this planet. Those who lie and cheat and steal, those who revel in immorality and pervert the ways of righteousness, those who mock and point the finger of scorn at the Saints of the Most High—all these will be burned at his coming, will die the death with which we are familiar, and their spirits will take up residence in the spirit world, there to await the last resurrection at the end of a thousand years. The second coming in glory is "the end of the world," meaning the end of the worldly, the destruction of the wicked (Joseph Smith–Matthew 1:4, 31).

Quoting an earlier prophet, Nephi wrote: "The time cometh speedily that Satan shall have no more power over the hearts of the children of men; for the day soon cometh that all the proud and they who do wickedly shall be as stubble; and the day cometh that they must be burned. For the time soon cometh that the fulness of the wrath of God shall be poured out upon all the children of men; for he will not suffer that the wicked shall destroy the righteous. Wherefore, *he will preserve the righteous by his power, even if it so be that the fulness of his wrath must come, and the righteous be preserved, even unto the destruction of their enemies by fire.* Wherefore, the righteous need not fear; for thus saith the prophet, they shall be saved, even if it so be as by fire" (1 Nephi 22:15–17; emphasis added; see also 1 Nephi 22:23; compare Malachi 4:1). Moroni explained that "they that come"—meaning the Lord and his destroying angels— "shall burn them, saith the Lord of Hosts, that it shall leave them neither root nor branch" (Joseph Smith–History 1:37).

The first resurrection will resume. The righteous dead from ages past—those who qualify for the first resurrection, specifically those who died true to the faith since the time the first resurrection was begun in the meridian of time—will come with the Savior when he returns in glory (JST, 1 Thessalonians 4:13–17). Victory over death will have been accomplished. In addition, when the Savior appears he will be clothed in red. Red is symbolic of victory—victory over the devil, death, and hell. It is the symbol of salvation, of being placed beyond the power of all one's enemies.[12] Christ's red apparel will also symbolize both aspects of his ministry to fallen humanity—his mercy and his justice. Because in Gethsemane he trod the wine press alone, "even the wine-press of the fierceness of the wrath of Almighty God" (D&C 76:107; 88:106), he has descended below all things and mercifully taken upon him our stains, our blood, or our sins (2 Nephi 9:44; Jacob 1:19, 2:2; Alma 5:22). In addition, he comes in "dyed garments" as the God of justice, even he who has trampled the wicked beneath his feet (D&C 133:48–51).

Those who are of at least a terrestrial level of righteousness will continue to live as mortals after the Lord returns. The Saints will live to "the age of man"—in the words of Isaiah, the age of one hundred (Isaiah 65:20)—and will then pass through death and be changed instantly from mortality to resurrected immortality (D&C 63:49–51; see also JST, Isaiah 65:20). Speaking of those mortals who remain on earth when the Lord comes in glory, President Joseph Fielding Smith pointed out that "the inhabitants of the earth will have a sort of translation. They will be transferred to a condition of the terrestrial order, and so they will have power over disease and they will have power to live until they get to a certain age and then they will die."[13]

The earth will be transformed from a telestial to a terrestrial glory, to that paradisiacal condition of which the scriptures and the prophets speak, that glorious condition that prevailed in Eden

---

12. *Joseph Smith* [manual], 211–12.
13. *Signs of the Times*, 42.

before the Fall (Articles of Faith 1:10). There will indeed be a new heaven and a new earth (Isaiah 65:17; Revelation 21:1). When "the face of the Lord shall be unveiled," then, in that day, "the saints that are upon the earth, who are alive, shall be quickened and be caught up to meet him" (D&C 88:95–96). Sin and iniquity will be burned away by the brightness of the coming of the King of Zion, and the earth will finally rest (Moses 7:48; compare Romans 8:22). The Savior will be in our midst (3 Nephi 20:22; 21:25). He will reign over Zion and minister among his chosen people in both the Old and the New Jerusalem. He will dwell among his Saints, no doubt teach them in their congregations, and see to it that his doctrine is declared from one end of this earth to the other.

A PARADISIACAL EARTH

Isaiah declared prophetically that in that day "the wolf also shall dwell with the lamb, and the leopard shall lie down with the kid; and the calf and the young lion and the fatling together; and a little child shall lead them. And the cow and the bear shall feed; their young ones shall lie down together: and the lion shall eat straw like the ox. And the sucking child shall play on the hole of the asp, and the weaned child shall put his hand on the cockatrice' den. They shall not hurt nor destroy in all my holy mountain" (Isaiah 11:6–9; compare 65:25). That is, "in that day the enmity of man, and the enmity of beasts, yea, the enmity of all flesh"—an animosity, a natural tension and unrest that came as a result of the Fall—"shall cease from before my face" (D&C 101:26). One can hardly imagine, although it is glorious to try, a life without physical pain or premature death, an existence without the sorrow that accompanies sin and waywardness, without the disappointment associated with dishonesty and greed.

Mortals will inhabit the earth alongside immortals, during the entirety of the thousand years. Persons who abide the day of the

Lord's coming in glory will continue to live on this earth in an Edenic state. They will labor and study and grow and interact and love and socialize as before, but such things will be undertaken in a totally moral environment. "When the Savior shall appear," the Prophet Joseph Smith taught in Ramus, Illinois, "we shall see him as he is. We shall see that he is a man like ourselves. And *that same sociality which exists among us here will exist among us there, only it will be coupled with eternal glory, which glory we do not now enjoy*" (D&C 130:1–2; emphasis added). "And they shall build houses, and inhabit them; and they shall plant vineyards, and eat the fruit of them. They shall not build, and another inhabit; they shall not plant, and another eat" (Isaiah 65:21–22). That is, in the Millennium individuals will enjoy the fruits of their labors. In a world where there is no extortion, no bribery, no organized crime, where there are no unjust laws, no class distinctions according to income or chances for learning, people will no longer be preyed upon by the perverse or the malicious. Our longings for stability, for longevity, and for permanence will largely be satisfied, for the father of lies and those who have spread his influence will have no place on the earth during the thousand years.

A modern apostle, Elder Dallin H. Oaks, taught: "We know that many wonderful and worthy Latter-day Saints currently lack the ideal opportunities and essential requirements for their progress. Singleness, childlessness, death, and divorce frustrate ideals and postpone the fulfillment of promised blessings. In addition, some women who desire to be full-time mothers and homemakers have been literally compelled to enter the full-time work force. But these frustrations are only temporary. The Lord has promised that in the eternities no blessing will be denied His sons and daughters who keep the commandments, are true to their covenants, and desire what is right.

"Many of the most important deprivations of mortality will be set right in the Millennium, which is the time for fulfilling all that is incomplete in the great plan of happiness for all of our Father's worthy children. We know that will be true of temple ordinances. I believe it will also be true of family relationships and experiences."[14]

Our Lord and God will govern his people from two world capitals, "for out of Zion shall go forth the law, and the word of the Lord from Jerusalem" (Isaiah 2:3). "And he shall utter his voice out of Zion"—meaning Independence, Missouri—"and he shall speak from Jerusalem, and his voice shall be heard among all people; and it shall be a voice as the voice of many waters, and as the voice of a great thunder, which shall break down the mountains, and the valleys shall not be found" (D&C 133:21–22). In that day the latter-day David, even Jesus Christ, the true son of David, will unite Ephraim and Judah and preside over all Israel, from one end of the earth to the other. Thus will be fulfilled the divine decree: "Be subject to the powers that be, *until he reigns whose right it is to reign, and subdues all enemies under his feet*" (D&C 58:22; emphasis added).

Those who have accepted the fulness of the gospel in that day will know their God and be constrained to obey his will and keep his commandments. "And they shall teach no more every man his neighbour, and every man his brother, saying, Know the Lord: for *they shall all know me, from the least of them unto the greatest of them,* saith the Lord: for I will forgive their iniquity, and I will remember their sin no more" (Jeremiah 31:34; emphasis added). "How is this to be done?" Joseph Smith asked. "It is to be done by this sealing power, and the other Comforter spoken of"—the Second Comforter, the Lord Jesus himself—"which will be manifest by revelation."[15]

It will be a day when Christ and the resurrected Saints will dwell on earth. Brother William T. McIntire reported hearing the Prophet teach: "That Jesus will be a resident on the earth a thousand [years] with the Saints *is not the case,* but will reign over the

---

14. *With Full Purpose of Heart,* 35.
15. *Words of Joseph Smith,* 4.

Saints and come down and instruct, as he did the five hundred brethren [1 Corinthians 15:6], and those of the first resurrection will also reign with him over the Saints."[16] It will be a time in which all will have grown up in the Lord (Helaman 3:21), will have cultivated the gifts of the Spirit, and will have received a fulness of the Holy Ghost (D&C 109:15). The Holy Spirit will have taught and sanctified them until they are prepared to come into the presence of Christ and even unto the Father.[17] It will be the day of the Second Comforter, the day when the Saints whose eyes are single to the glory of God will see him (D&C 88:67–68).

Though Satan will have been dismissed from the earth by the true King of kings and though he will have been bound by the righteousness of the people, all humankind will have their moral agency. They will exercise the power of choice. For reasons that have not been fully revealed, there will come a time at the end of the thousand years when "men again begin to deny their God" (D&C 29:22), when the devil will be loosed for a "little season" (Revelation 20:7–8; D&C 29:22; 43:31; 88:111). That is, individuals will choose, despite the light and the truth that surround them, to come out in open rebellion against our Father, his Beloved Son, and the great plan of happiness. Satan will again "be loosed, for a little season, that he might gather together his armies" (D&C 88:111; see also 43:31).[18]

---

16. *Joseph Smith* [manual], 258; emphasis added.

17. See *Words of Joseph Smith*, 14–15.

18. President George Q. Cannon taught: "After the thousand years [Satan] will regain some of his present power. It will be as it was among the Nephites. . . . Men will arise who will object to working for the benefit of others; class distinctions will once more make themselves apparent" (*Gospel Truth*, 71). On another occasion President Cannon explained that "when Satan is loosed again for a little while, when the thousand years shall be ended, it will be through mankind departing from the practice of those principles which God has revealed, and this Order of Enoch probably among the rest. He can, in no better way, obtain power over the hearts of the children of men, than by appealing to their cupidity, avarice, and low, selfish desires" (in *Journal of Discourses*, 16:120).

Satan's final conquest over the souls of men at the end of the Millennium will be limited to mortals. Exalted, immortal beings—those who have been changed in the twinkling of an eye, or resurrected personages who minister on earth from time to time—cannot fall, cannot apostatize. Their salvation is secure.[19] The "end of the earth" (D&C 88:101; Joseph Smith–Matthew 1:55) is the final cleansing and celestialization of the planet. Having been baptized by water in the days of Noah and confirmed, or baptized by fire, at the time of the Second Coming, the earth will pass through the equivalent of a death and resurrection. It will become a glorified celestial orb, inasmuch as it will have filled the measure of its creation (D&C 88:25). The earth will then be a fit abode for the true and faithful, "that bodies who are of the celestial kingdom may possess it forever and ever; for, for this intent was it made and created, and for this intent are they sanctified" (D&C 88:20).

CONCLUSION

The Prophet Joseph Smith and his followers rejoiced in the supernal truth that a time was coming when everyone would see eye to eye, when suspicion and persecution would be no more, when "all that was promised the Saints will be given, / And none will molest them from morn until ev'n."[20] In short, they found comfort and peace in the assurance that one day things will change. Goodness and honesty and integrity will be the order of the day; morality and decency will characterize men and women across the globe. Though there were and are many tight places through which the Saints would be required to pass,[21] though trials and difficulties would abound on every side, though disease and death and despair

---

19. See Orson Pratt, in *Journal of Discourses*, 16:322; see also Smith, *Doctrines of Salvation*, 2:56–57.

20. "Now Let Us Rejoice," *Hymns*, no. 3.

21. See Whitney, *Life of Heber C. Kimball*, 449–50.

would be rampant before the Lord's coming, yet one day the King of kings and Lord of lords would take control of things, and a new day would dawn. "For I, the Almighty, have laid my hands upon the nations, to scourge them for their wickedness. And plagues shall go forth, and they shall not be taken from the earth until I have completed my work, which shall be cut short in righteousness— until all shall know me, who remain, even from the least unto the greatest, and shall be filled with the knowledge of the Lord, and shall see eye to eye" (D&C 84:96–98). The principal message of the book of Revelation is a message to us, just as it was to the seven churches of Asia: Hold on! Be steadfast and immovable. Endure faithful to the end. The time of deliverance will come.

Nauvoo, April 1844. Dissidents reacted adversely to the Prophet's growing political power and influence in Nauvoo, the teaching of salvation for the dead through temple ordinances, and the practice of plural marriage among some of the leading elders. Perhaps just as troublesome to this element of the community were teachings about the nature of God and the ultimate glorification of man. These ideas were communicated by Joseph principally in a memorial service held on 7 April 1844 for a member of the Latter-day Saint community who had died in an accident, a man named King Follett. The sermon, given in what was known as the East Grove, was delivered to several thousand people.

Hundreds of hours of interfaith involvement have been not only intellectually challenging and spiritually rewarding to me but also incredibly revealing. By that I mean, interacting with individuals of other faiths has taught me a great deal about how we as Latter-day Saints are perceived by them—what they think we think, what they think we believe and practice, who they think we are. Having stood before what must be by now thousands of persons of various faith traditions and seeking to respond to their questions has crystalized for me which elements of the Latter-day Saint faith are most attractive, most compelling and persuasive, and of course which ones are most troublesome and problematic. Matters that have come up regularly would certainly include our belief in extrabiblical scripture, why we build temples, why Latter-day Saint women are not ordained to the priesthood, the Church's moral standards, unusual statements or teachings from early Church leaders, plural marriage, and why men of African descent were not able to hold the priesthood until 1978.

Now, though I cannot speak for others who have been in similar situations—and acknowledging that their experiences may have been different from my own—perhaps the one question that has been raised most often, most consistently, and in some cases with curiosity bordering on suspicion, is some variation of the following: "Is it true that you people believe that you will one day become God?" Others may phrase it this way: "Do you really believe that you will create and govern your own worlds?" And behind those questions is occasionally an unspoken but apparent air of "What audacity!" Once again, we reiterate that this doctrine was restored in gradual, incremental pieces, one piece of the puzzle after another, precept upon precept.

TRUTH UPON TRUTH

Let us remember that Latter-day Saints read and study the same Bible as our friends of other Christian faiths. All humankind, like Christ, are made in the image and likeness of God (Genesis 1:27; Moses 2:27), and so Latter-day Saints feel it is neither audacity nor heresy for the children of God to aspire to be like God. Consider the implications of the following scriptural passages:

"Be ye therefore perfect, even as your Father which is in heaven is perfect" (Matthew 5:48).

"For as many as are led by the Spirit of God, they are the [children] of God. For ye have not received the spirit of bondage again to fear; but ye have received the Spirit of adoption, whereby we cry, Abba, Father. The Spirit itself beareth witness with our spirit, that we are the children of God: and *if children, then heirs: heirs of God, and joint-heirs with Christ*; if so be that we suffer with him, that we may be also glorified together" (Romans 8:14–17; emphasis added).

"Where the Spirit of the Lord is, there is liberty. But we all, with open face beholding as in a glass [mirror] the glory of the Lord, are changed into the same image [of Christ] from glory to glory, even as by the Spirit of the Lord" (2 Corinthians 3:17–18).

"Grace and peace be multiplied unto you through the knowledge of God, and of Jesus our Lord. According as his divine power hath given unto us all things that pertain unto life and godliness, through the knowledge of him that hath called us to glory and virtue: whereby are given unto us exceeding great and precious promises: that by these *ye might be partakers of the divine nature,* having escaped the corruption that is in the world through lust" (2 Peter 1:2–4; emphasis added).

"Behold, what manner of love the Father hath bestowed upon us, that we should be called the [children] of God: therefore the world knoweth us not, because it knew him not. Beloved, now are we the [children] of God, and it doth not yet appear what we shall be: but we know that, *when he shall appear, we shall be like him;* for we shall see him as he is" (1 John 3:1–2; emphasis added).

One simply need ask, What do these biblical passages mean? Is it even conceivable that frail and weak mortals could ever hope to become perfect as God the Father is perfect? If not, why would his Beloved Son call and challenge the children of God to become such? Further, is it reasonable that followers of the Christ who live in a world of sin could somehow become a joint heir, a co-inheritor, with Christ to all the Father has? What do we make of Peter's fascinatingly cryptic remark that through the gospel of Jesus Christ mortals might become partakers of the divine nature? Can mortals become divine? And finally, should Christian disciples take seriously John's proposition that when the Savior does appear in glory, those who see him as he is will be like him?

It appears that the first revelation of the doctrine of deification to the restored Church came in the vision of the glories on 16 February 1832 at Father John Johnson's home in Hiram, Ohio. Those who attain unto the highest heaven are described as people who "overcome by faith, and are sealed by the Holy Spirit of promise, which the Father sheds forth upon all those who are just and true. They are they who are the church of the Firstborn. They are they into whose hands the Father has given all things—they are they who are priests and kings, who have received of his fulness, and of his glory; . . . wherefore, as it is written [Psalm 82:6; John 10:34], *they are gods, even the sons* [and daughters] *of God*" (D&C 76:53–58; emphasis added).

I say cautiously that the vision *appears* to be the first revelation of this doctrine because, as we discussed in Chapter 17, we know that many parts of the revelation on eternal marriage, recorded in Doctrine and Covenants 132, were made known to the Prophet during his inspired translation of the Bible as early as 1831. In that revelation we are told that those whose marriages and lives are sealed by the Holy Spirit of Promise, who receive the two major blessings of eternal life—the fulness of the Father and the eternal continuation of the family, eternal lives (D&C 132:19, 24)—are "*gods, because they have no end; therefore shall they be from everlasting to everlasting, because they continue; then shall they be above all, because all things are subject unto them. Then shall they be gods, because they have all power, and the angels are subject unto them*" (D&C 132:20; emphasis added).

In September of 1832, in the midst of the Lord's explanation of the terms and conditions of the oath and covenant of the Melchizedek Priesthood, the Lord said: "For he that receiveth my servants receiveth me; and he that receiveth me receiveth my Father; and he that receiveth my Father receiveth my Father's kingdom; therefore *all that my Father hath shall be given unto him*" (D&C 84:36–38; emphasis added). Three months later, as a part of the marvelous revelation we call the Olive Leaf, the Prophet was told: "And again, another angel shall sound his trump, . . . saying: It is finished; it is finished! The Lamb of God hath overcome and trodden the wine-press alone, even the wine-press of fierceness of the wrath of Almighty God." Now note this language: "And then shall the angels be crowned with the glory of his might, and *the saints shall be filled with his glory, and receive their inheritance and be made equal with him*" (D&C 88:106–107; emphasis added).

As we saw earlier, the Lectures on Faith were delivered in the winter of 1834–35 in Kirtland, Ohio. Lecture Five is not only a deep and profoundly significant discussion of the Godhead but also specifically refers to men and women becoming like God through being graced and endowed with the power and might and glory and mind of Deity. We are instructed in it that "all those who keep [God's] commandments shall grow up from grace to grace, and become heirs of the heavenly kingdom, and joint heirs with Jesus Christ; possessing the same mind, being transformed into the same image or likeness, even the express image of him who fills all in all; being filled with the fullness of his glory, and become one in him, even as the Father, Son and Holy Spirit are one." The Saints therefore "have a sure foundation laid for the exercise of faith unto life and salvation, through the atonement and mediation of Jesus Christ." This comes as we partake "of the fullness of the Father and the Son through the Spirit. As the Son partakes of the fullness of the Father through the Spirit, so *the saints are, by the same Spirit, to be partakers of the same fullness, to enjoy the same glory;* for as the Father and the Son are one, so, in like manner, the saints are to be one in them. Through the love of the Father, the mediation of Jesus

Christ, and the gift of the Holy Spirit, they are to be heirs of God, and joint heirs with Jesus Christ."[1]

In speaking of an experience her brother Lorenzo had before his baptism into the restored Church in June 1836, Eliza R. Snow wrote: "Being present at a 'Blessing meeting,' in the [Kirtland] Temple, previous to his baptism into the Church; after listening to several patriarchal blessings pronounced upon the heads of different individuals with whose history he was acquainted, and of whom he knew the Patriarch was entirely ignorant; he was struck with astonishment to hear the peculiarities of those persons positively and plainly referred to in their blessings. And, as he afterwards expressed, he was convinced that an influence, superior to human prescience, dictated the words of the one who officiated." On that occasion Lorenzo became acquainted with the Patriarch, Joseph Smith Sr., and Father Smith said to Lorenzo "that he would soon be convinced of the truth of the latter-day work, and be baptized; and he said: 'You will become as great as you can possibly wish— even as great as God, and you cannot wish to be greater.'"[2] In the spring of 1840, just before leaving on a mission to England, Lorenzo found himself in a doctrinal conversation with Henry G. Sherwood. Brother Sherwood was attempting to explain the Savior's parable of the laborers in the vineyard (Matthew 20:1–16). "While attentively listening to his explanation," Lorenzo stated, "the Spirit of the Lord rested mightily upon me—the eyes of my understanding were opened, and I saw as clear as the sun at noonday, with wonder and astonishment, the pathway of God and man. I formed the following couplet which expresses the revelation, as it was shown me . . . :

> *As man now is, God once was:*
> *As God now is, man may be.*

---

1. *Lectures on Faith*, 60–61; emphasis added.
2. *Biography and Family Record of Lorenzo Snow*, 9–10.

Lorenzo Snow "felt this to be a sacred communication, which I related to no one except my sister Eliza, until I reached England, when in a confidential private conversation with President Brigham Young, in Manchester, I related to him this extraordinary manifestation."[3] In later reflecting on this profound doctrine, Lorenzo confessed: "I did not know that I had come into possession of knowledge that I had no business with; but I knew it was true. Nothing of this kind had ever reached my ears before." Then, in referring to a private meeting of Church leaders some time later, he said: "It was preached a few years after that; at least, *the Prophet Joseph taught this idea to the Twelve Apostles.*"[4]

And of course it was in the King Follett Sermon that Joseph the Seer discussed the matter in a public setting.

THE KING FOLLETT DISCOURSE

On 7 April 1844, less than three months before his martyrdom, the Prophet Joseph Smith delivered a funeral address for King Follett, a Nauvoo resident and member of the Church who had died in an accident while digging a well. The memorial service for Brother Follett was held in conjunction with the general conference of the Church and was attended by thousands of the Latter-day Saints. The Prophet's sermon addressed the following doctrines:

- God, an exalted man, once lived on an earth, just as we do now.
- It is possible for every person to become, through the transforming powers of the Almighty extended to us, like our Heavenly Father.
- To create is not to make out of nothing but rather to organize or form from preexisting materials.

---

3. *Biography and Family Record of Lorenzo Snow*, 46–47; see also *Teachings of Lorenzo Snow*, 1.

4. *Teachings of Lorenzo Snow*, 2; emphasis added.

- In the premortal existence our Heavenly Father, the Head of the gods, called a council of the gods to contemplate and prepare for the creation of the earth.
- The mind of man is co-eternal with God. God is a self-existent being, and so is the eternal, uncreated part of man.
- The greatest responsibility God has placed upon us is to seek after our dead.
- The unpardonable sin is a grievous offense that will not be forgiven in this world or the next.
- Little children who die before the age of accountability are saved in the highest heaven. Worthy parents who lose little children will have the privilege of raising their little ones to maturity.

The King Follett Sermon is, without doubt, a most memorable, certainly a most distinctive, address delivered by Joseph Smith. For the Latter-day Saints, this sermon suggests a relationship with Deity that expands our minds and broadens our perspectives on life here and hereafter. For those of other faiths, particularly traditional Christians, the discourse tends to elicit strong reactions: a theological antagonism, a cry of heresy. In this discourse, the Prophet Joseph dismissed as unsuitable and unacceptable the unknowable, unreachable, and unattainable god of Plato. This sermon introduces us to a God who is, as the revelations affirm, "infinite and eternal, from everlasting to everlasting the same unchangeable God" who sits "enthroned, with glory, honor, power, majesty, might, dominion, truth, justice, judgment, mercy, and an infinity of fulness, from everlasting to everlasting" (D&C 20:17; 109:77). This glorious Being also delights to honor his children, is unselfish with his glory and power, and desires for his children, the whole human family, to become as he is.

This sermon is not a part of the canon of scripture, not found within the standard works, and so it does not carry the same weight in determining and explicating doctrine as do the teachings in the Bible, Book of Mormon, Doctrine and Covenants, and Pearl of Great Price. Also, because Joseph Smith died a short time after this discourse was delivered, we do not have his supplementary prophetic insights into some of the more difficult doctrinal matters. For example, we have no problem as a people accepting the truth that God was once a man; indeed, we believe him to be a man now. We do not, however, have doctrinal details about God's mortal life beyond what the Prophet taught. In addition, it remains for Joseph's apostolic and prophetic successors to expound upon how our Father in heaven can be a man who became exalted (which we accept) and eternally God (which we also accept). Nonetheless, we do not know specifically what it means to become as God beyond gaining exaltation and eternal life, which entails receiving a fulness of the glory and power of the Father, as well as enjoying the continuation of the family unit in eternity (D&C 132:19–20).

Because many of those who were in attendance reported listening to a message that may have taken as long as two hours to deliver (and which takes thirty to forty-five minutes to read) and because there has been no official proclamation or declaration to expand upon, clarify, or even refine the teachings of the sermon by those holding the keys of priesthood authority, we read it as a very significant historical address, one that in many ways illustrates the spiritual and intellectual heights to which the Saints in Nauvoo, the City of Joseph, aspired. We read it today as a people who are unafraid of engaging serious theological matters, at times daring to think above and beyond where cautious creedal Christians dare not go. And we read it as believers of "all that God has revealed, all that He does now reveal, and we believe that He will yet reveal many great and important things pertaining to the Kingdom of God" (Articles of Faith 1:9).

We begin our discussion here with the Prophet's profound

insight into both God and man: "If men do not comprehend the character of God, they do not comprehend themselves."[5] Joseph sought to raze the colossal Christian belief that had been in place for centuries upon centuries—that God is wholly other, that he is of a different species than man, that God is Creator and we are creatures. Joseph boldly and unhesitatingly proposed that if a man or woman sincerely desires to understand the nature of humanity, he or she must delve into holy scripture, must search the prophetic word, to uncover exactly what Deity is like. If you know what the One who has arrived is like, you can begin to understand more clearly what the one who is in process can eventually become. Latter-day Saint philosopher Truman Madsen put it beautifully: "One begins mortality with the veil drawn, but slowly he is moved to penetrate the veil within himself. He is, in time, led to seek the 'holy of holies' within the temple of his own being."[6]

GOD WAS ONCE A MAN

Joseph the Seer asked, "What sort of being was God in the beginning?" The starkness of his reply has delighted his followers while at the same time scandalizing his critics: "God himself was once as we are now, and is an exalted man, and sits enthroned in yonder heavens! That is the great secret. If the veil were rent today, and the great God who holds this world in its orbit, and who upholds all worlds and all things by his power, was to make himself visible—I say, if you were to see him today, you would see him like a man in form—like yourselves in the person, image, and very form as a man; for Adam was created in the very fashion, image, and likeness of God, and received instruction from, and walked, talked and conversed with him, as one man talks and communes with another." He added, "It is the first principle of the Gospel to know

5. *Joseph Smith* [manual], 40.
6. *Eternal Man*, 20.

for a certainty the Character of God, and to know that we may converse with him as one man converses with another, and that he was once a man like us; yea, that God himself, the Father of us all, dwelt on an earth, the same as Jesus Christ himself did."[7]

This doctrine is stunning, to be sure. But is it irreverent or blasphemous, as so many contend? I think not. What is the Prophet saying, and what is he not saying? First, God is more than a word, an essence, a force, a law, more than the great first cause; he has form, shape, an image, a likeness. He is a he; he has gender. This is not so strange, for the Prophet made clear in 1843 that "the Father has a body of flesh and bones as tangible as man's" (D&C 130:22). Again, that he was "once a man" is not so surprising, given that Latter-day Saints believe *he is still a man,* an exalted human being, to be sure, a glorified Man of Holiness (Moses 6:57). He has form and shape, human form and shape. This is what Latter-day Saints mean when they say that God and man are of the same species.

The concept that God has a physical body (D&C 130:22) is inextricably tied to such doctrines as the immortality of the soul, the incarnation of Christ, the literal resurrection, eternal marriage, and the continuation of the family unit into eternity. In his corporeal or physical nature, God can be in only one place at a time. His divine nature is such, however, that his glory, his power, and his influence, meaning his Holy Spirit, fills the immensity of space and is the means by which he is omnipresent and through which law and light and life are extended to us (D&C 88:6–13). The Father's physical body does not limit his capacity or detract one whit from his infinite holiness, any more than Christ's resurrected body did so (Luke 24:36–39; John 20–21). The risen Lord said of himself: "All power is given unto me in heaven and in earth" (Matthew 28:18). That does not sound at all as if Jesus was in some way limited by his

---

7. *Joseph Smith* [manual], 40.

physicality. "In Joseph's view," historian Richard Bushman pointed out, "making God corporeal did not reduce Him: Joseph had little sense of the flesh being base. In contrast to conventional theologies, Joseph saw embodiment as a glorious aspect of human existence."[8] Interestingly enough, research by Professor David Paulsen of the Brigham Young University Philosophy Department indicated that the idea of God's corporeality was taught in the early Christian church into the fourth and fifth centuries, before being lost to the knowledge of the people.[9]

Scholars of other faiths have commented on the possibility of God's corporeality. For example, James L. Kugel, professor emeritus of Hebrew literature at Harvard University, wrote that some scholars' "most basic assumptions about God," including the idea "that he has no body but exists everywhere simultaneously," are not "articulated in the most ancient parts of the Bible. . . . We like to think that what our religions say nowadays about God is what people have always believed." Further, "biblical narratives did not like to speak of God actually appearing to human beings directly and conversing with them face-to-face. The reason was not that God in those days was thought to be invisible, and certainly not that He was (as later philosophers and theologians were to claim) altogether spiritual and therefore had no body to be seen. Rather, God in the Bible is not usually seen by human beings for an entirely different reason; especially in the earliest parts: catching sight of Him was believed to be extremely dangerous." Kugel observed that "the same God who buttonholes the patriarchs and speaks to Moses face-to-face is perceived in later times as a huge, cosmic deity—not necessarily invisible or lacking a body, but so huge as to surpass our own capacities of apprehension, almost our imagination." In time

---

8. *Rough Stone Rolling*, 420.
9. "Early Christian Belief in a Corporeal Deity," 105–16; "Doctrine of Divine Embodiment," 7–94.

the God who spoke to Moses directly "became an embarrassment to later theologians. It is, they said, really the great, universal God" who is "omniscient and omnipresent and utterly unphysical." Kugel asked, "Indeed, does not the eventual emergence of Christianity— in particular Nicene Christianity, with its doctrine of the Trinity— likewise represent in its own way an attempt to fill the gap left by the God of Old?"[10]

The late Christian theologian Clark Pinnock wrote that if we "are to take biblical metaphors seriously, is God in some way embodied? . . . *I do not believe that the idea is as foreign to the Bible's view of God as we have assumed. In tradition, God is thought to function primarily as a disembodied spirit but this is scarcely a biblical idea.* . . . [I]n the theophanies of the Old Testament God encounters humans in the form of a man. . . . Add to that the fact that God took on a body in the incarnation and Christ has taken that body with Him into glory. It seems to me that the Bible does not think of God as formless."[11]

What do we know of a time before God was God? What do we know of the time when he dwelt on an earth? Nothing. We really do not know more than what was stated by Joseph Smith. Insights concerning God's life before Godhood are not found in our canon of scripture (Bible, Book of Mormon, Doctrine and Covenants, and Pearl of Great Price), in official doctrinal declarations or proclamations, in current handbooks or curricular materials, nor are doctrinal expositions on the subject delivered in general conference today. In speaking of this sensitive matter in an interview, President Gordon B. Hinckley stated: "I haven't heard it discussed for a long time in public discourse. I don't know all the circumstances under

---

10. *The God of Old*, xi–xii, 5–6, 61, 195; see also 81, 104–6, 134–35.
11. *Most Moved Mover*, 33–34; emphasis added. See also a fascinating book by Webb, *Jesus Christ, Eternal God*, particularly chapter 9, which deals with the teachings of the Latter-day Saints.

which the statement was made. I understand the philosophical background behind it, but I don't know a lot about it, and I don't think others know a lot about it."[12] It is important to point out that President Hinckley was *not* denying that the Latter-day Saints believe in theosis, or deification, as some of our critics have suggested; rather, President Hinckley was stating that we know little or nothing regarding Joseph Smith's statement that God once dwelt on an earth. We will see later how President Hinckley himself affirmed the doctrine of deification in a general conference of the Church.

MORTALS MAY BECOME AS GOD

Joseph went on to say, "Here, then, is eternal life—to know the only wise and true God; and you have got to learn how to be Gods yourselves, and to be kings and priests to God, the same as all Gods have done before you, namely, by going from one small degree to another, and from a small capacity to a great one; from grace to grace, from exaltation to exaltation, until you attain to the resurrection of the dead, and are able to dwell in everlasting burnings, and to sit in glory, as do those who sit enthroned in everlasting power."[13]

Note it carefully: to be like God is to receive a fulness of the priesthood, to be a king and a queen, a priest and a priestess, to have received the ordinances of the house of the Lord and to have kept the covenants associated therewith. As we saw in the vision of the glories, it is to have become, in the fullest sense—through the sanctifying power of the atonement of Jesus Christ—a son or daughter of God (D&C 76:56–58).

Our God is not possessive, not one who hoards his power, glory, and gifts. God has *the power and the desire* to extend his grace, including the gifts, fruit, and blessings of the Spirit, to his children, and he does not hesitate to do so. The scriptures do not speak of

---

12. In Ostling and Ostling, *Mormon America*, 296.
13. *Joseph Smith* [manual], 221.

396 PRECEPT UPON PRECEPT

a barrier beyond which individuals may not progress spiritually. Followers of Christ are not told by the writers and speakers in either ancient or modern scripture that they can progress and grow and mature and develop "thus far and no more." Eternal Life, exaltation, salvation—all are equivalent terms. In the words of Elder Bruce R. McConkie, "to be saved, to gain exaltation, to inherit eternal life, all mean to be one with God, to live as he lives, to think as he thinks, to act as he acts, to possess the same glory."[14] To gain eternal life or exaltation is to gain godhood.

Elder Jeffrey R. Holland explained that "Jesus did not come to improve God's view of man nearly so much as He came to improve man's view of God and to plead with them to love their Heavenly Father as He has always and will always love them."[15] Similarly, one of Joseph Smith's most significant efforts was to make the Father of the universe more accessible to his family members within that universe, to retrieve the unreachable, unknowable, timeless, and impassible Deity that had been pushed to the grand beyond by traditional Christians. As my friend Richard Mouw of Fuller Theological Seminary observed, "While Joseph [Smith] and Mary Baker Eddy espoused very different—indeed opposing—metaphysical systems, with Joseph arguing for a thorough-going physicalism and the founder of Christian Science insisting on a thorough-going mentalism—they each were motivated by a desire to reduce the distance between God and human beings. . . .

"These two reduce-the-distance theologies emerged in an environment shaped significantly by the high Calvinism of New England Puritanism. I think it can be plausibly—and rightly, from an orthodox Christian perspective—argued that New England theology, which stressed the legitimate *metaphysical* distance between God and his human creatures, nonetheless at the same time fostered

14. *Promised Messiah*, 129–30.
15. "The Grandeur of God," *Ensign*, Nov. 2003, 72.

an unhealthy *spiritual* distance between the Calvinist deity and his human subjects."[16]

More than once I have heard the Latter-day Saint view of Deity described as a belief in a "finite God." I suppose because of the statement by Joseph Smith that God was once a man, people jump to the conclusion that the God in whom Latter-day Saints put their complete trust is not the same Being Christians know as the God of the omnis. I am one, however, who is very uncomfortable with stating that we believe in a finite God; all of scripture states otherwise. From the Doctrine and Covenants, for example, we learn that Latter-day Saints worship "a God in heaven, who is infinite and eternal, from everlasting to everlasting, the same unchangeable God, the framer of heaven and earth, and all things which are in them" (D&C 20:17). Our Father in heaven is indeed omnipotent, omniscient, and, by the power of His Holy Spirit, omnipresent. He is a gloried, exalted, resurrected being, "the only supreme governor and independent being in whom all fullness and perfection dwell; . . . in Him every good gift and every good principle dwell; He is the Father of lights; in Him the principle of faith dwells independently, and He is the object in whom the faith of all other rational and accountable beings center for life and salvation."[17] The Almighty sits "enthroned, with glory, honor, power, majesty, might, dominion, truth, justice, judgment, mercy, and an infinity of fulness" (D&C 109:77). He is not a student, an apprentice, or a novice. In short, our God is God.

Further, while Latter-day Saints certainly accept the teachings of Joseph Smith regarding man becoming like God, we do not fully comprehend all that is entailed by such a bold declaration. Church leaders have spoken very little concerning what qualities

16. "Possibility of Joseph Smith," in Neilson and Givens, *Joseph Smith,* 195; emphasis in original.
17. *Lectures on Faith,* 10.

or attributes of Deity can or may be conveyed to and acquired by glorified human beings and which reside and rest solely and forever with Almighty God. What we do know is that through the atonement of Jesus Christ and the sanctifying power of the Spirit, we may develop and mature in Christlike attributes, the divine nature—that is, become more like our Savior Jesus Christ—until we are prepared and comfortable to dwell in the presence of God and Christ, together with our families, forever. That is eternal life or godhood.[18]

Although we believe that becoming like God is entailed in eternal life (D&C 132:19–20), we do not believe we will ever, worlds without end, unseat or oust God the Eternal Father or his Only Begotten Son, Jesus Christ; those holy Beings are and forever will be the Gods we worship. I am unaware of any authoritative statement in Latter-day Saint literature that suggests that we will ever worship any being other than the ones in the Godhead. In describing those who are glorified and attain eternal life, Elder Parley P. Pratt stated: "The difference between Jesus Christ and another immortal and celestial man is this—the man is subordinate to Jesus Christ, does nothing in and of himself, but does all things in the name of Christ, and by his authority, being of the same mind, and ascribing all the glory to him and his Father."[19] We believe in "one God" in the sense that we love and serve one Godhead, one divine Presidency, each of whom possesses all of the attributes of Godhood in perfection (Alma 11:44; D&C 20:28). While we do not believe that God and man are of a different species, we readily acknowledge that the chasm between a fallen, mortal being and an immortal, resurrected, and glorified Being is immense (D&C 20:17; 109:77).

18. For an official statement from The Church of Jesus Christ of Latter-day Saints on theosis or deification, see lds.org/topics, "Becoming Like God."
19. *Key to the Science of Theology*, 21–22.

Many critics of Mormonism have been eager to question the couplet of Lorenzo Snow, the fifth President of the Church:

> As man is, God once was.
> As God is, man may become.[20]

Truman Madsen asked me once, "What if this couplet were stated differently?" He then suggested an alternate rendering:

> As man is, Christ once was.
> As Christ is, man may become.

President Snow explained on one occasion that "as man now is, God once was—even the Babe of Bethlehem, advancing to childhood—thence to boyhood, manhood, then to the Godhead. This, then, is the 'mark of the prize of man's high calling in Christ Jesus.'"[21] For all intents and purposes, we become as God is by striving to become as Jesus Christ is, by seeking to emulate the sinless Son of God; indeed, the great quest for all humankind is "the imitation of Christ." Beloved Christian churchman and writer John Stott explained: "I want to share with you where my mind has come to rest as I approach the end of my pilgrimage on earth and it is— *God wants his people to become like Christ.* Christlikeness is the will of God for the people of God. . . . In other words, if we claim to be a Christian . . . God's way to make us like Christ is to fill us with his Spirit."[22]

The other point to be made is that we are certainly not the only professing Christian group that holds to this tenet: Eastern Orthodox churches, with numbers of adherents exceeding 300 million, have done so for centuries. Jordan Vajda, formerly a Roman

---

20. *Teachings of Lorenzo Snow,* 1; see also Snow, *Biography and Family Record of Lorenzo Snow,* 46–47.

21. *Teachings of Lorenzo Snow,* 5.

22. "The Model"; emphasis added.

Catholic, noted that "what was meant to be a term of ridicule has turned out to be a term of approbation, for the witness of the Greek Fathers of the Church . . . is that they also believed salvation meant 'becoming a god.' It seems that if one's soteriology [study of salvation] cannot accommodate a doctrine of human divinization, then it has at least implicitly, if not explicitly, rejected the heritage of the early Christian church and departed from the faith of first-millennium Christianity. However, if that is the case, those who would espouse such a soteriology also believe, in fact, that Christianity, from about the second century on, has apostatized and 'gotten it wrong' on this core issue of human salvation."[23]

Ex Nihilo Creation

Christian theologian Emil Brunner spoke of the divide between God and man: "There is no greater sense of distance than that which lies in the words Creator-Creation. Now this is the first and fundamental thing which can be said about man: He is a creature, and as such he is separated by an abyss from the Divine manner of being. The greatest dissimilarity between two things which we can express at all—more dissimilar than light and darkness, death and life, good and evil—is that between the Creator and that which is created."[24]

It is only natural for those who believe that God and humanity are basically of a different race and that God is a totally unattached and uncreated being to also believe that there was a time when only God existed and thus that the Creation had to be *ex nihilo,* out of nothing. For there to be anything in the universe to which God would turn or upon which he would rely in constructing the worlds, for example, is to suggest the unthinkable—that element is as eternal as he is, which notion theologians could never even

---

23. "Partakers of the Divine Nature," 56–57.
24. *Man in Revolt,* 90, in Norman, "Ex Nihilo," 294.

entertain. The Prophet Joseph Smith responded to such ideas by suggesting that the Hebrew word translated as "create" really means to organize, implying that Deity drew upon already existing matter. He taught: "Learned doctors tell us God created the heavens and earth out of nothing. They account it blasphemy to contradict the idea. They will call you a fool. You ask them why and they say: Doesn't the Bible say that [God] created the world, and they infer that it must be out of nothing. The word create . . . means to organize, the same as a man would use [previously existing materials] to build a ship. Hence we infer that God had materials to organize from—chaos, chaotic matter; element had an existence from the time he had. The pure principles of element are principles which can never be destroyed; they may be organized and re-organized, but not destroyed."[25]

CHILDREN IN THE RESURRECTION

In speaking of the status of children in the resurrection, the Prophet said, "A question may be asked—'Will mothers have their children in eternity?' Yes! Yes! Mothers, you shall have your children; for they shall have eternal life, for their debt is paid. Children . . . must rise just as they died; we can there hail our lovely infants with the same glory—the same loveliness in the celestial glory."[26] According to Mary Isabella Horne, Joseph "told us that we should receive those children in the morning of the resurrection just as we laid them down, in purity and innocence, and we should nourish and care for them as their mothers. He said that children would be raised in the resurrection just as they were laid down, and that they would [eventually] obtain all the intelligence necessary to occupy thrones, principalities and powers."[27]

---

25. *Words of Joseph Smith,* 359.
26. *Joseph Smith* [manual], 177.
27. *Joseph Smith* [manual], 178.

Some confusion arose over the years after the Prophet's death concerning his teachings on the status of children in the resurrection. Some erroneously claimed that the Prophet taught that children would be resurrected as children and *never grow,* but would remain in that state through all eternity. President Joseph F. Smith collected testimonies and affidavits from persons who themselves had heard the King Follett Sermon, and it was his powerful witness that Joseph Smith Jr. had taught the truth but had been misunderstood by some. President Smith said in 1895 at the funeral of Daniel W. Grant, son of Heber J. Grant:

"Such children are in the bosom of the Father. They will inherit their glory and their exaltation, and they will not be deprived of the blessings that belong to them; . . .

"Joseph Smith, the Prophet . . . declared that the mother who laid down her little child . . . would after the resurrection, have all the joy, satisfaction and pleasure, and even more than it would have been possible to have had in mortality, in seeing her child grow to the full measure of the stature of its spirit. . . . [T]he body will develop, either in time or in eternity, to the full stature of the spirit, and when the mother is deprived of the pleasure and joy of rearing her babe to manhood or womanhood in this life, through the hand of death, that privilege will be renewed to her hereafter, and she will enjoy it to a fuller fruition than it would be possible for her to do here. When she does it there, it will be with certain knowledge that the results will be without failure; whereas here, the results are unknown until after we have passed the test."[28]

In the beautifully hopeful words of Brother Joseph, "All your losses will be made up to you in the resurrection, provided you continue faithful. By the vision of the Almighty I have seen it."[29]

---

28. *Gospel Doctrine,* 452–54; see also Smith, "Status of Children in the Resurrection," in Clark, *Messages of the First Presidency,* 5:91–98.
29. *Joseph Smith* [manual], 51.

CONCLUSION

On the one hand, we worship a divine Being with whom we can identify, a Being whose infinity does not preclude either his immediacy or his intimacy. "In the day that God created man," the Prophet's inspired translation of Genesis attests, "in the likeness of God made he him; in the image of his own body, male and female, created he them" (Moses 6:8–9). We believe that God is not simply a spirit influence, a force in the universe, or the Prime Mover. When we pray, "Our Father which art in heaven" (Matthew 6:9), we mean what we say. We believe God is comprehendible, knowable, approachable, and, like his Beloved Son, touched with the feeling of our infirmities (Hebrews 4:15).

On the other hand, our God is God. There is no truth he does not know and no power he does not possess. Scriptural passages that speak of him being the same yesterday, today, and forever clearly refer to his divine attributes—his love, justice, constancy, and willingness to bless his children. God is our Heavenly Father, the Father of our spirits (Numbers 16:22; 27:16; Hebrews 12:9). He is a glorified, exalted man. God is in every way a divine Being. He possesses in perfection every godly attribute. He is omnipotent, omniscient, and, by the power of his Holy Spirit, omnipresent. These things we have come to know principally through the revelations and translations that came through Joseph Smith, as well as the poignant and inspiring sermons he delivered.

And we also know something infinitely sublime about our destiny. Elder Hyrum Mack Smith, son of Joseph F. Smith and also a member of the Quorum of the Twelve Apostles, along with an associate, Janne M. Sjodahl, offered the following commentary on Doctrine and Covenants 132:20, "Then shall they be gods": "What a wonderful revelation this is when compared with the narrow ideas held in the world! Children of kings are princes and princesses, associating on terms of equality with their royal parents, and having a good chance of becoming kings and queens themselves. But when we say that the privilege of God's children is to associate with Him in the eternal mansions, and that they may become gods, then the world does not understand us, and many deem us guilty of blasphemy. *They seem to think that they honor God by supposing that His children are infinitely inferior to Him. What kind of father is He, then, that He should feel it an honor to be the progenitor of an inferior offspring?* Is there a king on earth that would feel honored by having degenerates and beggars for children? Do not fathers and mothers rejoice in the progress of their children? Is it not their ambition to educate and train their loved ones, until these shall reach the highest possible degree of intelligence and efficiency? Surely, we can do no greater honor to God, our Father, than to admit the divine possibilities which He has planted in His offspring, and which will be developed under His tuition in this life and hereafter, until His children are perfect as He is perfect."[30]

"The whole design of the gospel," President Gordon B. Hinckley declared, "is to lead us onward and upward to greater achievement, even, eventually, to godhood. This great possibility was enunciated by the Prophet Joseph Smith in the King Follett sermon and emphasized by President Lorenzo Snow. . . . Our enemies have criticized us for believing in this. Our reply is that this lofty concept in no way diminishes God the Eternal Father. He is the Almighty. He is the Creator and Governor of the universe. He is the greatest of all and will always be so. But just as any earthly father wishes for his sons and daughters every success in life, so I believe our Father in Heaven wishes for his children that they might approach him in stature and stand beside him resplendent in godly strength and wisdom."[31]

Through Joseph Smith has come the knowledge concerning God and man that had been lost for centuries, precious knowledge that helps to unveil the otherwise mysterious Being we worship,

---

30. *Doctrine and Covenants Commentary,* 826–27; emphasis added.
31. "Don't Drop the Ball," *Ensign,* Nov. 1994, 48.

sublime knowledge that lifts the human soul from existential despair to a quiet confidence that accompanies the correct knowledge of what and who human beings really are. My late friend and colleague Rodney Turner wrote some years ago: "To know what God is, is to know what man is—and what he may become. The loss of this knowledge goes far to explain the present plight of humanity. *Man, like water, cannot rise higher than his beginnings.* If an ever-increasing number of men and women are choosing to wallow in the mire of carnality, we must not forget that they are taught that the human race was spawned in mire. *We have little desire to reach for the stars if we do not believe that we came from the stars.* That we did is the message of the Restored Gospel. This is why The Church of Jesus Christ of Latter-day Saints testifies that where the valiant are concerned, *the origin of man is the destiny of man.*"[32]

We might well ask, Does God want His children to be like him? Or is this something repulsive to him? Is it something inappropriate? Does God possess the power to transform mortals into his own image? What parts of the "divine nature" or "being like him" are out of bounds or off base? What scriptural injunctions preclude the children of God from aspiring to be like him in every way possible?

"What the Eternal Father wants for you and with you," Truman G. Madsen pointed out, "is the fullness of your possibilities. And those possibilities are infinite. He did not simply make you from nothing into a worm; he adopted and begat you into his likeness in order to share his nature. And he sent his Firstborn Son to exemplify just how glorious that nature can be—even in mortality. That is our witness."[33] What a significant witness, a deeply important religious truth that has come to us through the instrumentality of a modern prophet, Joseph Smith! It is but one more doctrinal evidence of his prophetic calling.

---

32. "The Visions of Moses," 45; emphasis added.
33. *The Highest in Us,* 5–6.

Chapter 2-1

THE DEATH
OF THE TESTATOR

Carthage, Illinois, June 1844. As Joseph Smith the Prophet became more and more an object of controversy, derision, and division, he sensed the need to prepare himself and his people for what seemed the inevitable. Thus in the weeks preceding the martyrdom, the leaders of the Church spent scores of hours together in sober contemplation and instruction on such matters as the keys of the kingdom of God, apostolic succession, and the relocation of the Latter-day Saints to the West. As a result, the Choice Seer could go to his grave in peace.

M any factors led to the death of Joseph Smith the Prophet. "Doctrinal developments at Nauvoo introduced beliefs that . . . would not endear Mormons to their neighbors," historian Davis Bitton explained. "These included baptism for the dead, the temple endowment ceremony, eternal marriage, exaltation and potential divine status for humans, and plural marriage. It was especially plural marriage—usually known as polygamy—that aroused hatred. The other beliefs could be dismissed as bizarre or ridiculous, but the taking of more than one wife was an affront to the inherited moral code of their neighbors. . . .

"In a more general sense, . . . the Mormon Church simply

appeared to outsiders as a monolithic entity incompatible with American pluralism. In other words, even with religious and political matters set aside, the Mormons were a growing, unified group that just did not fit in. As they grew in number and their beliefs appeared less and less mainstream, it became increasingly easier for others to see the Mormons as a nuisance or a threat. And at their head stood their leader, the cause of it all, Joseph Smith."[1]

Add to all that Joseph's decision to destroy the printing press that produced the *Nauvoo Expositor* on the grounds that it was a "public nuisance," and the fears, suspicions, and paranoia were raised to fever pitch. I will leave to the historians the recitation of the painful and poignant details surrounding the martyrdom of the Prophet and the Patriarch and turn instead to a consideration of how Brother Joseph prepared the Church and its leaders to continue on after his death.

FINAL PREPARATIONS

Many of us have served in positions of responsibility in which decisions had to be made, hard decisions, decisions that would not be popular. A certain loneliness is associated with leadership in all fields of endeavor, but perhaps it is even more penetrating when it comes to spiritual things. Joseph Smith knew those feelings only too well. The First Vision was a theophany that he alone had witnessed, and one can only imagine how painfully difficult it was to know what you had experienced, to know of its import, and to realize after brief experience that the sharing of such matters brought ridicule and marginalization.

One of Joseph's experiences that is particularly moving to me, one that took place early in the Church's history, is when Joseph was able to finally have three credible and respected witnesses join

---

1. *The Martyrdom Remembered,* xiii–xv.

him in testifying to the reality of golden plates and angels and divine translation. After Joseph, in company with Oliver Cowdery, David Whitmer, and Martin Harris, had seen the angel Moroni and the plates, according to Lucy Mack Smith, Joseph went into his home and "threw himself down beside me, and exclaimed, 'Father, mother, you do not know how happy I am: the Lord has now caused the plates to be shown to three more besides myself. They have seen an angel, who has testified to them, and they will have to bear witness to the truth of what I have said, for now they know for themselves, that I do not go about to deceive the people, and I feel as if I was relieved of a burden which was almost too heavy for me to bear, and it rejoices my soul, that I am not any longer to be entirely alone in the world."[2]

Oliver Cowdery was with the Prophet when he received the Aaronic and Melchizedek Priesthoods in 1829 and also when Moses, Elias, and Elijah appeared in the Kirtland Temple to restore sacred priesthood keys in 1836. Sidney Rigdon saw the vision of the glories just as Joseph did in the John Johnson home in 1832.

Having begun to administer the blessings of the temple endowment and to confer upon select individuals the fulness of the blessings of the priesthood (see Chapter 16) and sensing that his time was short, Joseph began to prepare the Twelve for his death. He "seemed depressed and opened his heart about his 'presentiments of the future.' He explained that 'some important scene is near to take place,' that perhaps he would be killed, and that as a precaution he must give the Twelve all other keys and powers that he held. Then, if God wills, 'I can go with all pleasure and satisfaction, knowing that my work is done, and the foundation laid on which the kingdom of God is to be reared."[3] Or, as George Q. Cannon, an

2. *History of Joseph Smith by His Mother,* 152.
3. Undated draft statement in Brigham Young Papers, in Arrington, *Brigham Young,* 109–10.

early biographer, put it, "During the winter of 1843–4 superhuman power rested upon the Prophet in his teachings and administrations. He was impelled to constant labor in his ministry as if he had the briefest possible time to accomplish his work."[4]

Wilford Woodruff recalled with clarity the occasion of the Prophet's last meeting with them, on or about 26 March 1844: "I remember the last speech that [Joseph] ever gave us before his death. . . . He stood upon his feet some three hours. The room was filled as with consuming fire, his face was as clear as amber, and he was clothed upon by the power of God."[5] At another time Brother Woodruff spoke of that same meeting: "The Prophet Joseph, I am now satisfied, had a thorough presentiment that that was the last meeting we would hold together here in the flesh. We had had our endowments; we had had all the blessings sealed upon our heads that were ever given to the apostles or prophets on the face of the earth. On that occasion the Prophet Joseph rose up and said to us: 'Brethren, I have desired to live to see this temple built. I shall never live to see it, but you will. I have sealed upon your heads all the keys of the kingdom of God. . . . Now, no matter where I may go or what I may do, the kingdom rests upon you.' Joseph added: "'Ye apostles of the Lamb of God, my brethren, upon your shoulders this kingdom rests; now you have got to round up your shoulders and bear off the kingdom.' And he also made this very strange remark, 'If you do not do it you will be damned.'"[6]

THE TRANSFER OF THE MANTLE OF LEADERSHIP

Many of the Twelve were away from the city of Nauvoo in late June 1844, and the Prophet Joseph communicated with them, encouraging them to return. He and Hyrum were murdered in the

---

4. *Life of Joseph Smith the Prophet*, 516.

5. *Joseph Smith* [manual], 532.

6. *Discourses of Wilford Woodruff*, 71–72.

jail in Carthage on 27 June 1844 (D&C 135). By August most of the brethren had arrived in Nauvoo to find that Sidney Rigdon had returned from Pennsylvania, claiming a vision from God and a commission from Joseph to lead the Church as its duly appointed "guardian." On 7 August Sidney spoke in the Seventies Hall to the Twelve, the high council, and the high priests. "I propose to be a guardian to the people," Sidney said. "In this I have discharged my duty, and done what God had commanded me, and the people can please themselves whether they accept me or not." Brigham Young, president of the Council of the Twelve Apostles then spoke: "I do not care who leads the church, . . . but one thing I must know, and that is what God says about it. I have the keys and the means of obtaining the mind of God on the subject. . . . Joseph conferred upon our heads all the keys and powers belonging to the apostleship which he himself held before he was taken away, and no man or set of men can get between Joseph and the Twelve in this world or the world to come."[7]

The next day, 8 August, a special meeting of the members of the Church was convened at 10:00 A.M. "Sidney Rigdon took his position in a wagon, about two rods in front of the stand, and harangued the saints for about one and a half hours, upon choosing a guardian for the Church." At a 2:00 P.M. meeting that afternoon, President Young arose and said, among other things: "For the first time in my life, for the first time in your lives, for the first time in the Kingdom of God in the 19th century, without a prophet at our head, do I step forth to act in my calling in connection with the quorum of the Twelve, as apostles of Jesus Christ unto this generation. . . . [D]o you, as individuals at this time want to choose a prophet or a guardian? . . .

---

7. History, 1838–1856, volume F-1 [1 May 1844–8 August 1844], The Joseph Smith Papers, accessed 15 Mar. 2016, http://josephsmithpapers.org/paperSummary/history -1838-1856-volume-f-1-1-may-1844-8-august-1844&p=280.

"Here is President Rigdon who was counselor to Joseph. I ask, where are Joseph and Hyrum? They are gone beyond the veil, and if Elder Rigdon wants to act as his counselor, he must go beyond the veil where he is. . . .

"The Twelve are appointed by the finger of God. Here is Brigham, have his knees ever faltered? Have his lips ever quivered? Here is Heber, and the rest of the Twelve, an independent body, who have the keys of the priesthood. . . . You cannot fill the office of a Prophet, Seer and Revelator: God must do this."[8]

Recent research indicates that well over one hundred Latter-day Saints recorded a most unusual experience as Brigham Young spoke.[9] Typical is the testimony of William Lampard Watkins: "It was at this [August 8th] meeting Sidney Rigdon made a lengthy and tedious speech presenting his claims, telling the people what wonderful things he had planned for them.

" . . . The Darkness was soon dispelled, for Brigham Young explained before the people on that day, the order of the Priesthood. He was filled with the power of the Holy Ghost. He stood before the people as the Prophet Joseph Smith often had done and we heard the voice of the true shepherd, for he spoke with the voice of Joseph. His manner and appearance were like unto Joseph's and it was manifested to all those present upon whom the responsibility rested to carry on the work of God and lead the Saints."[10]

Robert Taylor Burton observed, "At that time I was not acquainted with President Young, but his voice, manner, expression, and in fact, his personal appearance was so strikingly that of the

---

8. History, 1838–1856, volume F-1 [1 May 1844–8 August 1844], The Joseph Smith Papers, accessed 15 Mar. 2016, http://josephsmithpapers.org/paperSummary/history-1838-1856-volume-f-1-1-may-1844-8-august-1844&p=281.

9. Welch and Carlson, *Opening the Heavens*, 375–480.

10. In Welch and Carlson, *Opening the Heavens*, 377.

martyred Prophet, that I rose from my seat, as did hundreds of others, to look at the Prophet Joseph Smith Jr."[11]

Notice the specificity of the report by Homer Duncan: "Not only did the voice of Brigham [sound] like that of Joseph, but the very gestures of his right hand when he was saying anything very positive reminded me of Joseph."[12]

Benjamin F. Johnson, a man intimately acquainted with Brother Joseph, provided the following detail: "Suddenly, and as from Heaven, I heard the voice of the Prophet Joseph, that thrilled my whole being, and quickly turning around *I saw in the transfiguration of Brigham Young, the tall, straight and portly form of the Prophet Joseph Smith, clothed in a sheen of light,* covering him to his feet; and I heard the real and perfect voice of the Prophet, *even to the whistle,* as in years past [March 1832] caused by the loss of a tooth said to have been broken out by a mob at Hyrum [sic]."[13]

Also of interest is the testimony of George Morris, who remarked that when Brigham "arose to speak I was sitting right before him holding down my head—reflecting about what Rigdon had said—when I was startled by hearing Joseph's voice—he had a way of clearing his throat before he began to speak—by a peculiar effort on his own—like Ah-hem—I raised my head suddenly—and the first thing I saw was Joseph—as plain as I ever saw Him in my life."[14] In short, recalled Nancy Naomi Alexander Tracy, "as the mantle of Elijah fell upon Elisha, so the mantle of Joseph fell upon Brigham."[15]

Joseph had taught the members of the Twelve the principles of priesthood government, including the matter of apostolic

---

11. In Welch and Carlson, *Opening the Heavens,* 412.

12. In Welch and Carlson, *Opening the Heavens,* 414.

13. In Welch and Carlson, *Opening the Heavens,* 426; emphasis added. A similar observation regarding the broken tooth was made by Joseph Stacy Murdock, in Welch and Carlson, *Opening the Heavens,* 432.

14. In Welch and Carlson, *Opening the Heavens,* 431.

15. In Welch and Carlson, *Opening the Heavens,* 439.

succession. As early as January 1836 Joseph had explained that the Twelve were next in authority to the First Presidency and that "the Twelve are not subject to any other than the First Presidency, . . . and where I am not, there is no First Presidency over the Twelve."[16] Though there were many aspirants, many claiming the right to lead the Church,[17] one thing was perfectly clear to those who had sat in council with the Prophet Joseph—no man could properly succeed Joseph Smith who had not been endowed or had not received the fulness of the priesthood.[18] The visible transfiguration of Brigham Young before a large crowd in Nauvoo but confirmed what the leaders knew—that the Quorum of the Twelve Apostles, with Brigham Young as their senior member, now held the keys of the kingdom of God and that revelation for the management and direction of the restored Church rested with them.

"The Prophet Joseph held the keys of this dispensation on this side of the veil," President Wilford Woodruff explained, "and he will hold them throughout the countless ages of eternity. He went into the spirit world to unlock the prison doors and to preach the Gospel to the millions of spirits who are in darkness, and every Apostle, every Seventy, every Elder, etc., who has died in the faith as he passes to the other side of the veil, enters into the work of the ministry, and there is a thousand times more to preach there than there is here."[19]

CONCLUSION

In the April 1916 general conference of the Church, President Joseph F. Smith opened the conference on Friday with a profound

---

16. History, 1838–1856, volume B-1 [1 September 1834–2 November 1838], The Joseph Smith Papers, accessed 15 Mar. 2016, http://josephsmithpapers.org/paperSummary /history-1838-1856-volume-b-1-1-september-1834-2-november-1838?p=145.

17. See Shields, *Divergent Paths of the Restoration.*

18. See Ehat, "Joseph Smith's Introduction of Temple Ordinances."

19. In *Journal of Discourses,* 22:333–34.

message to the members of The Church of Jesus Christ of Latter-day Saints. It was now the twentieth century, plural marriage had been discontinued, many of the charismatic and powerful leaders of the Church had passed on to their reward, and, as is inevitably the case with the operation of the living Church, there were new developments, alterations in programs and procedures— change. President Smith said: "I feel quite confident that the eyes of Joseph the Prophet, and of the martyrs of this dispensation, and of Brigham and John and Wilford, and those faithful men who were associated with them in their ministry upon the earth, are carefully guarding the interests of the kingdom of God in which they labored and for which they strove during their mortal lives. . . . I have a feeling in my heart that I stand in the presence not only of the Father and of the Son, but in the presence of those whom God commissioned, raised up, and inspired, to lay the foundations of the work in which we are engaged."[20]

Historian Jan Shipps observed that this conference took place "at a point where the demise of the Mormon political kingdom was marked by a demonstrable shift in the nature of LDS politics that made possible the election in 1916 of Utah's first non-Mormon governor." Shipps also notes that President Joseph F. Smith "knew that the fifteen years of his presidency had been hard years for the Latter-day Saints too. He knew that they were worried about what had happened in the church as well as to the church and that they were concerned about the changes that were rushing in upon the Mormon world." President Smith's sermon "called up the sacred past and brought it forward to vindicate the present." His message *"established a basis for a metaphysical bonding between the nineteenth-century Mormon experience and its distinctly dissimilar twentieth-century counterpart."* Truly, "calling the roll of the names of his

---

20. "In the Presence of the Divine," in Clark, *Messages of the First Presidency*, 5:5–6.

predecessors in office . . . President Smith assured his hearers that the church's former leaders continued to watch over the Saints."[21]

The transfiguration of Brigham Young in 1844 was a visible and dramatic manifestation to the Saints that the reins of authority had passed from Joseph to Brigham. And though Joseph would no longer be seen walking the streets of Nauvoo, pulling sticks and playing ball with the boys, or preaching in the grove, the members of The Church of Jesus Christ of Latter-day Saints knew that from the other side of the veil their beloved Brother Joseph would continue to exercise all the righteous influence he could in behalf of the Saints of the Most High. But a transition was necessary. An era had passed, and the loyalty of the people now needed to shift to another prophet leader. And for good reason.

President Harold B. Lee passed away suddenly and unexpectedly on 26 December 1973, after serving as President of the Church for less than a year and a half. In January 1974 Elder Bruce R. McConkie delivered an insightful sermon to the students at Brigham Young University regarding principles of apostolic succession: "The Lord, in his infinite wisdom and goodness, knows what ought to be done with his servants. The other thing to note is that when the Lord calls a new prophet, he does it because he has a work and a labor and a mission for the new man to perform.

"I can imagine," he continued, "that when the Prophet Joseph Smith was taken from this life the Saints felt themselves in the depths of despair. To think that a leader of such spiritual magnitude had been taken from them! . . . And yet when he was taken the Lord had Brigham Young. Brigham Young stepped forth and wore the mantle of leadership. With all respect and admiration and every accolade of praise resting upon the Prophet Joseph, still *Brigham*

---

21. *Mormonism*, 138–42; emphasis added.

Young came forward and did things that then had to be done in a bet-
ter way than the Prophet Joseph could have done them."[22]

"The testators are now dead," John Taylor declared, "and their
testament is in force" (D&C 135:5; compare Hebrews 9:16–17). It
was necessary, the Lord said through Joseph's immediate successor, "that [Joseph] should seal his testimony with his blood, that he
might be honored and the wicked might be condemned" (D&C
136:39). With the martyrdom of the Smith brothers the indel-
ible witness was planted, and now, for a change, the world was on
trial—people on earth bore the responsibility to open their minds
and hearts, ponder and reflect, search and pray, about the unusual
message that had been given through the instrumentality of Joseph
Smith Jr. Joseph's invitation to a world desperately in need of greater
light and knowledge was simply to follow the admonition of James:
"If any of you lack wisdom, let him ask of God, that giveth to all
men liberally, and upbraideth not; and it shall be given him" (James
1:5).

---

22. "Succession in the Presidency," 24; emphasis added.

Conclusion

BECAUSE OF
JOSEPH SMITH

O n one occasion Joseph Smith pointed out, "If you wish to go where God is, you must be like God, or possess the principles which God possesses, for if we are not drawing towards God in principle, we are going from Him and drawing towards the devil." He then gave this charge to his followers: "Search your hearts, and see if you are like God. I have searched mine, and feel to repent of all my sins."[1] Indeed, one of the many admirable qualities of the Prophet of the Restoration was his willingness to confess his own humanity and acknowledge that despite the magnificent visions and revelations that had been unfolded to him as the head of this final dispensation, he walked the paths of mortality and struggled with the pull of the flesh like every other son and daughter of God.

In November of 1835 he noted: "I was this morning introduced to a man from the east. After hearing my name, he remarked that I was nothing but a man, indicating by this expression, that he had supposed that a person to whom the Lord should see fit to receive His will, must be something more than a man."[2] Joseph knew different. He certainly knew that his calling was divine when

1. *Joseph Smith* [manual], 72.
2. *Joseph Smith* [manual], 521.

the Father and the Son had appeared in the Sacred Grove. "I had actually seen a light," he recorded in his official account, "and in the midst of that light I saw two Personages, and they did in reality speak to me. . . . I had seen a vision; I knew it, and I knew that God knew it, and I could not deny it, neither dared I do it" (Joseph Smith–History 1:25). He was fully aware that by means of the Urim and Thummim he had accomplished a miraculous task in translating and publishing the Book of Mormon. He knew by personal experience that angels had been sent from the courts of glory, that they had laid their physical hands upon his head, delivered to him power and authority, had given him knowledge, and had broadened and deepened his understanding. He knew, in short, that he was human but that he had been appointed to undertake a superhuman mission.

Joseph understood only too well what a prophetic successor, President David O. McKay, would state quite simply by quoting John Locke: "God, when he makes the prophet, does not unmake the man."[3]

Elder D. Todd Christofferson of the Quorum of the Twelve Apostles reminded us that "not every statement made by a Church leader, past or present, necessarily constitutes doctrine. It is commonly understood in the Church that a statement made by one leader on a single occasion often represents a personal, though well-considered, opinion, not meant to be official or binding for the whole Church. The Prophet Joseph Smith taught that 'a prophet [is] a prophet only when he [is] acting as such.'"[4]

Joseph said: "I told them I was but a man, and they must not expect me to be perfect; if they expected perfection from me, I should expect it from them; but if they would bear with my

---

3. Locke, *Essay on Human Understanding*, 537. See McKay, in Conference Report, Apr. 1907, 11–12; Apr. 1962, 7.
4. "The Doctrine of Christ," *Ensign*, May 2012, 88.

infirmities and the infirmities of the brethren, I would likewise bear with their infirmities."[5] And so the warning the Prophet extended to the Saints, and one he took responsibility to heed himself, was, "As far as we degenerate from God, we descend to the devil and lose knowledge, and without knowledge we cannot be saved, and while our hearts are filled with evil, and we are studying evil, there is no room in our hearts for good, or studying good. Is not God good? Then you be good; if He is faithful, then you be faithful."[6]

The first prophet and president of The Church of Jesus Christ of Latter-day Saints was not a perfect man, but he was a man whose whole soul delighted in the things of God, one whose deepest yearning was to build a bridge between the least Saint and the Almighty God, to prepare individuals and whole congregations to enjoy the highest and grandest blessings that Deity can confer on mortals. One of my favorite tributes to the Prophet was delivered by Elder B. H. Roberts of the Presidency of the Seventy: "Joseph Smith . . . claimed for himself no special sanctity, no faultless life, no perfection of character, no inerrancy for every word spoken by him," he wrote. "And as he did not claim these things for himself, so can they not be claimed for him by others. . . . *Yet to Joseph Smith was given access to the mind of Deity, through the revelations of God to him.*"[7]

Or, in the Prophet's own words, uttered less than two months before his death, "I never told you I was perfect; but there is no error in the revelations which I have taught."[8] Repeated encounter with the Divine would allow the Prophet, a man who balanced

---

5. *Joseph Smith* [manual], 522. Elder Robert D. Hales spoke of the apostolic office: "To be an Apostle of the Lord is a process—a process of repentance and humility, of looking inward and asking for forgiveness and strength to be what I should be. Unfortunately, I am not a perfect man, and infallibility does not come with the call" (*Return,* 56).

6. *Joseph Smith* [manual], 72.

7. *Comprehensive History of the Church,* 2:360–61; emphasis added.

8. *Joseph Smith* [manual], 522.

humility and certitude admirably, to remark: "I know the scriptures and understand them."[9] Joseph Smith knew the scriptures, he knew their precepts, he knew their prophets, and he knew their central character—Jesus Christ.

Because of Joseph Smith,

- We understand that God our Heavenly Father is a personal Being, the Father of the spirits of all humankind, that he has a body of flesh and bones as tangible as our own, and we can approach him and know him.
- We know the nature and purpose of the Fall of Adam and Eve, that it was in fact a "fortunate fall," a fall downward but forward. The Fall opened the way for the powers of the Atonement to re-create the human family and restore the image of God to each of earth's inhabitants.
- We know that mortals are not born as depraved creatures and that the physical body is not evil.
- We understand the saving grace of Jesus Christ and know that through our faith in him, our trust in his redemptive labors, and our dedicated discipleship, we can be redeemed from our fallen condition and eventually inherit eternal life.
- We know that we are members of the house of Israel and heirs to all the blessings promised to Abraham, Isaac, and Jacob.
- We know that revelation has not ceased, either for the prophetic guidance of the Church of Jesus Christ or for personal direction for our lives.
- We know that life did not begin with this second estate we call mortality and that we existed as spirits long before coming to earth.
- We know there is purpose in life, that God has a plan of

---

9. *Joseph Smith* [manual], 294.

salvation for our happiness and fulfillment here and our eternal reward hereafter.

- We know that God desires to save all of his children and that no person comes to this earth who is not capable of attaining the highest heaven hereafter.
- We can have a meaningful understanding of the world to come, the nature of its purpose, sociality, and glory.
- We know that angels have been sent to earth to bestow divine priesthood authority and that apostolic power and authority will never be lost from the earth again through apostasy.
- We know that the saving principles of the gospel will be taught to all who died without the opportunity to hear them while in the flesh and that in holy temples the ordinances essential to the fulness of salvation can be performed in their behalf.
- We know that as a result of the authority restored to Joseph Smith, the family unit will be preserved throughout the eternities, that love truly can be eternal, and that the privileges of fatherhood and motherhood can continue through all eternity.

Elder Joseph F. Merrill of the Quorum of the Twelve Apostles spoke of some of the significant contributions of Joseph Smith and added: "In the short space of fifteen years [from 1830 until his death in 1844], Joseph Smith, unschooled in the learning and the methods of the world, did all these important things. How was it possible? Does not the only rational explanation lie in the claim that he was God-taught? . . . Joseph Smith, his claims, his teachings, and his achievements are so very remarkable in character that they challenge every . . . human being able to do so, to make an honest and thorough investigation of them."[10]

As early as 1837 Wilford Woodruff stated: "There is not so great a man as Joseph standing in this generation. The gentiles look upon him as he is like a bed of gold, concealed from human view. They

---

10. "Joseph Smith Did See God," *Ensign*, Dec. 2015, 70–71.

know not his principles, his spirit, his wisdom, his virtues, his philanthropy, nor his calling. His mind, like Enoch's, expands as eternity, and only God can comprehend his soul."[11]

☙❦

I express without reserve my love, admiration, and loyalty to Joseph Smith Jr. His was an onerous burden to carry, a monumental weight to bear, and my heart goes out to him as I reflect on how challenging his task must have been. I have great difficulty imagining that Brother Joseph could have delivered to the Saints some of the most doctrinally magnificent gems in human history, answers to many of the world's most vexing issues, if he was a charlatan, a philanderer, and a deceiver, if he was untrue to his prophetic call, if he was immoral or unworthy; God simply does not work that way. Because I accept wholeheartedly the *revelations,* I must and do accept in that same spirit the *revelator.* On Saturday, 6 April 1844, the day before he delivered the King Follett Sermon, the Prophet said: "The great Jehovah has ever been with me, and the wisdom of God will direct me. . . . *I feel in closer communion, and better standing with God than ever I felt before in my life,* and I am glad of this opportunity to appear in your midst. I thank God for the glorious day that he has given us."[12] John Taylor, a man who stood by Joseph all his mature years and was with him in the jail at Carthage, stated: "I testify before God, angels, and men, that [Joseph] was a good, honorable, [and] virtuous man—. . . [and] that his private and public character was unimpeachable—and that he lived and died as a man of God."[13]

As members of The Church of Jesus Christ of Latter-day Saints, we worship God the Eternal Father and his Only Begotten Son, Jesus Christ, and there are no competitors; they are the ultimate

---

11. Journal History, 9 Apr. 1837.

12. *Words of Joseph Smith,* 339.

13. *John Taylor* [manual], 83; emphasis added.

object of our veneration, our adoration, our faith. No person need ever be confused on that point.

In that same spirit, we acknowledge the plowboy who became a prophet as the preeminent prophetic revealer of God, Christ, and the plan of salvation in these last days. President Thomas S. Monson emphasized that "we do not worship the Prophet Joseph; however he left behind a legacy that enables [his] followers today on every continent to proclaim him as a prophet of God. May we, each of us, strive to continue the Prophet Joseph's vision for this work and to magnify his legacy through our works and testimonies to others, that they may know him as we do and that they may experience the peace and joy of the gospel he restored."[14]

Now I do not expect that the attacks upon the name and life and work of Joseph Smith will decrease with the passing of time, for it was the angel Moroni who foretold that Joseph's name would be known for good and evil among all nations, kindreds, tongues, and people (Joseph Smith–History 1:33). That same Moroni explained to Brother Joseph that "those who are not built upon the Rock will seek to overthrow this church; but *it will increase the more opposed.*"[15] Elder Neil L. Andersen offered the following advice to Latter-day Saints, in particular: "Questions concerning the Prophet Joseph Smith are not new. They have been hurled by his critics since this work began. To those of faith who, looking through the colored glasses of the 21st century, honestly question events or statements of the Prophet Joseph from nearly 200 years ago, may I share some friendly advice: For now, give Brother Joseph a break! In a future day, you will have 100 times more information than from all of today's search engines combined, and it will come from our

---

14. *Teachings of Thomas S. Monson,* 161.

15. Cowdery, "Letter VIII," *Messenger and Advocate* 2, no. 1 (Oct. 1835): 199; emphasis added.

all-knowing Father in Heaven. . . . I testify that Joseph Smith was a prophet of God. Settle this in your mind, and move forward!"[16]

In his first general conference after becoming the tenth President of the Church, Joseph Fielding Smith said: "I desire to say that no man of himself can lead this church. It is the Church of the Lord Jesus Christ; he is at the head. . . .

"He chooses men and calls them to be instruments in his hands to accomplish his purposes, and he guides and directs them in their labors. But men are only instruments in the Lord's hands, and the honor and glory for all that his servants accomplish is and should be ascribed unto him forever.

"If this were the work of man, it would fail, but it is the work of the Lord, and he does not fail."[17]

The same Spirit that has borne witness to me that God is our Father, the Father of the spirits of all humankind, and that Jesus Christ is our Savior and Redeemer, our only hope for peace in this world and salvation in the world to come—that same Spirit has confirmed to my soul that our Father in heaven, in his mercy and grace, has chosen to restore the fulness of the gospel of Jesus Christ in this final dispensation. That Holy Spirit prompts and impels me to bear witness that the work Joseph Smith began, under the direction of the Almighty, is proceeding according to a divine plan; that the Prophet Joseph's influence is still being felt; and that his successors in the leading councils of the Church today are being directed by the same Lord and Savior, led by that same kindly Light that led Brother Joseph while he presided over the beginning stages of the Restoration. These things I know, as plainly as I know that I live. May we always be true and loyal to all that God has seen fit to reveal.

---

16. "Faith Is Not by Chance, but by Choice," *Ensign,* Nov. 2015, 66.
17. In Conference Report, Apr. 1970, 113.

Appendix 1

DOCTRINES, PRINCIPLES, AND PRECEPTS FROM THE BOOK OF MORMON

The following is a sample of the great doctrinal reservoir to be found in the Book of Mormon. These are doctrinal gems. Careful reflection on these truths will edify many and astonish others.

- God will always provide a way for his children to accomplish whatever he commands them (1 Nephi 3:7).
- Very often we are led by the Spirit, not knowing the things we should do (1 Nephi 4:6).
- Israel is grafted in as they come to the knowledge of the true Messiah (1 Nephi 10:14).
- The Holy Ghost, or the third member of the Godhead, is in the form of a man (1 Nephi 11:11).
- The tree of life is a symbol of Jesus Christ (1 Nephi 11:4–7, 21–22).
- Jesus is the God of Abraham, Isaac, and Jacob (1 Nephi 19:10).
- Salvation is free (2 Nephi 2:4; 26:25, 27, 28).
- We are saved through the merits, mercy, and grace of the Holy Messiah (2 Nephi 2:8; Helaman 14:13).
- There is a sense in which all of God's children will be redeemed. After the resurrection, all are brought back into the presence of God to be judged (2 Nephi 9:15; Helaman 13:15–18).
- The ordinances of salvation, including baptism, are essential (2 Nephi 31).

- The doctrine of Christ or gospel of Jesus Christ consists of faith, repentance, baptism, reception of the Holy Ghost, enduring to the end, resurrection, and eternal judgment (2 Nephi 31; 3 Nephi 27).
- Israel is scattered when she rejects the true Messiah. Israel is gathered whenever she accepts the true Messiah, his gospel, his Church, and his doctrine (1 Nephi 15:12–19; 2 Nephi 6:8–11; 9:1–2; 10:5–7; 15).
- The Fall of Adam and Eve is as much a part of the plan of salvation as the Atonement. "Adam fell that men might be, and men are that they might have joy" (2 Nephi 2:25).
- Joseph Smith is the foreordained Choice Seer in the last days (2 Nephi 3).
- The Atonement of Christ is infinite because it overcomes physical death and brings to pass the resurrection of all humankind (2 Nephi 9:6–15).
- If there is no resurrection, there is no Atonement; we would all be subject to Satan forever (2 Nephi 9:8–9).
- We are to worship God the Father in the name of Jesus Christ (2 Nephi 25:16; Jacob 4:5).
- Satan is versatile. With some of us he rages in our hearts and stirs us up to anger against the things of God. Others he pacifies and lulls into a state of carnal security: they perceive that "all is well in Zion" (2 Nephi 28:20–24).
- Those who are truly built on the rock of Christ are eager for new revelation, even new scripture (2 Nephi 28–29).
- Remission of sins comes after baptism of water through the conferral of the Holy Ghost; the Holy Ghost is the Sanctifier (2 Nephi 31:17).
- The members of the Godhead are so united that they are occasionally referred to as "one eternal God" (2 Nephi 31:21; Alma 11:44; 3 Nephi 11:23–25; Mormon 7:7).
- People speak with the tongue of angels when they speak the words of Christ, that is, when they speak by the power of the Holy Ghost (2 Nephi 31:13–14; 32:1–5).

- True disciples *experience* Christ—they believe in him, view his death, suffer his cross, and bear the shame of the world (Jacob 1:8).
- Before we seek for riches, we should seek for the kingdom of God. After we have obtained a hope in Christ, we will obtain riches if we seek them, and we will seek them so that we may clothe the naked, feed the hungry, liberate the captive, and administer relief to the sick and afflicted (Jacob 2:18–19).
- Christ and his Atonement have been preached since the beginning of time (Jacob 4:5; 7:11; Jarom 1:11; Alma 39:17–19).
- Spiritual darkness comes by looking beyond the mark (Jacob 4:14).
- God has an everlasting love for his chosen people; he simply will not let Israel go (Jacob 5–6).
- We become unshaken in the faith as we have frequent spiritual experiences (Jacob 7:5; Enos 1:2–11).
- We are eternally indebted to God and, even if we should serve God with all the abilities we possess, we would still be unprofitable servants (Mosiah 2:20–25).
- The natural man is an enemy to God and to himself (Mosiah 3:19; Alma 41:11).
- We know that we have been forgiven of our sins when the Spirit dwells with us once again and when we feel joy and peace of conscience (Mosiah 4:3).
- When we are born again, we become the sons and daughters of Jesus Christ (Mosiah 5:7).
- Jesus Christ is both the Father and the Son—the Father because he was conceived by the power of the Father, and the Son because of the flesh, his physical body (Mosiah 15:1–4; Alma 11:38–39; Helaman 14:12; Mormon 9:12; Ether 3:14).
- The first resurrection consists of the rising from the dead of the prophets and those who gave heed to their words (Mosiah 15:21–22).
- At the time of baptism, we covenant to bear one another's burdens, mourn with those that mourn, comfort those who stand in need of

comfort, stand as witnesses of God at all times and in all places; in addition, we take upon us the name of Christ (Mosiah 18:8–10).

- The Lord can lighten the burdens we bear without removing the burdens from us (Mosiah 24:13–14).

- When we are born again, we are changed from a carnal and fallen state to a state of righteousness; we become "new creatures" in Christ (Mosiah 27:23–26).

- The only way to reclaim some who have wandered or left the faith is to bear pure testimony (Alma 4:19).

- Christ came to earth to experience everything every other mortal experiences—pains, afflictions, temptations, sicknesses, infirmities—so that he could empathize with his people and thus succor them (Alma 7:11–13).

- All those who receive the Melchizedek Priesthood in this life were foreordained to do so in the premortal existence (Alma 13:1–12).

- We become persons of sound understanding and are able to teach the gospel with power and authority as we search the scriptures, pray, and fast (Alma 17:1–3).

- Predestination is a false doctrine (Alma 31).

- Faith is not to have a perfect knowledge but rather to have hope for things that are not seen but are true (Alma 32:21).

- The Atonement of Christ is infinite because Jesus Christ is an infinite Being (Alma 34:13–14).

- This life is the time to prepare to meet God, the time for us to perform our labors (Alma 34:32).

- The same spirit we have at the time of death will continue with us as we go into the postmortal spirit world (Alma 34:33–35).

- By small and simple means great things are brought to pass (1 Nephi 16:29; Alma 37:6).

- The only sins more serious to God than sexual immorality are murder and the sin against the Holy Ghost (Alma 39:5).

- At the time of death, one experiences a partial judgment and goes either to paradise or to hell/outer darkness (Alma 40:11–14).

- In the resurrection the body and the spirit are reunited, and the body is raised in its perfect form (Alma 11:43; 40:23).
- Wickedness never was happiness; this is what is known as the law of restoration (Alma 41).
- Mercy cannot rob justice (Alma 42:12–15).
- We are sanctified by yielding our hearts unto God (Helaman 3:35).
- We must build our foundation on the rock of our Redeemer if we hope to be able to withstand the onslaught of the devil (Helaman 5:12).
- Those who have sought all their days for that which cannot be obtained—to be happy while caught up in iniquity—will find that their destruction is made sure (Helaman 13:38).
- The offering we are to make to God is a broken heart and a contrite spirit (3 Nephi 9:20).
- When the fulness of the times of the Gentiles comes, the gospel will then be taken on a preferential basis to the house of Israel (3 Nephi 16:10).
- When we take the sacrament of the Lord's Supper, we take these emblems to our soul; that soul will never hunger nor thirst but will always be filled (3 Nephi 18:8).
- The sign that the work of the Father (the work of gathering Israel) has commenced in the last days is the coming forth of the Book of Mormon (3 Nephi 21:1–7; 29:1; Ether 4:17).
- Those who reject the Lord's latter-day servant (Joseph Smith) will be cut off from the Lord's covenant (3 Nephi 21:11).
- Jesus expounded all the scriptures in one (3 Nephi 23:14).
- In order for a church to be the Lord's church it must be called after his name and be built on his gospel. Then the works of the Father will be manifest in it (3 Nephi 27:7–10).
- The gospel is the good news that Christ came into the world to do the will of the Father, to be lifted up on the cross that he might draw all men unto him, that they might be raised from the dead and then stand before him to be judged (3 Nephi 27:13–16).

- Only those whose garments have been washed clean in the blood of the Lamb can enter the kingdom of God and enter into his rest (3 Nephi 27:19–20).
- Translated beings are changed so that they do not experience death or the pains of this life, except sorrow for the sins of the world. They remain in a translated state until the second coming of Jesus Christ, at which point they are changed in the twinkling of an eye from mortality to resurrected immortality (3 Nephi 28).
- True and lasting happiness comes as people are converted to the Lord; they then deal justly with one another and look to the needs of their neighbors. Such persons are made truly free and become partakers of the heavenly gift (4 Nephi 1:2–3).
- Sorrow that does not lead to repentance is merely the sorrowing of the damned—people simply cannot find happiness in sin (Mormon 2:13).
- An awful fear of death fills the breasts of the wicked (Mormon 6:7).
- The eternal purposes of the Lord will roll on until all his promises are fulfilled (Mormon 8:22).
- God has not ceased to be a God of miracles (Mormon 9:15, 19–20).
- We have been charged to do all things in worthiness and to do them in the name of Jesus Christ (Mormon 9:29).
- Although because of the Fall our natures have become evil continually, we have been commanded to call upon God, that we may receive according to our desires (Ether 3:2).
- We should not dispute simply because we cannot see, for we receive no witness until after the trial of our faith (Ether 12:6).
- If we come unto Christ, he will make known unto us our weakness; if we have faith in him, then he will make weak things become strong unto us (Ether 12:27).
- Christ has laid down his life for the world and gone to prepare a place for us; the love that motivated this selfless sacrifice is charity, the pure love of Christ (Ether 12:33–34).

- If we seek Christ, then the grace of the Father, Son, and Holy Ghost will abide in us forever (Ether 12:41).
- We remain spiritually vigilant, watchful unto prayer, through relying alone upon the merits of Christ, who is the author and finisher of our faith (Moroni 6:4).
- Members of the Church of Jesus Christ are charged to be peaceable followers of Christ who have sufficient hope to enter into the rest of the Lord here, in preparation for entering into his rest hereafter (Moroni 7:3).
- The Spirit of Christ is given to every person that each may know good from evil. Everything that invites to do good and to believe in Christ is sent forth by the gift and power of Christ and is of God (Moroni 7:16).
- Angels have not ceased to minister to the children of God. They are subject to Christ and minister to those who have strong faith and a firm mind. The office of their ministry is to call people to repentance, first by declaring the word of Christ to the chosen vessels, who then minister to the residue of humankind (Moroni 7:30–31).
- The only reason that miracles cease and that angels do not minister is that faith has ceased also (Moroni 7:36–37; 10:24).
- Charity is the pure love of Christ and endures forever. We are to pray unto the Father with all the energy of our hearts to be filled with this love, which the Father always bestows upon all who are true followers of his Son. By and through the transforming power of this love, we will be like him when he appears and we will see him as he is (Moroni 7:47–48).
- Infant baptism is a false doctrine and a wicked practice, for baptism is only for those who have faith and require repentance, those who are accountable. Since little children are redeemed from the foundation of the world, they are innocent (Moroni 8:10–12).
- It matters not how bleak a situation may appear to be or how wicked the world may become; we have a labor to perform while we are in this mortal condition—namely, to conquer the enemy

of all righteousness and rest our souls in the kingdom of God (Moroni 9:6).

- By the power of the Holy Ghost we may know the truth of all things (Moroni 10:5).
- We must never deny the gifts of God or gifts of the Spirit; they are given for our profit (Moroni 10:8–18).
- If we deny ourselves of all ungodliness and love God with our whole soul, then his grace is sufficient for us, so that by that grace we become perfected and sanctified in Christ (Moroni 10:32–33).

What a feast! "Anyone who has done much reading," Elder Neal A. Maxwell pointed out, "finds himself grateful for books that contain two or three significant truths or great ideas. Sometimes we settle for articulate restatement or re-phrasings. . . . Thus the density of the spiritual truths of the Book of Mormon is especially impressive."[1]

After many readings of the Book of Mormon, President Boyd K. Packer observed: "I found these scriptures to be plain and precious. I wondered how young Joseph Smith could have such insights. The fact is, I do not believe he had such penetrating insights. He did not have to have them. He just translated what was written on the plates." President Packer continued: "Such plain and precious insights are everywhere in the Book of Mormon. They reflect a depth of wisdom and experience that is certainly not characteristic of a 23-year-old."[2]

---

1. *Plain and Precious Things*, 14.
2. "The Book of Mormon: Another Testament of Jesus Christ," *Ensign*, May 2005, 7.

BRIGHAM YOUNG

I honor and revere the name of Joseph Smith. I delight to hear it; I love it. I love his doctrine.

What I have received from the Lord, I have received by Joseph Smith; he was the instrument made use of. If I drop him, I must drop these principles; they have not been revealed, declared, or explained by any other man since the days of the Apostles. If I lay down the Book of Mormon, I shall have to deny that Joseph is a Prophet; and if I lay down the doctrine and cease to preach the gathering of Israel and the building up of Zion, I must lay down the Bible; and, consequently, I might as well go home as undertake to preach without these three items. . . .

Not that Joseph was the Savior, but he was a Prophet. As he said once, when someone asked him, "Are you the Savior?" "No, but I can tell you what I am—I am his brother." So we can say.[1]

JOHN TAYLOR

Who was Joseph Smith? The Book of Mormon tells us he was of the seed of Joseph that was sold into Egypt, and hence he was selected as Abraham was to fulfil a work upon the earth. God chose this young man. He was ignorant of letters as the world has it, but the most profoundly

---

1. *Discourses of Brigham Young,* 458.

learned and intelligent man that I ever met in my life, and I have traveled hundreds of thousands of miles, been on different continents and mingled among all classes and creeds of people, yet I never met a man so intelligent as he was. And where did he get his intelligence from? Not from books, not from the logic or science or philosophy of the day, but he obtained it through the revelation of God made known to him through the medium of the everlasting gospel.[2]

WILFORD WOODRUFF

It has been my faith and belief from the time that I was made acquainted with the gospel that no greater prophet than Joseph Smith ever lived on the face of the earth save Jesus Christ. He was raised up to stand at the head of this great dispensation—the greatest of all dispensations God has ever given to man. . . . Joseph Smith was ordained before he came here, the same as Jeremiah was.[3]

LORENZO SNOW

A word or two about Joseph Smith. Perhaps there are very few men now living who were so well acquainted with Joseph Smith the Prophet as I was. I was with him oftentimes. I visited with him in his family, sat at his table, associated with him under various circumstances, and had private interviews with him for counsel. I know that Joseph Smith was a prophet of God; I know that he was an honorable man, a moral man, and that he had the respect of those who were acquainted with him. The Lord has shown me most clearly and completely that he was a prophet of God, and that he held the holy priesthood.[4]

JOSEPH F. SMITH

God lives, and Jesus is the Christ, the Savior of the world. Joseph Smith is a prophet of God—living, not dead; for his name will never perish. . . . He laid the foundations in this dispensation for the restoration

2. *The Gospel Kingdom*, 353.
3. *Discourses of Wilford Woodruff*, 43.
4. *Teachings of Lorenzo Snow*, 55.

of the principles that were taught by the Son of God, who for these principles lived, and taught, and died, and rose from the dead. Therefore I say, as the name of the Son of God shall be held in reverence and honor, and in the faith and love of men, so will the name of Joseph Smith eventually be held among the children of men, gaining prestige, increasing in honor and commanding respect and reverence, until the world shall say that he was a servant and Prophet of God. The Lord God Omnipotent reigneth. Peace on earth, good will to men, is the proclamation that Joseph the Prophet made, and that is the same as his Master, the Lord Jesus Christ, made to the world.[5]

Heber J. Grant

I have met hundreds of men who have said: "If it were not for Joseph Smith I could accept your religion." Any man who does not believe in Joseph Smith as a prophet of the true and the living God has no right to be in this Church. That revelation to Joseph Smith is the foundation stone. If Joseph Smith did not have that interview with God and Jesus Christ, the whole Mormon fabric is a failure and a fraud. It is not worth anything on earth. But God did come, God did introduce His Son; God did inspire that man to organize the Church of Jesus Christ, and all the opposition in the world is not able to withstand the truth. It is flourishing; it is growing, and it will grow more.[6]

George Albert Smith

Many of the benefits and blessings that have come to me have come through that man [Joseph Smith] who gave his life for the gospel of Jesus Christ. There have been some who have belittled him, but I would like to say that those who have done so will be forgotten and their remains will go back to mother earth, if they have not already gone, and the odor of their infamy will never die, while the glory and honor and majesty and

5. *Gospel Doctrine*, 479–80.
6. *Gospel Standards*, 15.

courage and fidelity manifested by the Prophet Joseph Smith will attach to his name forever.[7]

DAVID O. MCKAY

The boldness of [Joseph Smith's] assertions was remarkable. Many of those were in direct opposition to the belief of the orthodoxy of his day. He contradicted doctrines advocated by learned divines—a rash thing for an unlearned youth to do unless he had an assurance that he was right. If he had this assurance, whence did it come? . . .

Other men with noble aspirations, with power and popularity, failed utterly in attempting to establish their ideals. Joseph Smith was favored intellectually by inspiration. Brother Joseph knew he was chosen of Almighty God to establish in this dispensation the Church of Jesus Christ which he, as Paul, declared to be the power of God unto salvation—social salvation, moral salvation, spiritual salvation.[8]

JOSEPH FIELDING SMITH

Mormonism, as it is called, must stand or fall on the story of Joseph Smith. He was either a prophet of God, divinely called, properly appointed and commissioned, or he was one of the biggest frauds this world has ever seen. There is no middle ground. . . .

There is no possibility of his being deceived, and on this issue we are ready to make our stand. I maintain that Joseph Smith was all that he claimed to be. His statements are too positive and his claims too great to admit of deception on his part. No imposter could have accomplished so great and wonderful a work. Had he been such, he would have been detected and exposed, and the plan would have failed and come to naught. . . .

No man, in and of himself, without the aid of the Spirit of God and the direction of revelation, can found a religion, or promulgate a body of doctrine, in all particulars in harmony with revealed truth. If he has not the inspiration of the Lord and the direction of messengers from his

---

7. *Teachings of George Albert Smith*, 45.
8. *Gospel Ideals*, 82–83.

presence, he will not comprehend the truth, and therefore such truth as he teaches will be hopelessly mixed with error.[9]

HAROLD B. LEE

As one of the humblest among us, and from the depths of my soul, I too want to add my humble testimony. I know that Joseph Smith was a prophet of the living God. I know that he lived and died to bring to this generation the means by which salvation could be gained. I know that he sits in a high place and holds the keys of this last dispensation. I know that for those who follow him and listen to his teachings and accept him as a true prophet of God and his revelations and teachings as the word of God, the gates of hell will not prevail against them.[10]

SPENCER W. KIMBALL

Of all the great events of the century, none compared with the first vision of Joseph Smith. . . . Nothing short of this total vision to Joseph could have served the purpose to clear away the mists of the centuries. Merely an impression, a hidden voice, a dream could [not] have dispelled the old vagaries and misconceptions. . . .

The God of all these worlds and the Son of God, the Redeemer, our Savior, in person attended this boy. He saw the living God. He saw the living Christ. Few of all the man-creation had ever glimpsed such a vision. . . . Joseph now belonged to an elite group—the tried and trusted, and true. He was in a select society of persons whom Abraham describes as "noble and great ones" that were "good" and that were to become the Lord's rulers.[11]

EZRA TAFT BENSON

The world has generally revered the ancient dead prophets and rejected the living ones. It was so with Joseph Smith. Truth is often on the

---

9. *Selections from Doctrines of Salvation,* 252–55.

10. *Teachings of Harold B. Lee,* 371.

11. *Teachings of Spencer W. Kimball,* 428, 430.

scaffold—error on the throne. But time is on the side of truth, for truth is eternal.

The greatest activity in this world or in the world to come is directly related to the work and mission of Joseph Smith—man of destiny, prophet of God. That work is the salvation and eternal life of man. For that great purpose this earth was created, prophets of God are called, heavenly messengers are sent forth, and on sacred and important occasions even God, the Father of us all, condescends to come to earth and to introduce His beloved Son.[12]

HOWARD W. HUNTER

Time vindicates the words and acts of a prophet. The passing of time has turned faith into knowledge. . . . One who accepts the doctrine commonly known or referred to as Mormonism must accept . . . those writings which have been left to us by the Prophet Joseph Smith—a prophet, seer, and revelator.

This is the time of the year [December] when we are reminded of his birth. I am grateful for his teachings, for his revelations, for the heritage he has left us. Through him the gospel was restored to the earth. There is no story in all of history more beautiful than the simple, sweet story of the lad who went into the woods near his home, kneeled in prayer, and received heavenly visitors. . . .

As time went by, this young man, without scholarly achievements and formal education, was educated by the Lord for the things to come. . . .

I am grateful for my membership in the Church. My testimony of its divinity hinges upon the simple story of the lad under the trees kneeling and receiving heavenly visitors. If it is not true, Mormonism falls. If it is true—and I bear witness that it is—it is one of the greatest events in all history.[13]

---

12. *Teachings of Ezra Taft Benson*, 103–4.
13. *Teachings of Howard W. Hunter*, 189.

GORDON B. HINCKLEY

It is a constantly recurring mystery to me how some people speak with admiration for the Church and its work, while at the same time disdaining him through whom, as a servant of the Lord, came the framework of all that the Church is, of all that it teaches, and of all that it stands for. They would pluck the fruit from the tree while cutting off the root from which it grows. . . .

Great was the Prophet Joseph Smith's vision. It encompassed all the peoples of mankind, wherever they live, and all generations who have walked the earth and passed on. How can anyone, past or present, speak against him except out of ignorance? They have not tasted of his words; they have not pondered about him, nor prayed about him. As one who has done these things, I add my own words of testimony that he was and is a prophet of God, raised up as an instrument in the hands of the Almighty to usher in a new and final gospel dispensation.[14]

THOMAS S. MONSON

Through Joseph Smith, the gospel—which had been lost through centuries of apostasy—was restored, the priesthood and its keys were received, the doctrines of salvation were revealed, the gospel and temple ordinances—along with the sealing power—were returned and, in 1830, the Church of Jesus Christ was re-established on the earth.

Though reviled and persecuted, the Prophet Joseph never wavered in his testimony of Jesus Christ. His peers watched him lead with dignity and grace, endure hardships, and time and again rise to new challenges until his divine mission was completed. Today that heritage he established still shines for all the world to see. The teachings he translated and his legacy of love for his fellow man continue in the millions of hearts touched by the message he declared so long ago.[15]

---

14. *Teachings of Gordon B. Hinckley,* 501–3.
15. *Teachings of Thomas S. Monson,* 160.

SOURCES

Ahlstrom, Sydney E., ed. *Theology in America: The Major Protestant Voices from Puritanism to Neo-Orthodoxy.* Indianapolis, Ind.: Bobbs-Merrill, 1967.

Anchor Bible Dictionary. Edited by David Noel Freedman. 6 vols. New York: Doubleday, 1992.

Andersen, Neil L. "Faith Is Not by Chance, but by Choice." *Ensign,* Nov. 2015, 65–68.

———. "It's True, Isn't It? Then What Else Matters?" *Ensign,* May 2007, 74–75.

Anderson, Karl Ricks. *The Savior in Kirtland: Personal Accounts of Divine Manifestations.* Salt Lake City: Deseret Book, 2012.

Anderson, Richard Lloyd. "Parallel Prophets: Paul and Joseph Smith." *1982–83 Brigham Young University Fireside and Devotional Speeches.* Provo, Utah: BYU Publications, 1983.

Andrus, Hyrum L. *Doctrines of the Kingdom.* Salt Lake City: Bookcraft, 1973.

———. "The Field Is White Already to Harvest." In Andrus, *Doctrinal Themes of the Doctrine and Covenants.*

———. *The Glory of God and Man's Relationship to Deity.* Provo, Utah: Brigham Young University Publications, 1970.

———. *God, Man, and the Universe.* Salt Lake City: Bookcraft, 1968.

———. Personal correspondence with Robert L. Millet, Sept. 21, 1982.

———, ed. *Doctrinal Themes of the Doctrine and Covenants.* Provo, Utah: Brigham Young University Press, 1970.

Andrus, Hyrum L., and Helen Mae Andrus. *They Knew the Prophet.* Salt Lake City: Bookcraft, 1974.

Arrington, Leonard J. *Brigham Young: American Moses.* New York: Alfred A. Knopf, 1985.

———. "Early Mormon Communitarianism: The Law of Consecration and Stewardship." *Western Humanities Review* 7 (Autumn 1953): 344.

Bachman, Danel. "New Light on an Old Hypothesis: The Ohio Origins of the Revelation on Eternal Marriage." *Journal of Mormon History* 5 (1978): 22.

Backman, Milton V., Jr. *American Religions and the Rise of Mormonism.* Rev. ed. Salt Lake City: Deseret Book, 1970.

———. *The Heavens Resound: A History of the Latter-day Saints in Ohio, 1830–1838.* Salt Lake City: Deseret Book, 1983.

———. *Joseph Smith's First Vision: Confirming Evidences and Contemporary Accounts.* 2d ed. Salt Lake City: Bookcraft, 1980.

———. "Truman Coe's 1836 Description of Mormonism." *Brigham Young University Studies* 17, no. 3 (1977): 347–54.

[Ballard, Melvin R.] *Melvin J. Ballard—Crusader for Righteousness.* Salt Lake City: Bookcraft, 1966.

Ballard, M. Russell. "Men and Women in the Work of the Lord." *New Era,* Apr. 2014, 2–5.

———. "The Miracle of the Holy Bible." *Ensign,* May 2007, 80–82.

Balmer, Randall. *Mine Eyes Have Seen the Glory: A Journey into the Evangelical Subculture in America.* 3d ed. New York: Oxford University Press, 2000.

Bartholomew, Calvin H. "A Comparison of the Authorized Version and the Inspired Revision of Genesis." Master's thesis, Brigham Young University, 1949.

Baugh, Alex. "The Practice of Baptism for the Dead Outside of Temples." *Religious Studies Center Newsletter* 13, no. 1 (Sept. 1998): 3–6.

Bedell, George C., Leo Sandon Jr., and Charles T. Wellborn. *Religion in America.* New York: Macmillan, 1975.

Bednar, David A. "Ask in Faith." *Ensign,* May 2008, 94–97.

———. "Faithful Parents and Wayward Children: Sustaining Hope While Overcoming Misunderstanding." *Ensign,* Mar. 2014, 28–33.

Benson, Ezra Taft. "Civic Standards for the Faithful Saints." *Ensign,* July 1972, 59–61.

———. *Come unto Christ.* Salt Lake City: Deseret Book, 1983.

———. *Ezra Taft Benson* [manual]. Teachings of Presidents of the Church series. Salt Lake City: The Church of Jesus Christ of Latter-day Saints, 2014.

———. *Teachings of Ezra Taft Benson.* Salt Lake City: Bookcraft, 1988.

———. "What I Hope You Will Teach Your Children about the Temple." *Ensign,* Aug. 1985, 6–10.

———. *A Witness and a Warning: A Modern-Day Prophet Testifies of the Book of Mormon.* Salt Lake City: Deseret Book, 1988.

Bestor, Arthur E., Jr. "The Ferment of Reform." In Andrus, *Doctrinal Themes of the Doctrine and Covenants.*

Bitton, Davis. *The Martyrdom Remembered: A One Hundred Fifty Year Perspective on the Assassination of Joseph Smith.* Salt Lake City: Aspen Books, 1994.

Bloom, Harold. *The American Religion: The Emergence of the Post-Christian Nation.* New York: Simon & Schuster, 1992.

Boston Quarterly Review. 3 vols. Boston: Cambridge Press, 1840.

Boyd, Gregory. *God of the Possible.* Grand Rapids, Mich.: Baker, 2000.

Brandt, Edward J. "The Origin and Importance of the Articles of Faith." In *The Pearl of Great Price,* edited by Robert L. Millet and Kent P. Jackson, 407–19. Vol. 2 of Studies in Scripture series. Salt Lake City: Randall Book, 1985.

Briggs, E. C., and J. W. Peterson. "Another Testimony. Statement of William Smith, concerning Joseph, the Prophet." *Deseret News,* 20 Jan. 1894, 11.

Brunner, Emil. *Man in Revolt: A Christian Anthropology.* Translated by Olive Wyon. Philadelphia: Westminster Press, 1947.

Bushman, Richard L. "A Joseph Smith for the Twenty-First Century." *Brigham Young University Studies* 40, no. 3 (2001), 155–71.

———. *Joseph Smith, Rough Stone Rolling: A Cultural Biography of Mormonism's Founder.* New York: Alfred A. Knopf, 2005.

Butler, Jon, Grant Wacker, and Randall Balmer. *Religion in American Life: A Short History.* New York: Oxford University Press, 2003.

Campbell, Alexander. *The Christian Baptist.* Revised by D. S. Burnet. 7 vols. Bethany, W.V.: H. S. Bosworth, 1861.

Cannon, George Q. *Gospel Truth.* Edited by Jerreld Newquist. 2 vols. in 1. Salt Lake City: Deseret Book, 1987.

———. *Life of Joseph Smith the Prophet.* Salt Lake City: Deseret Book, 1964.

Cartwright, Peter. *Autobiography of Peter Cartwright, the Backwoods Preacher.* Edited by W. P. Strickland. New York: Carlton & Porter, 1856.

Christensen, Matthew B. *The First Vision: A Harmonization of 10 Accounts from the Sacred Grove.* Springville, Utah: CFI, 2014.

Christofferson, D. Todd. "The Doctrine of Christ." *Ensign,* May 2012, 86–89.

———. "Justification and Sanctification." *Ensign,* June 2001, 18–25.

"A Chronology of the Life of Joseph Smith." *Brigham Young University Studies* 46, no. 4 (2007): 6–173.

Church History in the Fulness of Times. Salt Lake City: The Church of Jesus Christ of Latter-day Saints, 1989.

Clark, J. Reuben, Jr. *J. Reuben Clark Jr.: Selected Papers on Religion, Education, and Youth.* Edited by David H. Yarn. Provo, Utah: Brigham Young University Press, 1984.

Clark, James R., comp. *Messages of the First Presidency.* 6 vols. Salt Lake City: Bookcraft, 1965–75.

———. *The Story of the Pearl of Great Price.* Salt Lake City: Bookcraft, 1955.

Cook, Lyndon W. *Joseph Smith and the Law of Consecration.* Provo, Utah: Grandin Book, 1985.

———. *The Revelations of the Prophet Joseph Smith.* Salt Lake City: Deseret Book, 1985.

Cowdery, Oliver. "Letter I." *Messenger and Advocate* 1, no. 1 (Oct. 1834): 13–16.

———. "Letter IV." *Messenger and Advocate* 1, no. 5 (Feb. 1835): 77–79.

———. "Letter VIII." *Messenger and Advocate* 2, no. 1 (Oct. 1835): 195–202.

Cowley, Matthias F. *Wilford Woodruff.* Salt Lake City: Bookcraft, 1964.

De Tocqueville, Alexis. *Democracy in America.* 2 vols. 1835, 1840. Reprint, New York: Alfred A. Knopf, 1945.

Dew, Sheri L. *Go Forward with Faith: The Biography of Gordon B. Hinckley.* Salt Lake City: Deseret Book, 1996.

Dodge, Samuel Alonzo, and Steven C. Harper, ed. *Exploring the First Vision.* Provo, Utah: BYU Religious Studies Center, 2012.

Durham, Reed C., Jr. "A History of Joseph Smith's Revision of the Bible." Ph.D. diss., Brigham Young University, 1965.

Ehat, Andrew F. "'It Seems like Heaven Began on Earth': Joseph Smith and the Constitution of the Kingdom of God." *Brigham Young University Studies* 20, no. 3 (1980): 253–80.

———. "Joseph Smith's Introduction of Temple Ordinances and the 1844 Mormon Succession Question." Master's thesis, Brigham Young University, 1981.

Ehrman, Bart D. *The Orthodox Corruption of Scripture.* New York: Oxford University Press, 1993.

Emerson, Ralph Waldo. "The Editors to the Reader." *Dial* 1, no. 1 (July 1840): 2.

Eyring, Henry B. *Because He First Loved Us.* Salt Lake City: Deseret Book, 2002.

———. *To Draw Closer to God.* Salt Lake City: Deseret Book, 1997.

Far West Record: Minutes of The Church of Jesus Christ of Latter-day Saints. Edited by Donald Q. Cannon and Lyndon W. Cook. Salt Lake City: Deseret Book, 1983.

Faulring, Scott H., Kent P. Jackson, and Robert J. Matthews, eds. *Joseph Smith's New Translation of the Bible: Original Manuscripts.* Provo, Utah: BYU Religious Studies Center, 2004.

Faust, James E. "Dear Are the Sheep That Have Wandered." *Ensign,* May 2003, 61–68.

———. "Father, Come Home." *Ensign,* May 1993, 35–37.

The First Presidency and Quorum of the Twelve Apostles. "The Family: A Proclamation to the World." *Ensign,* Nov. 2010, 129.

Fish, Carl Russell. *The Rise of the Common Man.* New York: Macmillan, 1927.

Fluhman, J. Spencer. "'A Subject That Can Bear Investigation': Anguish, Faith, and Joseph Smith's Youngest Plural Wife." In *No Weapon Shall Prosper: New Light on Sensitive Issues,* edited by Robert L. Millet. Provo, Utah, and Salt Lake City: BYU Religious Studies Center and Deseret Book, 2011.

Fortman, Edward J. *The Triune God: A Historical Study of the Doctrine of the Trinity.* Philadelphia: Westminster Press, 1972.

Foster, Lawrence. *Religion and Sexuality: Three American Communal Experiments of the Nineteenth Century.* New York: Oxford University Press, 1980.

Garrison, W. E., and A. T. DeGroot, *The Disciples of Christ.* St. Louis, Mo.: Bethany Press, 1958.

Geddes, Joseph A. *The United Order among the Mormons.* Salt Lake City: Deseret News Press, 1924.

Givens, Terryl L. *By the Hand of Mormon: The American Scripture That Launched a New World Religion.* New York: Oxford University Press, 2002.

———. *When Souls Had Wings: Pre-Mortal Existence in Western Thought.* New York: Oxford University Press, 2010.

———. *Wrestling the Angel—The Foundations of Mormon Thought.* New York: Oxford University Press, 2015.

Givens, Terryl L., and Fiona Givens. *The God Who Weeps: How Mormonism Makes Sense of Life.* Salt Lake City: Ensign Peak, 2012.

Givens, Terryl L., and Matthew J. Grow. *Parley P. Pratt, the Apostle Paul of Mormonism.* New York: Oxford University Press, 2011.

Grant, Heber J. *Gospel Standards.* Compiled by G. Homer Durham. Salt Lake City: Deseret Book, 1976.

Greenlee, J. Harold. *Scribes, Scrolls, and Scripture*. Grand Rapids, Mich.: Eerdmans, 1985.

Grossberg, Michael. *Governing the Hearth: Law and the Family in Nineteenth-Century America*. Chapel Hill: University of North Carolina Press, 1985.

Gutjahr, Paul C. *The Book of Mormon: A Biography*. Princeton, N.J.: Princeton University Press, 2012.

Hafen, Bruce C. *The Broken Heart: Applying the Atonement to Life's Experiences*. Salt Lake City: Deseret Book, 1989.

Hales, Brian C. *Joseph Smith's Polygamy*. 3 vols. Salt Lake City: Greg Kofford Books, 2013.

Hales, Brian C., and Laura H. Hales. *Joseph Smith's Polygamy: Toward a Better Understanding*. Salt Lake City: Greg Kofford Books, 2015.

Hales, Robert D. *Return*. Salt Lake City: Deseret Book, 2010.

Hancock, Levi. Journal. Typescript. Harold B. Lee Library, Brigham Young University, Provo, Utah.

Hardy, Grant, ed. *The Book of Mormon, a Reader's Edition*. Urbana: University of Illinois, 2003.

———. *Understanding the Book of Mormon: A Reader's Guide*. New York: Oxford University Press, 2010.

Harper, Steven C. *Joseph Smith's First Vision: A Guide to the Historical Accounts*. Salt Lake City: Deseret Book, 2012.

Harper's Bible Dictionary. Edited by Paul J. Achtemeier. San Francisco: Harper & Row, 1985.

Harris, James R. "A Study of the Changes in the Content of the Book of Moses from the Earliest Available Sources to the Current Edition." Master's thesis, Brigham Young University, 1958.

Hatch, Edwin. *The Influence of Greek Ideas on Christianity*. Gloucester, Mass.: Peter Smith Publishers, 1970.

Hatch, Nathan O. *The Democratization of American Christianity*. New Haven, Conn.: Yale University Press, 1989.

Hills, Margaret T. *The English Bible in America*. New York: American Bible Society, 1961.

Hilton, John, III. "Jacob's Textual Legacy." *Journal of Book of Mormon and Restoration Scripture* 22, no. 2 (2013): 52–65.

———. "Textual Similarities in the Words of Abinadi and Alma's Counsel to Corianton." *Brigham Young University Studies* 51, no. 2 (2012): 39–60.

Hilton, John, III, and Jana Johnson. "Who Uses the Word *Resurrection* in the Book of Mormon and How Is It Used?" *Journal of Book of Mormon and Restoration Scripture* 21, no. 2 (2012): 30–39.

Hinckley, Gordon B. "Believe His Prophets." *Ensign*, May 1992, 50–53.

———. "The Continuous Pursuit of Truth." *Ensign*, Apr. 1986, 2–6.

———. "Don't Drop the Ball." *Ensign*, Nov. 1994, 46–48.

———. *Faith, the Essence of True Religion*. Salt Lake City: Deseret Book, 1989.

———. "Inspirational Thoughts." *Ensign*, Aug. 1997, 2–7.

———. *Teachings of Gordon B. Hinckley*. Salt Lake City: Deseret Book, 1997.

———. "What Are People Asking about Us?" *Ensign*, Nov. 1998, 70–72.

Holland, Jeffrey R. *Christ and the New Covenant.* Salt Lake City: Deseret Book, 1997.

———. "The Grandeur of God." *Ensign,* Nov. 2003, 70–73.

———. "The Laborers in the Vineyard." *Ensign,* May 2012, 31–33.

———. "My Words . . . Never Cease." *Ensign,* May 2008, 91–94.

———. "The Only True God and Jesus Christ Whom He Hath Sent." *Ensign,* Nov. 2007, 40–42.

———. "Our Most Distinguishing Feature." *Ensign,* May 2005, 43–45.

Holman Bible Dictionary. Nashville, Tenn.: Holman Bible Publishers, 1991.

Hopkin, Shon D., and John Hilton III. "Samuel's Reliance on Biblical Language." *Journal of Book of Mormon Studies* 24 (2015): 31–52.

Howard, Richard P. *Restoration Scriptures: A Study of Their Textual Development.* Independence, Mo.: Herald Publishing House, 1969.

Howe, Daniel Walker. *What Hath God Wrought: The Transformation of America, 1815–1848.* New York: Oxford University Press, 2012.

Hunter, Howard W. *The Teachings of Howard W. Hunter.* Edited by Clyde J. Williams. Salt Lake City: Bookcraft, 1997.

Hutson, James H., ed. *The Founders on Religion: A Book of Quotations.* Princeton, N.J.: Princeton University Press, 2005.

Hyde, Orson. "Letter from Elder O. Hyde." *Times and Seasons* 2, no. 23 (1 Oct. 1841): 551–57.

Hymns of The Church of Jesus Christ of Latter-day Saints. Salt Lake City: The Church of Jesus Christ of Latter-day Saints, 1985.

Jackson, Kent P., comp. *Joseph Smith's Commentary on the Bible.* Salt Lake City: Deseret Book, 1994.

Jessee, Dean C., ed. *Personal Writings of Joseph Smith.* Rev. ed. Salt Lake City: Deseret Book, 2002.

Jones, Josiah. "History of the Mormonites," *Evangelist* 9 (June 1841): 132–34.

Jones, Timothy Paul. *Misquoting Truth.* Downers Grove, Ill.: IVP Books, 2007.

The Joseph Smith Papers. http://josephsmithpapers.org/.

Journal of Discourses. 26 vols. London: Latter-day Saints Book Depot, 1854–86.

Journal History of The Church of Jesus Christ of Latter-day Saints. Compiled by Andrew Jensen et al. Salt Lake City: Historical Department of The Church of Jesus Christ of Latter-day Saints, 1906.

Karkkainen, Veli-matti. *One with God: Salvation as Deification and Justification.* Collegeville, Minn.: Liturgical Press, 2004.

Keller, Roger R. *Book of Mormon Authors: Their Words and Messages.* Provo, Utah: BYU Religious Studies Center, 1996.

Kimball, Spencer W. *Faith Precedes the Miracle.* Salt Lake City: Deseret Book, 1972.

———. In Manchester England Area Conference Report, 21 June 1976.

———. *The Miracle of Forgiveness.* Salt Lake City: Bookcraft, 1969.

———. "Our Great Potential." *Ensign,* May 1977, 49–51.

———. *Teachings of Spencer W. Kimball.* Edited by Edward L. Kimball. Salt Lake City: Bookcraft, 1982.

———. "Welfare Services: The Gospel in Action." *Ensign,* Nov. 1977, 76–78.

Kimball, Stanley B. *Heber C. Kimball: Mormon Patriarch and Pioneer.* Urbana: University of Illinois Press, 1981.

Kirkham, Francis W. *A New Witness for Christ in America.* 2 vols. Salt Lake City: Zion's Printing and Publishing Co., 1951.

Kirtland High Council Minutes, 21 April 1834, 43–44. http://josephsmithpapers .org/paperSummary/minute-book-1&p=48.

Kugel, James L. *The God of Old: Inside the Lost World of the Bible.* New York: The Free Press, 2003.

Launius, Roger D. *Joseph Smith III: Pragmatic Prophet.* Urbana: University of Illinois Press, 1988.

Lectures on Faith. Salt Lake City: Deseret Book, 1985.

Lee, Harold B. *Stand Ye in Holy Places.* Edited by Clyde J. Williams. Salt Lake City: Deseret Book, 1973.

———. *The Teachings of Harold B. Lee.* Salt Lake City: Bookcraft, 1996.

———. "Understanding Who We Are Brings Self-Respect." *Ensign,* Jan. 1974, 2–6.

Lewis, C. S. *Mere Christianity.* New York: Touchstone, 1996.

———. *Miracles.* New York: Touchstone, 1996.

Locke, John. *An Essay Concerning Human Understanding.* 1689. Reprint, London: T. Tegg and Son, 1836.

Lund, Gerald N. *The Coming of the Lord.* Salt Lake City: Bookcraft, 1971.

MacArthur, John F., Jr. *Charismatic Chaos.* Grand Rapids, Mich.: Zondervan, 1992.

———. *The Glory of Heaven: The Truth about Angels, Heaven, and Eternal Life.* Wheaton, Ill.: Crossway Books, 1996.

MacKay, Michael Hubbard, and Gerrit J. Dirkmaat. *From Darkness unto Light: Joseph Smith's Translation and Publication of the Book of Mormon.* Provo, Utah, and Salt Lake City: BYU Religious Studies Center and Deseret Book, 2015.

Madsen, Truman G. *Eternal Man.* Salt Lake City: Deseret Book, 1966.

———. *The Highest in Us.* Salt Lake City: Bookcraft, 1978.

———. *Joseph Smith the Prophet.* Salt Lake City: Bookcraft, 1989.

Matthews, Robert J. "The Book of Mormon as a Co-Witness with the Bible and as a Guide to Biblical Criticism." *Religious Educators Symposium on the Book of Mormon.* Salt Lake City: The Church of Jesus Christ of Latter-day Saints, 1982.

———. "The Joseph Smith Translation: A Primary Source for the Doctrine and Covenants." In *Hearken, O Ye People: Discourses on the Doctrine and Covenants.* Sidney B. Sperry Symposium series. Salt Lake City: Randall Book, 1984.

———. *"A Plainer Translation": Joseph Smith's Translation of the Bible, a History and Commentary.* Provo, Utah: Brigham Young University Press, 1975.

———. "A Study of the Doctrinal Significance of Certain Textual Changes Made by the Prophet Joseph Smith in the Four Gospels of the Inspired Version of the New Testament." Master's thesis, Brigham Young University, 1960.

———. "A Study of the Text of the Inspired Revision of the Bible." Ph.D. diss., Brigham Young University, 1968.

———. *Unto All Nations: A Guide to the Book of Acts and the Writings of Paul.* Salt Lake City: Deseret Book, 1975.

Maxwell, Neal A. *But for a Small Moment: Light from Liberty Jail, Inspired Contributions from the Prophet in Prison.* Salt Lake City: Bookcraft, 1986.

———. "Consecrate Thy Performance." *Ensign,* May 2002, 36–38.

———. "Meeting the Challenges of Today." *1978 Devotional Speeches of the Year.* Provo, Utah: Brigham Young University Press, 1979.

———. "Out of Obscurity." *Ensign,* Nov. 1984, 8–11.

———. *Plain and Precious Things.* Salt Lake City: Deseret Book, 1983.

———. *Things As They Really Are.* Salt Lake City: Deseret Book, 1978.

———. *A Wonderful Flood of Light.* Salt Lake City: Bookcraft, 1990.

McConkie, Bruce R. Address at the funeral for Elder S. Dilworth Young, 13 July 1981. Unpublished typescript in author's possession.

———. "The Bible: A Sealed Book." In *Religious Educators Symposium on the New Testament.* Salt Lake City: The Church of Jesus Christ of Latter-day Saints, 1984.

———. *Doctrinal New Testament Commentary.* 3 vols. Salt Lake City: Bookcraft, 1965–73.

———. "The Doctrine of the Priesthood." *Ensign,* May 1982, 32–34.

———. *Doctrines of the Restoration: Sermons and Writings of Bruce R. McConkie.* Edited by Mark L. McConkie. Salt Lake City: Bookcraft, 1989.

———. "The Foolishness of Teaching." Address to Church Educational System personnel. Salt Lake City: The Church of Jesus Christ of Latter-day Saints, 1981.

———. *The Lord God of Joseph Smith.* Brigham Young University Speeches of the Year. Provo, Utah, 4 Jan. 1972.

———. *The Millennial Messiah: The Second Coming of the Son of Man.* Salt Lake City: Deseret Book, 1983.

———. *Mormon Doctrine.* 2d ed. Salt Lake City: Bookcraft, 1966.

———. *The Mortal Messiah.* 4 vols. Salt Lake City: Deseret Book, 1979–81.

———. *A New Witness for the Articles of Faith.* Salt Lake City: Deseret Book, 1985.

———. *The Promised Messiah: The First Coming of Christ.* Salt Lake City: Deseret Book, 1978.

———. "The Salvation of Little Children." *Ensign,* Apr. 1977, 2–7.

———. "Succession in the Presidency." *1974 BYU Speeches of the Year.* Provo: BYU Publications, 1975.

———. "The Ten Blessings of the Priesthood." *Ensign,* Nov. 1977, 33–35.

McConkie, Joseph Fielding. "The Principle of Revelation." In *The Doctrine and Covenants,* edited by Robert L. Millet and Kent P. Jackson, 80–85. Vol. 1 of Studies in Scripture series. Salt Lake City: Randall Book, 1985.

———. *Sons and Daughters of God: The Loss and Restoration of Our Divine Inheritance.* Salt Lake City: Bookcraft, 1994.

McConkie, Joseph Fielding, and Robert L. Millet. *Joseph Smith, the Choice Seer.* Salt Lake City: Bookcraft, 1996.

McConkie, Mark L. *Remembering Joseph: Personal Recollections of Those Who Knew the Prophet Joseph Smith.* Salt Lake City: Deseret Book, 2003.

McKay, David O. In Conference Report, Apr. 1907, 10–14.

———. In Conference Report, Apr. 1962, 5–9.

McKiernan, F. Mark, and Roger D. Launius, eds. *An Early Latter Day Saint History: The Book of John Whitmer*. Independence, Mo.: Herald Publishing House, 1980.

Meldrum, Rod L. *Exploring Book of Mormon in America's Heartland Photobook*. Salt Lake City: Digital Legend Press, 2011.

Merrill, Joseph F. In Conference Report, Apr. 1947, 132–37.

———. "Joseph Smith Did See God," *Ensign*, Dec. 2015, 70–71.

Metzger, Bruce M. *The New Testament: Its Background, Growth, and Content*. 2d ed. Nashville, Tenn.: Abingdon, 1983.

Millet, Robert L. *Getting at the Truth: Responding to Difficult Questions about LDS Beliefs*. Salt Lake City: Deseret Book, 2004.

———. "Joseph Smith Encounters Calvinism." *Brigham Young University Studies* 50, no. 4 (2011): 123–40.

———. *Joseph Smith: Selected Sermons and Writings*. Sources of American Spirituality series. New York: Paulist Press, 1989.

———. *Life after Death: Insights from Latter-day Revelation*. Salt Lake City: Deseret Book, 1999.

———. *Living in the Eleventh Hour: Preparing for the Glorious Return of the Savior*. Salt Lake City: Deseret Book, 2014.

———. *Living in the Millennium*. Salt Lake City: Deseret Book, 2014.

———. *Restored and Restoring: The Unfolding Drama of the Restoration*. Salt Lake City: Eborn Books, 2014.

———. *When a Child Wanders*. Salt Lake City: Deseret Book, 1996.

———, ed. *By What Authority? The Vital Questions of Religious Authority in Christianity*. Macon, Ga.: Mercer University Press, 2010.

Millet, Robert L., and Shon D. Hopkin. *Mormonism: A Guide for the Perplexed*. London: Bloomsbury Academic, 2015.

Millet, Robert L., and Joseph Fielding McConkie. *The Life Beyond*. Salt Lake City: Bookcraft, 1986.

Millet, Robert L., Camille Fronk Olson, Andrew C. Skinner, and Brent L. Top. *LDS Beliefs: A Doctrinal Reference*. Salt Lake City: Deseret Book, 2011.

Millet, Robert L., and Larry E. Dahl, eds. *The Capstone of Our Religion: Insights into the Doctrine and Covenants*. Salt Lake City: Bookcraft, 1989.

Millet, Robert L., and Robert J. Matthews, eds. *Plain and Precious Truths Restored: The Doctrinal and Historical Significance of the Joseph Smith Translation*. Salt Lake City: Bookcraft, 1995.

Monson, Thomas S. *Teachings of Thomas S. Monson*. Compiled by Lynne F. Cannegieter. Salt Lake City: Deseret Book, 2011.

Moore, R. Laurence. *Religious Outsiders and the Making of Americans*. New York: Oxford University Press, 1986.

Mouw, Richard J. "The Possibility of Joseph Smith: Some Evangelical Probings." In *Joseph Smith: Reappraisals After Two Centuries*, edited by Reid L. Neilson and Terryl L. Givens. New York: Oxford University Press, 2008.

Mouw, Richard J., and Robert L. Millet, eds. *Talking with Mormons: An Invitation to Evangelicals*. Grand Rapids, Mich.: Eerdmans, 2012.

Nash, Marcus B. "The New and Everlasting Covenant." *Ensign,* Dec. 2015, 41–47.

"Nauvoo Baptisms for the Dead." Book A, Family History Archives, The Church of Jesus Christ of Latter-day Saints, Salt Lake City, 145, 149.

Neilson, Reid L., and Jed Woodworth, eds. *Believing History: Latter-day Saint Essays.* New York: Columbia University Press, 2004.

Nelson, Russell M. *Accomplishing the Impossible: What God Does, What We Do.* Salt Lake City: Deseret Book, 2015.

———. "Children of the Covenant." *Ensign,* May 1995, 32–35.

———. *Hope in Our Hearts.* Salt Lake City: Deseret Book, 2009.

———. "A New Harvest Time." *Ensign,* May 1998, 34–36.

———. *Perfection Pending.* Salt Lake City: Deseret Book, 1998.

———. *The Power within Us.* Salt Lake City: Deseret Book, 1988.

Nibley, Hugh. *Apostles and Bishops in Early Christianity.* Edited by John F. Hall and John W. Welch. Vol. 15 of Collected Works of Hugh Nibley. Provo, Utah, and Salt Lake City: Foundation for Ancient Research and Mormon Studies and Deseret Book, 2005.

———. *The Message of the Joseph Smith Papyri: An Egyptian Endowment.* Salt Lake City: Deseret Book, 1975.

———. *Mormonism and Early Christianity.* Edited by Todd M. Compton and Stephen D. Ricks. Vol. 4 of Collected Works of Hugh Nibley. Provo, Utah, and Salt Lake City: Foundation for Ancient Research and Mormon Studies and Deseret Book, 1987.

———. *Temple and Cosmos.* Edited by Don E. Norton. Vol. 12 of Collected Works of Hugh Nibley. Provo, Utah, and Salt Lake City: Foundation for Ancient Research and Mormon Studies and Deseret Book, 1992.

———. *The World and the Prophets.* Edited by John W. Welch, Gary P. Gillum, and Don E. Norton. Vol. 3 of Collected Works of Hugh Nibley. Provo, Utah, and Salt Lake City: Foundation for Ancient Research and Mormon Studies and Deseret Book, 1987.

Nibley, Hugh, and Michael D. Rhodes. *One Eternal Round.* Vol. 19 of Collected Works of Hugh Nibley. Provo, Utah, and Salt Lake City: Foundation for Ancient Research and Mormon Studies and Deseret Book, 2010.

Norman, Keith. "Ex Nihilo: The Development of the Doctrines of God and Creation in Early Christianity." *Brigham Young University Studies* 17, no. 3 (1977): 291–318.

Novak, Michael. *The Spirit of Democratic Capitalism.* New York: Simon & Schuster, 1982.

Nuttall, L. John. Diary. Vol. 1. Harold B. Lee Library, Brigham Young University, Provo, Utah.

Nyman, Monte S., and Robert L. Millet, eds. *The Joseph Smith Translation: The Restoration of Plain and Precious Things.* Provo, Utah: BYU Religious Studies Center, 1985.

Oaks, Dallin H. "The Challenge to Become." *Ensign,* Nov. 2000, 43–44.

———. "The Keys and Authority of the Priesthood." *Ensign,* May 2014, 49–52.

———. "Priesthood Authority in the Family and the Church." *Ensign,* Nov. 2005, 25–26.

———. *Pure in Heart.* Salt Lake City: Bookcraft, 1988.

———. "Scripture Reading, Revelation, and Joseph Smith's Translation of the Bible." In *Plain and Precious Truths Restored: The Doctrinal and Historical Significance of the Joseph Smith Translation,* edited by Robert L. Millet and Robert J. Matthews, 1–15. Salt Lake City: Bookcraft, 1995.

———. *With Full Purpose of Heart.* Salt Lake City: Deseret Book, 2002.

Odem, Mary E. *Delinquent Daughters: Protecting and Policing Adolescent Female Sexuality in the United States, 1885–1920.* Chapel Hill: University of North Carolina Press, 1995.

Olson, Roger E. *Arminianism: Myths and Realities.* Downers Grove, Ill.: IVP Academic, 2007.

———. *The Story of Christian Theology.* Downers Grove, Ill.: InterVarsity, 1999.

Osborn, David. "Recollections of the Prophet Joseph Smith." *Juvenile Instructor* 27, no. 6 (Mar. 15, 1892): 172–74.

Ostler, Craig James. *Refuge from the Storm: Living in the Last Days.* American Fork, Utah: Covenant Communications, 2012.

Ostling, Richard N., and Joan K. Ostling. *Mormon America.* San Francisco: Harper, 1999.

Packer, Boyd K. "The Book of Mormon: Another Testament of Jesus Christ." *Ensign,* May 2005, 6–9.

———. *The Holy Temple.* Salt Lake City: Bookcraft, 1980.

———. *Let Not Your Heart Be Troubled.* Salt Lake City: Bookcraft, 1991.

———. "Little Children." *Ensign,* Nov. 1986, 16–18.

———. "The Mystery of Life." *Ensign,* Nov. 1983, 16–18.

———. "Our Moral Environment." *Ensign,* May 1992, 66–68.

———. "The Plan of Happiness." *Ensign,* May 2015, 26–28.

———. "Prayers and Answers." *Ensign,* Nov. 1979, 19–21.

———. "Scriptures." *Ensign,* Nov. 1982, 51–53.

Pagels, Elaine. *Adam, Eve, and the Serpent.* New York: Random House, 1988.

Paulsen, David L. "The Doctrine of Divine Embodiment: Restoration, Judeo-Christian, and Philosophical Perspectives." *Brigham Young University Studies* 35, no. 4 (1996): 6–94.

———. "Early Christian Belief in a Corporeal Deity: Origen and Augustine as Reluctant Witnesses." *Harvard Theological Review* 83, no. 2 (1990): 105–16.

Penrose, Charles W. In Conference Report, Apr. 1921, 193–200.

———. *"Mormon" Doctrine, Plain and Simple; or, Leaves from the Tree of Life.* Salt Lake City: George Q. Cannon & Sons, 1897.

Peterson, H. Donl. *The Pearl of Great Price: A History and Commentary.* Salt Lake City: Deseret Book, 1987.

Phelps, William W. "Letter no. 8." *Messenger and Advocate* 1, no. 9 (June 1835): 130.

Pinnock, Clark H. *Most Moved Mover: A Theology of God's Openness.* Grand Rapids, Mich.: Baker, 2001.

Pinnock, Clark, and Delwin Brown. *Theological Crossfire.* Grand Rapids, Mich.: Zondervan, 1990.

Pinnock, Clark, Richard Rice, John Sanders, William Hasker, and David Basinger. *The Openness of God: A Biblical Challenge to the Traditional Understanding of God.* Downers Grove, Ill.: InterVarsity, 1994.

"Plural Marriage." *Millennial Star* 45, no. 29 (July 1833): 454–55.

Potter, Amasa. "A Reminiscence of the Prophet Joseph Smith." *Juvenile Instructor* 29, no. 4 (Feb. 15, 1894): 131–32.

Pratt, Orson. "The Holy Spirit." In *Orson Pratt: Writings of an Apostle.* Salt Lake City: Mormon Heritage Publishers, 1976.

———. *Masterful Discourses and Writings of Orson Pratt.* Edited by N. B. Lundwall. Salt Lake City: Bookcraft, 1962.

———. *Millennial Star* 40, no. 49 (Dec. 9, 1878): 788.

———. *Orson Pratt's Works.* Salt Lake City: Parker Pratt Robinson, 1965.

———. "The Pre-Existence of Man." *Seer* 1, no. 4 (Apr. 1853): 49–57.

Pratt, Parley P. *The Autobiography of Parley P. Pratt.* Salt Lake City: Deseret Book, 1975.

———. *Key to the Science of Theology.* Salt Lake City: Deseret Book, 1978.

———. *A Voice of Warning.* Salt Lake City: Deseret Book, 1978.

Quincy, Josiah. *Figures of the Past.* Boston: Roberts Brothers, 1883.

Rack, Henry D. *Reasonable Enthusiast: John Wesley and the Rise of Methodism.* Philadelphia: Trinity Press International, 1989.

Rahner, Karl. *The Trinity.* New York: Herder and Herder, 1970.

Remini, Robert. *Joseph Smith.* New York: Penguin, 2002.

Revelation given to Frederick G. Williams, 5 Jan. 1834, Joseph Smith Collection, Letters 1834, Church Historians Office, Salt Lake City.

Reynolds, Noel B. *Book of Mormon Authorship: New Light on Ancient Origins.* Provo, Utah: BYU Religious Studies Center, 1982.

———. *Book of Mormon Authorship Revisited: The Evidence for Ancient Origins.* Provo, Utah: Foundation for Ancient Research and Mormon Studies, 1997.

Richards, LeGrand. *A Marvelous Work and a Wonder.* Salt Lake City: Deseret Book, 1950.

Richards, Stephen L. In Conference Report, Oct. 1951, 109–18.

Ricks, Stephen D. "Apostles and Bishops: Puzzling Over the Problem of Priesthood Succession." In *By What Authority? The Vital Questions of Religious Authority in Christianity.* Edited by Robert L. Millet. Macon, Ga.: Mercer University Press, 2010.

Roberts, B. H. *A Comprehensive History of the Church of Jesus Christ of Latter-day Saints, Century One.* 6 vols. Salt Lake City: The Church of Jesus Christ of Latter-day Saints, 1930.

———. *Defense of the Faith and the Saints.* 2 vols. Salt Lake City: Deseret News, 1907.

———. *The Gospel and Man's Relationship to Deity.* Salt Lake City: Deseret Book, 1965.

Romney, Marion G. In Conference Report, Oct. 1965, 20–23.

Rust, Richard Dilworth. *Feasting on the Word: The Literary Testimony of the Book of Mormon.* Provo, Utah, and Salt Lake City: Foundation for Ancient Research and Mormon Studies and Deseret Book, 1997.

Sanders, John. *What about Those Who Have Never Heard?* Downers Grove, Ill.: InterVarsity, 1995.

Scoville, Lucius. "The Higher Ordinances." *Deseret News Semi-Weekly,* 15 Feb. 1884, 2.

Shields, Steven L. *Divergent Paths of the Restoration*. Bountiful, Utah: Restoration Research, Inc., 1982.

Shipps, Jan. *Mormonism: The Story of a New Religious Tradition*. Urbana: University of Illinois Press, 1985.

———. "The Reality of the Restoration and the Restoration Ideal in the Mormon Tradition." In *The American Quest for the Primitive Church*. Edited by Richard T. Hughes. Urbana: University of Illinois Press, 1988.

Silverman, Kenneth. *The Life and Times of Cotton Mather*. New York: Harper & Row, 1984.

Skinner, Andrew C. *To Become Like God: Witnesses of Our Divine Potential*. Salt Lake City: Deseret Book, 2016.

Smith, Adam. *The Theory of Moral Sentiments*. Indianapolis, Ind.: Liberty Classics, 1969.

Smith, Emma. Letter of Emma Smith Bidamon to Joseph Smith III, 2 Dec. 1867, Library-Archives, Community of Christ, Independence, Missouri.

Smith, George D., ed. *An Intimate Chronicle: The Journals of William Clayton*. Salt Lake City: Signature Books, 1995.

Smith, Hyrum M., and Janne M. Sjodahl. *Doctrine and Covenants Commentary*. Salt Lake City: Deseret Book, 1965.

Smith, Joseph. "The Answer." *Times and Seasons* 4, no. 6 (Feb. 1843): 82–84.

———. "Baptism." *Times and Seasons* 3, no. 21 (Sept. 1842): 903–5.

———. "Baptism for the Dead." *Times and Seasons* 3, no. 12 (Apr. 1842): 759–61.

———. "Books!!!" *Times and Seasons* 1, no. 9 (July 1840): 139–41.

———. "Church History." *Times and Seasons* 3, no. 9 (Mar. 1842): 706–10.

———. "Copy of a Letter from J. Smith Jr. to Mr. Galland." *Times and Seasons* 1, no. 4 (Feb. 1840): 51–56.

———. Diary, 10 Mar. 1844, Archives, The Church of Jesus Christ of Latter-day Saints, Salt Lake City.

———. *Elders' Journal* 1, no. 3 (July 1838): 42–44.

———. "Gift of the Holy Ghost." *Times and Seasons* 3, no. 16 (June 1842): 823–26.

———. *History of The Church of Jesus Christ of Latter-day Saints*. Edited by B. H. Roberts. 7 vols. 2d ed. rev. Salt Lake City: The Church of Jesus Christ of Latter-day Saints, 1931–52.

———. "History of Joseph Smith." *Millennial Star* 23, no. 31 (Aug. 3, 1861): 486–88.

———. *Joseph Smith* [manual]. Teachings of Presidents of the Church series. Salt Lake City: The Church of Jesus Christ of Latter-day Saints, 2007.

———. *Joseph Smith's New Translation of the Bible: Original Manuscripts*. Edited by Scott H. Faulring, Kent P. Jackson, and Robert J. Matthews. Provo, Utah: BYU Religious Studies Center, 2004.

———. Journal account dictated to Warren Parrish, 9 Nov. 1835.

———. "Millennium. No. X." *Messenger and Advocate* 1, no. 3 (Dec. 1834): 39–40.

———. *Teachings of the Prophet Joseph Smith*. Selected by Joseph Fielding Smith. Salt Lake City: Deseret Book, 1976.

———. "Try the Spirits," *Times and Seasons* 3, no. 11 (1 Apr. 1842): 743–48.

Smith, Joseph F. *Gospel Doctrine.* Salt Lake City: Deseret Book, 1971.

———. In Conference Report, Apr. 1912, 2–10.

———. "The Truth about 'Mormonism.'" *Millennial Star* 67, no. 40 (Oct. 5, 1905): 625–29.

Smith, Joseph Fielding. *Answers to Gospel Questions.* 5 vols. Salt Lake City: Deseret Book, 1957–66.

———. *Doctrines of Salvation.* Compiled by Bruce R. McConkie. 3 vols. Salt Lake City: Bookcraft, 1954–56.

———. Funeral of Elder Richard L. Evans, 4 Nov. 1971. Typescript.

———. In Conference Report, Apr. 1960, 72–75.

———. In Conference Report, Apr. 1970, 58–60, 113–14.

———. "Joseph Smith's 'Translation' of the Scriptures." *Improvement Era* 17, no. 6 (Apr. 1, 1914): 590–96.

———. *Man: His Origin and Destiny.* Salt Lake City: Deseret Book, 1954.

———. *The Progress of Man.* Salt Lake City: Deseret Book, 1964.

———. *The Restoration of All Things.* Salt Lake City: Deseret Book, 1945.

———. *Seek Ye Earnestly.* Salt Lake City: Deseret Book, 1970.

———. *Selections from Doctrines of Salvation.* Salt Lake City: The Church of Jesus Christ of Latter-day Saints, 2001.

———. *The Signs of the Times.* Salt Lake City: Deseret Book, 1952.

———. *The Way to Perfection.* Salt Lake City: Deseret Book, 1972.

Smith, Lucy Mack. *History of Joseph Smith by His Mother.* Edited by Preston Nibley. Salt Lake City: Bookcraft, n.d.

Smith, William. "Notes on Chambers' *Life of Joseph Smith.*" About 1875. Archives of The Church of Jesus Christ of Latter-day Saints, Salt Lake City.

Snow, Eliza R. *Biography and Family Record of Lorenzo Snow.* Salt Lake City: Deseret News Company, 1884.

Snow, Lorenzo. *The Teachings of Lorenzo Snow.* Compiled by Clyde J. Williams. Salt Lake City: Bookcraft, 1984.

Sorenson, John L. *An Ancient American Setting for the Book of Mormon.* Provo, Utah, and Salt Lake City: Foundation for Ancient Research and Mormon Studies and Deseret Book, 1985.

———. *Mormon's Codex: An Ancient American Book.* Provo, Utah, and Salt Lake City: Neal A. Maxwell Institute for Religious Scholarship and Deseret Book, 2013.

Spencer, Orson. "Letter of Orson Spencer." *Times and Seasons* 4, no. 4 (2 Jan. 1843): 49–59.

Sperry, Sidney B., and Merrill Y. Van Wagoner. "The Inspired Revision of the Bible." *Improvement Era* 43, no. 4 (Apr. 1940): 206–7.

St. Augustine. *The City of God.* Translated by Marcus Dods. New York: Random House, Modern Library, 1978.

Stein, Stephen J. *The Shaker Experience in America: A History of the United Society of Believers.* New Haven, Conn.: Yale University Press, 1992.

Stott, John. "The Model: Becoming More Like Christ." Sermon delivered at the Keswick Convention, 17 July 2007.

Sullivan, Francis. *From Apostles to Bishops: The Development of the Episcopacy in the Early Church.* New York: Paulist Press, 2001.

Swinton, Heidi S. *American Prophet: The Story of Joseph Smith.* Salt Lake City: Shadow Mountain, 1999.

Talmage, James E. *The Articles of Faith.* Salt Lake City: The Church of Jesus Christ of Latter-day Saints, 1961.

Taylor, John. *The Gospel Kingdom.* Compiled by G. Homer Durham. Salt Lake City: Bookcraft, 1987.

———. *John Taylor* [manual]. Teachings of Presidents of the Church series. Salt Lake City: The Church of Jesus Christ of Latter-day Saints, 2001.

———. *The Mediation and Atonement of Our Lord and Savior Jesus Christ.* Salt Lake City: Deseret News, 1882.

Taysom, Stephen C. *Shakers, Mormonism, and Religious Worlds: Conflicting Visions, Contested Boundaries.* Bloomington: Indiana University Press, 2011.

Top, Brent L. *The Life Before.* Salt Lake City: Bookcraft, 1988.

Tucker, Pomeroy. *Origin, Rise and Progress of Mormonism.* New York: D. Appleton, 1867.

Turley, Richard E., Jr., and William W. Slaughter. *How We Got the Book of Mormon.* Salt Lake City: Deseret Book, 2011.

Turley, Richard E., Jr., Robin S. Jensen, and Mark Ashurst-McGee. "Joseph the Seer." *Ensign,* Oct. 2015, 49–55.

Turner, Orasmus. *History of the Pioneer Settlement of Phelps and Gorham's Purchase, and Morris' Reserve.* Rochester, N.Y.: William Alling, 1851.

Turner, Rodney. "The Visions of Moses." In *The Pearl of Great Price,* edited by Robert L. Millet and Kent P. Jackson, 43–61. Vol. 2 of Studies in Scripture series. Salt Lake City: Randall Book, 1985.

Tyler, Daniel. "Recollections of the Prophet Joseph Smith." *Juvenile Instructor* 27, no. 3 (Feb. 1, 1892): 93–94.

Tyson, John R. *Assist Me to Proclaim: The Life and Hymns of Charles Wesley.* Grand Rapids, Mich.: Eerdmans, 2007.

Uchtdorf, Dieter F. "The Gift of Grace." *Ensign,* May 2015, 107–10.

———. "You Matter to Him." *Ensign,* Nov. 2011, 19–22.

Vajda, Jordan. "Partakers of the Divine Nature: A Comparative Analysis of Patristic and Mormon Doctrines of Divinization." Occasional Papers, series editor William J. Hamblin. Provo, Utah: Foundation for Ancient Research and Mormon Studies, 2002.

Walker, Charles L. *Diary of Charles L. Walker.* 2 vols. Compiled by A. Karl Larson and Catherine Miles Larson. Logan, Utah: Utah State University Press, 1980.

Walker, Kyle R. *William B. Smith: In the Shadow of a Prophet.* Salt Lake City: Greg Kofford Books, 2015.

Webb, Stephen H. *Jesus Christ, Eternal God: Heavenly Flesh and the Metaphysics of Matter.* New York: Oxford University Press, 2012.

———. *Mormon Christianity: What Other Christians Can Learn from the Latter-day Saints.* New York: Oxford University Press, 2013.

Webster, Noah. *An American Dictionary of the English Language.* 1828. Reprint, San Francisco: Foundation for American Christian Education, 1985.

Welch, John W. *Chiasmus in Antiquity: Structures, Analyses, Exegesis.* Provo, Utah: Foundation for Ancient Research and Mormon Studies, 1999.

————. *Illuminating the Sermon at the Temple and the Sermon on the Mount.* Provo, Utah: Foundation for Ancient Research and Mormon Studies, 1999.

Welch, John W., and Stephen D. Ricks. *King Benjamin's Speech: "That Ye May Learn Wisdom."* Provo, Utah: Foundation for Ancient Research and Mormon Studies, 1998.

Welch, John W., and David J. Whittaker. "'We Believe . . . ': Development of the Articles of Faith." *Ensign,* Sept. 1979, 51–55.

Welch, John W., and Erick B. Carlson, eds. *Opening the Heavens: Accounts of Divine Manifestations, 1820–1844.* Provo, Utah, and Salt Lake City: Brigham Young University Press and Deseret Book, 2005

White, O. Kendall. *Mormon Neo-Orthodoxy: A Crisis Theology.* Salt Lake City: Signature Books, 1987.

Whitney, Orson F. "The Aaronic Priesthood." *Contributor* 6, no. 1 (Oct. 1884): 1–9.

————. In Conference Report, Apr. 1928, 56–61.

————. In Conference Report, Apr. 1929, 109–15.

————. *Life of Heber C. Kimball.* 4th ed. Salt Lake City: Bookcraft, 1973.

Wilkinson, Bruce. *A Life God Rewards.* Sisters, Oreg.: Multnomah Publishers, 2002.

Williams, Rowan. *Christ on Trial: How the Gospel Unsettles Our Judgment.* Grand Rapids, Mich.: Eerdmans, 2000.

Woodruff, Wilford. *Discourses of Wilford Woodruff.* Compiled by G. Homer Durham. Salt Lake City: Bookcraft, 1969.

————. In Conference Report, Apr. 1898, 57–58.

————. *A String of Pearls.* Salt Lake City: Juvenile Instructor, 1880.

————. *Wilford Woodruff's Journal, 1833–1898: Typescript.* Edited by Scott Kenney. 9 vols. Salt Lake City: Signature Books, 1984.

Words of Joseph Smith: The Contemporary Accounts of the Nauvoo Discourses of the Prophet Joseph. Edited by Andrew F. Ehat and Lyndon W. Cook. Provo, Utah: BYU Religious Studies Center, 1980.

Wright, N. T. *Simply Christian.* New York: Harper San Francisco, 2006.

Young, Brigham. *Brigham Young* [manual]. Teachings of Presidents of the Church series. Salt Lake City: The Church of Jesus Christ of Latter-day Saints, 1997.

————. *Discourses of Brigham Young.* Compiled by John A. Widtsoe. Salt Lake City: Deseret Book, 1978.

Young, Joseph. *History of the Organization of the Seventies.* Salt Lake City: Deseret News Steam Printing Establishment, 1878.

SCRIPTURE INDEX

SUBJECT INDEX